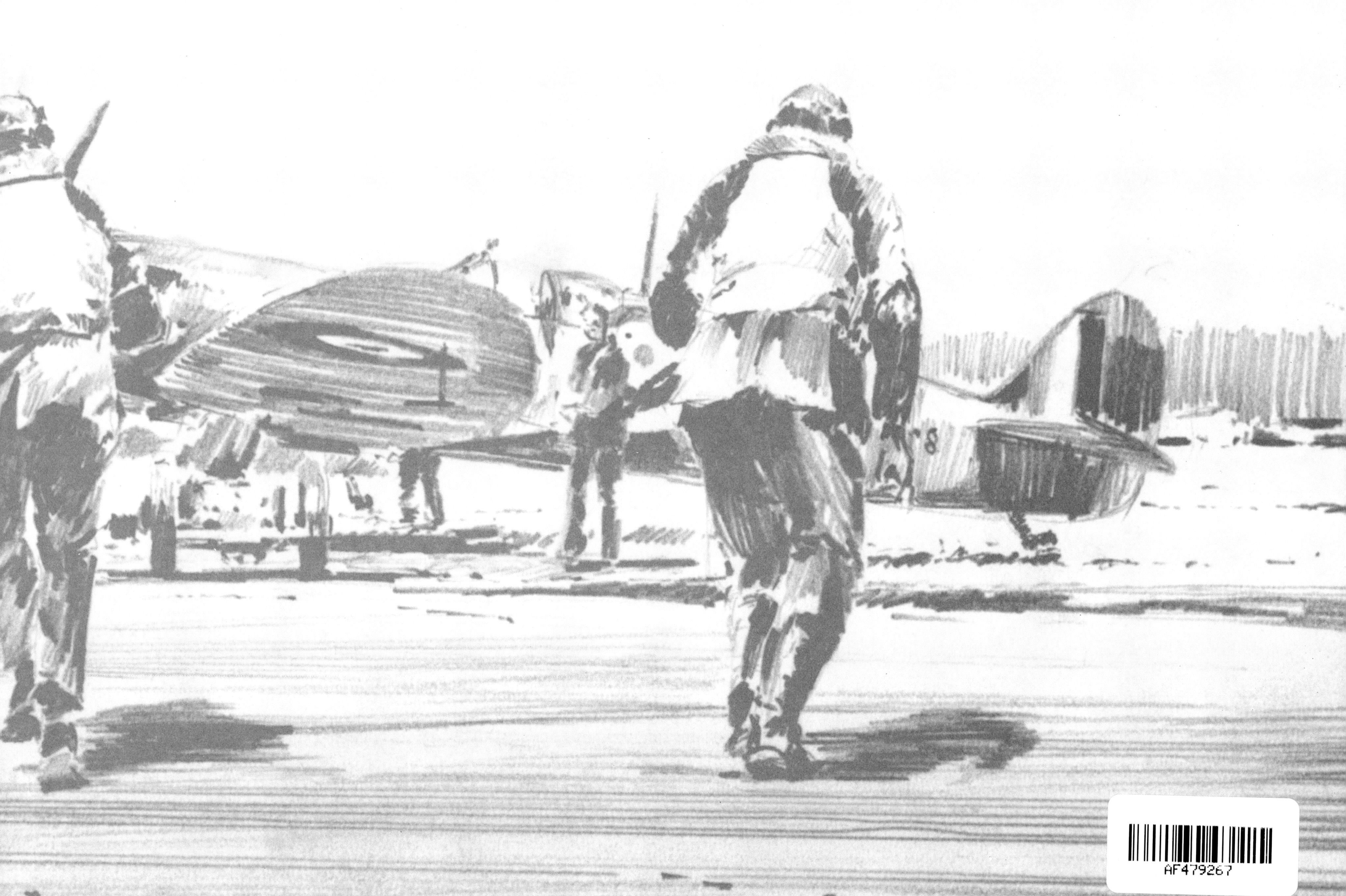

THE AIR COMBAT PAINTINGS OF ROBERT TAYLOR

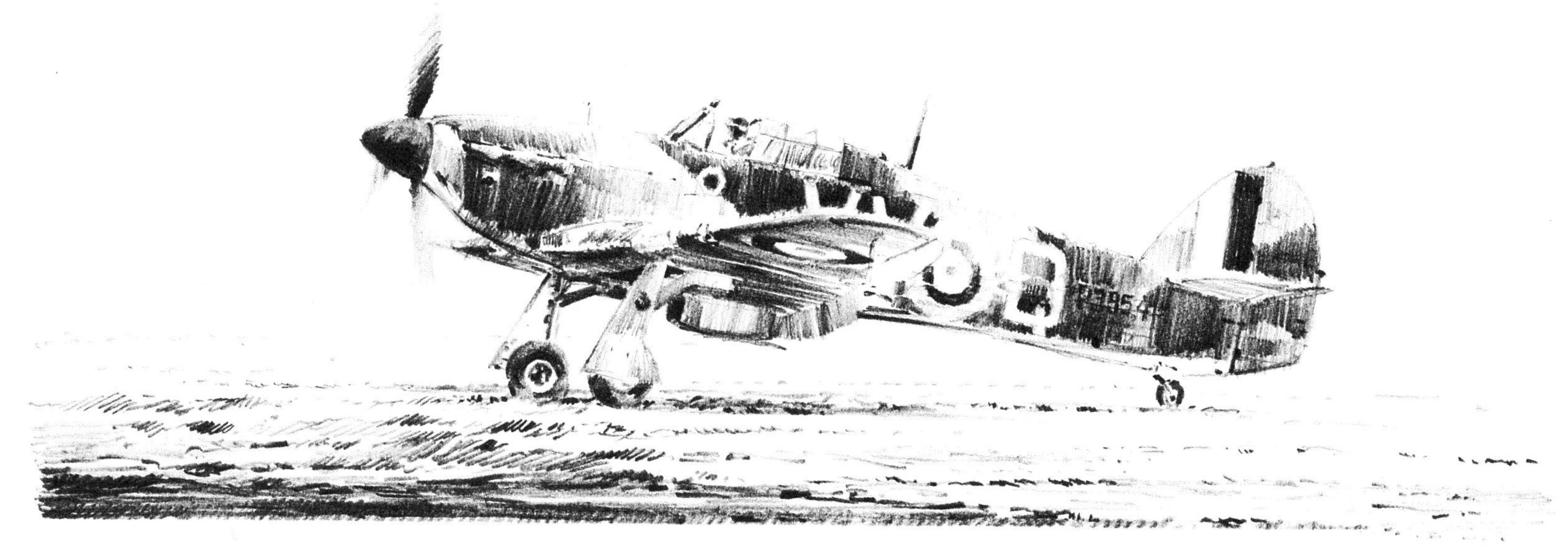

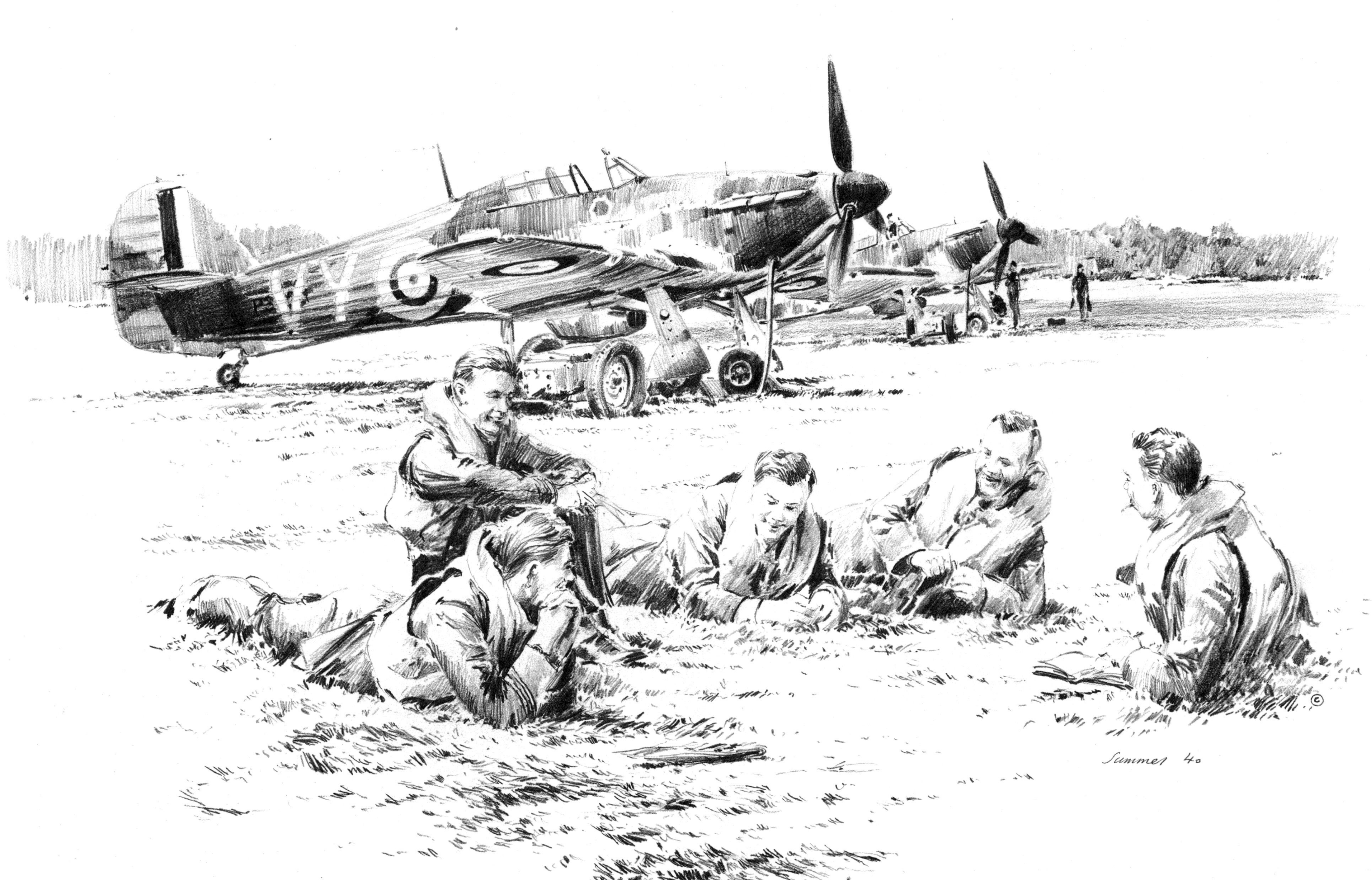
Summer 40

THE AIR COMBAT PAINTINGS OF ROBERT TAYLOR

Robert Weston and Robert Taylor

FOREWORD BY

Air Vice Marshal 'Johnnie' Johnson
CB, CBE, DSO, DFC, DL

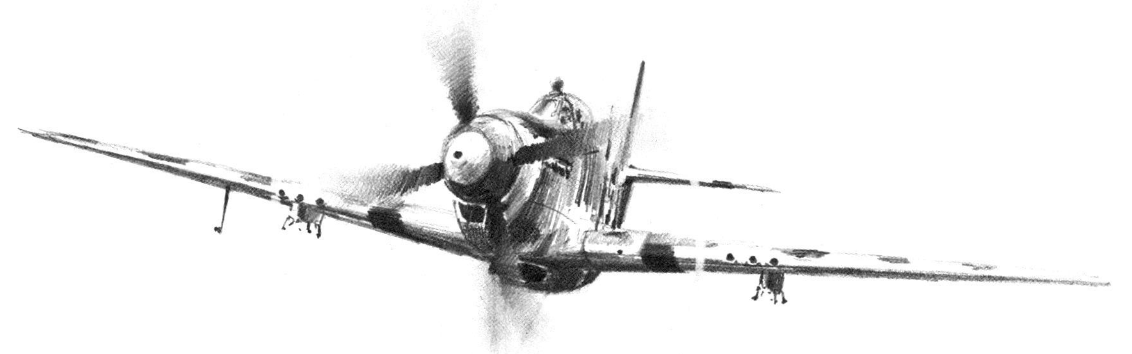

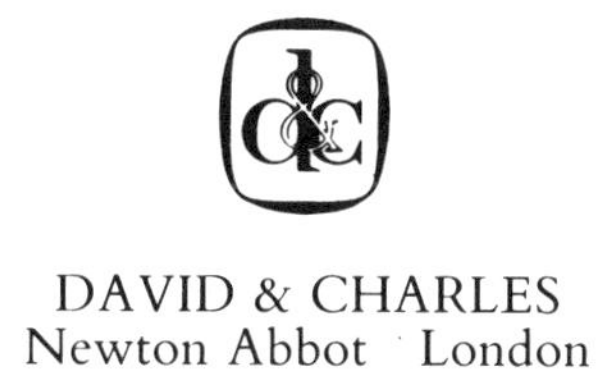

DAVID & CHARLES
Newton Abbot London

To my wife and family, and the friends who have helped and encouraged me so generously.

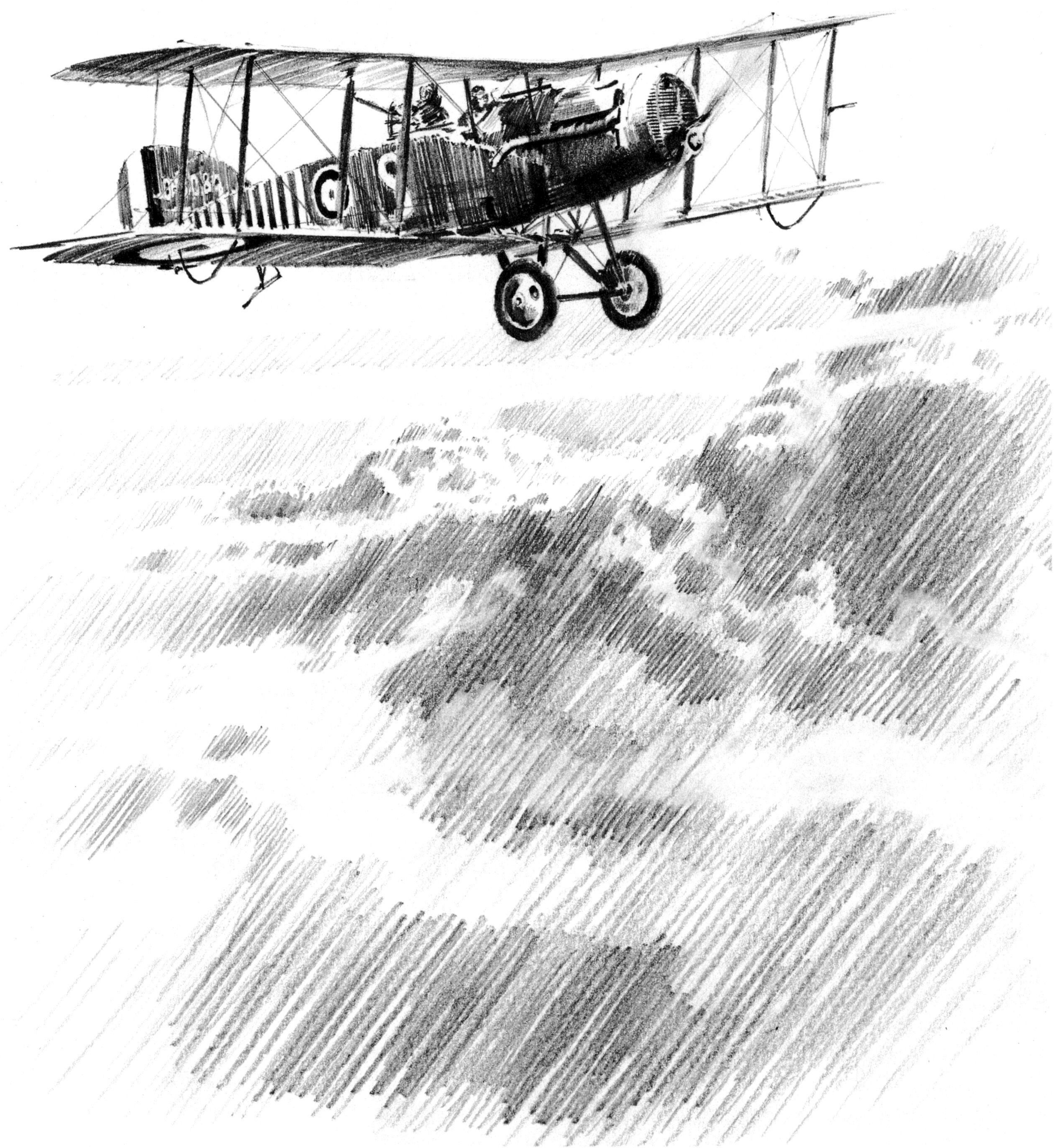

British Library Cataloguing in Publication Data
Taylor, Robert
The air combat paintings of Robert Taylor.
1. Taylor, Robert. 2. Airplanes, Military in art
I. Title II. Weston, Robert
759.2 ND497.T3/

ISBN 0–7153–9008–2

First published 1987
Second impression 1988
Third impression 1989
Fourth impression 1989
Fifth impression 1990

Designed by Universal Promotions, Bath, England

Printed in Singapore by Saik Wah Press
for David & Charles Publishers plc
Brunel House Newton Abbot Devon

CONTENTS

THE PAINTINGS

Introduced by the Artist

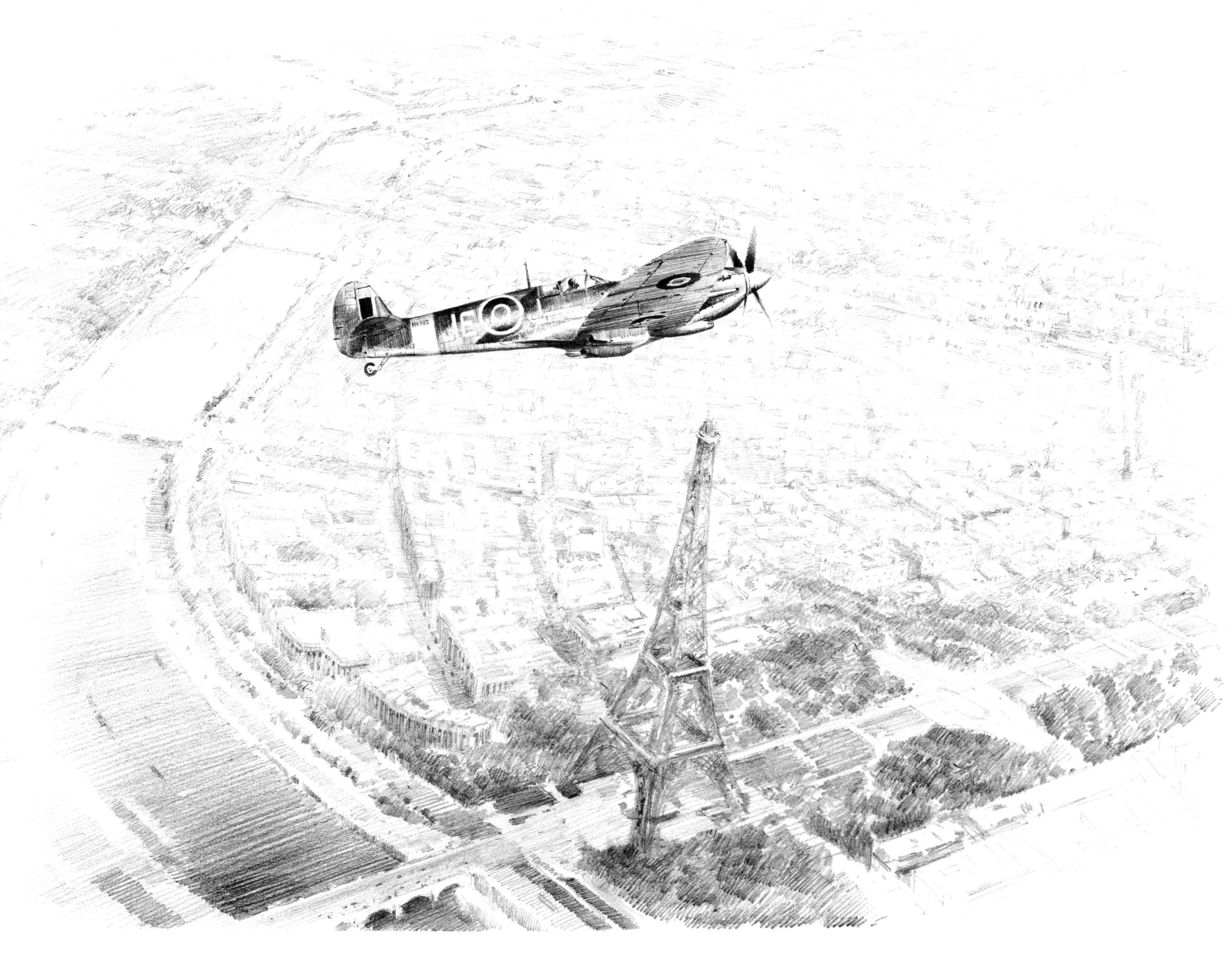
MK392
JE

FOREWORD

In this excellent book Robert Taylor explains the difficulties in portraying aircraft in combat and getting right the exact distance between aeroplanes. This was brought home to me when I first met him in 1979 when he was making his sketches for *Spitfire* which would depict Wing Commander Douglas Bader and Pilot Officer 'Johnnie' Johnson flying their Spitfires over the *Pas de Calais* in the early summer of 1941. Thus, one day Robert arrived with his publisher Pat Barnard at Ascot, where Douglas had an office, to discuss the artist's sketch.

Robert held the sketch in front of him, which Douglas and I studied. It was not quite right, since my Spitfire was too near to Douglas's, and consequently too big, and my shallow turn was not steep enough. Suddenly Douglas grabbed it from him, placed it on his desk, and with a biro (i.e. not a pencil!) proceeded to scrawl over the artist's precious drawing.

'That's how it should be, old boy' exclaimed Douglas, 'Johnnie's Spit should be about here turning like this' (more frantic biro strokes) 'and about this size!'

Pat Barnard was incredulous and speechless and I looked at the artist's face during this astonishing scene, but to his eternal credit Robert Taylor smiled and in his soft west country voice, said 'Yes, I see what you mean, I will make the necessary alteration'. Which he did, because eventually some 20,000 prints of his splendid painting were sold.

We had similar discussions for his powerful D-Day painting because, once again, the space between the Spitfires had to be right and had he shown us flying straight and level, with about 200 yards between each pair of our finger four, the painting would have been far too big. So Robert and I decided that the four leading Spitfires of 144 (Canadian) Wing, should be shown turning because when the cloud base was low, as it was on D-Day, and when there were hundreds of other aeroplanes in the vicinity, we closed up in the turn and, again, Robert got it just right.

I very much like *The Dambusters* and *Last Flight Home* because they symbolise the tremendous effort of Bomber Command during World War II and remind us that throughout that long contest 'night after night, undeterred by the fury of the guns and the new inventions of death' they battled their way over Germany and paid a terrible price for a total of 70,253 aircrew killed or missing on operations, 47,293 came from Bomber Command. At the end of the war Marshal of the Air Force, Sir Arthur Harris, said, 'There are no words with which I can do justice to the aircrews who fought under my command. There is no parallel in warfare to such courage and determination in the face of so prolonged a period of danger which, at times, was so great that scarcely one man in three could expect to survive his tour of thirty operations.'

My favourite painting from this outstanding collection must be *Memorial Flight* not only because of its wonderful composition and the serenity of a no longer hostile sky, but because to me these three splendid aeroplanes represent the Royal Air Force during World War II of whom John Terraine, concluding his excellent book *The Right of the Line* writes:

'And what of the aircrews, the flyers, the ones who left their burnt bones scattered over all of Europe. In those young men, we may discern the many faces of courage, the constitution of heroes: in lonely cockpits at dizzy altitudes, quartering the treacherous and limitless sea, searching the Desert's hostile glare, brushing the peaks of high mountains, in the ferocity of low-level attack or the long, tense haul of a bombing mission, in fog, in deadly cold, in storm . . . on fire . . . in a prison camp . . . in a skin grafting hospital . . . My title shows what I think of them: there is no prouder place, none deserving more honour, than the right of the line.'

Robert Taylor's paintings recapture the spirit of the wartime bravery of the combat aircrews and this book is a fitting tribute to their memory.

Johnnie Johnson.

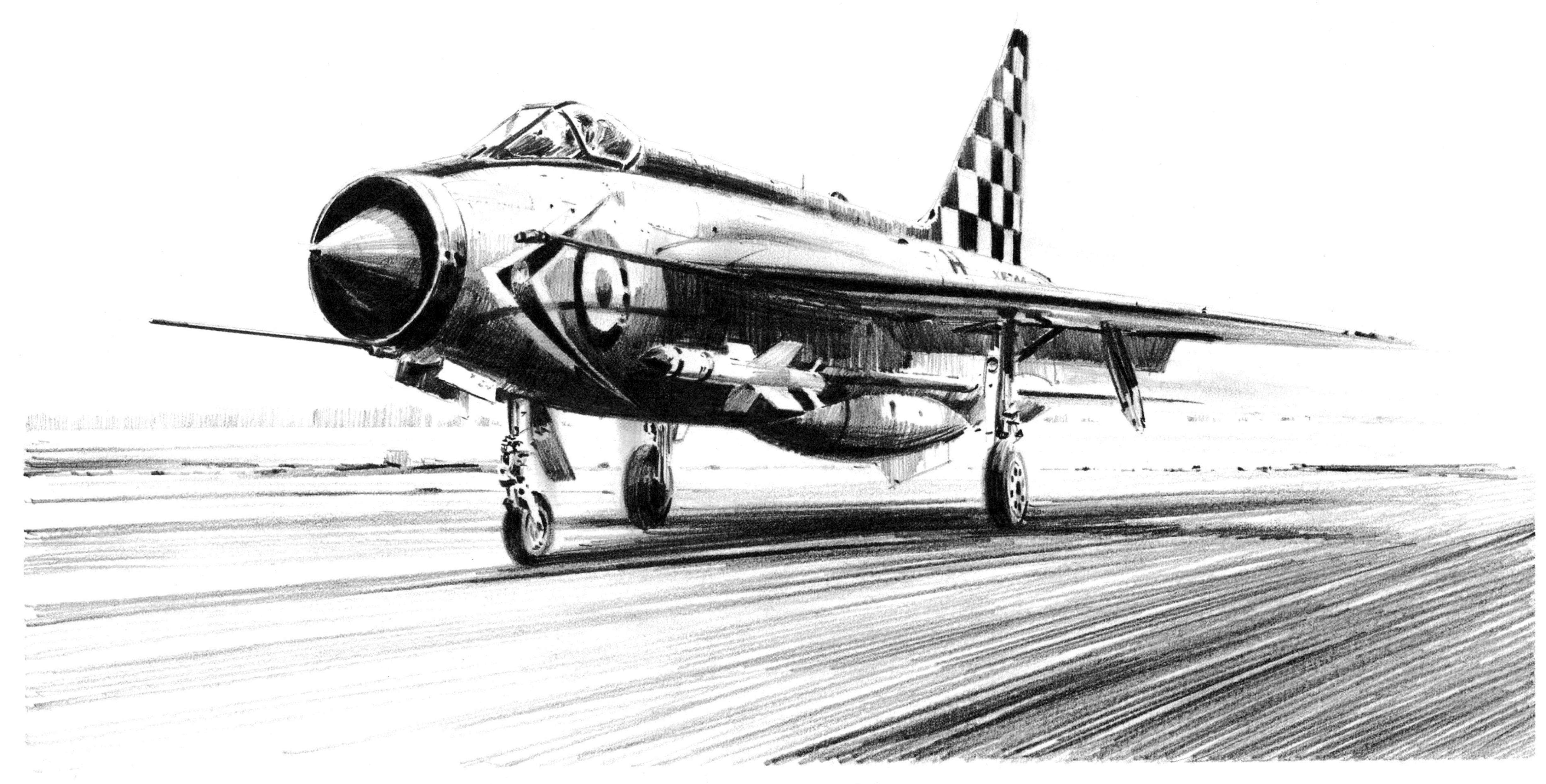

BAC LIGHTNING F.3. Wattisham based 56 Sqn 65.

INTRODUCTION

Very few people are lucky enough to make their living pursuing their favourite pastime. I am one!

As a young boy it was one of my most frequent daydreams that one day I would lead the life of a professional painter. All my life I have never really wanted to do anything else but paint, and I count myself amongst life's most fortunate that I have, since 1977, been able to achieve this ambition.

As a young art student I was made aware of the difficulties that confronted the budding young fine art painter. In the world of commercial art there were jobs available in design studios, advertising agencies and the like, but nobody ever offered a fine art painter a job! The painter, like his predecessors over the centuries, has always to find a way of achieving a living entirely by himself.

Starving in the proverbial garrett was not an option ever open to me, let alone one that I may have chosen – I was expected to earn a living when I reached the prescribed age! The fortunate sequence of events which have charted my life commenced with an unexpected opportunity which took me from school straight into the fine art business through an unexpected door.

I started my working career as an apprentice picture framer, which led me fairly quickly into the world of picture restoration. I enjoyed almost fifteen years with one company in the city of Bath, where I have lived all my life. During these happy years I spent every spare moment drawing and painting, and this activity, combined with my restoration work, provided me with the confidence to turn to painting professionally when the opportunity presented itself.

Believing that opportunities are always there for those looking for them, I again became the beneficiary of a sequence of fortunate events which allowed me to fulfil my boyhood dreams, and become a professional painter.

Even so I still wonder at my good fortune, for not only am I now able to paint the subjects I most enjoy – aircraft and ships in their environment – but I have met and become acquainted with many of my boyhood heroes, distinguished people who have excelled most in the fields of aviation and seafaring. My entire career as an artist has been a succession of delightful encounters with some of the most successful, fascinating and charming characters associated with these subjects. A number of these acquaintances, in addition to their indispensible help with the research for my paintings, have generously agreed to write first-hand accounts of their experiences for this book. I have acknowledged more fully these kind contributions later in the volume.

As a youngster I collected as many of the books of the great artists' work as I could afford. Reading their biographies, learning their techniques and simply marvelling at the wonderful colour plates illustrating their paintings was always a great inspiration to me. I confess that another of my boyhood dreams was that I too would one day have a book published of my own paintings. That this has happened is due to the kindness and help of many people, and to all of these friends I owe a huge debt of gratitude.

The publication of this book represents for me an important landmark in my painting career. I hope it gives as much enjoyment to the reader as it has given me in its preparation. But I hope most of all that it might inspire some young aspiring artist somewhere to daydream, then persevere so that one day he may too have a book of his own work published.

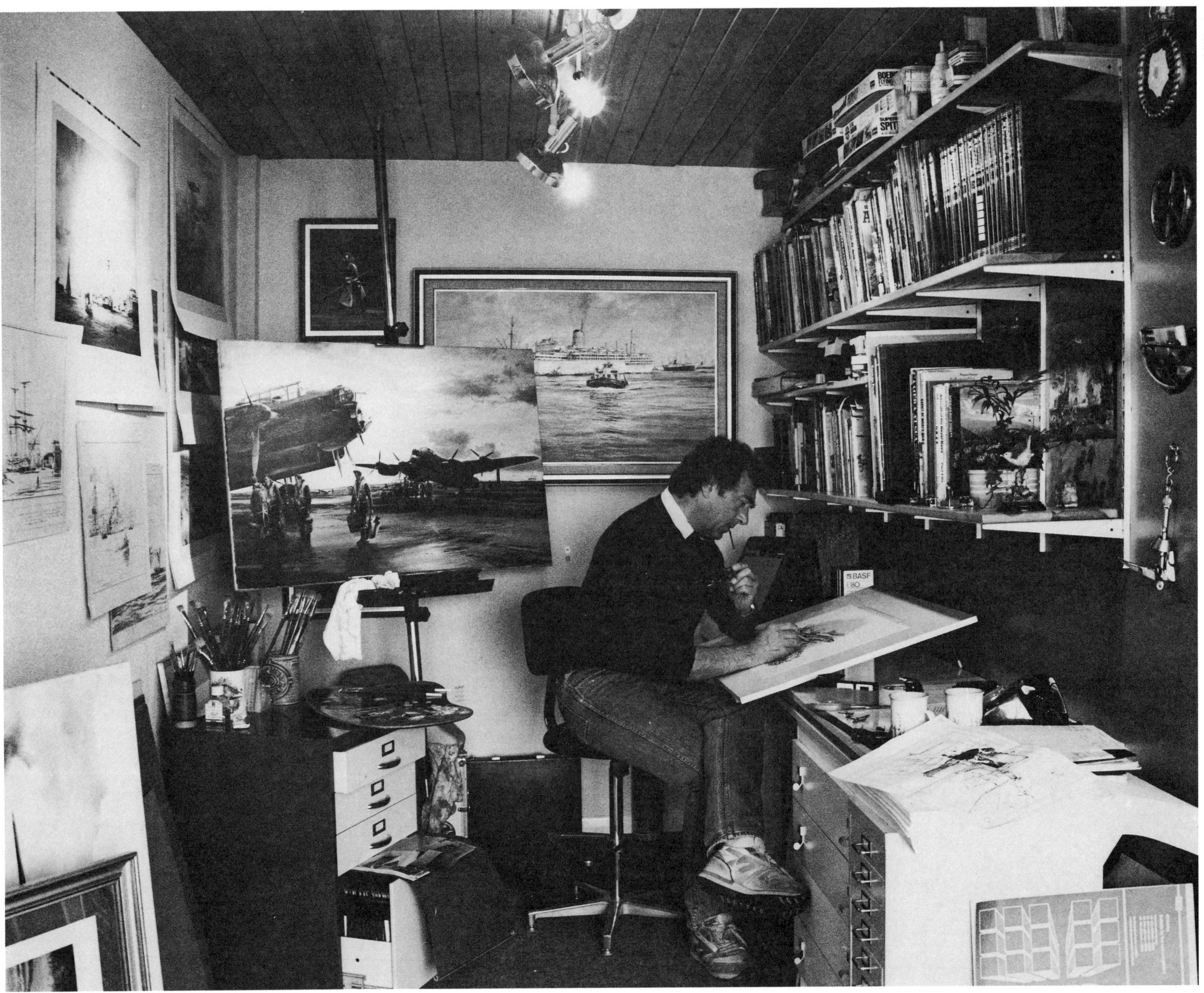
BASF

ROBERT TAYLOR

Robert Taylor is a man one might meet at a party, or pass in the street, and never suspect the magnitude of his reputation as an artist, nor imagine the intensity of his application to his art. Not for him the flamboyant dress, extravagant gestures and strident opinions of the archetypal 'creative genius'. He is a thoughtful, quietly-spoken and modest man whose most powerful statements are made in oil on canvas. In the last few years Robert's work has been exhibited in some of the world's most prestigious museums and galleries. At auction his prints have realised values many times their original published prices. He has become personally aquainted with many of the world's most eminent twentieth-century military figures, yet his attitude towards the prodigious skill which has brought him this recognition is one of mild surprise. He rarely expresses unqualified satisfaction with a piece of work he has completed and is constantly at pains to improve his technique.

The public acclaim which has accompanied this dramatic increase in the popularity of his work has had little effect on his outward manner and views. Indeed, if it has made any change at all to his attitude regarding his work, it has been to increase his commitment to his chosen career. He confesses to a strong disinclination to 'blunder in the limelight' and feels a powerful duty to his considerable audience to give his very best performance.

Robert Taylor was born in Bath in 1946. Coming into the world in the immediate post-war era gave him a unique view of life in his early years. Oblivious of the discomforts and privations caused by the recent turmoil – though many provisions were still scarce, he had never known any other way of life – the earliest impressions he can remember are of a happy and optimistic community, relieved of fear and suffering and in a celebratory mood. The stories he was raised upon were of daring exploits which coloured his vivid imagination. The soldiers, sailors and airmen who had fought so valiantly for his carefree existence were heroes. They were no different, in his eyes, from the glamorous knights of old whose chivalry and good humour were as essential to their character as was their determination in battle.

From an early age he could draw exceptionally well and he quickly began to employ this natural gift to portray his favourite subjects – aircraft, ships and occasionally locomotives. Having had numerous successes with art competitions, both at school and within the village-like community that was post-war Bath, his talent and industrious output were acknowledged to be more than a passing phase. Robert recalls one day meeting a friend who until quite recently had been at school with him, though in a higher form. His friend was now immaculately turned out in a blue uniform with grey piping. On the pocket was a school badge featuring an owl in flight. Robert asked his friend where he was going. 'To my new school where we do almost nothing but draw and paint!' was the reply. Robert remembers thinking then that this must be the ultimate form of education! He never imagined at the time that he might one day himself become a pupil at that very same school. He was entered for the scholarship examinations for the Bath School of Art a few years later, at the age of ten. Despite the high standards set by such a specialised establishment, Robert quickly found himself a member of this elite group and the formal development of his innate ability had begun. Suddenly he was more than a gifted child who happened to enjoy pursuing art as just another pastime, along with stamp-collecting, train-spotting and climbing trees. He was a full-time art student and he could not imagine a better life. Gone were the days when he was so often discovered sketching aircraft and ships under his desk top and reprimanded for neglecting the 'three Rs'. Now he was not only actively encouraged to follow his natural inclination towards art but was also provided with all the materials and sympathetic expert guidance he could wish for.

During the years he spent at the Bath School of Art, Robert completed all the standard foundation courses, and a personal preference began to emerge. He had studied sculpture, architecture, measured drawing, pottery, metalwork, woodwork and many other forms of visual art. He had discovered the wide variety of styles from Pre-Raphaelite to Impressionist, from Abstract-Expressionist to Surrealist.

'It was not so much that I had developed a distinct, recognisable style of my own', says Robert, 'but my preference for certain types of subject was growing very much stronger. More than this I was beginning to understand better how to exploit such strengths as I had so as to produce the best work I could. This in turn led to a focusing of method upon which I have based all my subsequent work over the years.'

Most people would probably agree that today the 'Robert Taylor style' is a real, recognisable phenomenon and that since he settled upon the portrayal of aircraft and ships this style has become a distinctive hallmark in all his paintings. Asked why he felt he had chosen these subjects and why they had remained a lifelong passion, Robert explained: 'Like any painter of natural scenes I have always found a fascination in the un-tamed elements – the raw power of the sea, the winds, rain, snow and sunshine, and the infinite range of character they reveal to us. But in addition to this I admire that aspect of human nature which is constantly striving to conquer those elements. Just as when a man breaks in a horse, he is trying to achieve control over it so as to put it to use for practical or pleasurable ends. However, even the greatest horseman can never be sure that he has total control. The horse, being physically much more powerful than the man, may at any moment throw him to the ground or take off with its rider, uncontrollably, in a direction of its own choosing. In the same way, man has made great steps towards conquering the elements, yet he can never rest on his laurels since his technical advances are nothing compared with the forces nature can bring to bear. Thus, even when I paint an aircraft in a sunlit sky or a ship making good speed in a calm sea, for me there is always a thrill of tension and expectancy. Man is showing a noble, pioneering and courageous facet of his character but is able to do so only so long as nature chooses to play along.'

So, having identified the beginnings of his artistic leanings and settled upon the direction in which he wanted to pursue them, the time inevitably arrived when Robert had to resolve an even more complex question – the course of his working career. As his mind became sharpened by the imminent completion of his time at the Bath School of Art he began to recognise more clearly that he faced a dilemma. He felt a very strong desire to make his way as a professional painter but knew that the proportion of artists able to support themselves from painting alone was very small indeed. He also had a yearning for a naval career having listened, enthralled, countless times over the years, to the tales told by his uncle – a Petty Officer in the Royal Navy – of fabulous travels to exotic lands during his days at sea. Robert was aware though that, at fifteen years of age, he was too

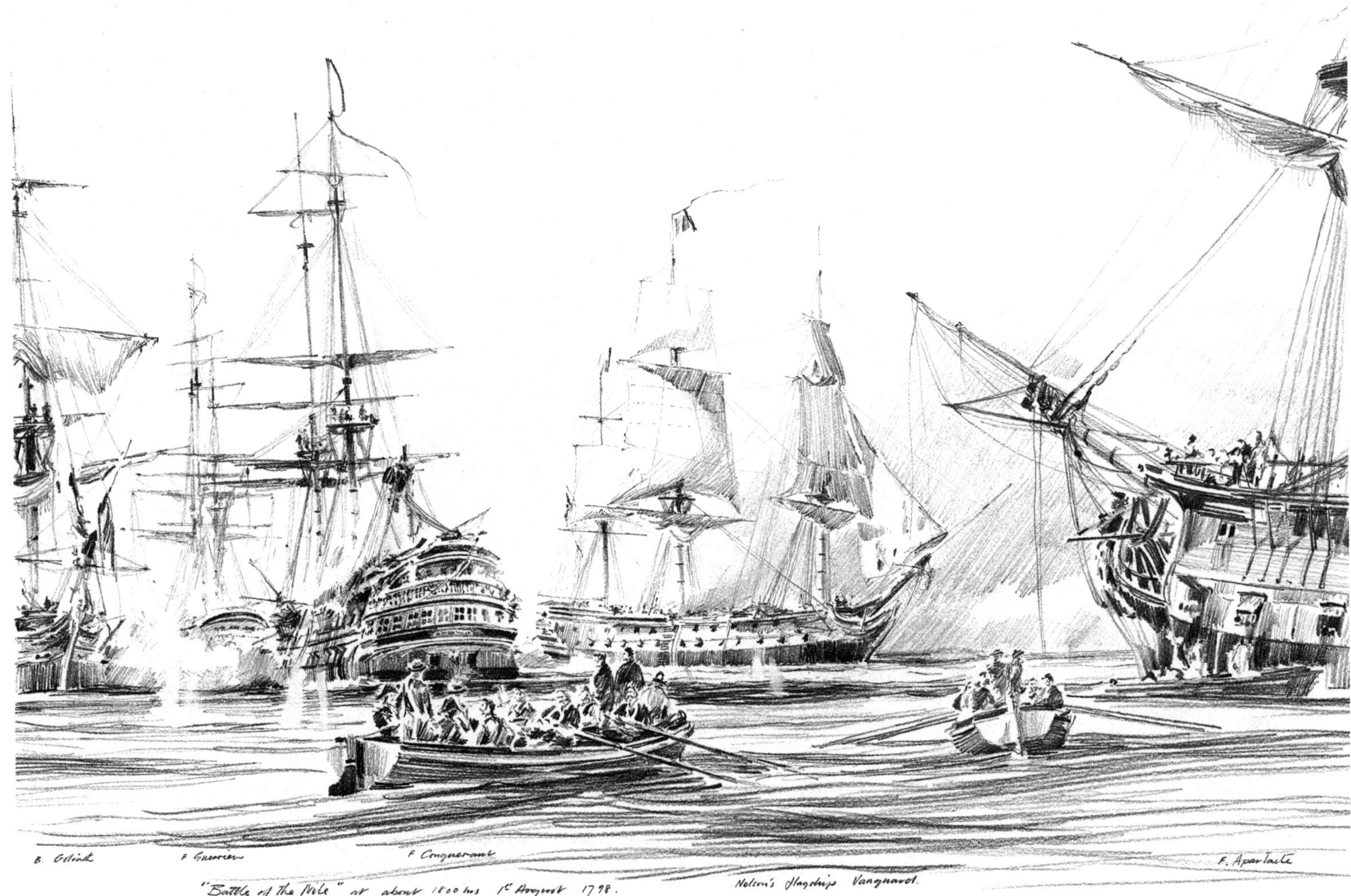

young to enter either the Royal Navy or the Merchant Navy in the type of post he would prefer. The need to find work of some sort was very pressing since his family badly needed a boost to their income and he felt that he owed it to them to provide whatever contribution he could.

Learning that there were vacancies at the local Clark's Shoes establishment, he applied for a job. An invitation to attend an interview with the Personnel Officer duly arrived.

Robert walked into the interview room at Clark's on the appointed day, feeling a mixture of apprehension and pride. He did not feel that such an establishment could provide him with the type of employment which would satisfy his idealistic dreams nor did he feel confident that he would be suitably qualified for the type of vacancy they had to offer. On the other hand, he was rapidly approaching the status of 'working man' and, to a fifteen-year-old, that phrase carried a great deal of prestige.

Despite his misgivings the interview was to prove instrumental, ultimately, in Robert's achieving his greatest ambition. The Personnel Officer was a friendly and sympathetic man and he rapidly dispelled all the nervousness Robert had felt. After a series of apparently unconnected questions regarding his family, school life, preferences and ambitions, he closed the file on his desk and looked up smiling.

'My feeling is, Mr Taylor', – Robert sat up a little at the first use of this title in his life – 'that I ought not to offer you a post with this company.' Unexpectedly deflated, he felt himself slip back down again.

'Please do not misunderstand me. There are openings here and you are capable of fulfilling our requirements in several areas but, with your abilities and ambitions, you would find the work less satisfying and neither of us would benefit.'

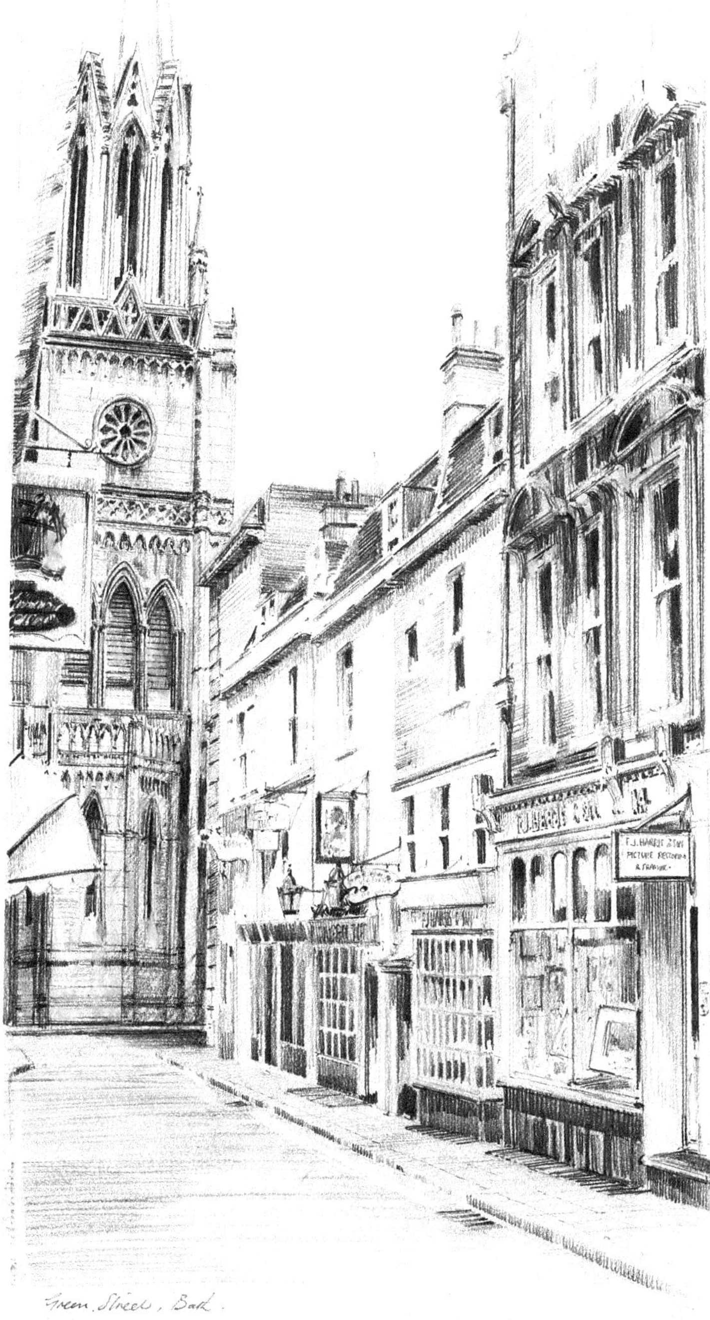

Green Street, Bath.

At this apparent mixture of encouragement and rejection, Robert must have been visibly confused, as his interviewer hurriedly continued: 'What I think you should do, since you are too young to pursue your proposed sea-going activities, is to contact the local Youth Employment Office and try to find a job in an art-related area. Should you find there is nothing available to suit you, then contact me again and I will re-consider your application.' Feeling it would be foolish to waste a rare occasion when he was already spruced up and wearing his 'Sunday best', Robert thanked the man and headed directly for the Youth Employment Office. Upon arriving he discovered there was no queue and he was able to walk straight into the office indicated by the receptionist and explain his situation for the second time that day.

After listening to what he had to say, the clerk he now faced opened a file before him and said, handing him a Situation Vacant form, 'I think we may have just the thing for you, Mr Taylor'. This time the use of the title 'Mr' did not have so pronounced an effect on his posture. What was written on the sheet of paper in his hand, however, brought him to his feet in a moment. He could hardly believe his luck. The vacancy had been registered by a Mr Cedric Harris, who was to conduct interviews personally at his business premises. Cedric Harris was then the owner of F. J. Harris and Son, art dealers, a firm which had received a great deal of Robert's pocket money in recent years in return for brushes, paints, watercolour blocks and all the other materials he needed to satisfy his passion for painting and drawing.

F. J. Harris and Son is an old family firm, established in 1821 by the then owner's grandfather. The business, situated in Green Street, in the centre of Bath, and occupied one of the city's oldest buildings.

At the arranged time Robert arrived and was met, in the ground floor showroom, by Mr Cedric Harris himself. He was a man whose lifelong involvement in the fine art trade had provided him with a wealth of experience and a love of all that it involved.

Mr Harris showed Robert around the wonderfully creaky old premises which housed the business and, as they moved from room to room, they discussed their respective views on many art-related issues. Each began to discover the depth of the other's interest in the creation and presentation of pictures. Upon discovering that he had met a young kindred spirit, Mr Harris offered Robert the job of Apprentice Picture Framer and Robert's career as a working man had begun.

Number 14, Green Street had not altered more than cosmetically in all of its three centuries and the rabbit warren of showrooms, offices, workshops and stores was like a treasure house to Robert.

Every aspect of the fine art trade was handled by Harris's and he could not have hoped for a more thorough introduction to this age-old tradition. He soon got to know the craftsmen and women engaged in designing and producing a vast variety of frames, preparing and stretching canvasses, renovating all types of paintings; the staff responsible for stocking and supplying artists' materials; those who manned the showrooms where a wide variety of finished work – old and new – was on sale; and the managing staff whose unenviable task it was to co-ordinate the skills of this rich collection of characters in their eccentrically arranged rooms on five rickety floors.

Robert quickly discovered how much more complex was the art of picture framing than he had ever realised. To the fifteen-year-old, his employer seemed a very wise old fellow and his ingenuity appeared to be limitless. He had even developed his own unique design for a woodturning lathe which enabled one to produce not circular but elliptical frames. From the production of simple picture frames using ready-made mouldings, Robert rapidly graduated to the more complex operations – he learned to produce his own mouldings from the exotic softwoods and hardwoods imported from all over the world, the list of whose names – makore, sapele, iroko, gelatung – seemed at first like a mysterious and barely pronounceable oriental menu. He also had to learn a wide range of traditional English woods – oak, elm, maple, rosewood and many others. It was not long, however, before he knew them all and was familiar with their delicate variations in grain, colour and texture. As his mastery of the art of framing continued to grow he was introduced to more and more of the sophisticated techniques available to the craftsman. He learned such arts as gilding, to produce a deep, burnished gold appearance, and the production of 'swept' frames with their ornamented 'compo-work' in infinite varieties.

The time came, after almost three years, when Robert had mastered all the skills required of an apprentice and was beginning to feel a diminution in the challenge which had stimulated him so deeply in his early days at Harris's. An astute employer, Cedric Harris quickly identified the problem and had also begun to realise that he had in his employ someone whose talent was potentially of very great value to the company. Ever since his arrival Robert had, from time to time, arrived at work with a sketch, watercolour or oil painting which he had produced himself. He would sometimes ask permission to use the firm's facilities to mount or frame these pieces and this gave Mr Harris the opportunity to inspect the work of his able young apprentice. Not only he but a number of his regular customers began to express an interest in the flair and increasing competence these works displayed.

One Friday afternoon as he was tidying up his workshop ready to leave the building, Robert was asked to visit Mr Harris before going home.

'Robert, I think it's time we had a chat about your career with the firm.'

'Yes Mr Harris?'

'Well you've been with us almost three years now and I don't think we can teach you very much more about framing. The point is we could use a gifted lad like yourself in restoration. What's more I am planning to retire in a few years' time and I need someone who will be able to carry on the work. What do you think of the idea?'

It was impossible at first for Robert to answer. This was just the sort of opportunity he had dreamed of and, though delighted, he was for a moment, spellbound. Eventually the words tumbled out – words of excitement, gratitude and enthusiasm.

'Of course you will have to begin training again but I think you will find the work more stimulating than the framing and if you prove you're up to it, there will be an increase in your wages of course!'

Robert went home that day a proud and supremely happy man. His prospects looked very good indeed. Still in his teens he was to learn, in much greater detail than ever he could at the School of Art, all the techniques of the artists he admired so much. He would be in the privileged position of giving new life to the neglected or damaged works of art of the masters, works he had only previously been able to admire at a respectful distance. He was to make a vast transition from picture framer to a status almost equal, in his estimation at the time, to that of a professional painter. All this and an increase in pay!

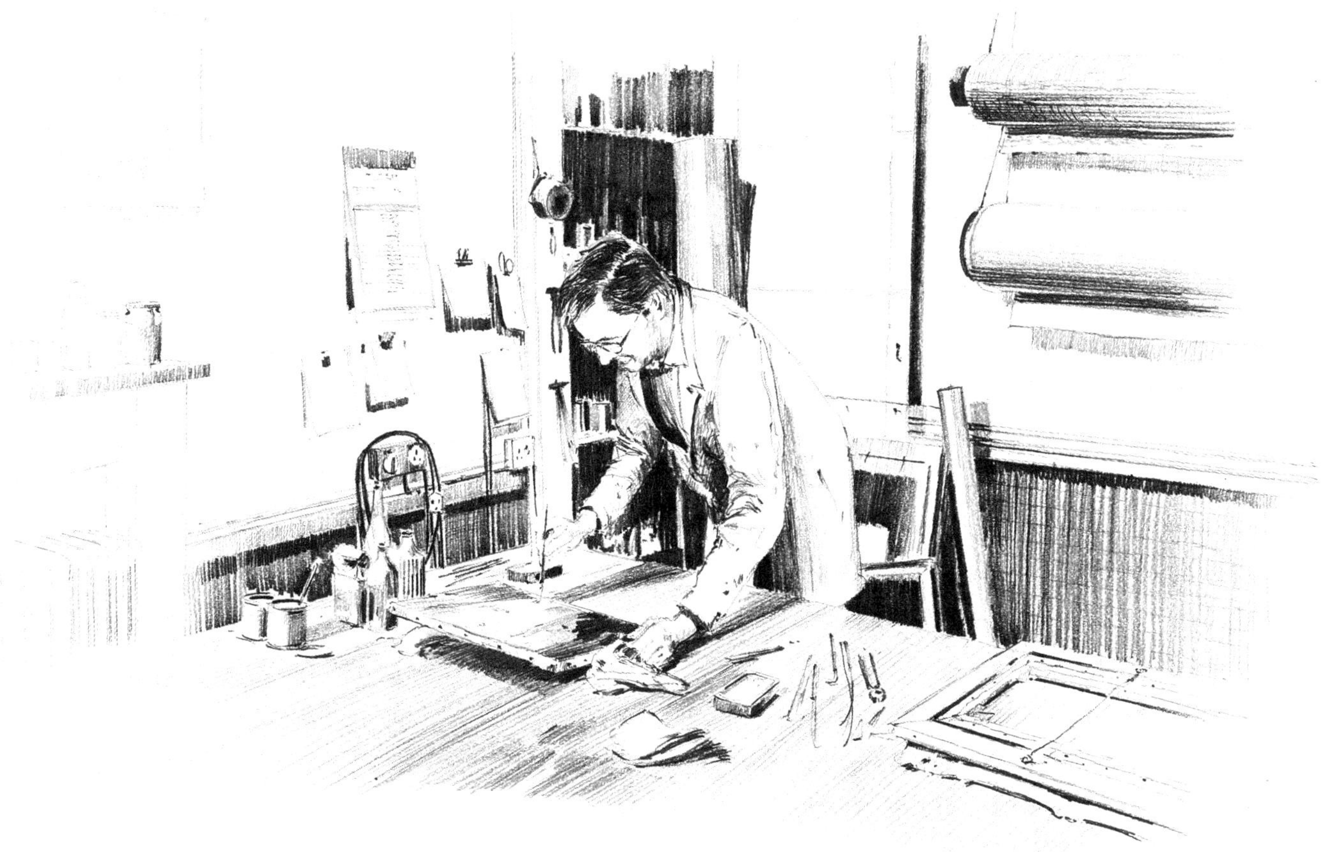

He felt he could not wait to begin.

The weekend, unlike most he had experienced recently, seemed to last for ever. When eventually Monday morning came, Robert arrived at Harris's full of enthusiasm and anticipation.

Until his decision to elevate Robert to his new position, Cedric Harris had carried out most of the restoration work himself. Trained by his grandfather in the intricacies of this complex craft, he was able to bring to bear a broad repertoire of skills in passing on his knowledge. A willing pupil, it was not long before Robert had mastered the techniques required to perform some of the more straightforward oil painting restorations. He and Mr Harris had a great deal in common and they worked together very well. Robert learned quickly and eased the considerable workload. He was also fascinated by the vast treasury of anecdotes and little-known details of local history which his employer related for hours at a stretch as they worked.

In addition to the benefits of his companions' friendship and experience, Robert enjoyed the familiarity which developed as his membership of this circle became firmly established. Though never an acutely shy young man, he had always found that it took him a considerable time to establish deep friendships. The necessary long periods in close contact with others had not often before been possible. As he came to know his workmates better and better, his reticence began to be replaced by a more confident and mischievous manner. Ingenious cartoon drawings – amusing scenes and caricatures of his friends – began to appear on walls and doors throughout the workshops. Booby traps would be sprung by unsuspecting members of staff without any warning. On one notable occasion, still described with great amusement by the staff at Harris's, Robert and a fellow from the framing department dangled a young apprentice out of an upper storey window by his ankles for being cheeky once too often. The shoppers in Bath's salubrious Green Street were stopped in their tracks by the sight of a young boy suspended upside down two floors above the pavement, squealing for his life!

Robert was certainly finding his work a great deal more fun than ever before but also his standing within the company continued to grow as he became more and more proficient at his job. His enjoyment of life outside working hours seemed to keep pace too. He took pleasure in helping the local church as a set designer and painter for the productions staged by their Amateur Dramatic Society. Furthermore his own spare-time painting provided the opportunity to continue developing his technique alongside his rapidly-growing understanding of the methods employed by the great masters of the past. On those rare occasions when his wide-ranging commitments left time for reflection he felt that, but for the constant self-questioning over the possibility of becoming a full-time professional artist, his was a very fortunate and contented existence. It was in such a happy frame of mind that he packed up his tools, brushes and paints and left for a long overdue summer holiday in Weymouth, where he spent many hours along the coast with his sketch book and camera.

Upon returning Robert made another discovery which was to have profound consequences for him. The discovery was Mary Richardson. Mary, having just left school, had been employed by Harris's as a trainee in the fitting shop. Upon seeing the pretty young girl Robert very quickly decided that it would be essential that he take every opportunity to combine his role as understudy to Mr Harris with a little teaching of his own. After all, he had trained for three years as a framer himself and he felt he would not be fulfilling his duty to his employer if he did not pass on the skills he had been taught!

There were two major impediments to his carrying out his obligations in this direction. The first was a rival in the form of a fellow worker – also a school-leaver – who had joined at the same time as Mary and whose lovestruck expression betrayed his feelings all too evidently. The second and more serious problem was Robert's intense shyness where girls were concerned. Whenever he found himself in the same room as the object of his secret affection, his mind seemed to seize up and he could not summon the words to express his feelings. Furthermore he worked on the third floor in the exalted atmosphere of the restoring rooms while Mary spent all her time in the fitting shop on the first floor.

Eventually, after countless visits to the fitting shop on a variety of pretexts, still with no success, Robert was beginning to run out of excuses for being there. He could also feel his rival hot on his heels. He braced himself for the ordeal and blurted out a stumbling suggestion that she might, perhaps, like to go to the local cinema with him.

It would certainly have been a great deal easier for him had he known at the time that not only would she accept his offer but that in a few years' time she would become his wife and, over the succeeding years, bear him five children!

Meanwhile, back on planet Earth, Robert's progress under the guidance of Mr Harris was proving to be rapid and sure. He had acquired a deep understanding of a wide range of styles and periods and could turn his hand to almost all the tasks assigned to the company by their appreciative clientele: oils, watercolours, prints, etchings, pastels. In addition to the more usual paper and canvas, he learned to work with wood, porcelain and glass. He worked on paintings of all styles and periods: Rubens, Corot, Canaletto, Raeburn, Augustus John, Gainsborough amongst them. The versatility required as a restorer was unbounded.

Surprisingly, cleaning was, in many cases, the most taxing of the tasks he faced. Gainsborough's technique, for example, often involved building up form, tone and shadow using base colour only – black, white and greys – and then adding colour over the top using glazes. The whole would be varnished and, over the years, with the mellowing process far advanced, it became almost impossible to determine where the varnish ended and the glaze began.

Mr Harris had, in the many years of perfecting his restoration techniques, pioneered several new methods which he gradually revealed to Robert. His pupil was soon able, in turn, to make further advances himself in response to the challenges thrown down by the customers. Paintings sometimes arrived having come through the most horrific ravages of the elements – floods, fires, storms and heavy seas. Also, human agency proved very helpful in keeping the art of the restorer alive – burglaries, arguments, clumsiness and ignorance all played a significant part in maintaining the flow of sad and sorry looking works of art arriving to be rejuvenated. One morning a local customer arrived with a painting which was so appallingly torn and covered in mud that Robert wondered whether it would be possible to restore it at all. Its unfortunate owner had set out from a nearby village with the six feet by four canvas, which had only needed cleaning, lashed to the roof of his car. On passing over the brow of the local Lansdown Hill, something in his rear view mirror had caught his eye. His painting had been wrenched from the roof of the car and was careering across a field in the wind!

On some occasions it was impossible for the paintings to be brought to the workshops so Robert would go to the paintings. Churches and stately homes, typically, required large numbers of works restored. He once completed the restoration of an entire collection of thirty paintings in one house. Elaborate memorial plaques in the nearby Lacock church, and even a number of very old Russian icons benefited from his expert touch.

Throughout the thirteen years Robert spent as a professional restorer, he continued to paint for pleasure in his spare time and occasionally undertook a commission for friends or family members. His constant exposure to the works of some of the greatest artists naturally had influenced his own style. He has always had a close affinity with the Dutch Masters and admires most of all their high-contrasting rich use of colour and fine detail. This influence, perhaps more than any other, permeates his work still today and can be seen in his treatment of both seascapes and aviation subjects with their formidable cloud formations and 'living' seas.

As time went by, his reputation grew and people he had never met, having heard of or seen examples of his work, began to commission paintings. The model museum at nearby Oakhill Manor, which housed a fine collection of model ships and trains, had asked Robert to produce, over a period of time, some eight large paintings each measuring six feet by three, depicting in lifelike settings the ships whose models were on show. This was at the time a considerable undertaking for so young a painter and the owner of the museum, Mr Harper, deserves credit for his astute judgement and the confidence he placed in the young

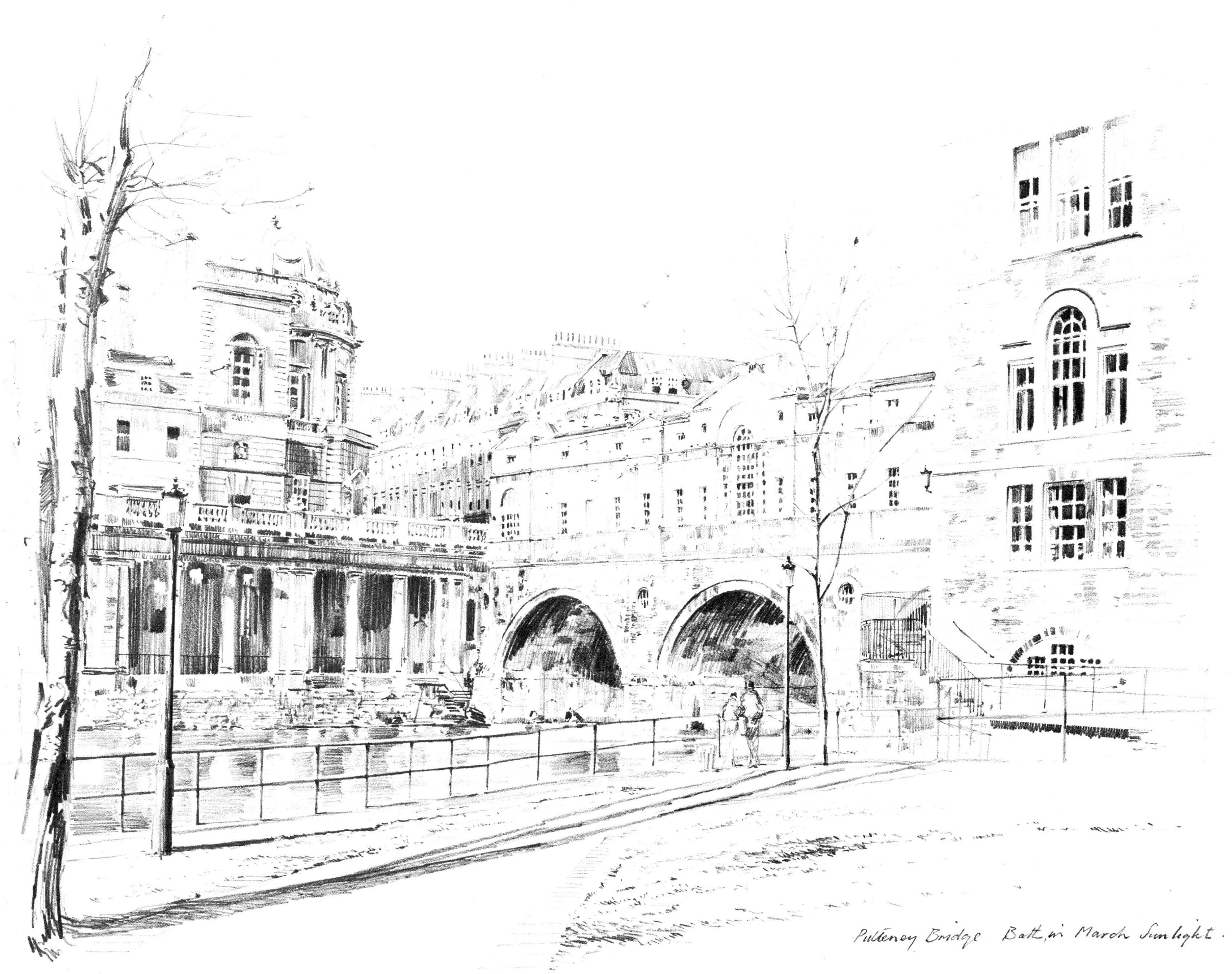
Pulteney Bridge Bath, in March Sunlight.

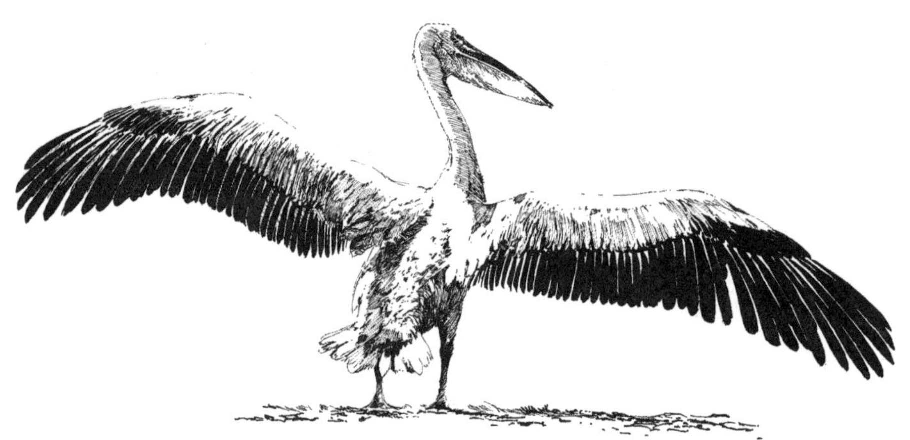

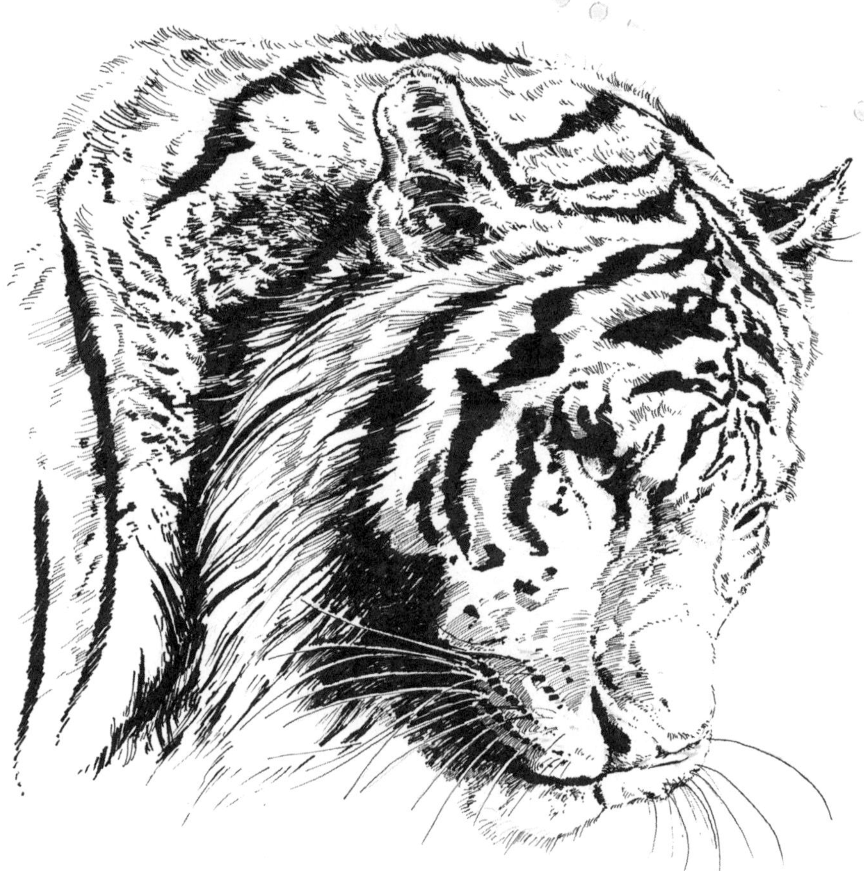

Robert Taylor. This was gratifying to the aspiring professional side of his nature but set up in his mind something of a conflict. With commitments such as those he was by then encumbered with, the only way to survive as a full-time professional painter would be to establish a reputation such that he would never be without commissioned work. Alternatively he had to be confident that speculative paintings would sell quickly and at a good price. While Robert had achieved very widespread acceptance the question of living purely from his paintings had never arisen. Now, however, his name was becoming better known and the possibility was becoming more of a reality. The matter tantalised him increasingly. His most serious concern, however, was that although, in his younger days, life in an artist's garret may have been a possible, if uncomfortable, prospect, he now had responsibilities which precluded this type of precarious existence. His regular salary cheques were required to provide for a wife and three children. He had also taken on a mortgage and other related financial commitments which made any such risks inconsiderate at best. Coincidentally, at this period of his life, when he was again thinking seriously about how he might break into the competitive and insecure world of the professional artist, he was introduced to the chairman of a fine art publishing company by a mutual friend. Another fortunate coincidence was that this company was based in the city of Bath.

The chairman of the company, Pat Barnard, recalls their first meeting: 'Robert came along to see me at my office, bringing with him a couple of examples of his paintings. They were both watercolours. I remember one was a study of an owl. I was immediately impressed by the detail and, although there was no composition about such a study, I wanted to see more of his work. I asked if he ever painted in oil, to which he replied that he did, and indeed much prefered to work in that medium.

I also remember immediately liking him. He was quiet, yet confident, and struck me as being a very level-headed young chap – which incidentally is a very important quality a publisher likes to see in an artist. I sensed he had a real ambition, and so I asked him if he would like to accept a rather testing commission. I proposed – "If you are prepared to paint me a picture in oil, and I think it has sufficient merit, I will buy the painting and publish prints from it. If I do not think it has the required quality, you keep the painting and I will pay you nothing."

I reckoned that if he was made of the right stuff, and had sufficient confidence in his own ability, he would demonstrate that he had the amount of ambition needed to succeed by taking up the challenge. Robert accepted the commission without hesitation.

When, a few weeks later, he returned with a painting (we had agreed it should depict a tiger), I knew instantly that if he truly wanted it he had a great future as a professional artist. The quality of the work in the painting he showed me was superior to that of many artists whose work was already being published regularly. I was sure that if this part-time painter had the fortitude of character and was prepared to make all the sacrifices necessary to succeed as a full-time professional, he certainly already had all the required natural talent.

We talked at length about his aspirations and the more we talked the more I felt sure that here was a big star of the future. In my opinion he showed, at that crucial time of his life, all the right ingredients in both character and ability.

Robert and I have had a wonderful working friendship ever since.'

What Pat Barnard did not tell Robert when issuing his challenging commission, was that if it came up to his expectations, it would be the first of four paintings featuring the Big Cats at Lord Bath's famous Longleat Safari Park. These would be published as prints and sold through a national TV promotion. Had Robert known all this at the time he probably would not have slept for a week!

After accepting Pat Barnard's commission for three more paintings, Robert returned home to discuss with his wife the implications of the project upon their future. He pointed out that painting for publishers, or to criteria laid down by their clients, might mean a threat to his choice of subject matter and style of execution. He added that, no matter how favourable the terms agreed with his publishers, the real benefits would not begin to accrue until his reputation was very much better established and this could take many years. He expressed his fears over the matter of paying the substantial bills generated by a growing family. He pointed out that he felt a great loyalty towards his present employers and was aware that their thriving restoration service would probably suffer if he were abruptly to leave the firm. Mary's reaction to his playing devil's advocate was more positive than he could have hoped for. She listened carefully to all his doubts and fears and agreed that if he were to go ahead and turn professional it would mean many changes in their lives. She acknowledged that there was a serious element of risk in abandoning a successful career in an area where few opportunities arose. She then turned to look at the expression on his face and pointed out that it was very difficult to reconcile the difficulties and dangers he was describing with the excitement and anticipation he was so unsuccessfully trying to hide. She knew that his overriding feeling was that this opportunity represented everything he had most hoped for in all the time she had known him and, smiling, she gave him her support.

The decision to move from Harris's was in many ways difficult and painful for Robert. Whilst he desperately wanted to become a full-time painter, he felt very close to the company and, in particular, to the Harris family. Happily this was resolved for him in the easiest possible way. The Harris family were, though concerned for his well-being, very helpful and made no attempt to stand in his way – despite the loss to their restoration business that his departure represented. So it was that Robert's career as a professional artist was launched.

Robert did not fall short of the judgement Pat Barnard had made in assessing his ability: all four paintings were to become national best-selling prints and these were to be the first of a whole succession of popular prints that would be published in the years to come. No amount of planning and soul-searching could have prepared Robert for the drama and speed of the changes that were to occur in his life. Within mere months he found himself at the ITV studios in London, discussing the preparations for a forthcoming series of TV advertisements for the prints from the Longleat paintings.

This was rapidly followed by the unexpected pleasure of seeing his work reproduced for the first time in print. When he saw the fresh, clean, identical sheets emerging from the press, each bearing the image of his own work, he experienced an exhilaration he had never before encountered. On the evening when the first advertisement for his prints appeared on television, and he watched on his screen Lord Bath strolling in the grounds of Longleat House, extolling 'the beauty and depth of feeling to be found in the work of the artist, Robert Taylor', he was still not fully prepared for the thought that his audience had expanded from a maximum of a dozen or so friends to millions across the country, all within a matter of months!

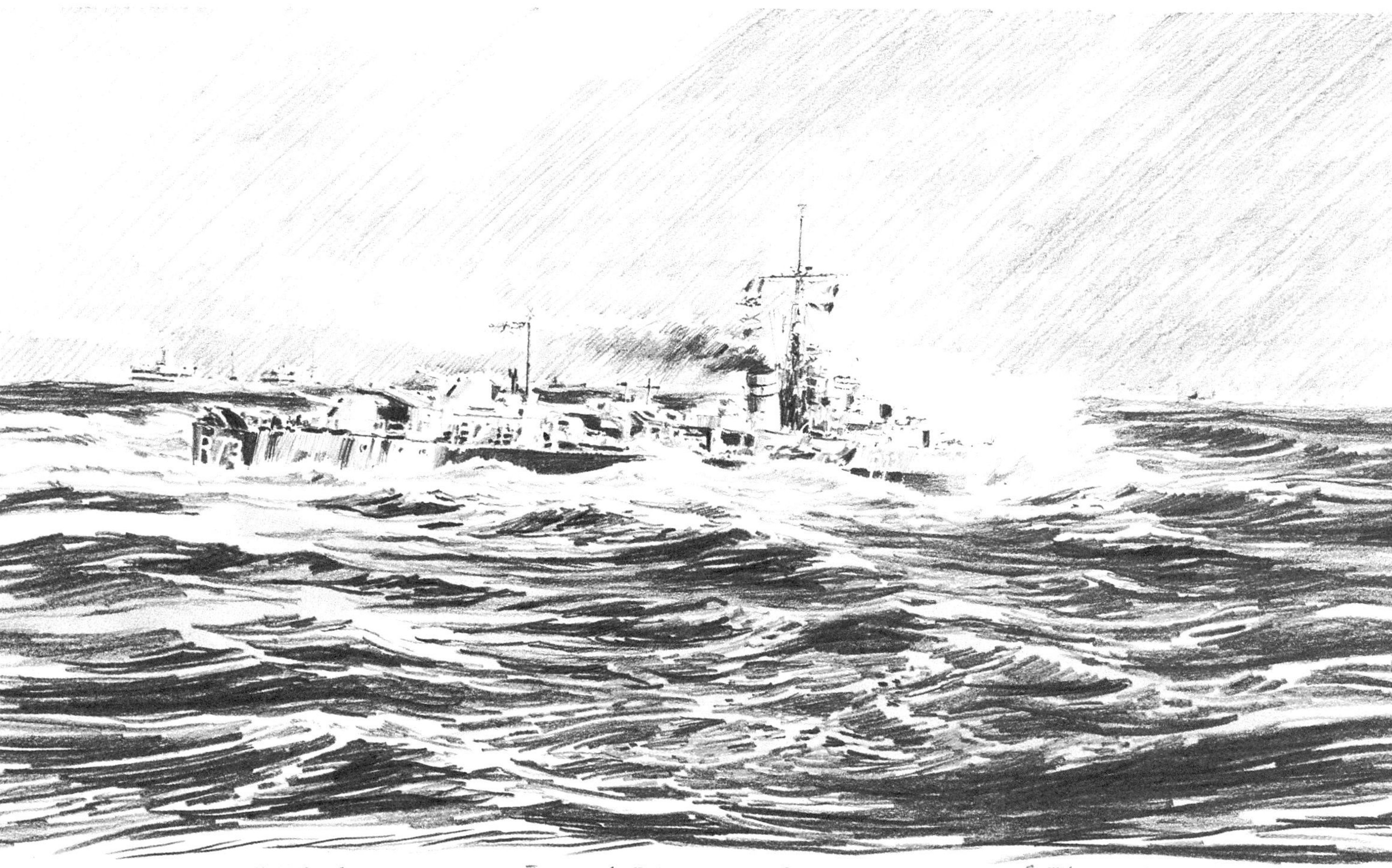
H.M.S. CAVALIER escorting Arctic convoy RA64, bound for Scotland from Murmansk.

As the popularity of his prints grew, Robert found that Boots, the major retail group, had elected to offer his prints to their customers and that these could now be found in hundreds of showrooms all over the country. His publishers continued to perform their role and his reputation was spreading like a forest fire. Perhaps best of all for him, Robert was able, at last, to spend all his time researching and painting. He designed and built a new studio extension to his house. He was a contented man.

On one occasion, when the first flush of excitement had subsided, Pat Barnard asked Robert 'If you had to choose one subject to paint for the rest of your life, what would it be?' It was not a question Robert was prepared for or indeed had ever asked himself directly, but it did not take him long to answer. 'It would be,' he said, 'ships and the sea.'

Like all gifted representational artists Robert Taylor can paint most subjects with great realism and flair. Some of his early wildlife paintings in oil rank very respectably alongside the best such paintings published as prints during the period, and he can paint a very accomplished landscape. His true love, though, is always closely associated with the elements, and man's eternal efforts to tether in some way their unlimited force.

The purpose of Pat Barnard's question was to establish the general direction in which Robert felt he wanted his art to move. Robert quickly realised this. More perhaps than most, an artist's career is closely scrutinised and Robert has, during his years as a professional painter, maintained a process of personal assessment and review. He is a constant critic of his own work and accepts constructive comment from others with intelligence and good grace. It is this continual process that has manifested itself in his style as it is known and recognised today. Knowing that no matter how versatile a painter may be, he will produce his best work in the area he most enjoys, Pat immediately proposed a series of marine paintings which Robert set about with very evident delight. He found it satisfying that the demand for his work was already such that by performing this most pleasant of tasks he could comfortably provide for his family and fulfil his greatest ambitions all at once.

As his reputation for works of marine art continued to develop, an increasing number of commissions began to arrive. One in particular excited him more than usual: Would he like to paint the two famous World War II destroyers HMS *Kelly* and HMS *Cavalier* as part of a fund-raising exercise for the HMS *Cavalier* Trust? HMS *Cavalier* was the last surviving World War II destroyer. She was in imminent danger of being scrapped and a Trust had been formed to preserve her, if possible, as a museum ship.

Robert's circle of eminent acquaintances was already by this time rapidly expanding, and this circle was significantly added to during the new project: President of the HMS *Cavalier* Trust was Admiral of the Fleet, Lord Louis Mountbatten. As President, Lord Mountbatten had agreed to sign each of the prints published from Robert's paintings. This valuable endorsement led to a rapid success for the project and £20,000 was raised for the Trust. Today HMS *Cavalier* is moored at Brighton where she is open to the public as a Museum Ship.

This enterprise generated a great deal of public interest and soon Robert's work became the subject of a prominent double-page feature article in a national newspaper – the *Daily Express*. Furthermore, Robert noted with delight, the press had quoted some extremely flattering remarks made about his work by Lord Mountbatten himself. An accolade indeed.

The paintings and prints for the *Cavalier* Trust were a great success and brought Robert to the notice of a new and much wider audience. It was not long before another similar commission arose. HMS *Ark Royal*, the last of the great British aircraft carriers, was de-commissioned in 1979 and Robert was asked to paint a picture to commemorate this famous naval vessel's service. It was an exciting project, and one which was to bring the young painter a degree of success which a couple of years earlier he would have never believed possible: prints from his painting of *Ark Royal* outsold all other prints published in the UK that year! It became a huge best-seller that broke all previous records. Orders were received from over 5000 individuals during the first two days following publication. The military publishing division of Pat Barnard's company – The Military Gallery – needed to take on extra staff to deal with the deluge of orders received for this latest Robert Taylor print.

As is so often the case, success bred further success and, as Robert's work reached a wider and wider audience, he became of increasing interest to the media. After the success of his *Ark Royal* print Robert was approached by BBC Television. Would he please appear on their nation-wide *Pebble Mill at One* programme to discuss his work and views and to show a number of his paintings. He was asked to bring along eight canvases to the BBC TV studios in Birmingham by mid-day on the agreed date. When the day came he arrived with plenty of time to spare and very quickly regretted his mistake. With a full hour to wait before going 'on air' he found his mind turning over the prospect of appearing live before millions of people in an unrehearsed programme. His natural nervousness turned to icy dread. As he was dismissing the one-hundred-and-first hollow excuse for calling the whole thing off, he was jerked back to reality with an abrupt 'You're on in ninety seconds, Mr Taylor. Please take your place.' Within a minute of the beginning of his 'nightmare' he found, to his amazement, that he had been put completely at ease. The professionalism and friendliness of the programme's presenter, Marion Foster, was such that he quickly forgot the cameras and studio audience. It was more as if he were chatting with friends in his own sitting room than being transmitted to television screens in millions of homes. The interview was a great success and before the programme ended there had been a substantial number of calls received from viewers who wanted to know where they could acquire copies of his prints.

Though somewhat overwhelmed by the speed with which he had become almost a 'household name', Robert found his popularity a pleasant experience. Yet an ambition remained which he had yet to fulfil. His widespread acceptance as a marine painter was already well established but he was keen to find a way of conveying to the art-buying public his love of aviation subjects. As his next great passion after painting ships and the sea, he felt there was much he wanted to express in this field. No sooner had he begun to feel the need to address this problem than the solution arrived 'out of the blue', so to speak. It came from the most appropriate quarter – the Fleet Air Arm. He was commissioned to paint one of the most famous of all Fleet Air Arm victories – The Battle of Taranto. Commander Dennis White, OBE, director of the Fleet Air Arm Museum at Yeovilton, introduced Robert to the two pilots who, in 1941, had flown their Swordfish biplanes through heavy barrages of fire to drop flares in advance of the main attacking force, during this daring wartime raid. With these two intrepid pilots, Commanders Charles Lamb

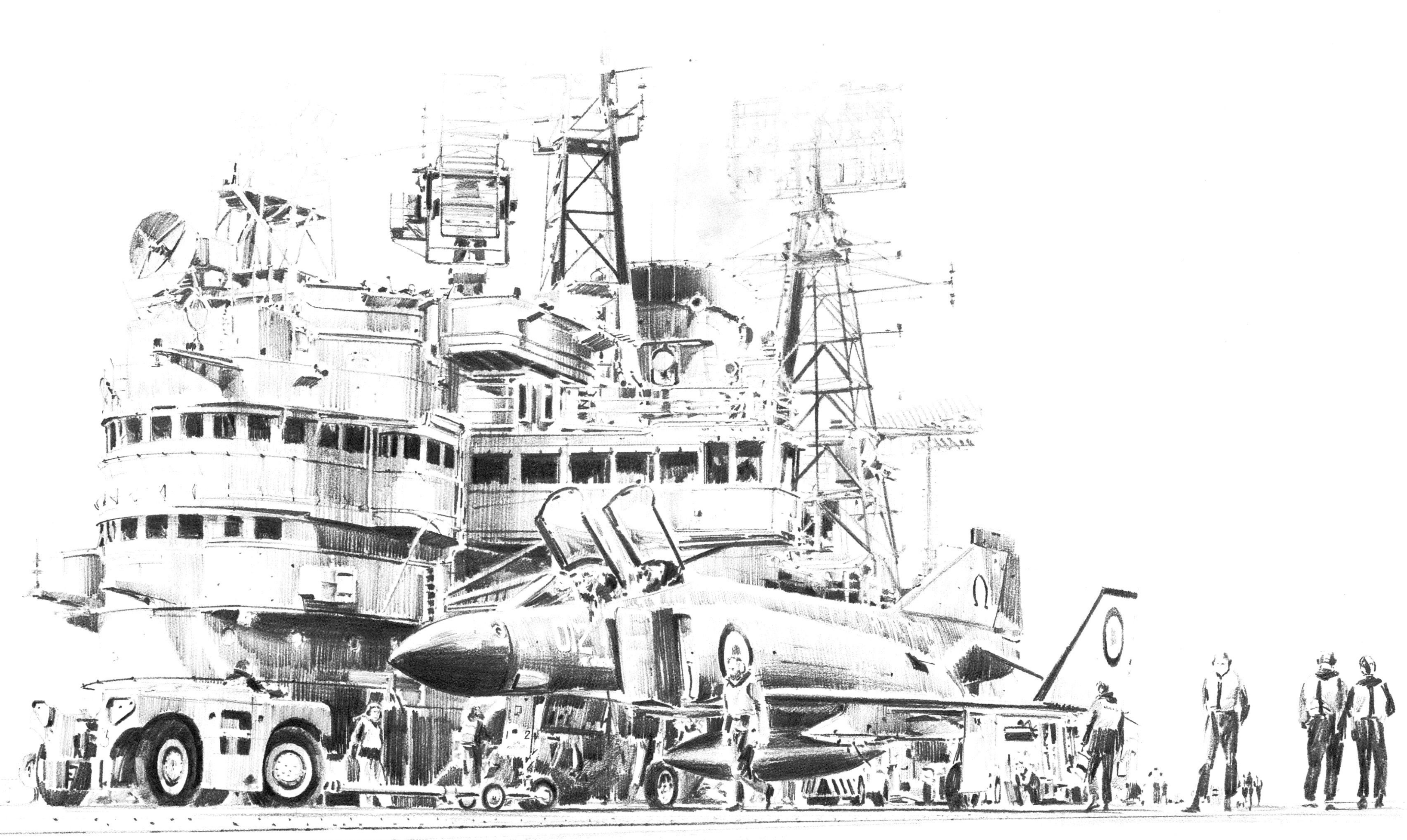

Phantom FG1 of 892 Squadron on Ark's flight deck

and Lancelot Kiggell, Robert went over every detail of that historic night's events. He remembers their enthusiasm for the project and the lively rapport between the two pilots. He recalls in particular Charles Lamb's remarkable talent as a raconteur and how this had brought the raid to life for him so vividly that he almost felt he had witnessed the event himself! The admiration Charles Lamb felt for his fellow airmen, together with his deep love of flying, permeated Robert's consciousness as they talked, and fanned the flames of his own feeling for the subject. He became determined to convey that feeling on canvas. Steeped in enthusiasm Robert painted what is generally considered today to be one of the finest recreations of that famous and heroic victory ever painted. The painting is now on permanent exhibition in the 'Taranto Room' at the Fleet Air Arm Museum.

The acceptance of a commission to paint for a specific and important event can be a daunting prospect for an artist. It took Robert many years as a professional painter before he entered contracts with the same confidence he shows today. He recalls, many years ago painting two pictures for Prime Minister Edward Heath, depicting his famous sailing victories. 'I was terrified when I took the first painting to his house in London. He stood and looked at it for what seemed like an eternity before he said a word. Finally he said "Robert, I think it's magnificent but in the interests of accuracy could you give me a haircut please, and also deepen my suntan".

I had to darken his face and shorten his hair slightly in the picture which I thought was a rather amusing request. Ted Heath was very kind and courteous. As we talked he showed me his collection of paintings, which included a Winston Churchill which had been badly damaged in a bomb attack by the IRA.'

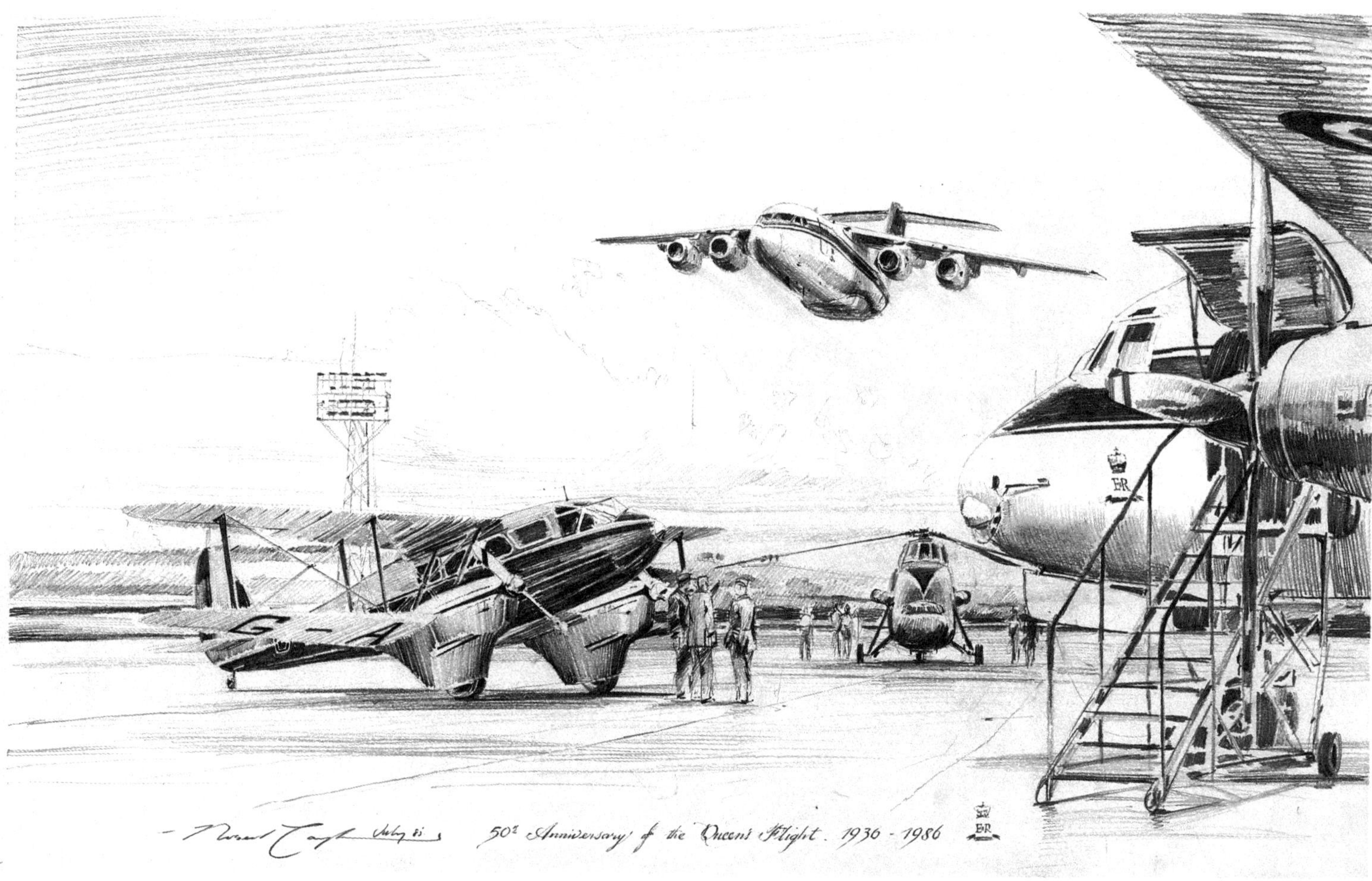

Despite his standing today as an artist it is indicative of his willingness to please that Robert still feels a certain apprehension at that telling moment when a finished painting is first presented to its new owner. Recently he confessed to that same apprehension when commissioned by Her Majesty The Queen's Flight to produce a painting to commemorate fifty years of royal flying. Though the subject matter commissioned was both clearly defined and to be kept within certain constraints, the result was greeted enthusiastically by Air Vice-Marshal John Severn, Captain of the Queen's Flight, at the handing-over ceremony.

As well as enjoying a rapidly-growing reputation among his appreciative public, Robert's status within the art establishment continued to increase. Early in his career he had submitted, and had accepted, paintings for the annual exhibitions of both the Royal Society of Marine Artists and the Guild of Aviation Artists. With his work represented at these and other important exhibitions, other institutions began to take notice of this fast-emerging artist. Today Robert has works on view in many of the most important museums and galleries around the world, where his standing as a military artist is considerable.

Most of Robert's published prints carry the signatures of the famous military people with whom he has consulted in the preparation of his paintings. Robert is proud of the authentication that this adds to his prints, many of which have become greatly sought after during recent years.

A remark often heard about Robert Taylor's painting is that the subjects he paints are 'so real'. It is this perhaps more than anything that makes his work so popular among those who took part in the events he portrays. It may be a rather obvious remark to make that any operational aircraft or ship bears all the outward signs of everyday use: scratches, dents, chips, cracks, missing chunks of paint, rust and other signs of the work for which the vehicle was designed, but few artists seem to achieve authentic portrayal of these scars. Giving his vehicles that look of reality is very important to Robert and accuracy of detail has become a hallmark of his paintings. His aircraft do indeed look as if they have been to war, and not just emerged from the factory: look at the leading edge of the wing of any of his aircraft and see how the paint has been chipped by the elements; study the fuselage behind the exhaust or the gun ports and note how the stains and marks of use are faithfully portrayed. This attention to realism is what gives a Robert Taylor its life.

However, all is not plain sailing: upon completion of a private commission of a Type-22 destroyer, pounding through a North Sea swell on her sea trials, a proud Captain exclaimed 'No ship of mine ever has that much rust on her hull!' Robert visualised a team of painters dangling over the side in all weathers with paint brushes, disguising rust as it appeared. A compromise was reached: some of the rust was removed and a slightly newer destroyer emerged from the swell!

It was Marshal of the RAF Sir Arthur Harris, who said: 'If ever an artist could make an aircraft live and fly on canvas, Robert Taylor can.' The great wartime chief of Bomber Command was not alone in noting Robert's ability not just to reproduce his subjects, but to set them in an environment that captures the exact spirit of the scene. He has that rare ability to transport his audience to the event in his painting and create an uncanny atmosphere of reality.

The talented fighter pilot Bob Stanford-Tuck, when he first saw the finished painting *Victory Over Dunkirk*, exclaimed: 'Robert, that's exactly what it was like!' That exclamation is the manifestation of all that Robert Taylor works for. It is the fruit of his prodigious efforts in research, imagination and attention to detail, coupled with his undoubted natural flair.

The ability to research thoroughly one's intended subject is as important to an artist as it is to an author. Except in the case of abstract art, where a momentary glimpse may inspire an imaginative work, the artist must get as close to experiencing the subject of the painting as is possible. In the case of a painter of 'realism' his or her talent must extend into this important area of research. A keen eye and an observant and inquisitive nature are essential – together with an inordinate amount of patience. Robert is no exception. When researching, his is a timeless world. Lost in his own thoughts, composing, imagining, stopping periodically to climb into, under, over, to touch, smell, to sketch from this angle and that. To photograph parts he will never need to paint, so as to understand the whole.

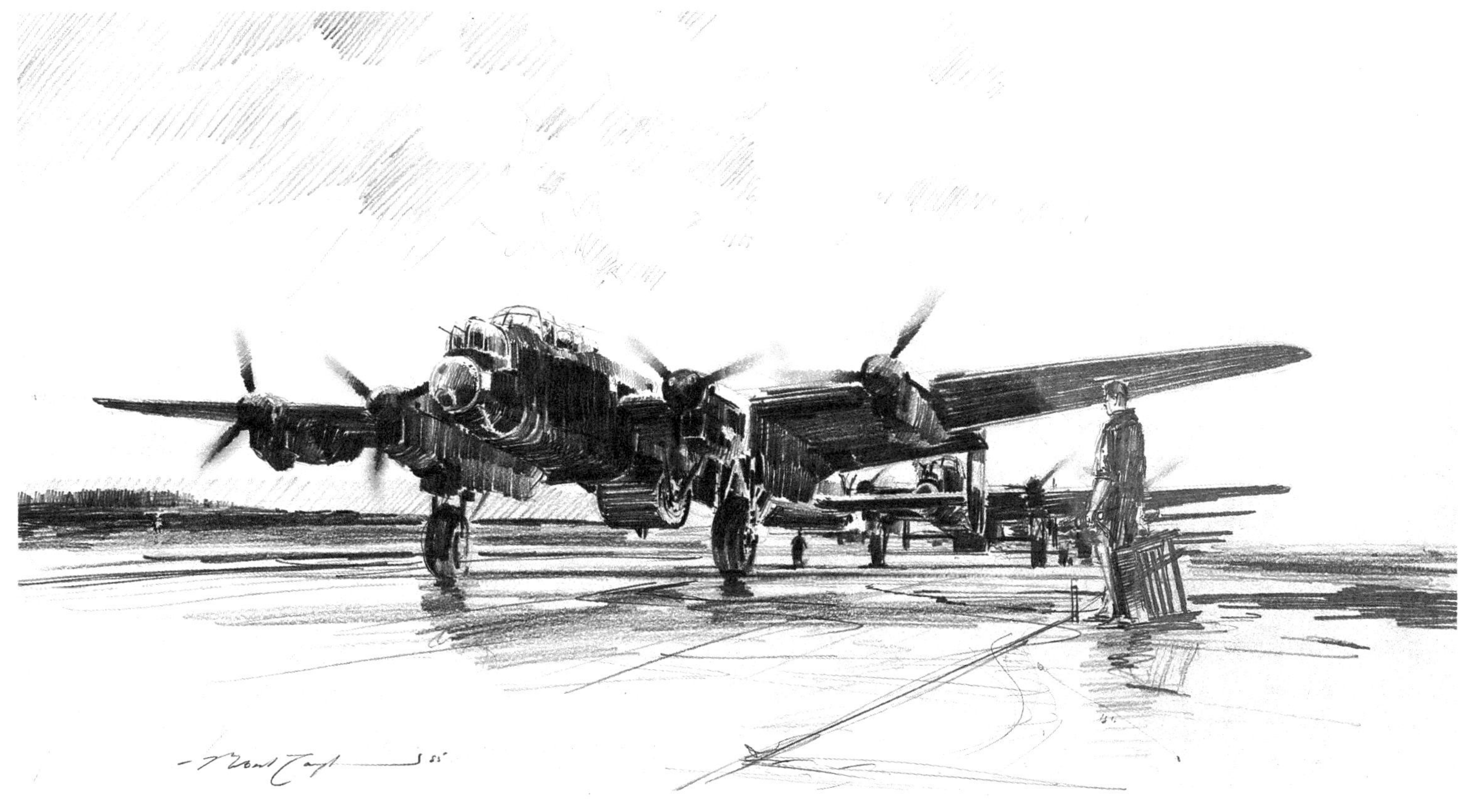

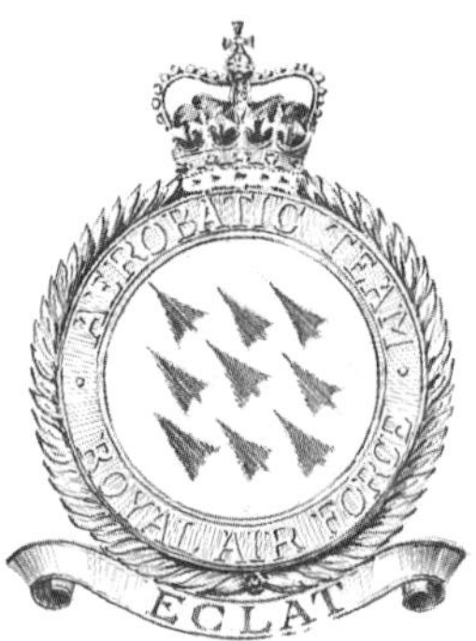

He re-creates in his own mind every detail of the scene to be painted.

It has its funny side. Spending a weekend with the Red Arrows in preparation for a book of drawings featuring the famous R.A.F. aerobatic team, Robert flew with them to RAF Wattisham, in Suffolk. After two days of constant flying, the pilots were relaxing in the Mess before the afternoon performance. Robert was bored. Off he went, dressed in his old hat and 'donkey' jacket to gather a little more research material. Finding a Lightning fighter aircraft parked nearby (Wattisham was at that time a high security fighter station), Robert couldn't believe his luck and busied himself with sketch book and camera. Within minutes a vehicle screeched to a halt and he was confronted by two military policemen. 'Who are you and what are you doing?' they demanded. 'I am Robert Taylor and I am with the Red Arrows'

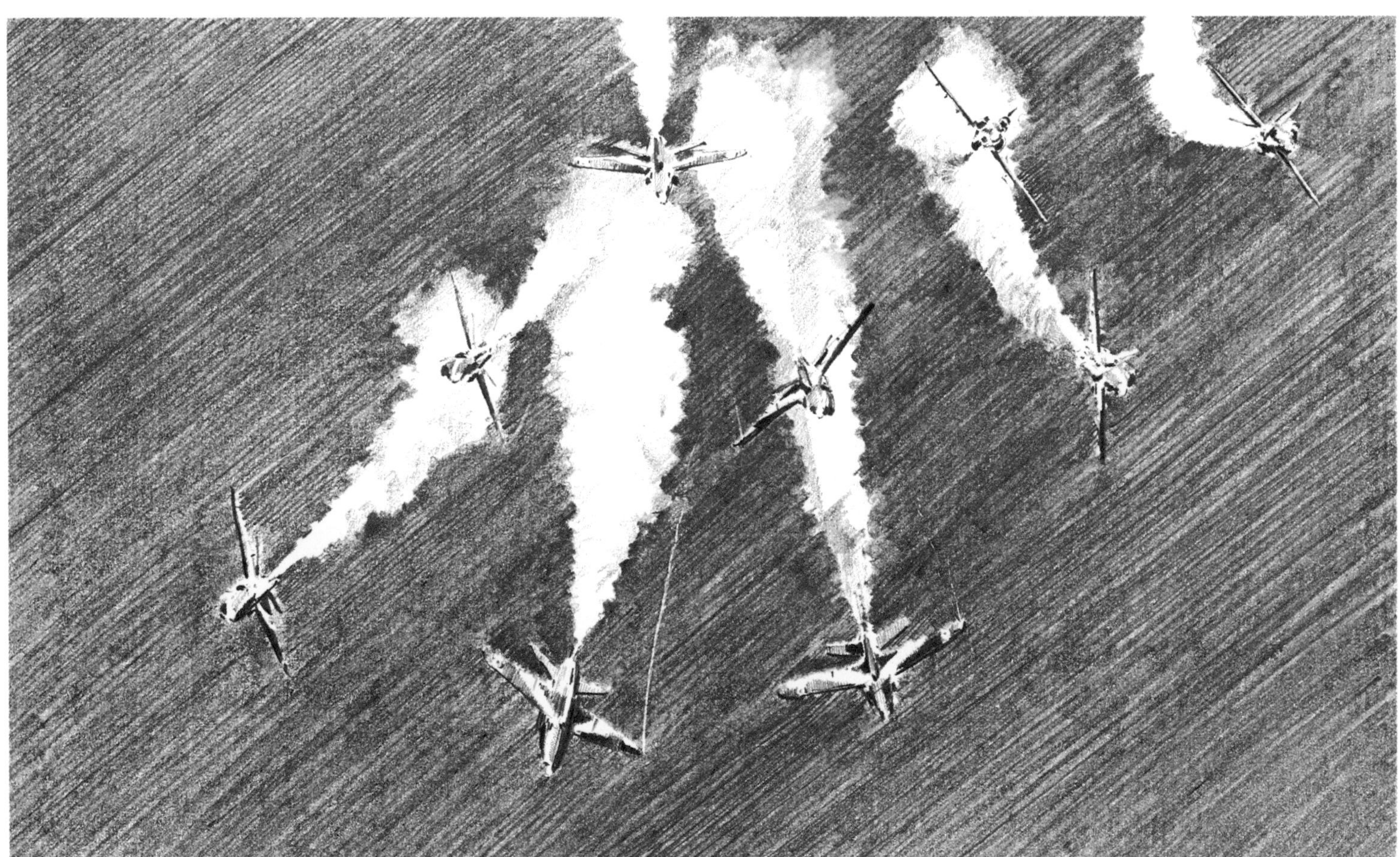

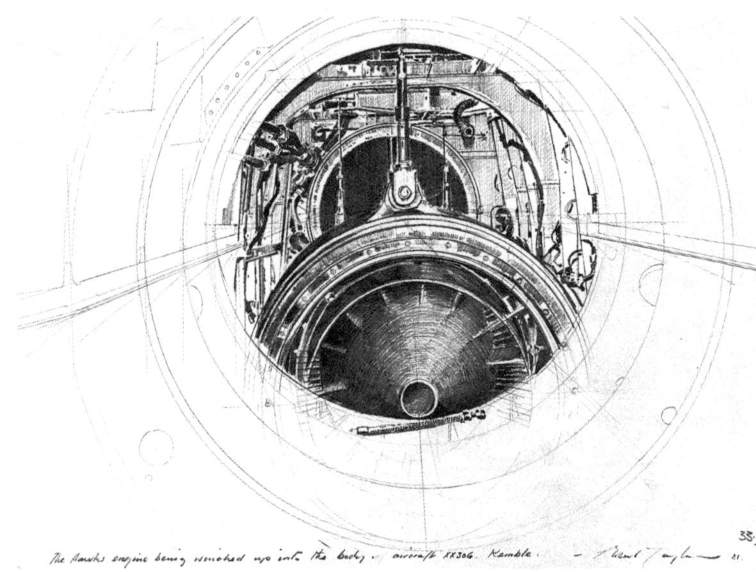

innocently replied the man in the scruffy jacket and the battered hat. 'Oh yes, and which one do you fly?' muttered the indignant policeman as he bundled Robert into the vehicle and headed for the guardroom. Convinced they had caught an enemy agent disguising his obviously foreign accent (the dialect differences between East Anglia and the West Country of England are considerable to say the least) it took Robert a little while to persuade his captors at least to telephone Squadron Leader Brian Hoskins. Back in the Mess a serious-faced team leader placed the phone down (having secured Robert's release) and announced to the assembled team 'Gentlemen, I have to announce that Robert has been arrested as a possible spy.' Moments later a sheepish artist appeared, to much hearty laughter and a generous round of applause from the Royal Air Force's top nine aerobatic pilots!

The whole event contains an important insight into Robert's character. Oblivious to the possible consequences he leapt at what to a serious artist represents his lifeblood – reference material. Within moments he was on the spot with his sketchbook.

Some say that unless an artist can draw he cannot paint. Generally speaking this is true though some forms of painting do not perhaps require that particular skill. Representational painting, the world of Robert Taylor, requires the ability to draw in no small measure.

Robert has loved to draw for as long as he can remember. His skill with the pencil ranges from quick 'thumb-nail' sketches, made, literally, in seconds, to full technical drawings, though he hates to use any instrument other than the pencil. Examples of his prowess abound in this volume. Some of his 'finished' drawings, as he calls them, are works of art in themselves. He invariably 'works-up' his paintings

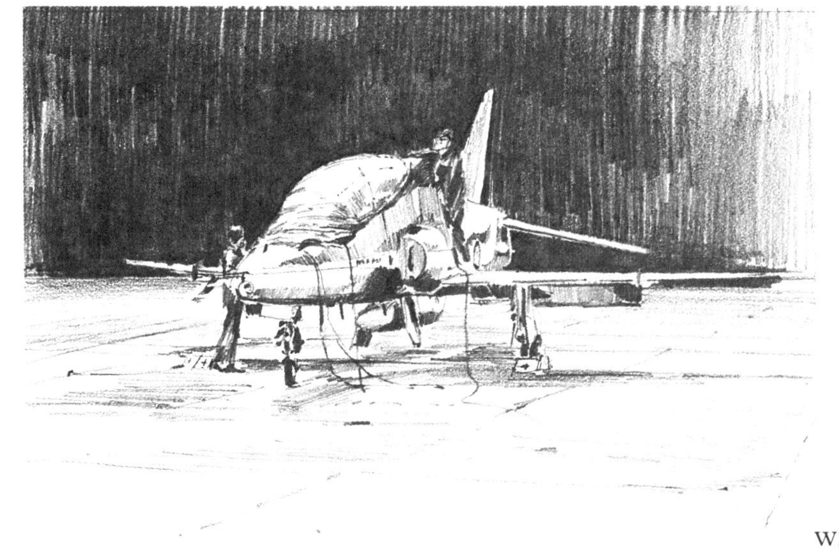

with a series of drawings, often trying as many as six or eight different compositions before deciding on the most appropriate. Questioned on this subject, he can become very enthusiastic: 'The lovely thing about drawing is that it is instant. It is a total contrast to painting in oil. It is essential to me and my work. It helps me in every possible way with my painting and I cannot commend enough the importance of sketching to any young aspiring artist. It is not really possible to paint a subject well if you don't understand it. Drawing helps me to understand better what I am about to paint. People sometimes ask why

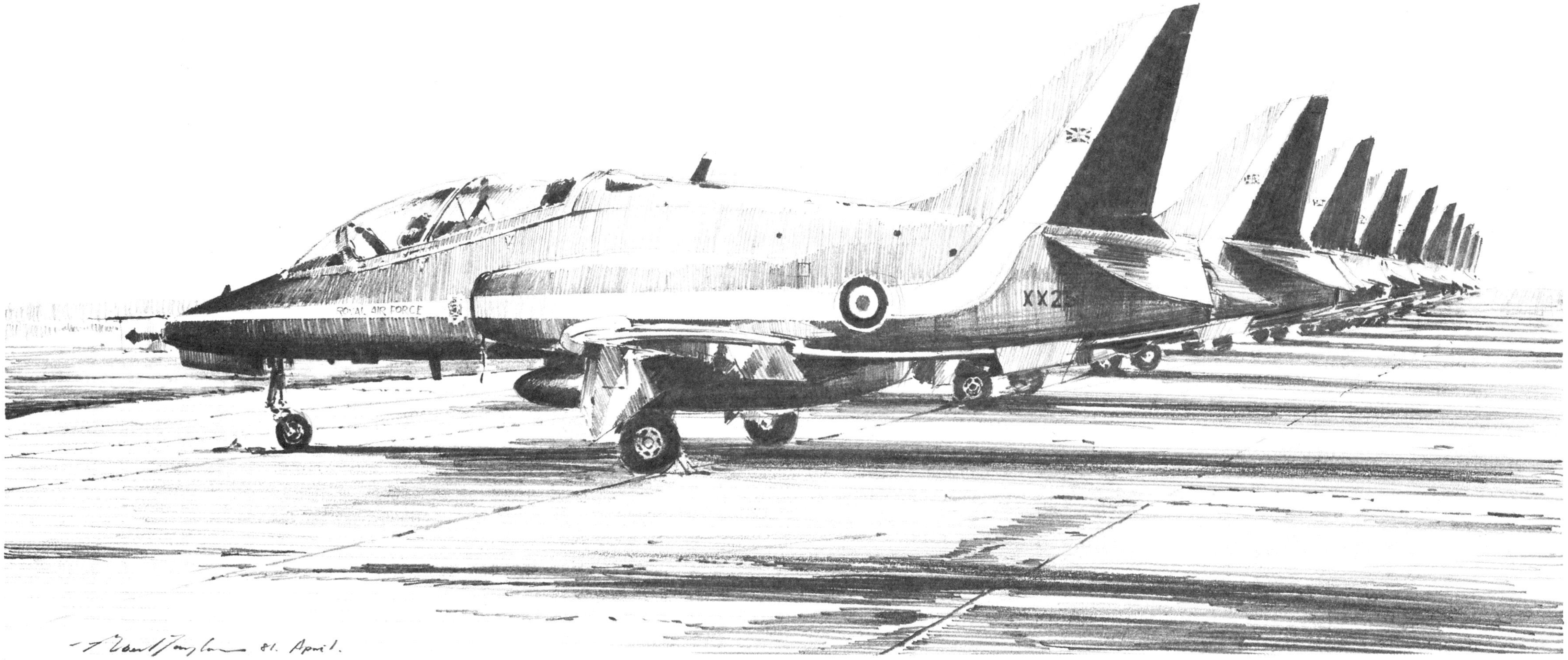

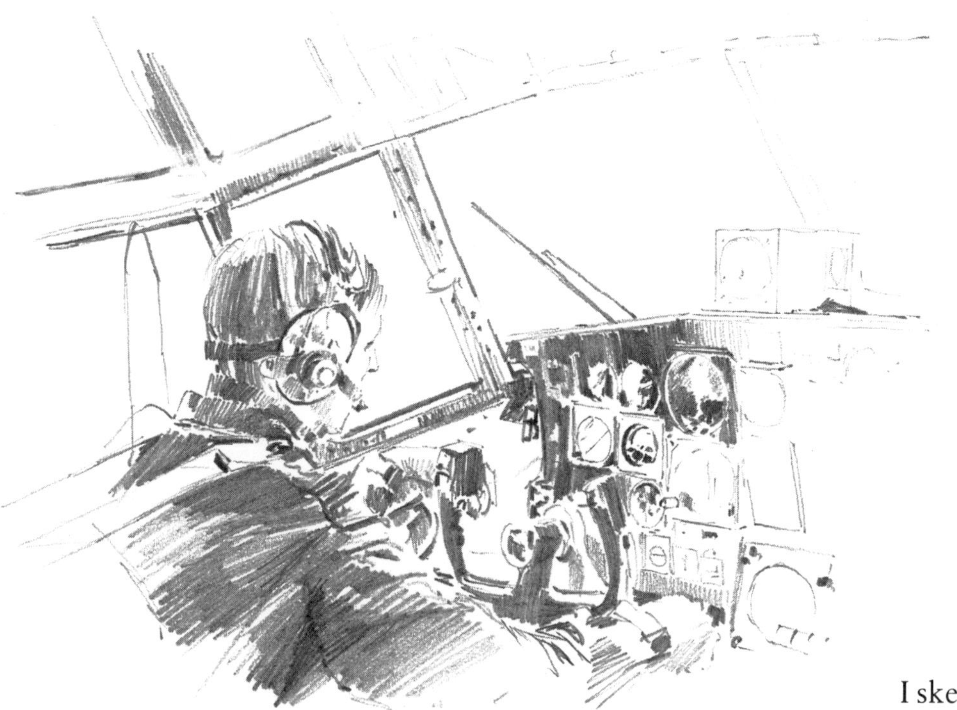

I sketch the back of an aircraft which I am about to paint from the front. The answer is simple: it is so as to understand better the whole of what I am to portray. I get a constant thrill drawing in pencil – it is so easy to get effect, to make use of light and shade, to experiment.'

Robert's love of drawing is demonstrated in the 'remarque' drawings which he adds to small numbers of his limited edition prints. I have never seen such beautiful and comprehensive sketches made by any artist remarquing prints. Often remarques are confined to small, apparently hurriedly sketched outline drawings, but in the case of Robert Taylor remarques his love of drawing and his skill with the pencil is self-evident. Taylor remarques demonstrate another quality in his character: it is a pride in his

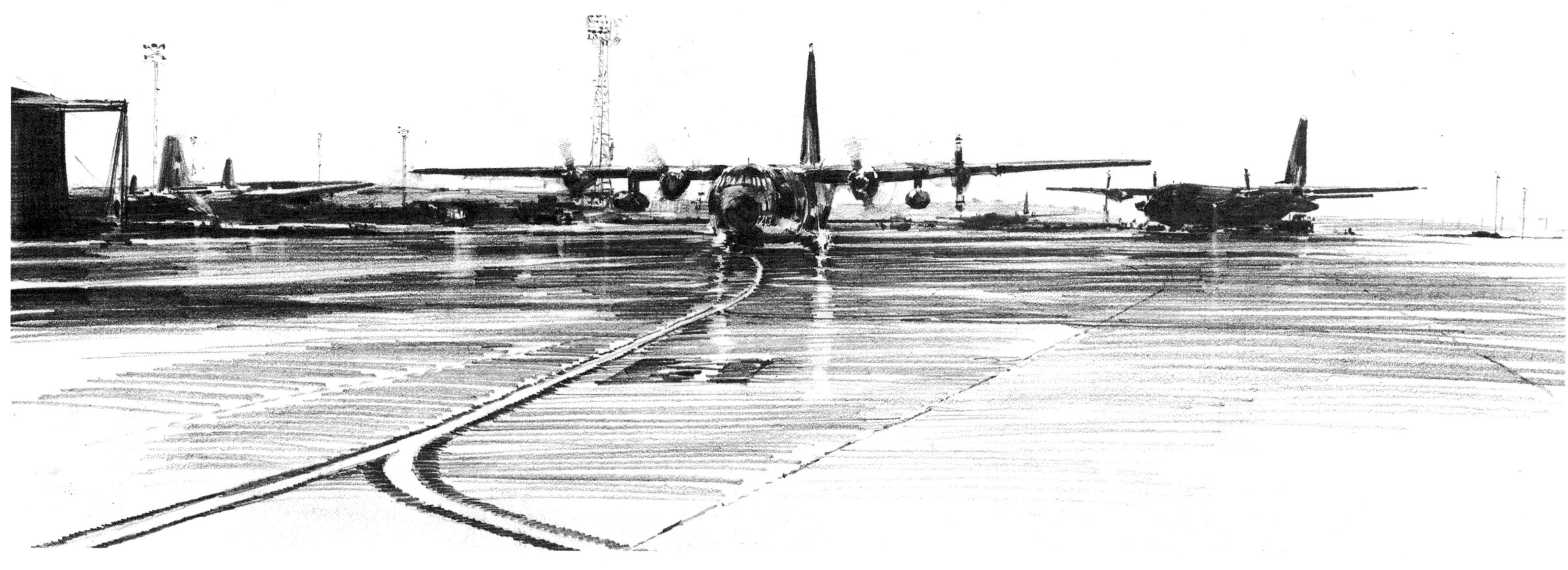

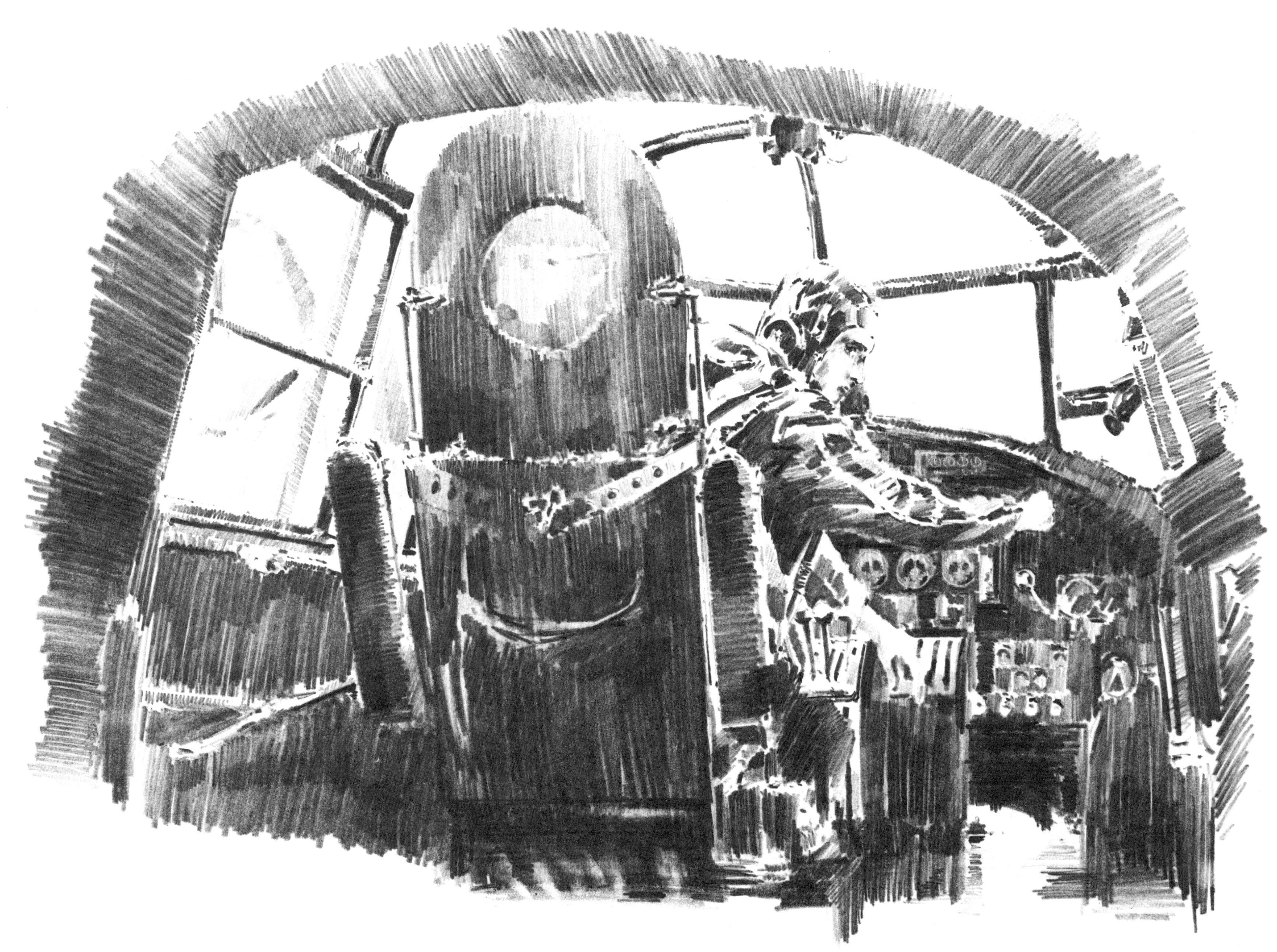

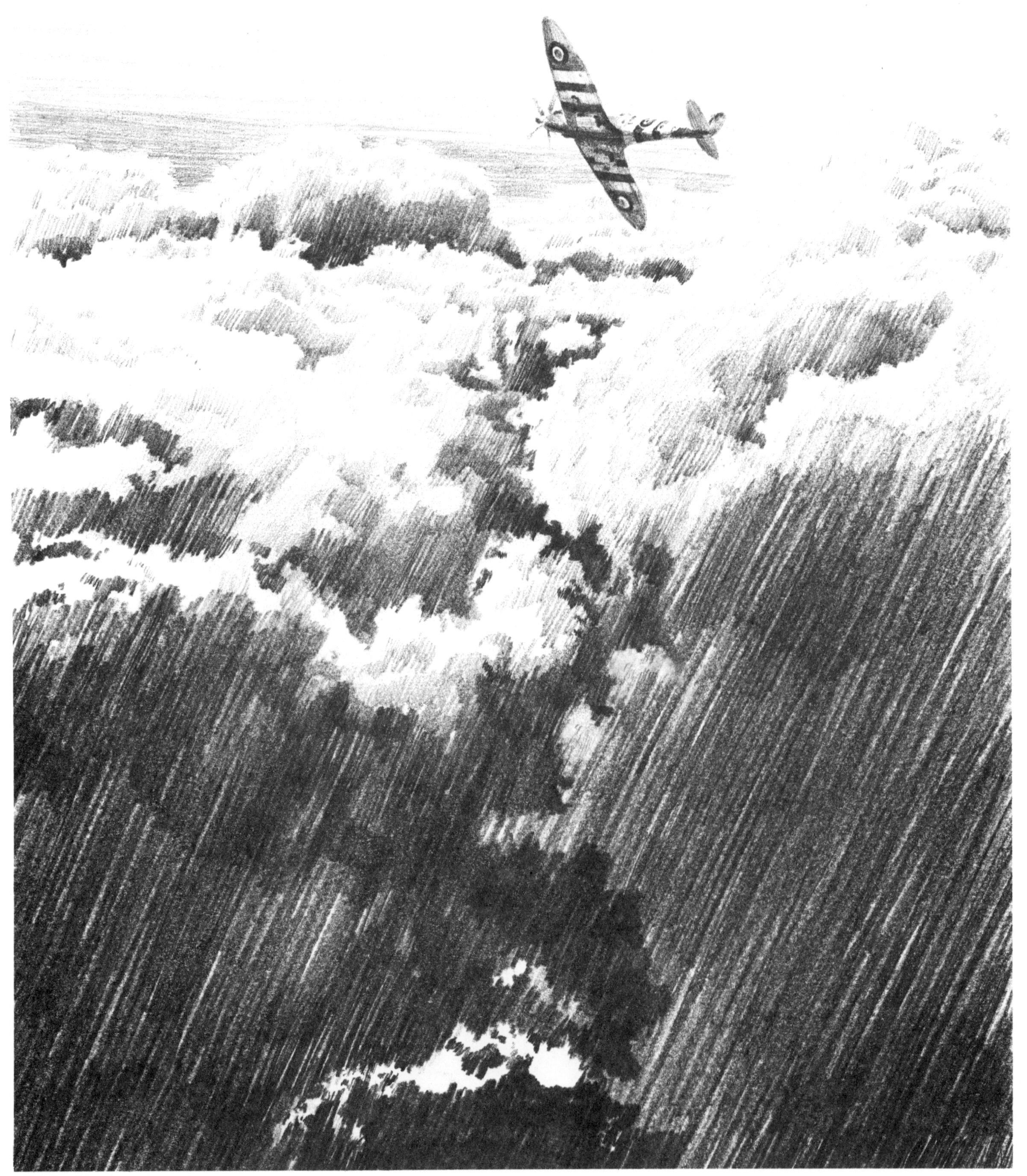

work almost to the point of passion. For Robert is a conscientious man. He takes pride in his work, his achievements, and his standards. Above all he is proud that people should want to collect his work, and like most truly talented artists, his personal reward comes in knowing that his efforts give pleasure to his audience.

He occasionally tells the story of an elderly client who, because of Robert's commitments, had waited two years for a particular commission to be completed. The painting was a small one, depicting a destroyer upon which the client had served during the war – and lost many of his close comrades. Neither he nor Robert had met until the day the new painting was to be handed over. When the client first saw the painting, he stood in silence gazing at it for several minutes. Robert had the sinking feeling that his client was disappointed when, without saying anything, the old man turned to Robert, his eyes filled with tears, and hugged him.

'To be able to give anybody that amount of pleasure must surely be the greatest reward an artist can attain. It is total fulfilment,' said Robert afterwards.

Nor is this depth of feeling confined to his clients. An intriguing result of Robert's success as a professional artist is that many of his childhood heroes now reciprocate his long-held admiration for them. This phenomenon is perfectly encapsulated in a comment made by World War II's top-scoring Allied Fighter Pilot, Air-Vice Marshal Johnnie Johnson: 'As a fighter pilot who flew the types of aircraft that Robert Taylor paints so brilliantly, I can only marvel at his ability. He paints more than just aircraft: he paints with spectacular reality the whole vista of the sky that is the world of the fighter pilot. He ranks with the best . . .'

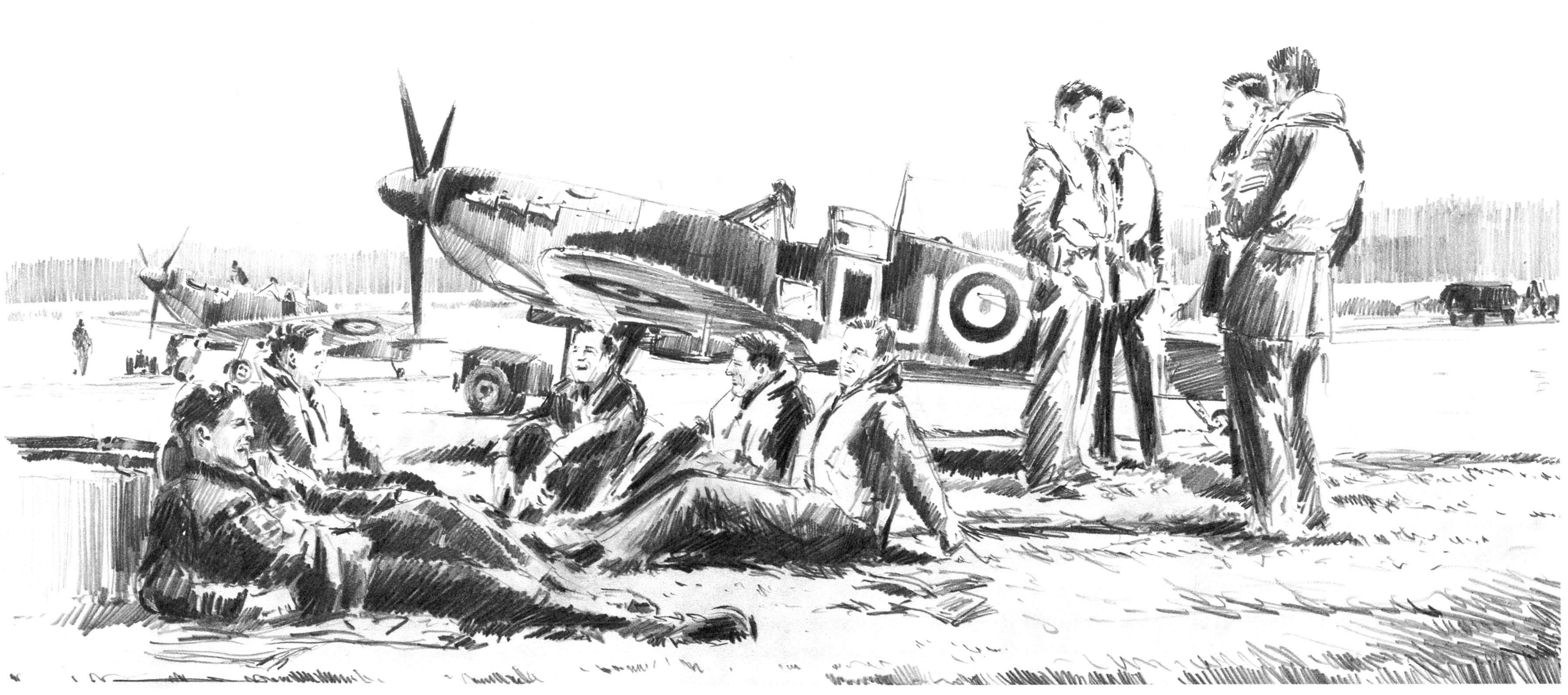

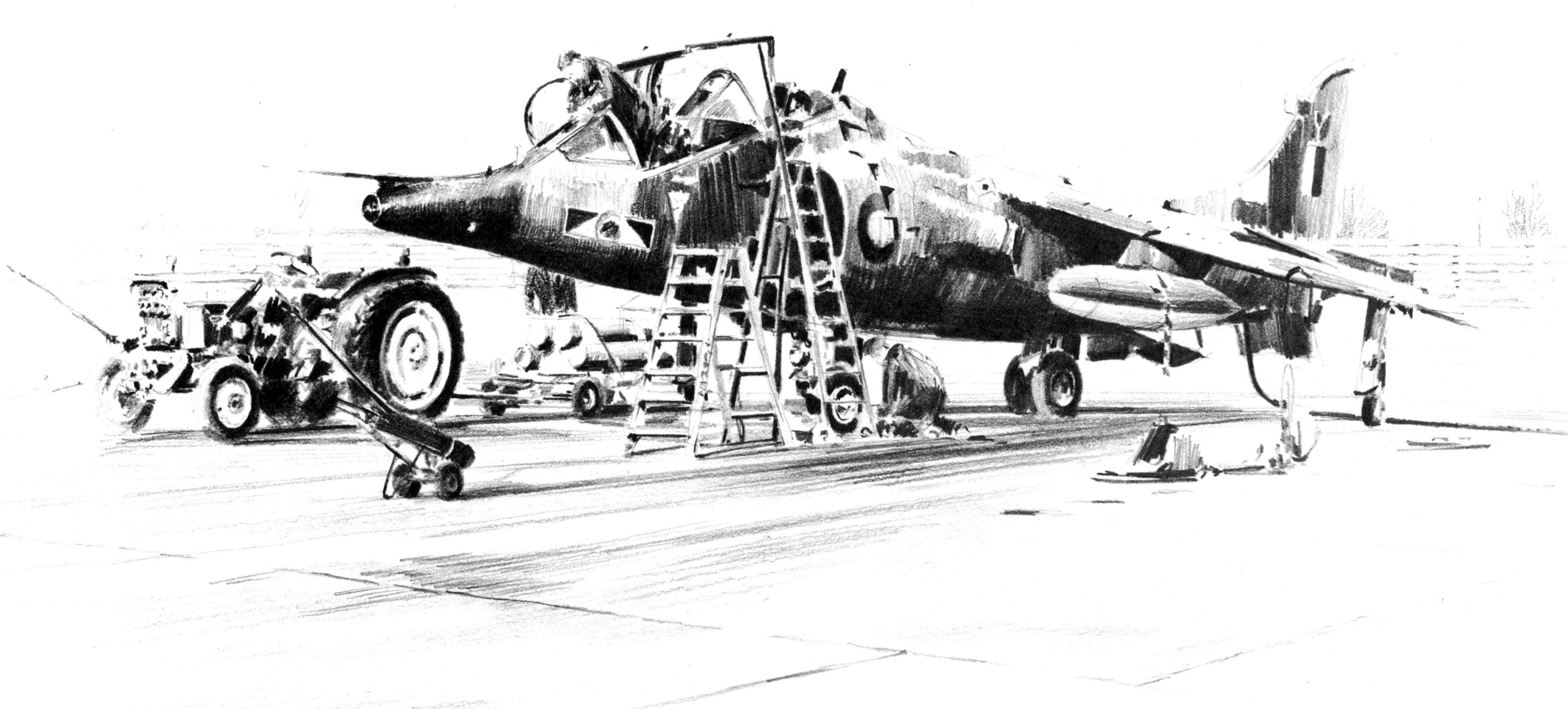

Harrier T.4. of No 233 OCU . YEOVILTON. ROYAL NAVY AIR STATION
DECEMBER 1982.

THE PAINTINGS

RETURN OF THE FEW

Johnnie in the cockpit of MK392

For a long time *Return of the Few* was a painting that had been in my mind. The idea was to paint a gaggle of Spitfires returning low over the English coast in a triumphant mood after a successful sortie. Beneath, also returning home, would be a small group of those wonderful old fishing trawlers, converted for wartime duties but otherwise virtually unchanged in their characterful configuration. The painting was perhaps a slightly selfish idea, because it contains a little of everything I enjoy painting most: aircraft, ships, the sea and the sky.

Although a clear vision of the picture was in my mind it was obviously necessary to make some drawings. Having committed the long held concept to my sketch book with pleasing results, I thought it important, as I had lived with the idea for so long, that a couple of variations on the theme, using water in the foreground, should be constructed by way of comparison. The two 'exercise' drawings shown on this page were the result. Having considered the alternatives I returned to the original idea which culminated in the finished painting. Everything went smoothly and the painting was completed within a few weeks.

People often ask me how long it takes to complete a painting. There is no general answer. Every painting is different. All paintings begin with research which usually tends to be a rather protracted affair. By the time painting actually commences on a canvas I may have spent weeks or even months getting all my facts together and planning the composition. Once a painting is started, however, I rarely do anything else until it is finished. For me this method works best. It allows me to work myself up during research to a sort of 'state of readiness'. When painting begins I usually become wholly immersed in what I am doing and do not like to break the concentration. Very occasionally during the project, if I need a rest from the work in hand, I will paint a small oil sketch or make some pencil drawings of a closely-related subject, but usually find I cannot leave a canvas for more than a couple of days before feeling a strong urge to continue working on it. This is not because of any feeling of pressure to get the picture completed. There is a kind of in-built motivation driven by enthusiasm for what I am doing. Perhaps I am a compulsive painter!

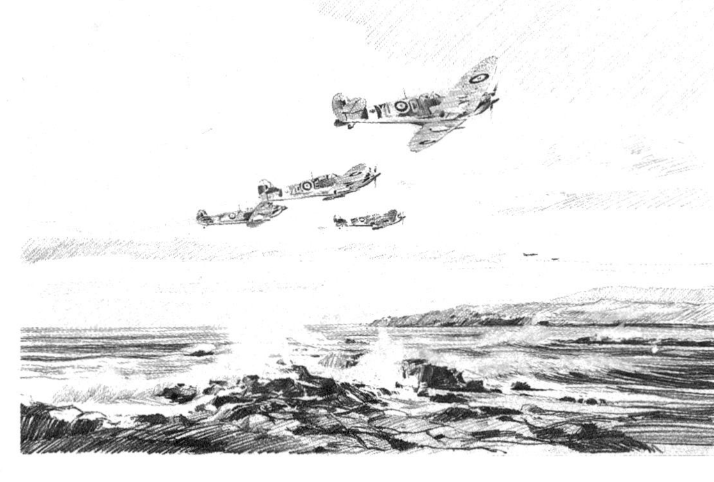

Both exercise drawings show Spitfires flying low over water as the main theme. The first drawing has a beach in the foreground where the thought was to use light shining through the breaking waves to create some interesting colours and activity in the foreground of the painting. Having studied the completed drawing I decided that this concept had no merit whatsoever!

The second drawing showed the Spitfires flying over an estuary or river, disturbing the local wildlife – in this case some wild duck. Such events must have happened a great many times over the lowlands of south east Britain during the war. Whilst choosing not to use this idea for *Return of the Few*, I decided the general plan had merit and may use it as the basis for a future painting.

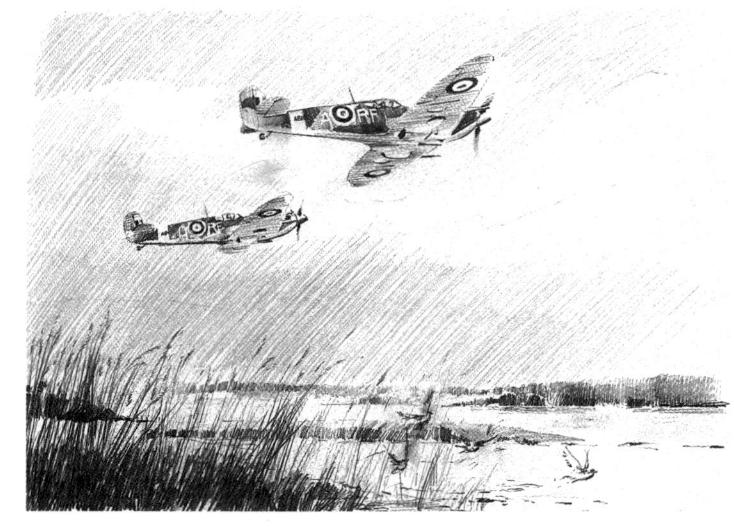

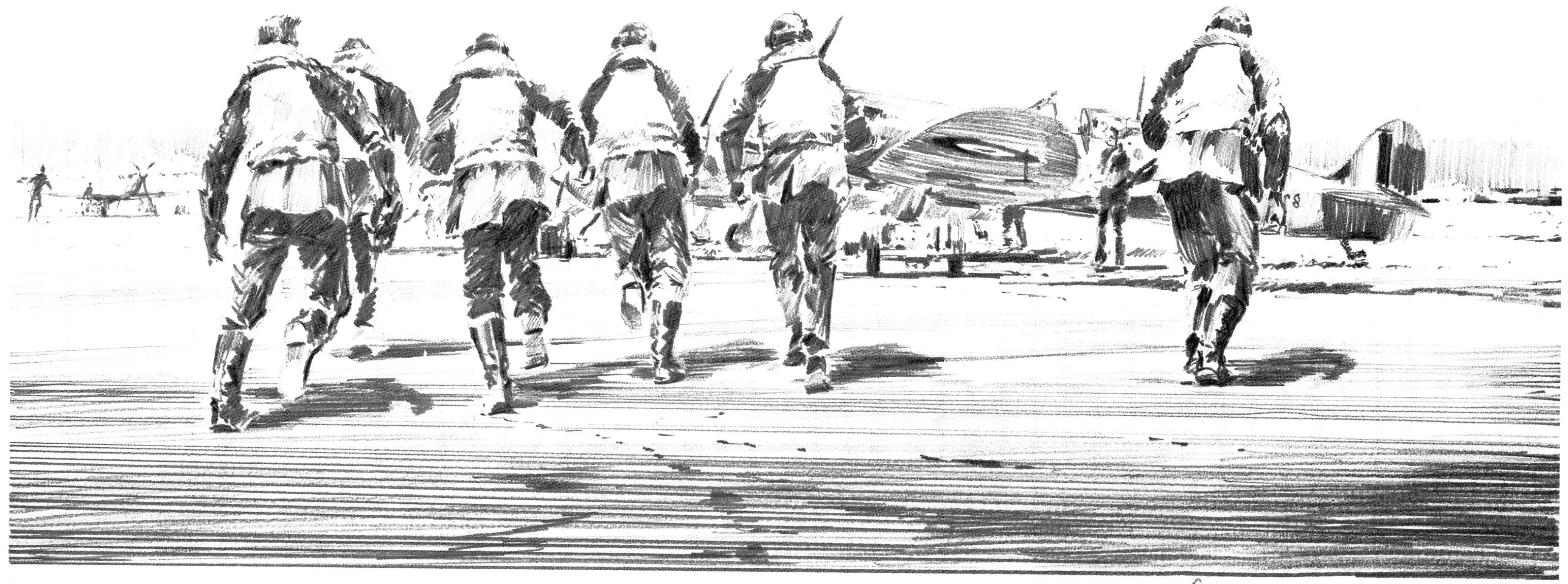

FLYING THE SPITFIRE IN COMBAT

By Air Vice-Marshal 'Johnnie' Johnson,
CB, CBE, DSO, DFC, DL

I first flew on Spitfire 1s in August, 1940, and after less than twenty Spitfire hours was posted to 616 (South Yorkshire) Squadron at Coltishall. They had been in the front line at Kenley, and had lost more than half their pilots in a few days, and were at Coltishall to train inexperienced fighters like me. This was a lucky break, because I could hardly fly the Spitfire properly and would not have lasted long against the experienced German fighter pilots – veterans of the Spanish Civil War, and Blitzkrieg in Poland, Holland, Belgium and France.

The average pilot needed at least fifty hours on Spitfires before becoming 'operational', and this was achieved in the less desperate times following the Battle of Britain.

Our Spitfire Is (1030 HP Rolls-Royce Merlin) with their eight .303 inch Browning machine guns had a ceiling of about 32,000 feet. The Messerschmitt 109E, our principal opponent, had a higher ceiling and better guns than either the Spitfire or the Hurricane; and the 109F, which was soon to make its debut over England, had one cannon firing through the hub of the airscrew so that the pilot had a great advantage of aiming and firing along his line of flight. Our Spitfires were more manoeuvrable, but manoeuvring does not win air battles, and tight turns are more of a defensive than an offensive tactic. The Spitfire's superior rate of turn would get you out of trouble – if you saw your attacker in time. On balance the Messerschmitt 109F was a slightly better fighting aeroplane than the Spitfire I.

Air fighting was tougher in 1941 because we flew over hostile territory and, apart from the Messerschmitt 109s, had to contend with light and heavy flak and a two-way sea crossing. Our Spitfire IIs carried eight .303 machine guns which did not compare with the excellent cannon on German fighters. Later that year we flew Spitfire VBs which, at last, had two 20mm cannon and four machine guns. The Spitfire VB had about the same performance as the Messerschmitt 109, but the elegant Spitfire could out-turn the angular enemy fighter.

In the summer of 1942 I was given command of 610 (County of Chester) Squadron, Auxiliary Air Force (Spitfire Vs). We were based at Ludham, hard by Hickling Broad, and our job was convoy patrols off the east coast, enemy shipping reconnaissances off the Dutch coast, a few fighter sweeps and plenty of those deadly low-level Rhubarbs.

That year, 1942, the redoubtable Focke-Wulf 190 entered the arena. This splendid fighter with its high speed, good ceiling, and four 20mm cannon completely out-classed our Spitfire Vs to the extent that although we restricted our offensive missions our casualties increased.

In the spring of 1943 I was promoted to lead the Kenley (Canadian) Wing, who were equipped with Spitfire IXs, which was the best defensive fighter of the day. The 1,600 HP Merlin 61 engine was designed for bombers but it was soon found that it could be housed in an extended Spitfire V airframe. It had a top speed of some 410 m.p.h. and was the best fighting aeroplane of the day. My (Canadian) Kenley Wing roamed far and wide over occupied Europe that year and, thanks to some excellent long-range controlling, downed a goodly number of FW 190s and Me 109Fs, especially when we escorted the B-17s of the famed US Eighth Air Force.

Later that year I flew the Spitfire XII which had a 2,000 HP Rolls-Royce Griffon engine and clipped wings. Its best fighting altitude was about 12,000 feet and the tactics of the Tangmere Wing were to fly below enemy formations; when the German leader began his attack Ray Harries, the wing leader, would 'break' into the 190s and out-turn them. However, I always preferred to be on top!

Towards the end of the war I commanded 125 Wing, equipped with three squadrons of Spitfire XIVs. This Spitfire was designed as a high altitude fighter, but its powerful engine produced a lot of torque, which meant that this fighter required constant trimming, especially when turning and twisting in combat. I preferred the trusty, graceful Spitfire IX – the best Spitfire ever – and beautifully illustrated by Robert Taylor.

Johnnie Johnson has helped me with advice for numerous paintings. Nobody had more success than he did flying Spitfires, or any other Allied fighter aircraft in Europe for that matter.

He was one of the outstanding Wing Leaders in World War II and is one of the great exponents of air combat. I am indebted to him for his generous help over the years, and for writing the fascinating notes about flying the Spitfire in combat.

The steam ships built between the wars had such wonderful characters – particularly the cargo ships and the trawlers. The first steam trawlers appeared as early as 1881 and were built right up to the 1930s. During World War II the Admiralty requisitioned around 300 trawlers, some similar to the type shown in my painting, which were used for offshore, coastal patrol and other duties. Some larger trawlers were armed and on one occasion a Yarmouth Drifter, when attacked by five German sea planes, brought two of them down. Amazingly they also sank more than twenty German submarines, though I cannot imagine how!

Fishing continued throughout the war, mostly off the north west coast of the British Isles. Although the fishing trawlers were given some protection they fished at considerable personal risk to the crews. In spite of these dangers they landed 400,000 tons of badly needed fish each year during the war.

The trawlers in my painting are viewed from a position right down at water level. The second trawler is partly obscured in order to emphasise the swell.

Return of the Few depicts Spitfires of 92 Squadron and they are seen over the south east coast of Britain on a summer evening in 1940. The Spitfires are pretty low and I suspect deliberately 'buzzing' the trawlers.

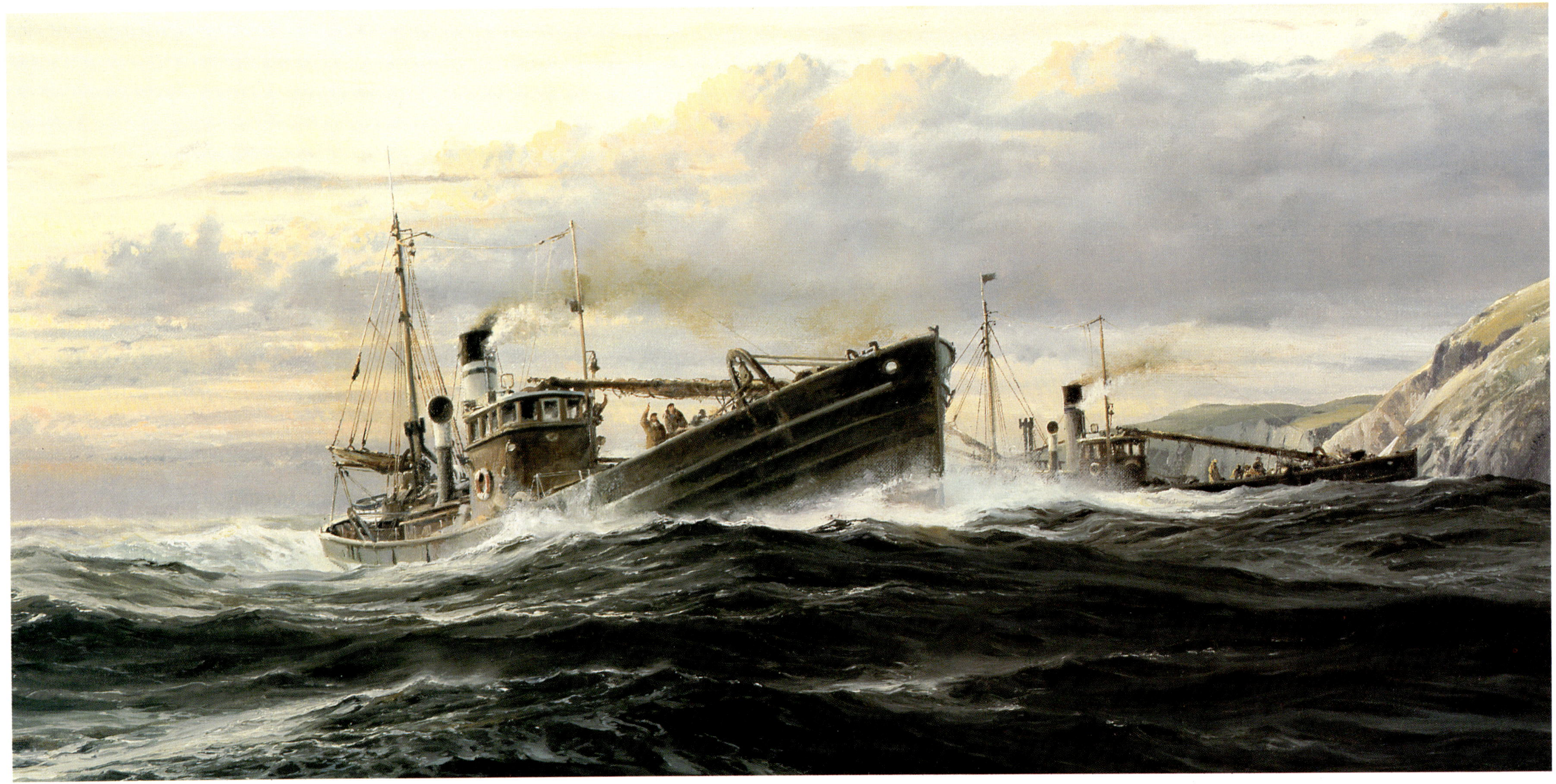

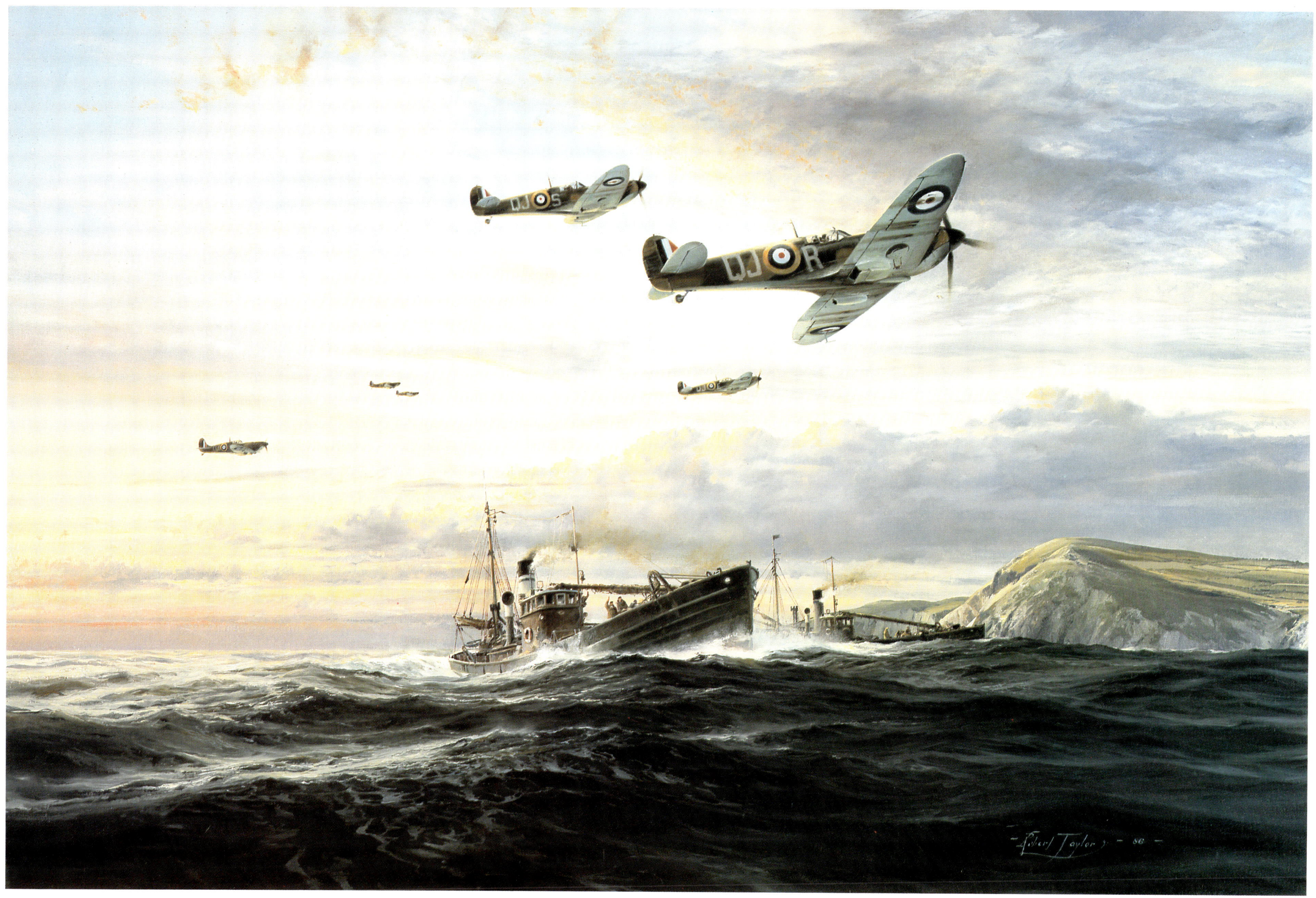

RETURN OF THE FEW
In the collection of The Military Gallery

THE DAMBUSTERS

The RAF attack on the Ruhr dams on the night of 16–17 May in 1943 became one of the most famous raids of the war. Under the command of Guy Gibson, who was awarded the Victoria Cross for his courage in leadership, nineteen Lancaster bombers of 617 Squadron attacked the Mohne, Eder and Sorpe dams. Using the ingenious 'bouncing' bomb, invented by the prolific and brilliant designer Barnes Wallis, the crews pressed home their attack against the heavily-defended dams with inordinate success. However, eight of the nineteen crews failed to return.

The Dams Raids have always caught the imagination of the public and the scene had been painted by several artists before I made my attempt. Most other paintings viewed the dams from the lower side, following the breach, with water cascading down. It seemed a good idea to try a different approach, but initially I was not sure how one might do this. Then I had the good fortune to be introduced to Air Marshal Sir Harold Martin.

'Mick' Martin, an Australian, had been Guy Gibson's deputy leader on the Dams Raids, and was known to be one of the most fearless and skilled bomber pilots in the RAF. Of great importance to me was the fact that he was also interested to help me with the research for the painting and kindly invited me to his home for lunch.

We talked throughout an excellent meal, prepared by Lady Martin and, by the time we had finished eating, Sir Harold was in full flow: the dining room table became the Mohne Reservoir, a line of cutlery the Dam, salt and pepper formed the twin turrets, a glass positioned the power station where the luckless Hopgood's bomb had landed, and a mustard pot fixed the position of the moon. Plates were used to plot the position of his own Lancaster and that of Guy Gibson's. During the following hours the entire raid was played out before me, move by move, by the pilot of the aircraft I was to paint. By the end of this totally absorbing afternoon I knew exactly how I wanted to paint the picture.

What was absolutely unique about the Dams Raids was the bomb used and its method of delivery. Apart from the astonishing bravery of the crews, it was this factor that set these attacks apart from all others of the war. I felt it essential for me somehow to construct my painting so as to portray these unique features.

The bomb was a barrel-shaped device, designed to be dropped on to the water from an absolutely critical height. Given the speed of the aircraft this would allow the bomb to bounce a certain number of times, finally coming to rest against the wall of the dam. It would then sink and explode below the surface, using a barometrically-controlled detonator. The precise height the aircraft needed to be above the water at the time of bomb release was judged by projecting two beams of light, from front and aft, on the water. At the correct height they shone a figure eight on the water surface. In addition to flying a large four-engined bomber into a barrage of gunfire, the pilot had to finely judge his height using this method.

When Sir Harold had taken me through the attack, I could visualise the painting, and had worked out where the light should come from (the attack was made on a moonlit night). I knew by this time that Mick Martin was third in line into attack. Gibson had gone in first and dropped his bomb, but the dam was still intact. Hopgood, second in line, had been brought down by enemy gunfire and his Lancaster had crashed beyond the dam. Gibson had circled around, turned on all his navigation lights and flown

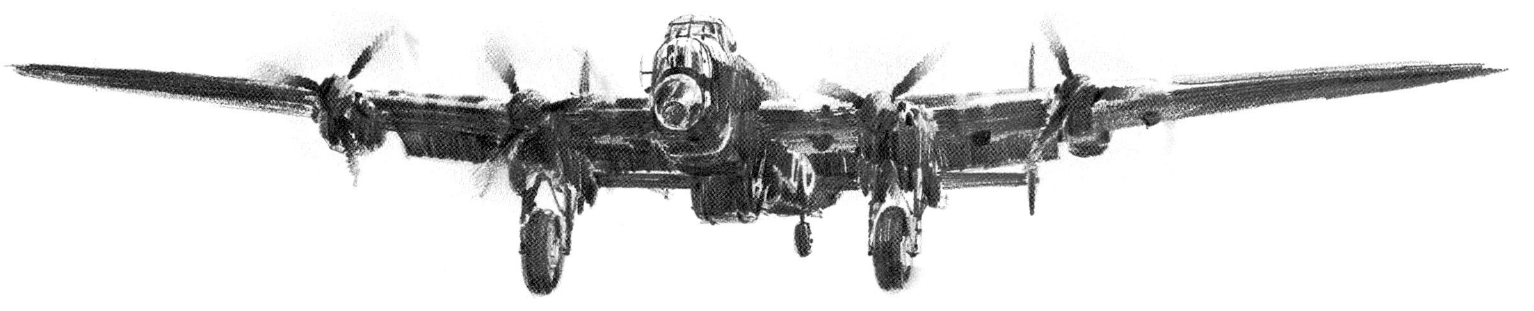

ED909 'P'. In the gathering darkness. 617 Squadron P- Popsie Thunders away from Scampton. "Brakes on - Brakes off; Undercarriage up; 2,850 r.p.m.

in with Martin in an effort to draw the enemy's fire. I would paint the moment when Mick Martin released his bomb. Armed with more information than I could have imagined I returned to my studio to prepare some drawings.

The sketch below shows how I interpreted Sir Harold Martin's account of the moment when he released his bomb. The moon was just out of the picture, to the left, and so I would be able to light the whole picture from its silver reflections on the water. I duly presented myself together with my drawing to Sir Harold. 'That's fine Robert, but Gibson flew off my starboard wing, not as you illustrate it.' In one sentence the Air Marshal had removed all the light source from the painting!

To include Gibson's aircraft in the painting, which both I and Sir Harold wanted to do, we had to view AJD from the port side, which would position the main light source, the moon, precisely behind the viewer. Reflections from the moon, even using every ounce of artist's licence I could muster would now be nil!

I discussed the problem with Sir Harold. He recalled that as he flew towards the dam there was an orange glow which lit up the top of the dam. This was the result of Hopgood's attack, the explosion of his bomb, and subsequent loss of his aircraft.

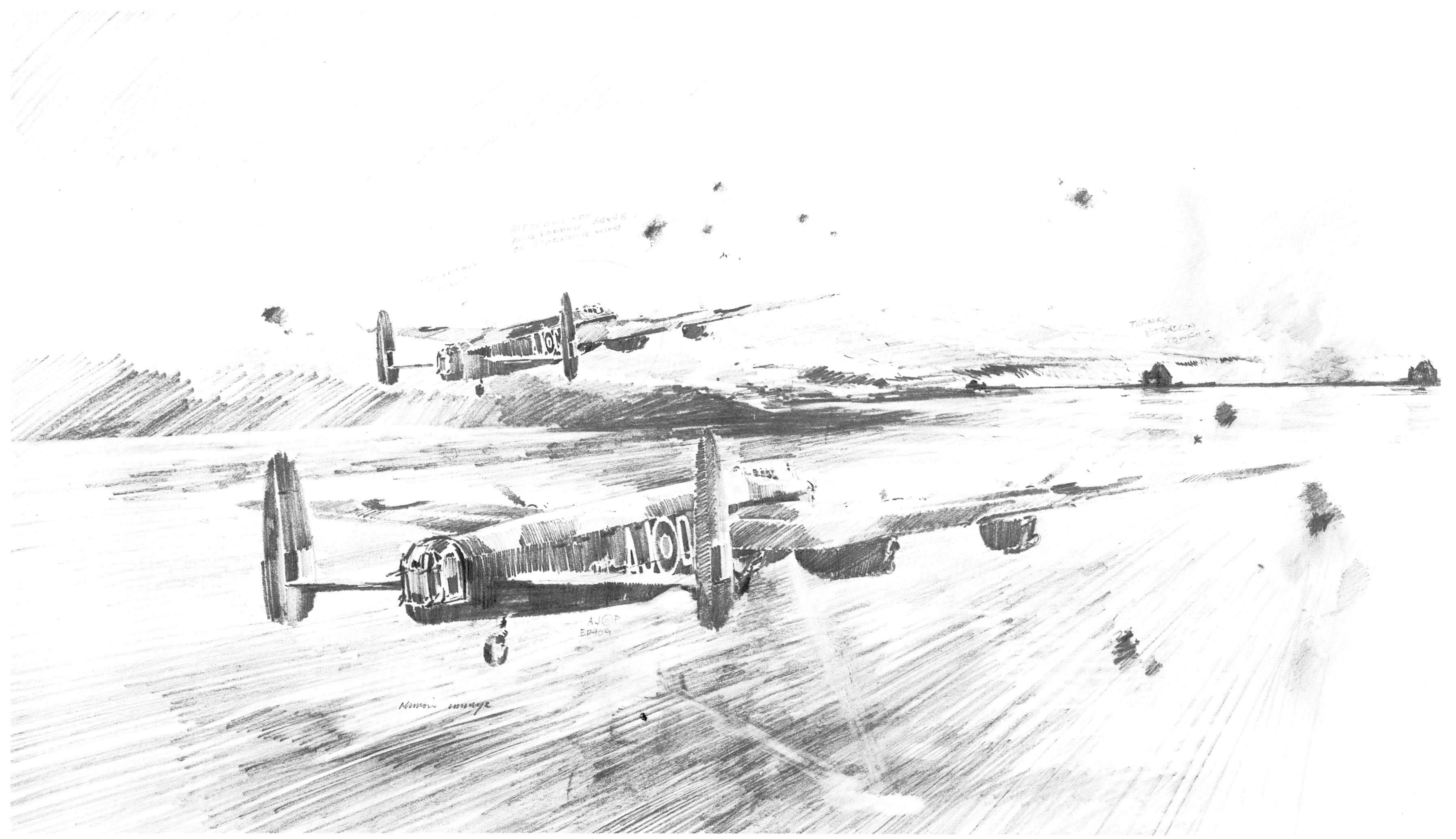

John Hopgood's aircraft had been caught in searchlights and hit by gunfire crossing Holland. Although Hopgood, along with others on board, had been injured he pressed on to the target. His was the second aircraft to attack the Mohne Dam and he faced a terrific barrage of gunfire from the defences. Just as he released his bomb, his aircraft was badly hit and the inner port engine set ablaze. The port outer was already dead, and his aircraft, unable to climb above its height of 300 feet, was doomed. He ordered his crew to bale out. Hopgood's bomb bounced right over the dam wall and exploded on the power station below, completely destroying it. Hopgood's aircraft crashed and exploded into flames a few miles past the dam and all those remaining on board were lost. It was these events which had caused the orange glow ahead of Mick Martin. Moving as the story was, it was a simple reality that, as Mick Martin flew in to make the third attack on the Mohne Dam, there was ahead of him all the light that any artist would need to depict that dramatic scene.

In the painting Mick Martin's Lancaster is seen flying into the attack. The 'figure eight' patch of light shows clearly on the water below that he is flying at the optimum height and he has just released his bomb. Gibson's Lancaster can be seen above and to starboard, with all lights on, drawing enemy fire. Mick Martin made a direct hit on the dam.

Illustrated on this page is a painting which I was privately commissioned to paint which depicts the Lancasters of 617 Squadron about to take off for the attack on the dams. Despatching a squadron of bomber aircraft depended always on a large number of ground staff, technical and otherwise. Many, in particular the armourers, were often at some personal risk when bombing-up an aircraft, and of course the aircrews depended greatly on the ground personnel. All played a vital role in getting the heavily-laden aircraft safely into the air. The dams bombs were armed just before they took off, and the man on the right of the picture (the title of the painting is *Green on, Go*) has just completed the task.

The Lancasters were modified to take the unusual barrel-shaped bouncing bomb, which was slung below the bomb bay position. The mid-upper turret was removed during these modifications in order to minimise weight.

GREEN ON GO

In the collection of Mr and Mrs G H Holsgrove

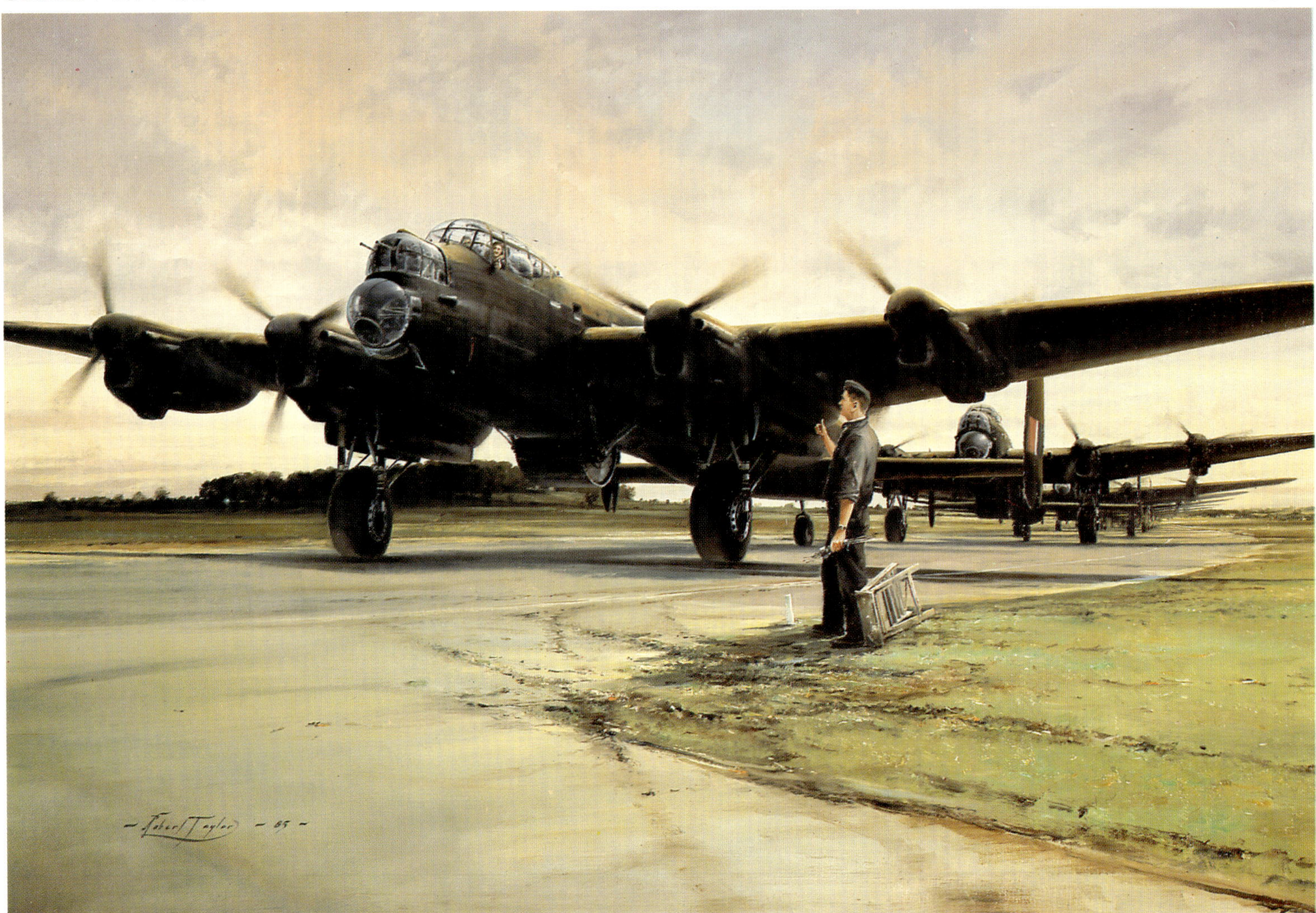

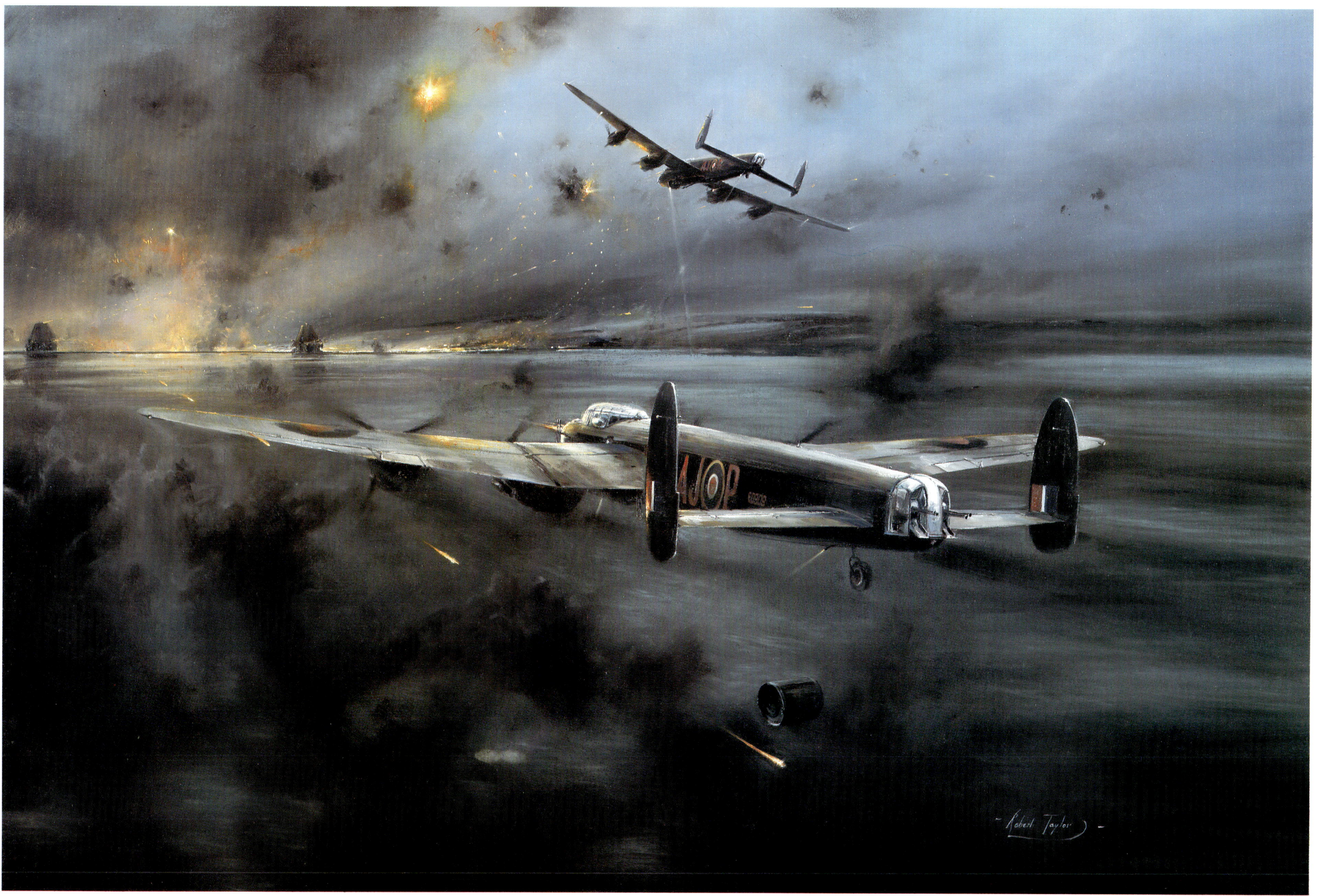

DAMBUSTERS

In the collection of RAF Bomber Command Museum, Hendon

MORAL SUPPORT

During the Battle of Britain, British fighter pilots were heavily outnumbered. There was an extreme shortage of trained new pilots to replace those being lost and there were in any case not nearly enough fighter aircraft for them to fly. Pilots knew this and, on many occasions, flew badly-damaged aircraft back to bases, when under more normal battle conditions, they would have taken to their parachutes. *Moral Support* depicts one such event as described to me by the commanding officer of No 85 Hurricane Fighter Squadron, Group Captain Peter Townsend.

One of the then Squadron Leader Townsend's pilots, a young enthusiastic extrovert named Jim Marshall had been left behind when the squadron scrambled to intercept incoming bombers over the South East of England. How he got left behind nobody is quite sure but, upset when he re-appeared on the squadron some minutes later to find his friends already departed, he climbed into the only remaining Hurricane and headed off into the summer sky in search of his comrades. Not only was he successful in finding them but he joined the wide-ranging dogfight which had developed. So enthusiastically did he dive into the fray that he collided with a Heinkel He111 with such force that it subsequently crashed. Mindful of the need to return his own badly-damaged aircraft in one piece, he headed for home.

Returning the squadron to refuel and re-arm, Squadron Leader Townsend quickly summed up the situation and closed in on Marshall's aircraft to assess the damage. It was flying. Just. In a nose-up attitude, Marshall was struggling to keep his Hurricane in the air. A large part of the port wing was missing, the tail-fin was badly smashed, and the radio was out. Townsend kept close station using hand-signals to communicate with Marshall and guided him back to their base at RAF Debden. Marshall and his Hurricane lived to fight another day.

Group Captain Townsend's description of events was so vivid that I was able to visualise the entire picture in my mind. Even the title was there – *Moral Support!*

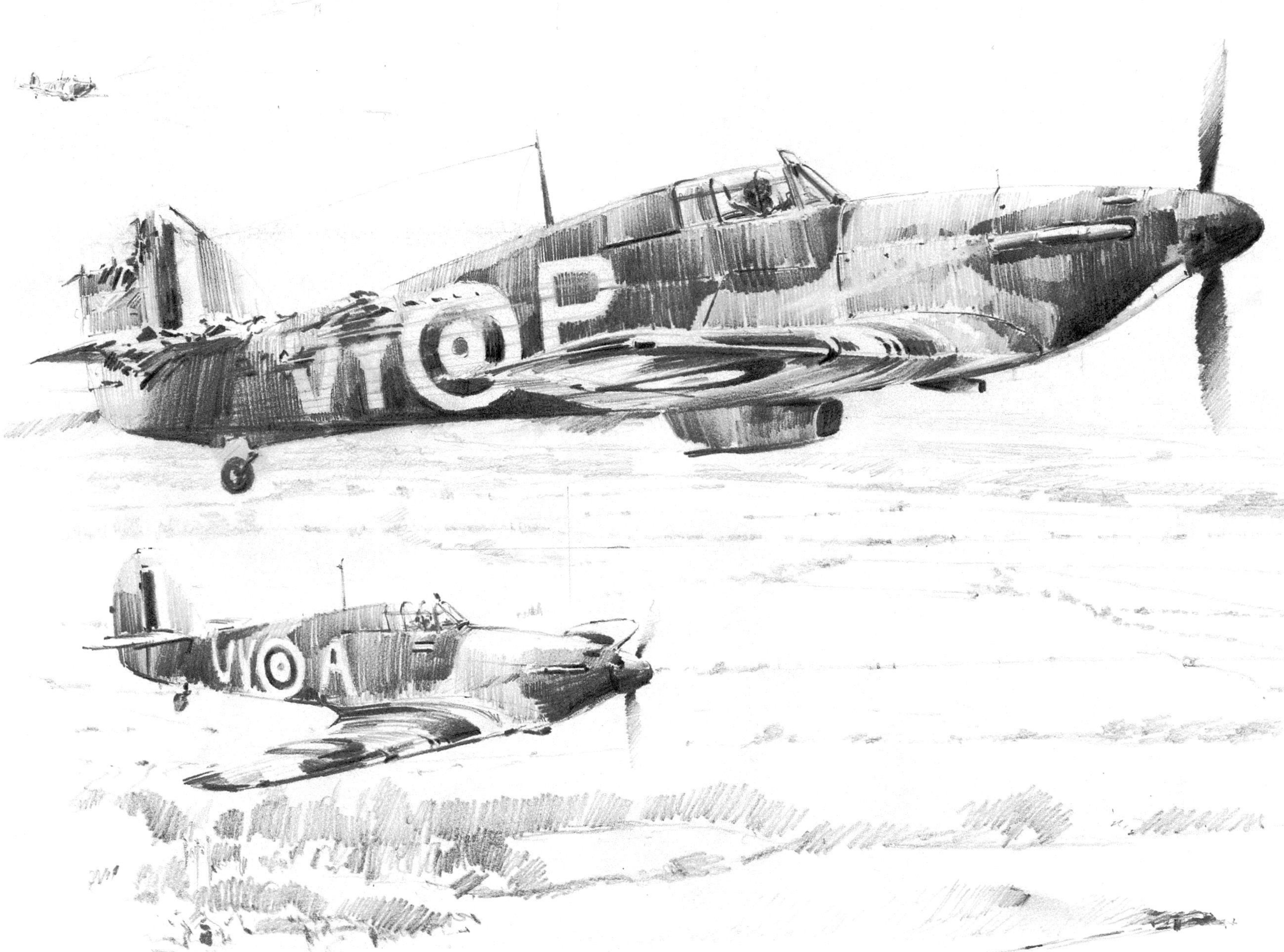

The sketch above is a section taken from the final drawing made prior to painting *Moral Support.* The drawing was concerned primarily with positioning the aircraft and obtaining the correct attitude for Marshall's Hurricane, which was flying just above stalling speed. Only a few pencil marks below the aircraft denote the ground, as in this painting I planned the landscape in a separate drawing. Marshall and Peter Townsend are seen flying in a north westerly direction over the Kent countryside at a height of about 1,000 feet. To obtain correct reference for this landscape I sifted through dozens of old photographs taken over this part of south east England during the 1940s. The English landscape has changed a great deal over the past forty years so a research-gathering reconnaisance in a light aircraft today would not have been much help to me. Many of the centuries old hedgerows have gone to create the larger fields which modern farming appears to dictate. The patchwork of tiny fields bordered by hedges and trees which were prevalent during the era of the Battle of Britain have, in most areas, disappeared. It is perhaps one of many ironies of war that much of the greatest and most desperately fought air battle in history was fought above the beautiful 'Garden of England'.

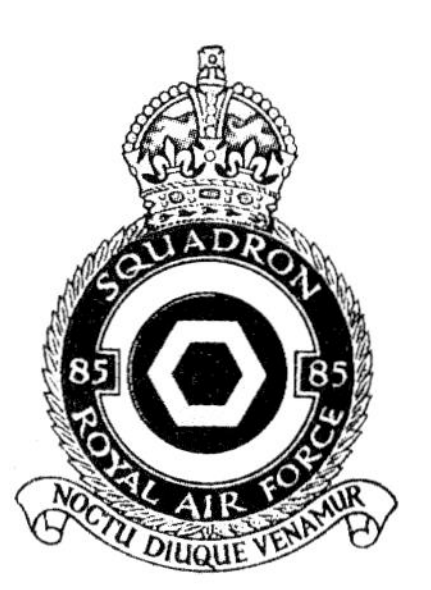

FLYING THE HURRICANE IN COMBAT
by Group Captain Peter Townsend, CVO, DSO, DFC

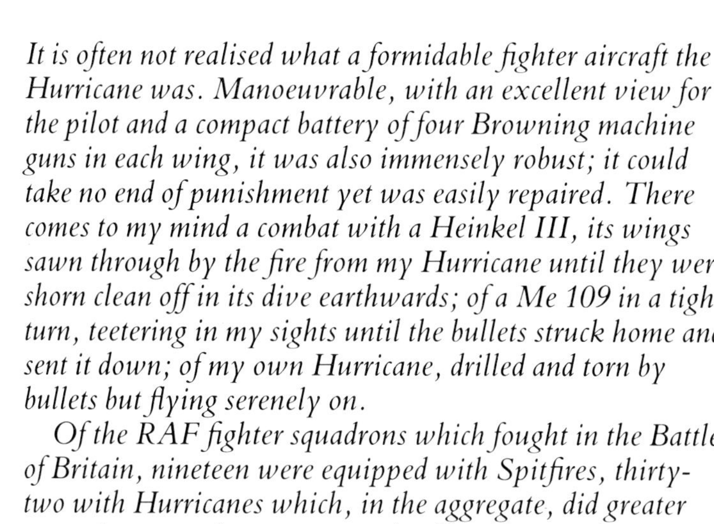

It is often not realised what a formidable fighter aircraft the Hurricane was. Manoeuvrable, with an excellent view for the pilot and a compact battery of four Browning machine guns in each wing, it was also immensely robust; it could take no end of punishment yet was easily repaired. There comes to my mind a combat with a Heinkel III, its wings sawn through by the fire from my Hurricane until they were shorn clean off in its dive earthwards; of a Me 109 in a tight turn, teetering in my sights until the bullets struck home and sent it down; of my own Hurricane, drilled and torn by bullets but flying serenely on.

Of the RAF fighter squadrons which fought in the Battle of Britain, nineteen were equipped with Spitfires, thirty-two with Hurricanes which, in the aggregate, did greater execution upon the enemy – and suffered heavier losses. The Hurricane, however, had not the legs of the Spitfire nor of the Messerschmitt 109. Moral: with a 109 on your tail, never dive or climb; keep turning and if he decides to stay, you will soon end up on his *tail. We faced the Luftwaffe's mass raids in squadrons of twelve aircraft, sometimes attacking head-on and, if possible, out of the sun.*

After the Battle of Britain, those marvellous Spitfires went on from strength to strength in Europe while the Hurricanes departed to fight on distant fronts: Russia, Greece, Malta, the North-African desert and in East Africa, in Burma and Indonesia. They were catapulted (minus undercarriage) from ships in the hard-pressed Atlantic convoys (the combat over, the pilot baled out into the sea).

The Hawker Hurricane was a faithful warhorse, mightily strong and a scourge to the enemy. So hats off to the Hurricane and its designer Sydney Camm.

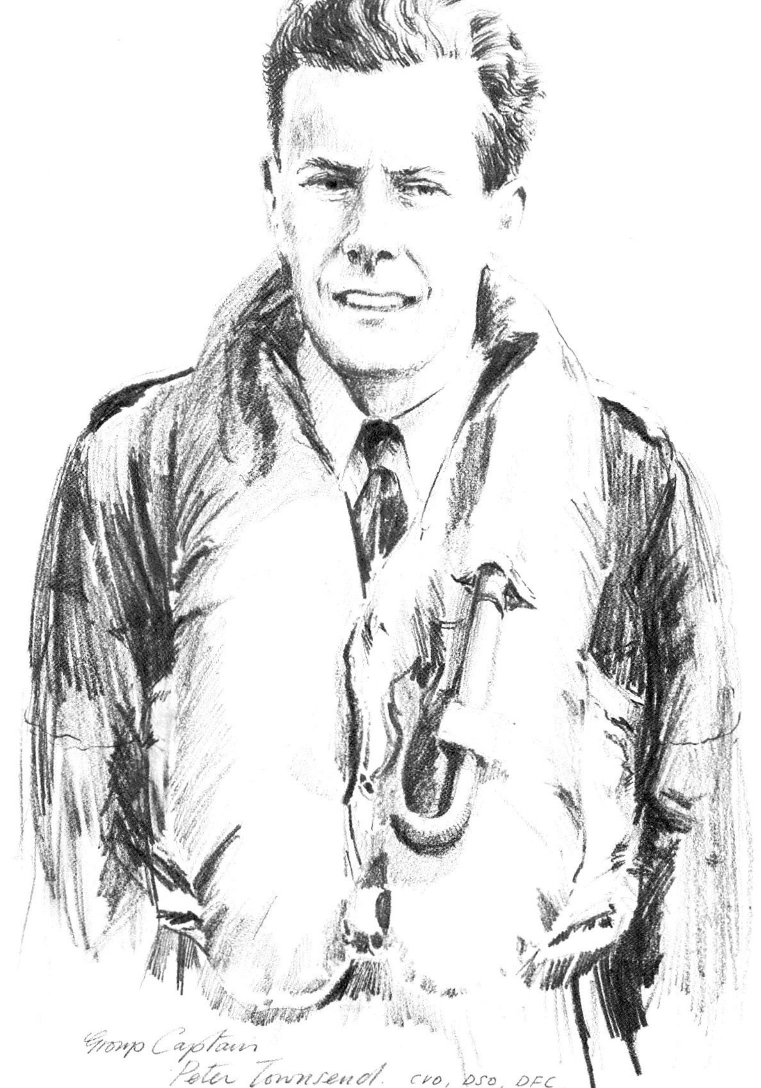

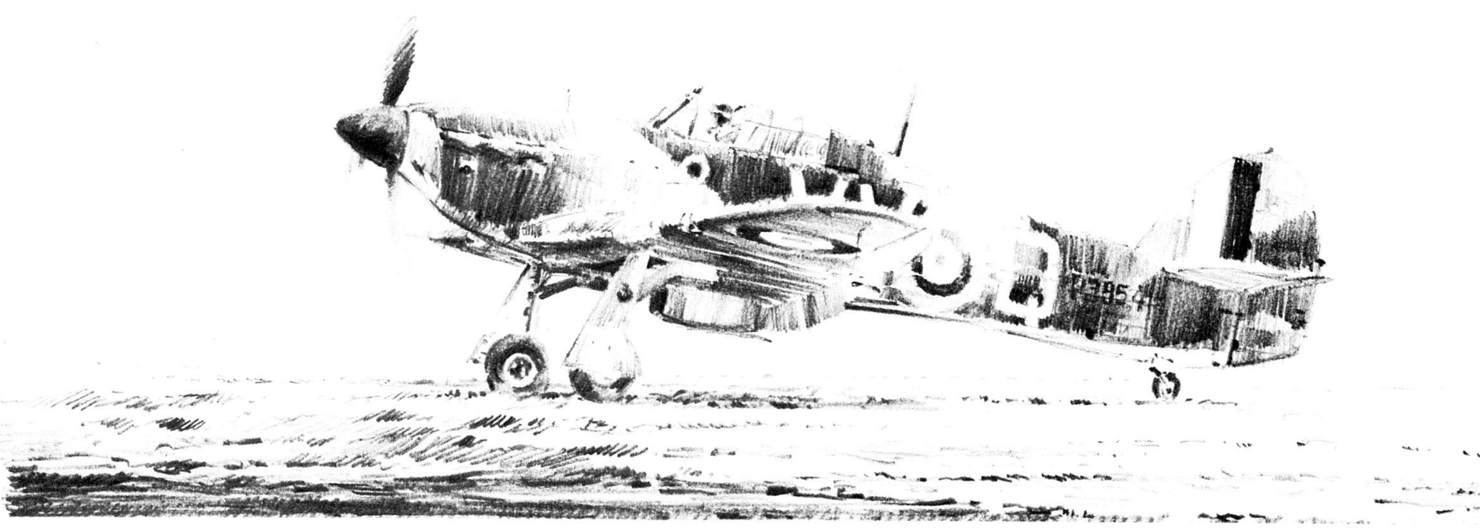

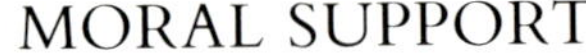

MORAL SUPPORT

In the collection of Mr Randall Gibson

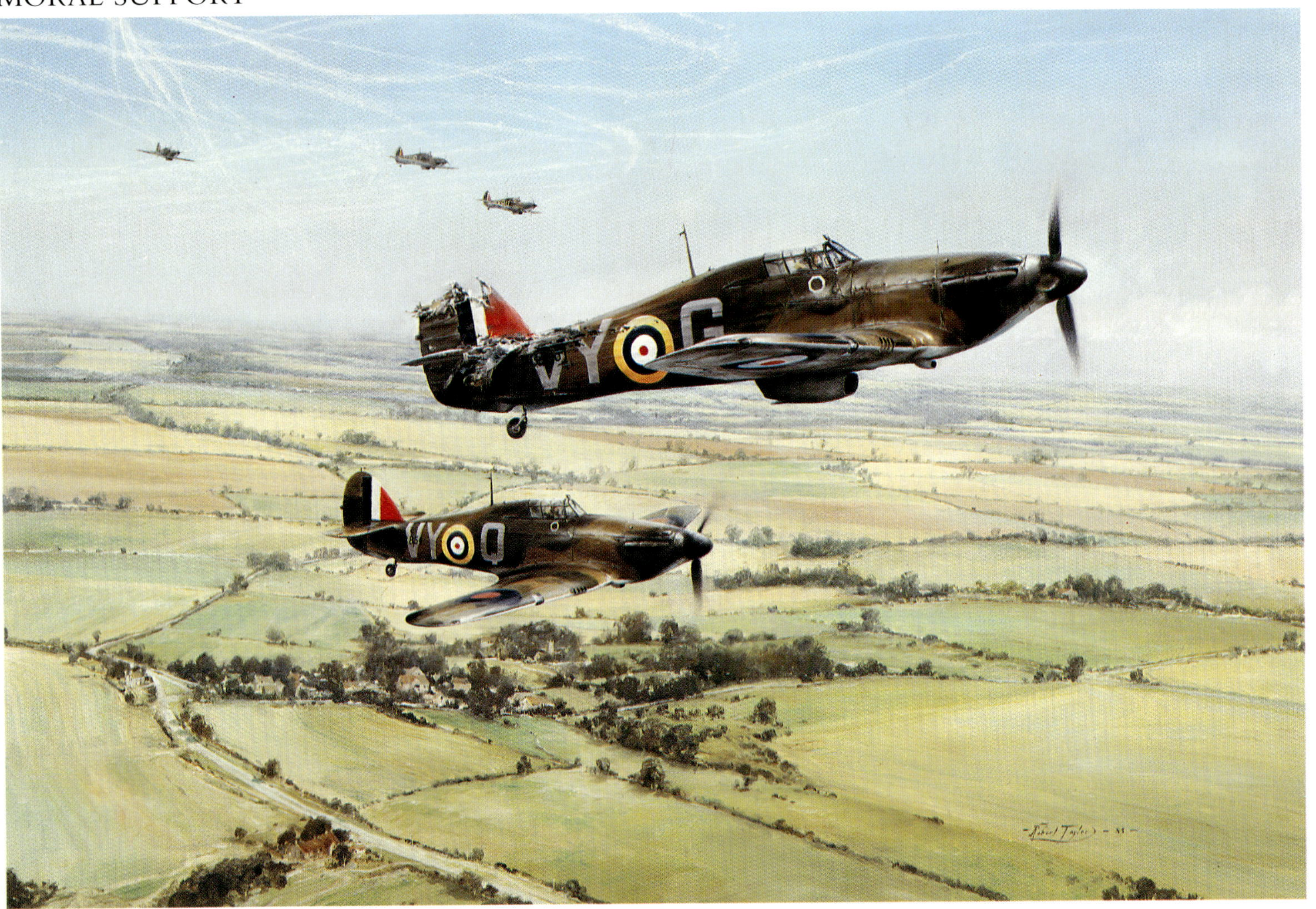

The colour detail on the right hand page is taken from *Moral Support*. The entire painting appears above. The original canvas measures 42 by 28 inches so it can be seen that quite a large area of canvas was covered painting Jim Marshall's Hurricane. The detail on the right is reproduced at exactly the same size as the print which was made from the painting, and shows some of the fairly intricate work that is necessary when painting an aircraft as large as this.

There were no photographs available showing the condition of Marshall's aircraft and so I had to 'construct' the damage from verbal descriptions. I am always careful to try to give my aircraft a 'used' look, even when commissioned by a manufacturer to paint his brand new aircraft. In this case it was no problem!

It took a lot of research and some careful painting to get the attitude of Marshall's aircraft portrayed accurately. His airplane was flying at only just above its stalling speed and it was important to convey this accurately. I wanted to depict the aircraft large enough in the painting so that both pilots could be clearly seen, as this would help convey what was going on and heighten the drama.

I have mentioned elsewhere the value to the aviation artist of first hand reports. Below is a wonderfully graphic account written by Peter Townsend describing a particular combat in which he was involved during the height of the Battle of Britain.

COMBAT REPORT.

31 August 1940

Croydon – Kenley controller. 'Please come to readiness immediately.' There was a mad rush by pilots in old cars, motor-bikes and bicycles to dispersal. I ordered pilots into cockpits, and to start-up, and I called controller. 'Can we go? I don't want to be bombed on the ground.' Controller: 'No hurry, old boy'. Looked round at my squadron, 12 Hurricanes, noses tilted skywards, propellers turning and glinting in the sun, all raring to go.

A moment later, controller: 'Off you go – and hurry!' As my undercarriage raised, the engine cut, spluttered, then recovered: caused by the blast from bombs exploding just behind, where the rest of my squadron somehow got airborne, obscured by smoke. Above were Dorniers, escorted by Me 110s and Me 109s. I climbed at full boost with hood open, (better to watch out for Me 109s) and reached the Me 110s first. As I attacked, a shower of Me 109s fell upon me spraying streams of tracer from behind. An Me 109 turned in front, I hit him and he streamed vapour and slowed up. Then another, I hit him too and he rolled over and, streaming vapour, dived. A third just below – I could easily see the pilot, but while manoeuvring to shoot, an Me 110 came at me, firing head-on. My Hurricane was badly hit in the windscreen and self-sealing centre tank but mercifully there was no fire. I was hit in the foot by a 20mm explosive shell, and momentarily lost control in dive. I baled out low down over woods, just missing some large oaks, and tumbling among fir saplings. After convincing the Home Guard and a policeman of my nationality, we all adjourned to the Royal Oak pub, Hawkhurst, for drinks all round and a wonderfully friendly little crowd to wave me off to hospital.

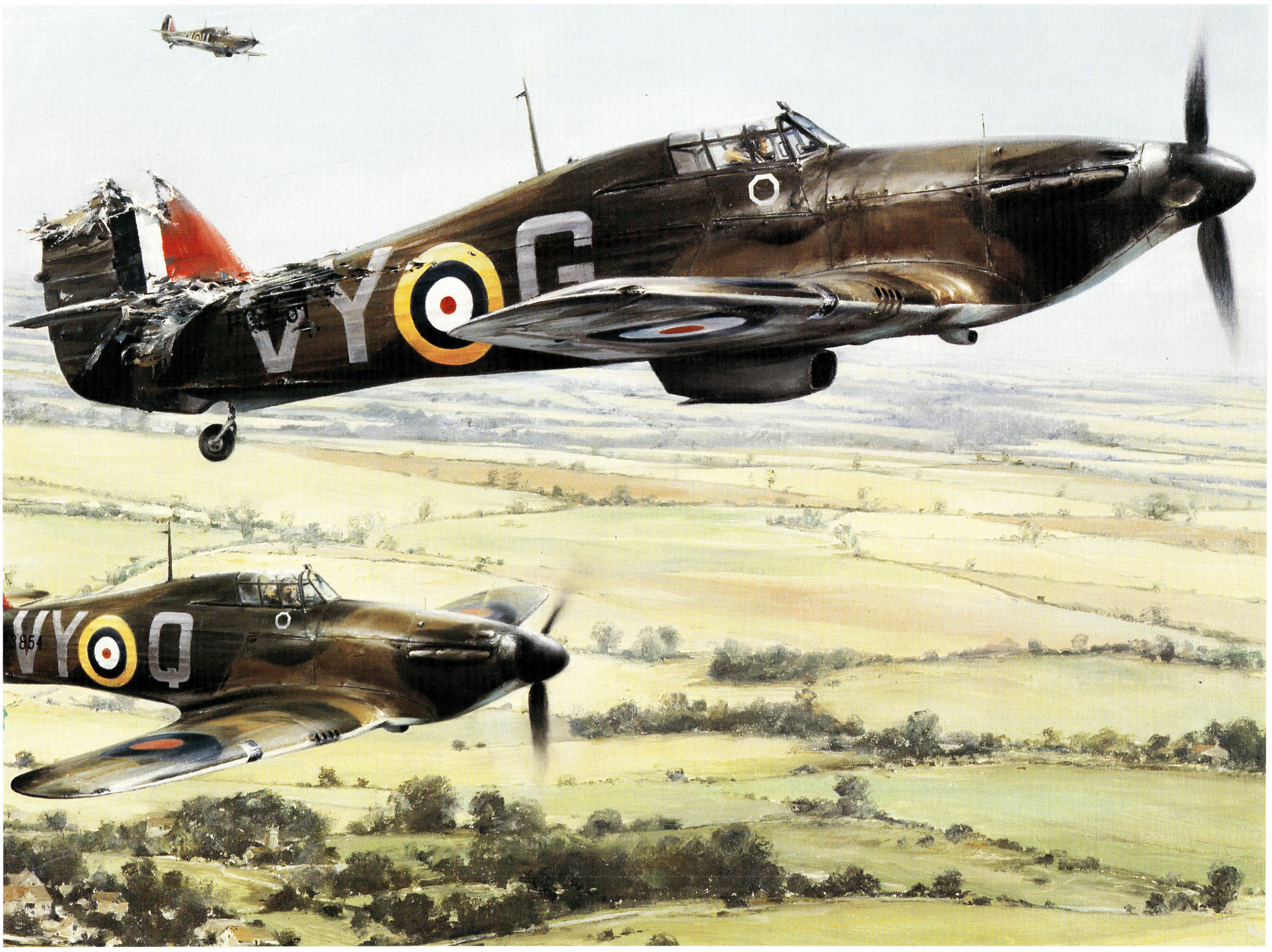
VY G
VY Q

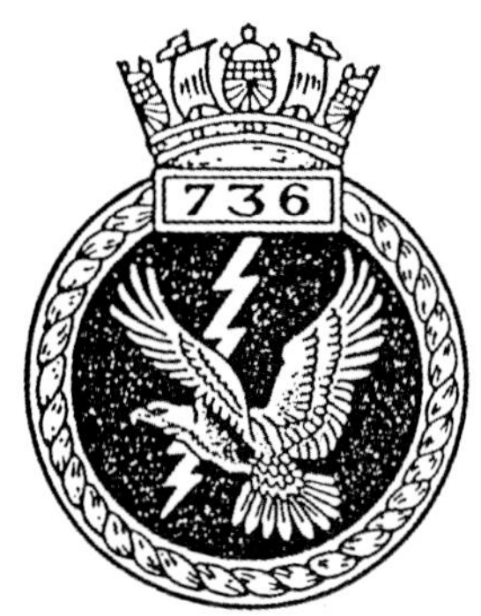

THE BATTLE OF TARANTO

On 11 November 1940 twenty Swordfish aircraft launched from HMS *Illustrious* and delivered a night attack on the Italian fleet at Taranto. Their torpedoes and bombs sank three battleships, two fleet auxiliaries, and badly damaged two cruisers, virtually crippling the Italian Fleet. With the loss of just two aircraft but no crews, it was a decisive victory which re-established British naval supremacy in the Mediterranean.

When commissioned to paint the attack on Taranto I was already familiar with the famous event but, as has happened to me on numerous occasions during my research for a painting, my admiration for those involved became unbounded when I discovered the full facts. When one sees the Navy's Swordfish aircraft – known affectionately as 'the Stringbag' – flying at the summer airshows it is difficult to imagine how this graceful old lady could even deliver an attack, let alone contribute to the demise of a navy. But that in fact is what she did.

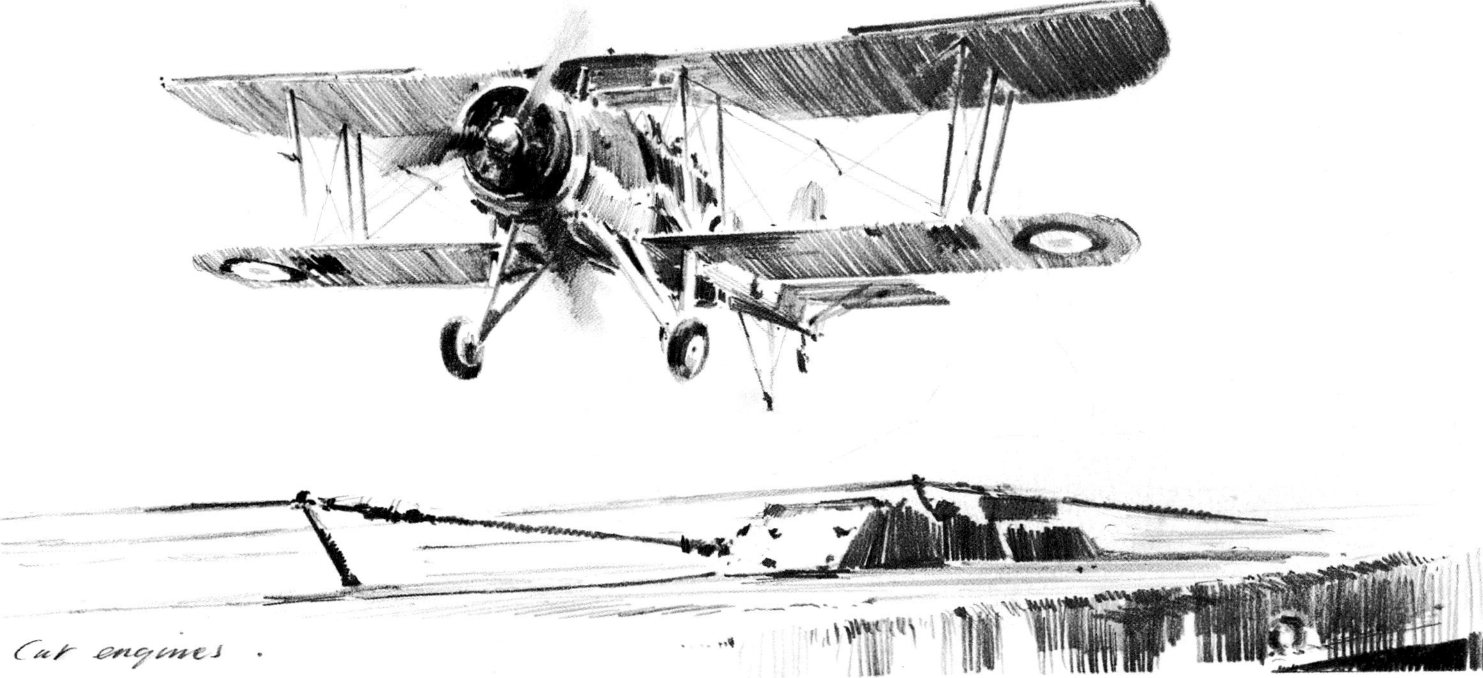

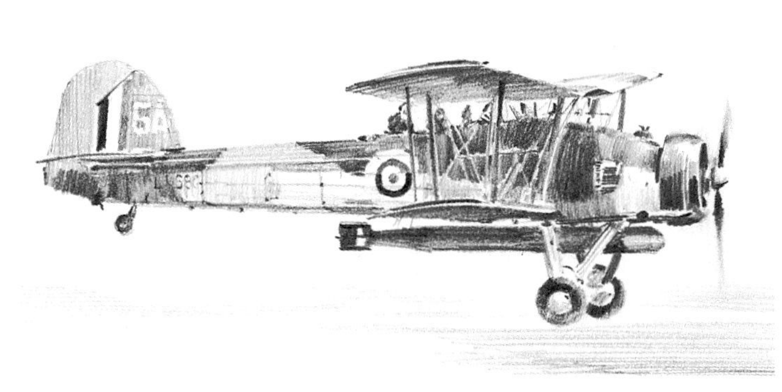

THE FAIREY SWORDFISH

The Fairey Swordfish is an aeroplane which inspired trust, admiration and affection in her pilots. Compared with other biplanes it was colossal, standing almost as high as a two-storey house and was affectionately nicknamed 'the Stringbag', for her size and considerable load-carrying capacity.

More than anything else this classic aircraft will be fondly remembered for its superb manoeuvrability and vice-free performance even under horrific conditions. Commander Charles Lamb, author of *War in a Stringbag*, had this to say:

'The Stringbag could be very roughly handled in incredible attitudes, provided the pilot knew what he was doing. To stall a Swordfish by mistake was almost an impossibility . . . given a stalling speed of 55 knots, and no pilot, however ham-handed, could allow his speed to drop to that extent without noticing. To induce it into a spin was quite hard work: the aircraft could be stood on its tail in mid-flight so that it became almost stationary before it would drop into a stalled turn, and then recovery could be instantaneous. Quick application of throttle and opposite rudder, and a speedy lowering of the nose, would provide almost immediate stability.'

This feature of the Swordfish's performance saved many lives during World War II. Even to attempt a landing-on with the deck of an aircraft carrier rising and falling by as much as sixty feet would have been considered suicidal in almost any other aircraft.

I had the good fortune to be introduced by Commander Dennis White of the Fleet Air Arm Museum, to the two pilots who flew the lead aircraft at Taranto, Commanders Charles Lamb and Lancelot Kiggell. As has been mentioned in the introduction to this book, these two colourful, amiable and courageous men gave me literally days of their time in my efforts to research the painting and I am indebted to them both. Sadly both are no longer with us but I shall never forget the amusing times we had together, and any success that I achieved in depicting the atmosphere at Taranto is largely due to them.

Normally the Swordfish carried a crew of three: pilot, observer (the navy's version of a navigator), and an airgunner. They sat in that order, behind the pilot. Because of the duration of the flight to Taranto and back, the Swordfish had to be fitted with an auxiliary fuel tank. This was placed in the observer's cockpit right behind the pilot. The observer moved aft to the airgunner's position, the airgunner being dispensed with on this occasion. The original working drawing missed this fact, but it was quickly pointed out to me by Charles Lamb. Another specialised modification for the raid was a cleverly-designed artificial horizon – a sort of forerunner of the modern head-up display. A tube was fitted in a horizontal position in front of the pilot at eye level. This was illuminated inside, with pin-holes drilled in the tube, which presented the pilot with an artificial horizon in the form of pin-pricks of light. It was important to have the wings of the Swordfish level at the point of release of the torpedo, and it was difficult to judge this in the dark. By lining up the pinpricks of light with the horizon – on this occasion well lit up by the flares dropped by Charles Lamb and Lancelot Kiggell – the pilot could maximise his chances of hitting the target.

During my research, no photographs or drawings could be found anywhere showing this ingenious and simple device, so I had to make sketches from the description given to me by Charles Lamb. The 'sight'

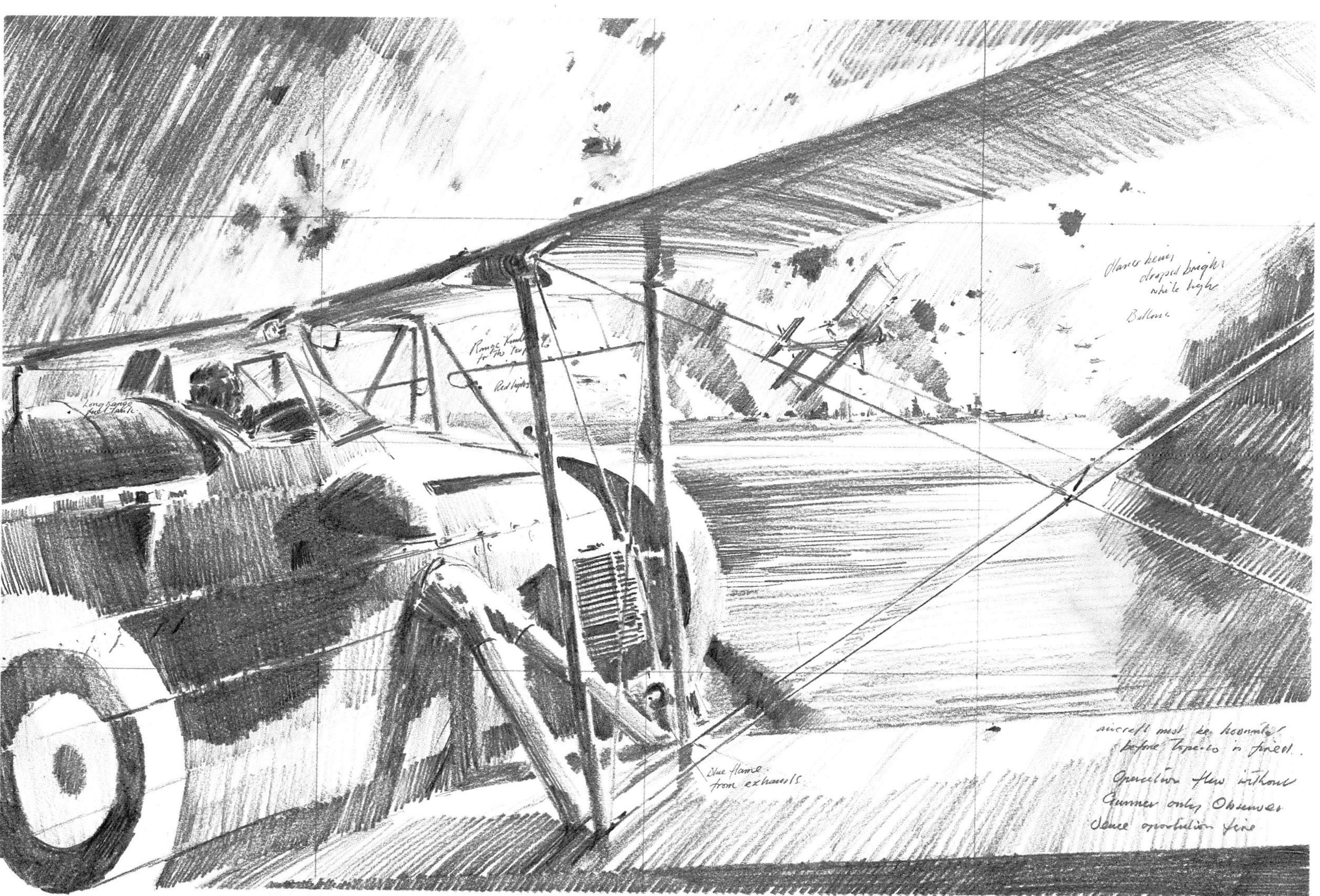

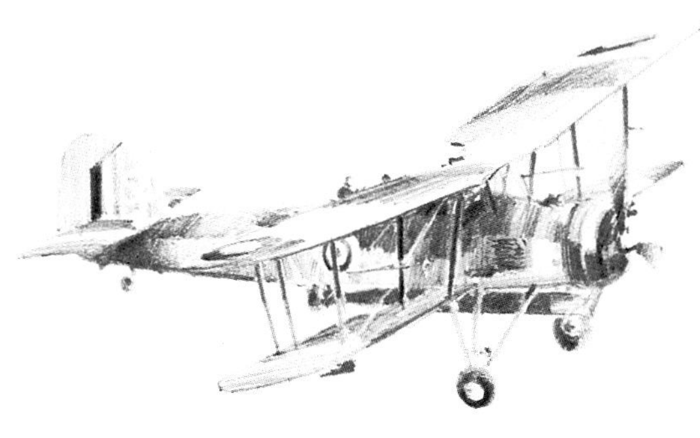

can be seen in my painting, directly in front of the pilot's line of vision.

The famous Swordfish attack at Taranto has been well painted many times by other artists and so it seemed particularly important to try a fresh approach. I tried a number of ideas. My final concept, seen above, came about by taking a 'detail' from a much larger drawing. By increasing the size of the aircraft so as to fill almost the whole canvas, it was possible to paint the attack looking through the wings of the 'Stringbag'. An entire Swordfish was included, ahead of the main aircraft, to heighten the action. Charles Lamb had likened the effect of the flares and gunfire to 'Piccadilly Circus', so there were no problems in lighting up the whole skyline ahead. The old Stringbag just oozes character and is a wonderful aircraft to paint. I enjoyed the enthralling time spent with Charles Lamb, and loved every minute of creating the painting. I am very proud that the Fleet Air Arm Museum saw fit to place it in their creatively-designed Taranto display.

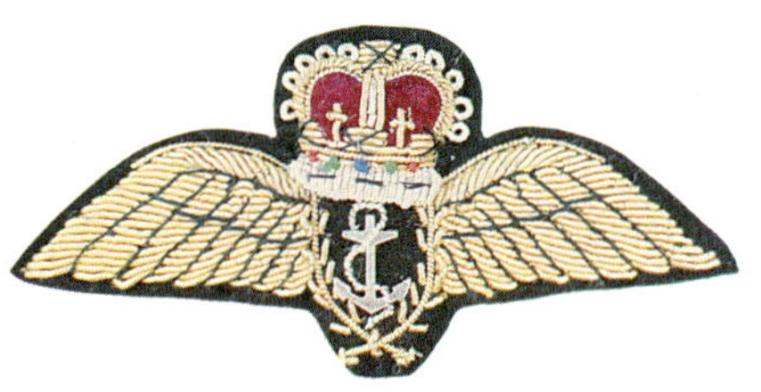

THE HISTORY OF THE FLEET AIR ARM 1907–1986 by Commander Dennis White, OBE, RN (Ret'd)

Despite the Board of Admiralty's opinion in 1907 that 'the aeroplane would not be of any practical use to the Naval Service' it was fortunate that there were officers on the Naval Staff who had the foresight to disagree. It is thanks to their tenacity and enthusiasm that aviation was firmly established in the Royal Navy during the momentous years that followed. Construction of No 1 Rigid Naval Airship, the Mayfly, started in 1909 and the first course of four naval pilots took place in 1911.

The Royal Flying Corps with its Military and Naval Wings was formed on 13 April 1912 and experiment, improvisation and trials went ahead with gathering momentum from ship and shore and by seaplane, landplane and airship. Two years later, on 1 July 1914 the Naval Wing became the Royal Naval Air Service thus marking the birth of naval flying as a coherent entity.

At the outbreak of the 1914–18 war the RNAS had 128 officers, 700 ratings, 40 land planes, 31 seaplanes and 7 airships operating from 10 bases. The following four years saw an astonishing expansion to 126 bases stretching from the Middle East to Scotland, 2,000 land planes, 650 seaplanes, 150 flying boats, 103 airships, 170 kite balloons and a complement of 55,000 officers and ratings. Much was accomplished during the war; operations in France and the Dardanelles, the air defence of Great Britain, the first strategic bombing attack, the development of sea plane tenders, the beginnings of the true aircraft carrier and many other aspects.

LAUNCH AGAINST THE BISMARCK

In the collection of The Fleet Air Arm Museum, Yeovilton

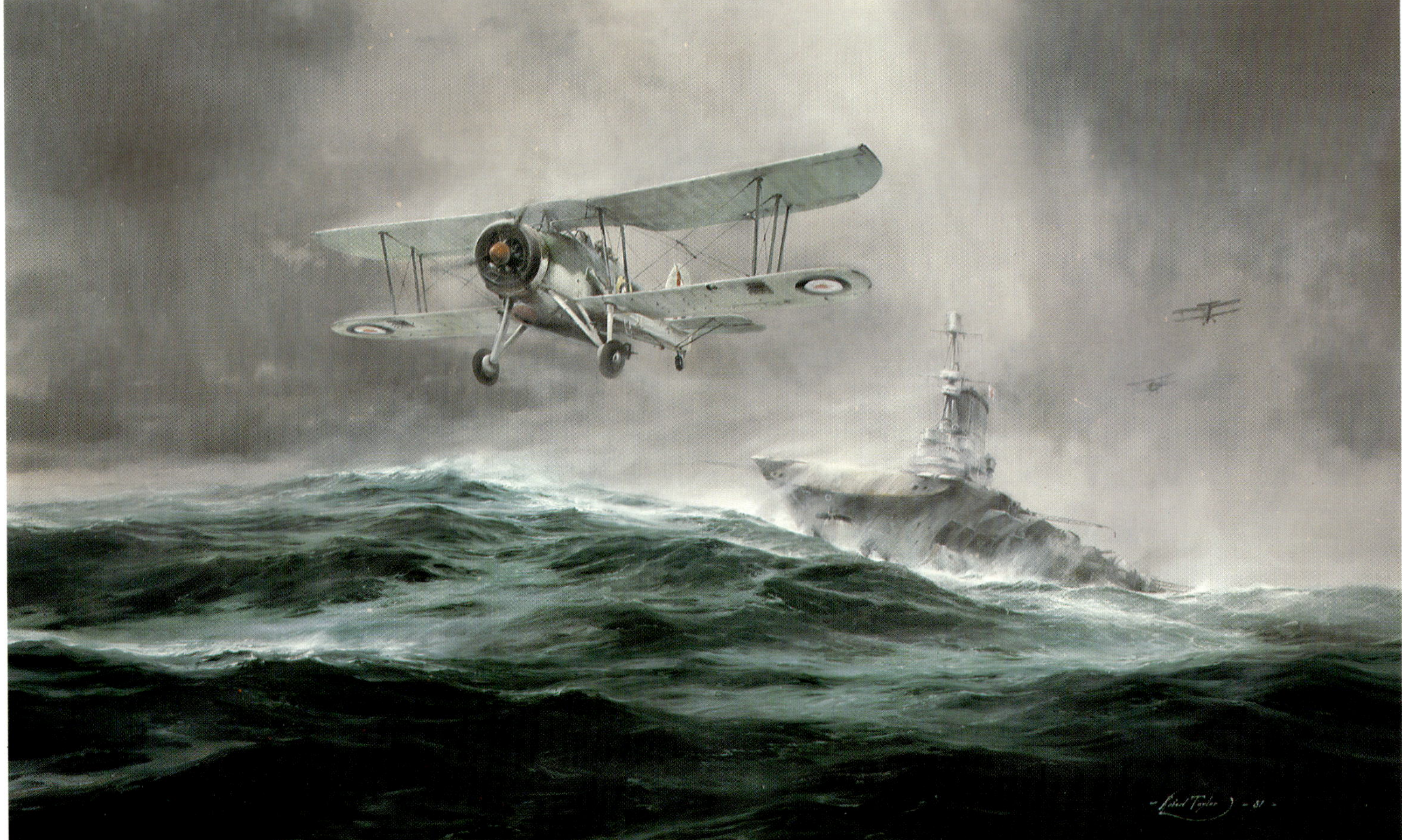

However, the involvement of the RNAS in air warfare other than that directly concerned with the support of the Fleet began to raise political questions. There was a groundswell of opinion that viewed the independence and size of the RNAS with suspicion, which led to the centralisation of British air power and the formation of the Royal Air Force on 1 April 1918 by combining the RFC and RNAS.

The RNAS thus became the Fleet Air Arm of the RAF and, having lost direct control by the Admiralty, it suffered in consequence. With few exceptions it had to accept aircraft primarily designed for the RAF and modified for use at sea. In addition the majority of pilots serving in FAA squadrons were RAF officers who returned to their parent service after a tour at sea. This led to a dearth of officers with aviation experience reaching the higher ranks of the Navy. Despite these disadvantages and reduced size the FAA pressed ahead during the inter war years with developing the aspects of Fleet support.

Almost from the day that the RNAS became a part of the RAF the battle to regain control began. The fight was to last until 1937, when full control of the Fleet Air Arm was returned to the Admiralty.

Once again the war years of 1939–45 saw a rapid expansion and, although poorly equipped initially, the Fleet Air Arm acquitted itself well, with the night attack on the Italian fleet at Taranto being worthy of particular mention. With the European war drawing to a close, attention was turned to the Pacific Ocean and the defeat of Japan.

The post war years saw the introduction of the angled flight deck, the mirror landing sight and steam catapult all of which made the introduction of jet aircraft a practical proposition and went a long way towards reducing the inherent dangers of deck landing.

The past twenty years have seen a radical change with the introduction of helicopters for anti-submarine warfare and Royal Marine Commando support and the advent of the VSTOL Sea Harrier. These changes were put to the test and proved right in the Falkland Islands in 1982.

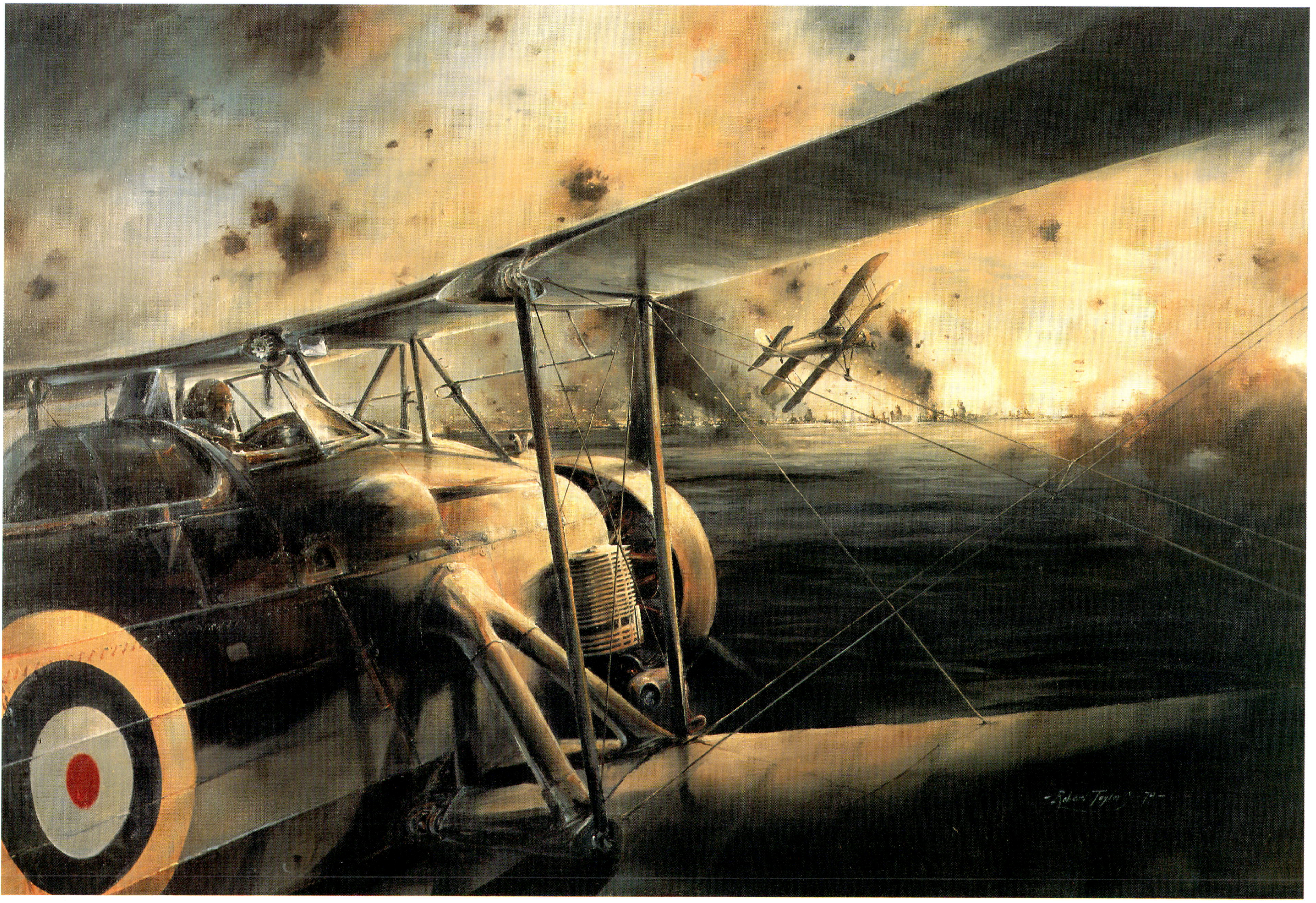

BATTLE OF TARANTO
In the collection of The Fleet Air Arm Museum, Yeovilton

EAGLE SQUADRON SCRAMBLE

In 1985 the British Prime Minister, Mrs Margaret Thatcher, unveiled a memorial to the American Eagle Squadron pilots in Grosvenor Square, London. Quite why it took 45 years to organise this is a mystery to most people, but of one thing all are convinced. It was fully deserved.

Eagle Squadron Scramble is one of my favourite pictures of Spitfires from the many I have painted over the years. Everything seemed to go well for me with this picture and when the painting was purchased and presented to the International Aerospace Hall of Fame, in San Diego, I was truly delighted. It now hangs in that wonderful museum, the brainchild of Colonel Ed Carey and his team, where the Eagle Squadrons are specially remembered.

I usually make a fairly comprehensive pencil sketch for all my paintings before I start applying any paint to canvas. This is because I like to know exactly what I am going to paint before starting. In this case I made a finished drawing, featured on the next page, on a sheet of cartridge paper measuring 23 by 15 inches. The painting itself measured 42 by 28 inches and although my finished work is always much larger than the drawing, I rarely vary the finished work much from the final pencil-drawn concept. While drawing, I am often planning exactly how the paint will be applied to a specific part of the canvas in order to achieve the effect I am aiming for. Before starting the final drawing for a picture, I may have completed dozens of smaller drawings and sketches, so it is often the culmination of many hours of previous work.

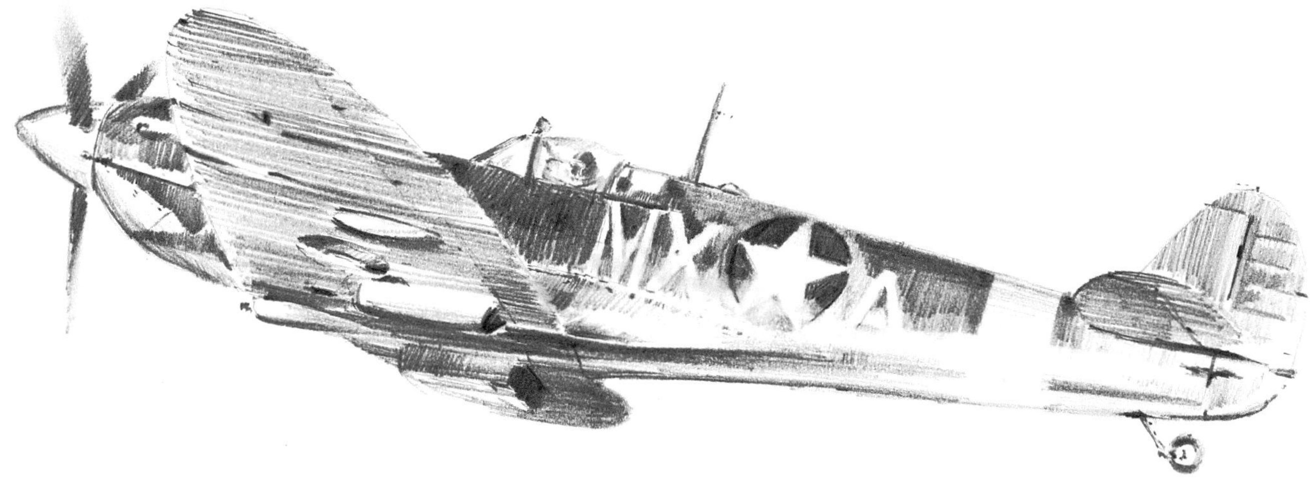

The first USAAF fighter unit to see action in Europe, as distinct from the R.A.F controlled 'Eagle' Squadrons was the 31st Fighter Group which became operational in August 42. above 307 Squadron Spitfire V .. based Manston.

THE EAGLE SQUADRONS

There were certain young men in the United States, shortly after Dunkirk, who, for a variety of reasons, felt that it was time to go to the aid of the pilots of Fighter Command. Some felt that such measures were made necessary by the threat the Nazis posed to the free world. Others simply found the promise of danger and adventure too thrilling a prospect to resist. Almost all of them risked serious legal consequences by enlisting with a foreign power: often it involved evasion of the US draft and violated neutrality laws.

Many of those who arrived in 1940 and formed No 71 Squadron – the first Squadron of 'Eagles' – were only one jump ahead of the ever-vigilant men of the FBI. Finally, each by his own unique route, 240 brave and boisterous young Americans arrived in England and formed the three famous Eagle Squadrons. Number 71 Squadron was joined by numbers 121 and 133. Between them, over the next eighteen months, they accounted for an official total of 73 enemy aircraft. In fact, historians are almost unanimous today in believing the actual figure to be considerably higher than this. Even so, this conservative estimate of their contribution to the Allied war effort shows that the RAF had at least the equivalent of six Luftwaffe squadrons fewer to worry about!

During the time the three squadrons were operative as 'Eagles', many pilots were shot down and taken prisoner. After America's entry into the war the Eagle Squadrons were incorporated within the US Army Air Forces and many more former Eagles suffered the same fate.

Despite the controversial nature of their enlistment and their reputation for a 'hard fighting, hard playing' philosophy, the men of the Eagle Squadrons provided a vitally-needed morale boost for the hard-pressed pilots of the RAF and, indeed, for the entire nation. They flew and fought for all they were worth and earned the admiration and respect of their fellow pilots of the RAF. When the United States joined the war in Europe it was to the experienced fighter pilots of the Eagle Squadrons that the USAAF looked to form the backbone of their new fighter wings.

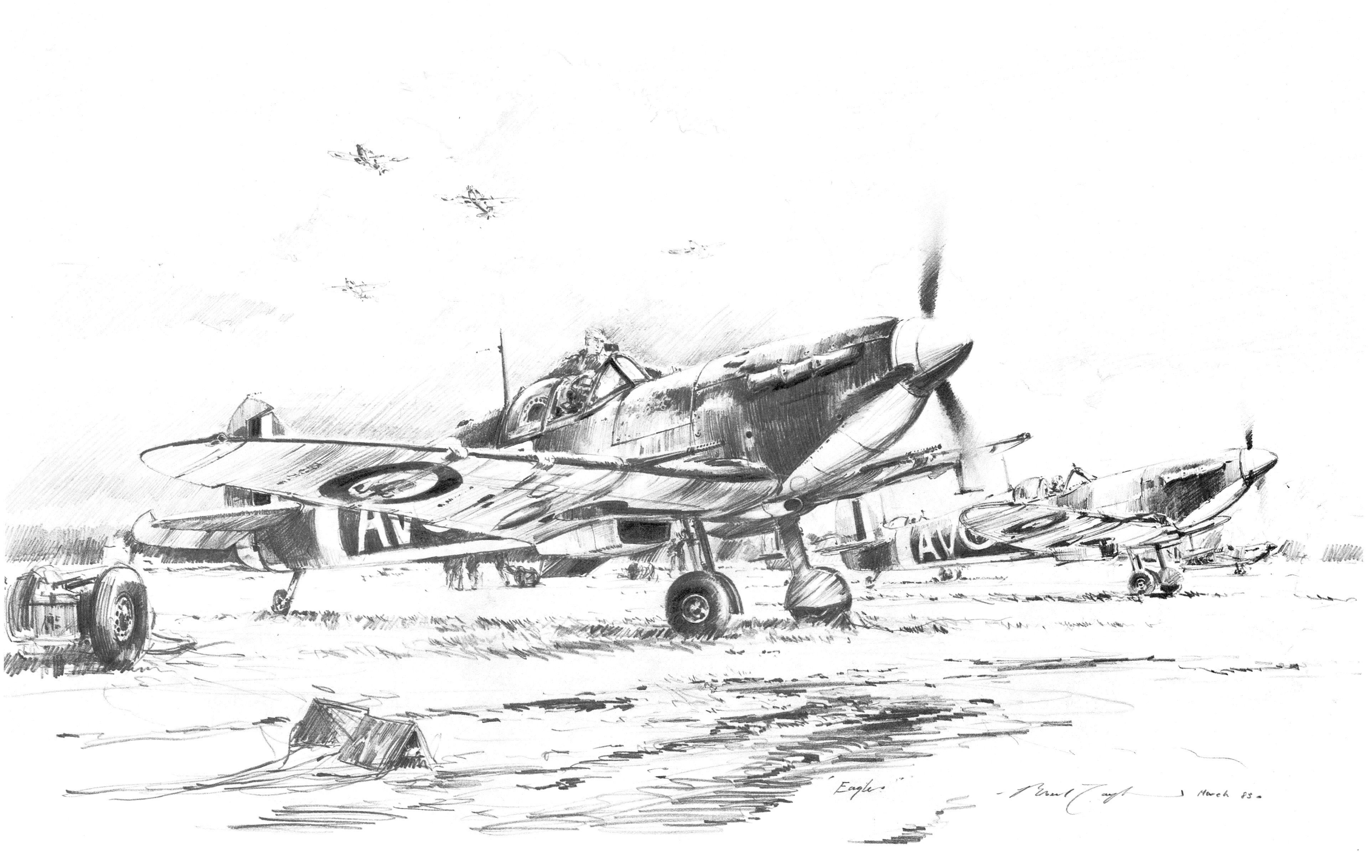
AV
AV
"Eagles"
March 83.

Having completed the final drawing, before starting to paint, I draw the picture accurately on the canvas using an HB pencil. First comes the outline, in pencil, of the main items of subject matter, to ensure that everything is positioned as in the finished pencil sketch. I then add in all the smaller items of detail before I start work with the paint. I place enormous importance on painting the sky and sometimes spend as long working on this part of a painting as on the aircraft that feature in them. The skyscapes are planned very carefully and I do my best to ensure that the cloud formations are correct. (Some cloud types never appear at the same time as others!) I usually sketch the cloud formations on the canvas last.

The Spitfires in *Eagle Squadron Scramble* are painted fairly large on the canvas, and this meant a great deal of detailed work. Painting fine detail in oil on a grained canvas is not easy, but very rewarding. There is always a tendency, when painting small detail, to over-emphasise everything and if one is not careful the resulting aircraft can look like models suspended in space – or in this case glued to the ground. I hope I have avoided such an effect in this painting. The detail below will make it easier to decide!

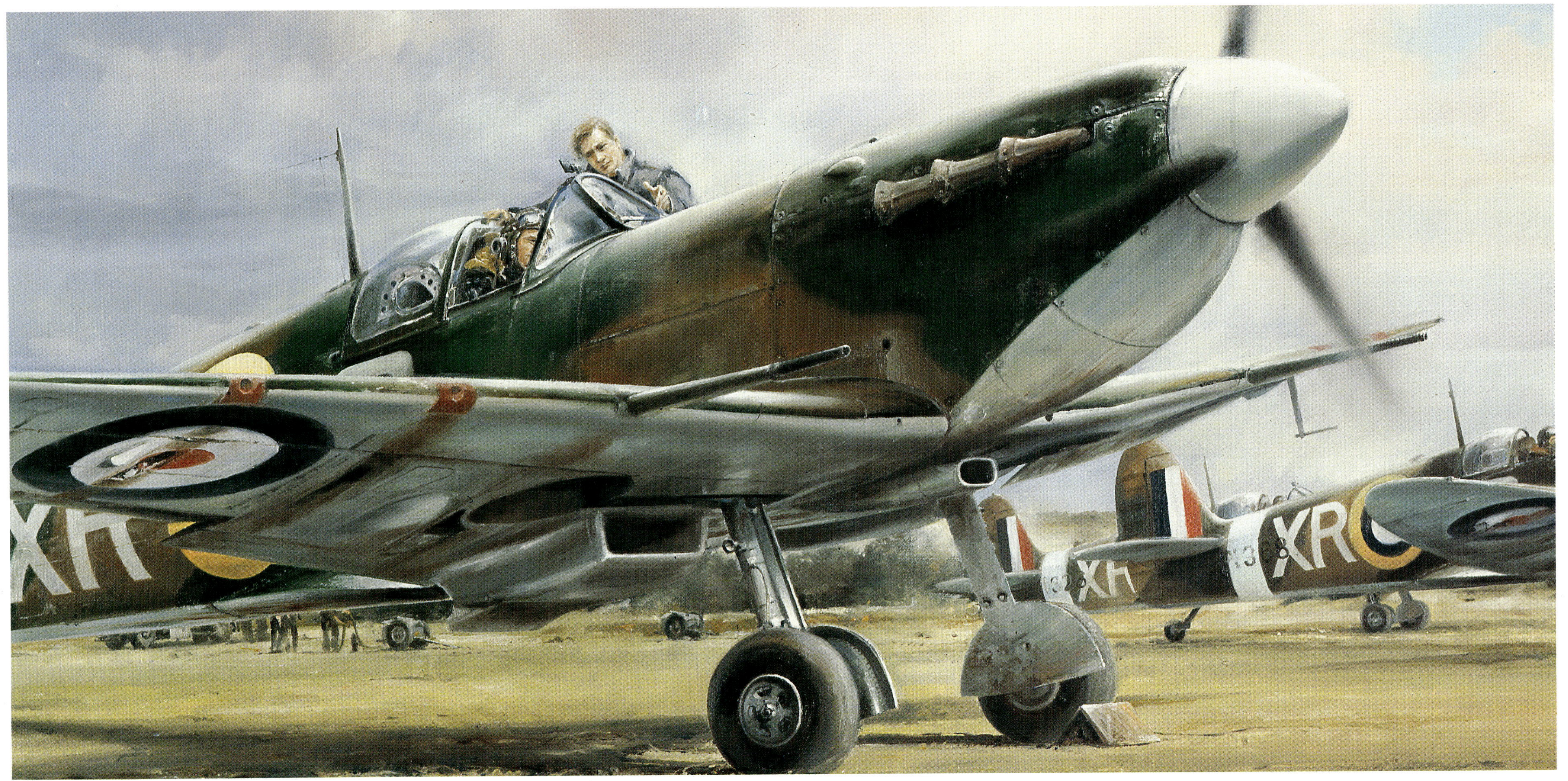

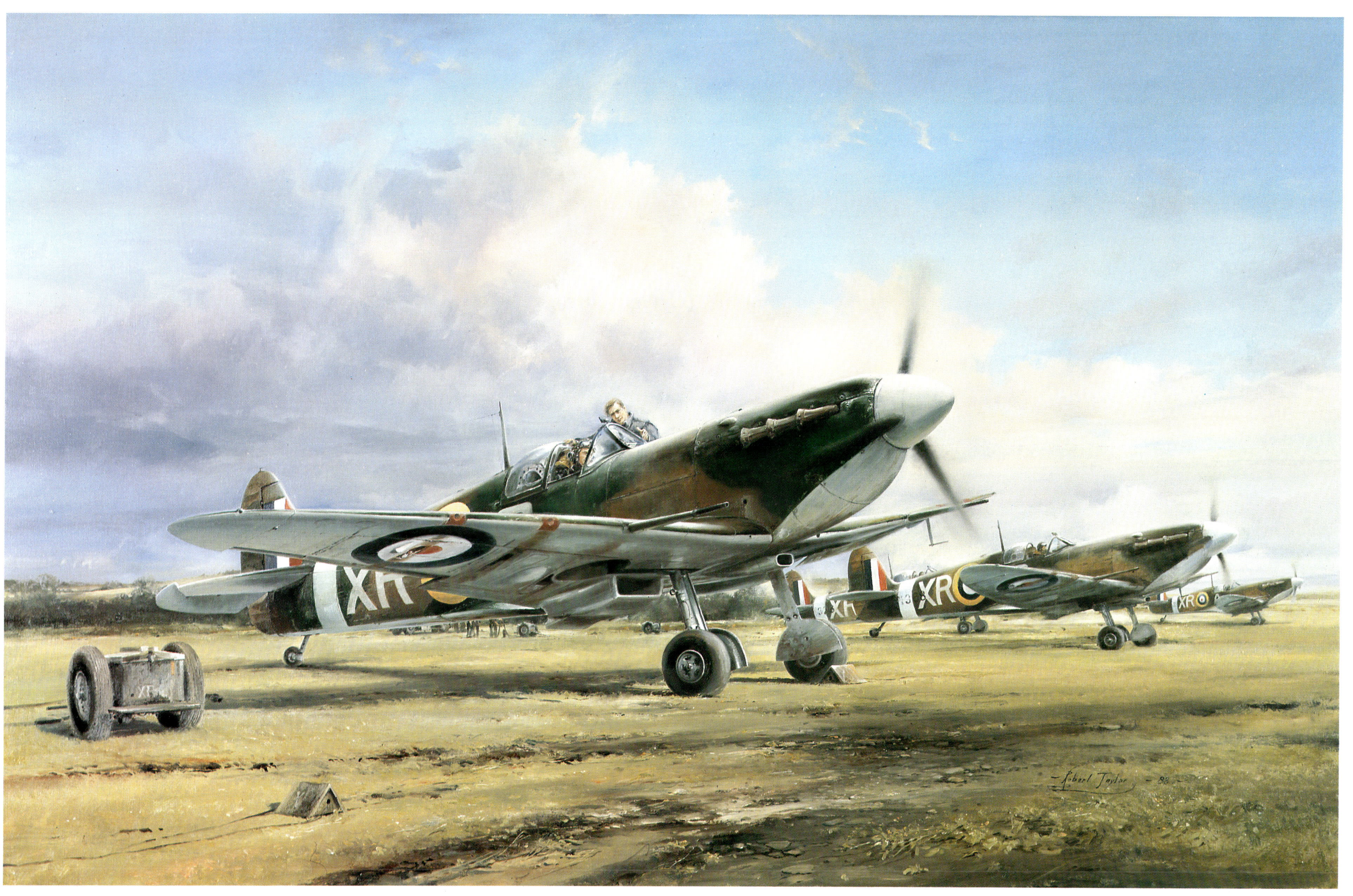

EAGLE SQUADRON SCRAMBLE

In the collection of The International Aerospace Hall of Fame, San Diego

SEA KING RESCUE

During the Falklands War in 1982, and during the year following, I received many requests to paint scenes depicting all manner of events which had taken place in that South Atlantic war. Amongst these requests at least half were to portray helicopters in action. Prior to the Falklands War nobody seemed interested in them at all!

Helicopters, it is claimed by many, are not very beautiful to look at, which perhaps accounts for the lack of demand for paintings of them, but I imagine that if you are on the aft end of a burning ship, they are about the most beautiful sight you could wish for!

Army helicopters played a significant part in the Falklands War, landing assault troops, moving stores and equipment, and in general assisting with communications. The naval helicopters were involved too in most of these activities, but also in radar detection using Sonar, and search and rescue. Possibly the most dramatic moments of their war in the South Atlantic were seen by millions on television as helicopter pilots manoeuvred perilously close to burning ships to rescue stranded crews.

One of the most challenging of these Falklands-related commissions was to portray the part played by His Royal Highness Prince Andrew and his Sea King crew in the rescue of those aboard the stricken *Atlantic Conveyor*, after she had been hit by an Exocet missile. Piloting a Sea King helicopter on Sonar duty, Prince Andrew was first on the scene after the missile struck.

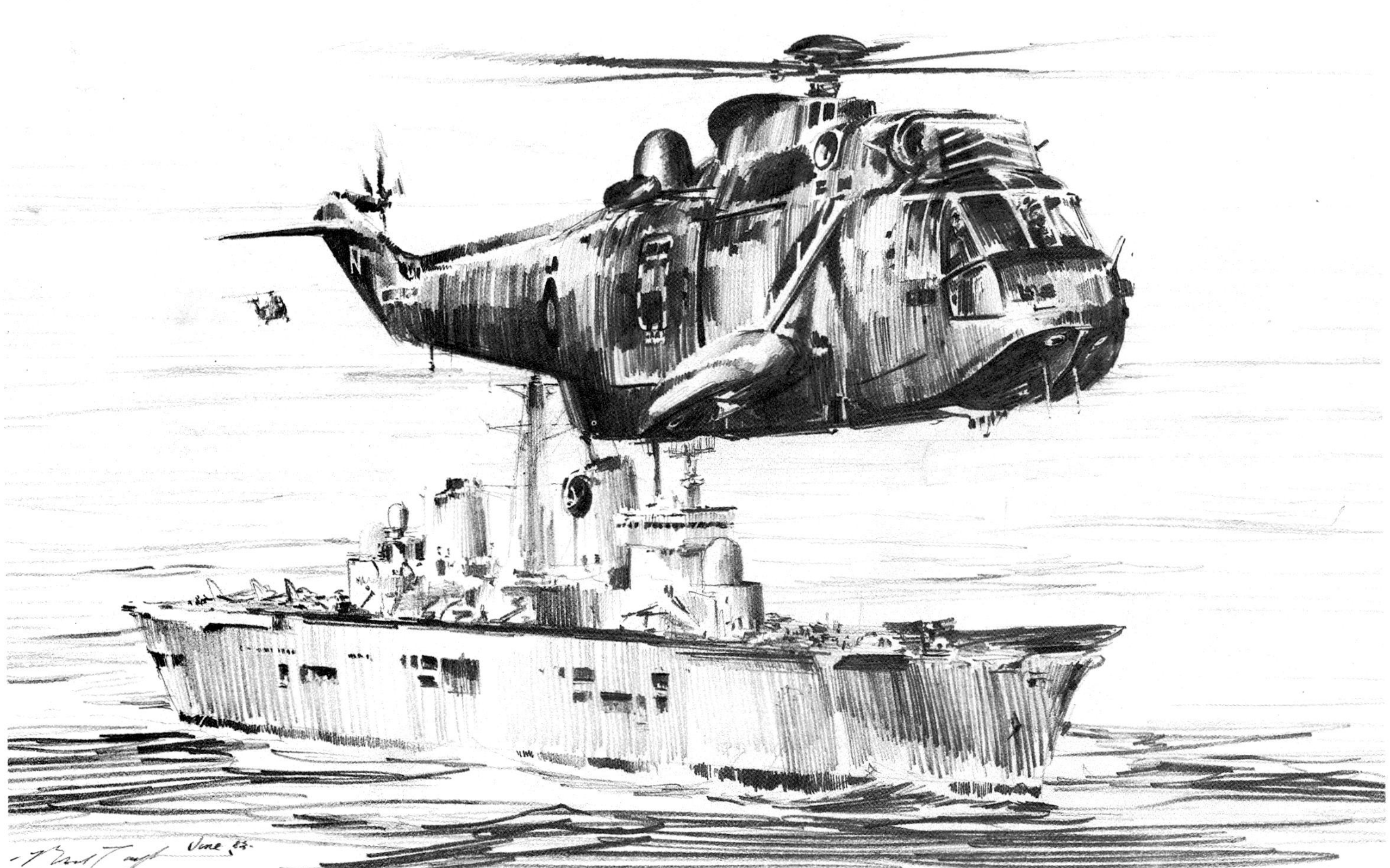

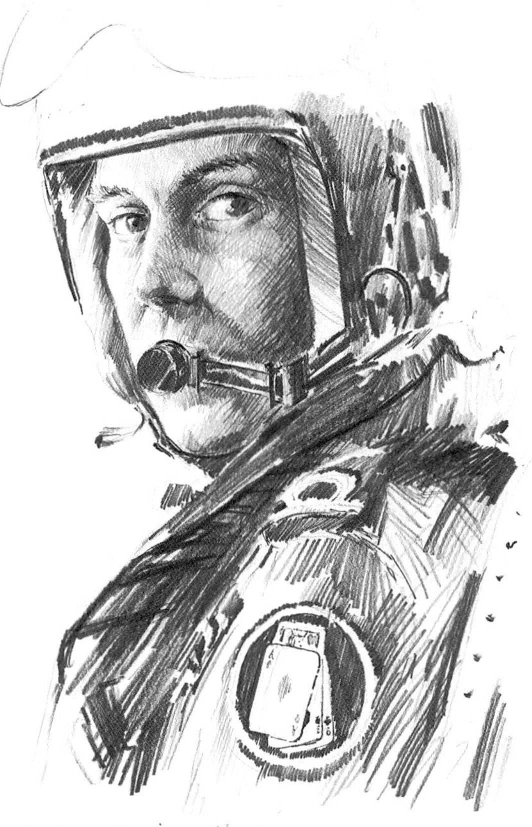

I had the honour to be presented to Prince Andrew when he opened the Falklands Exhibition at the Fleet Air Arm Museum. He said to me 'Ah, now you are the artist who is to paint my aircraft. Please remember that there are only four people who can give you the accurate information about the incident, (his crew totalled four) and I am one of them'. I was left in no doubt that His Royal Highness wished to be kept informed as to my progress and furthermore that I had better get it right!

After a good deal of very thorough research and a series of preparatory drawings, painting finally commenced. When my work was nearing completion Prince Andrew invited me to bring the painting to Buckingham Palace for him to check on progress. The visit was of great value because Prince Andrew was able to correct at least one major discrepancy – I had to remove a Lynx helicopter astern of the *Atlantic Conveyor*, and replace it with a Wessex – and add a further Wessex helicopter.

This, together with a few other smaller corrections requested by Prince Andrew, was duly completed and prints were published from the painting. His Royal Highness generously consented to sign, with his crew, 100 copies of the resulting print which subsequently – and very quickly – raised a substantial sum of money for the King George V Fund for Sailors. The entire project was very gratifying for me.

Several drawings of the Sea King in flight were necessary in order to decide upon the concept. I had not painted this particular aircraft before and felt a need to familiarise myself fully with it. After making preliminary drawings, my first thought was to show the aircraft looking at it from just slightly below, more or less at the angle shown in the drawing on the left hand page. Although HMS *Invincible* was not to appear in the painting I drew it into the sketch just for the exercise!

The next approach was a study looking down slightly on the aircraft, which seemed better than the original angle. This sketch, on the right, again includes part of the *Invincible*. I was pleased with this view of the Sea King. I thought this angle would work for the painting so I drew my next sketch (above) using the same view of the helicopter, and this time sketching in the burning *Atlantic Conveyor* below. This provided quite a nice 'grandstand' view of the action, but it left an uneasy feeling that Prince Andrew's helicopter had become a little too 'detached' from the events beneath.

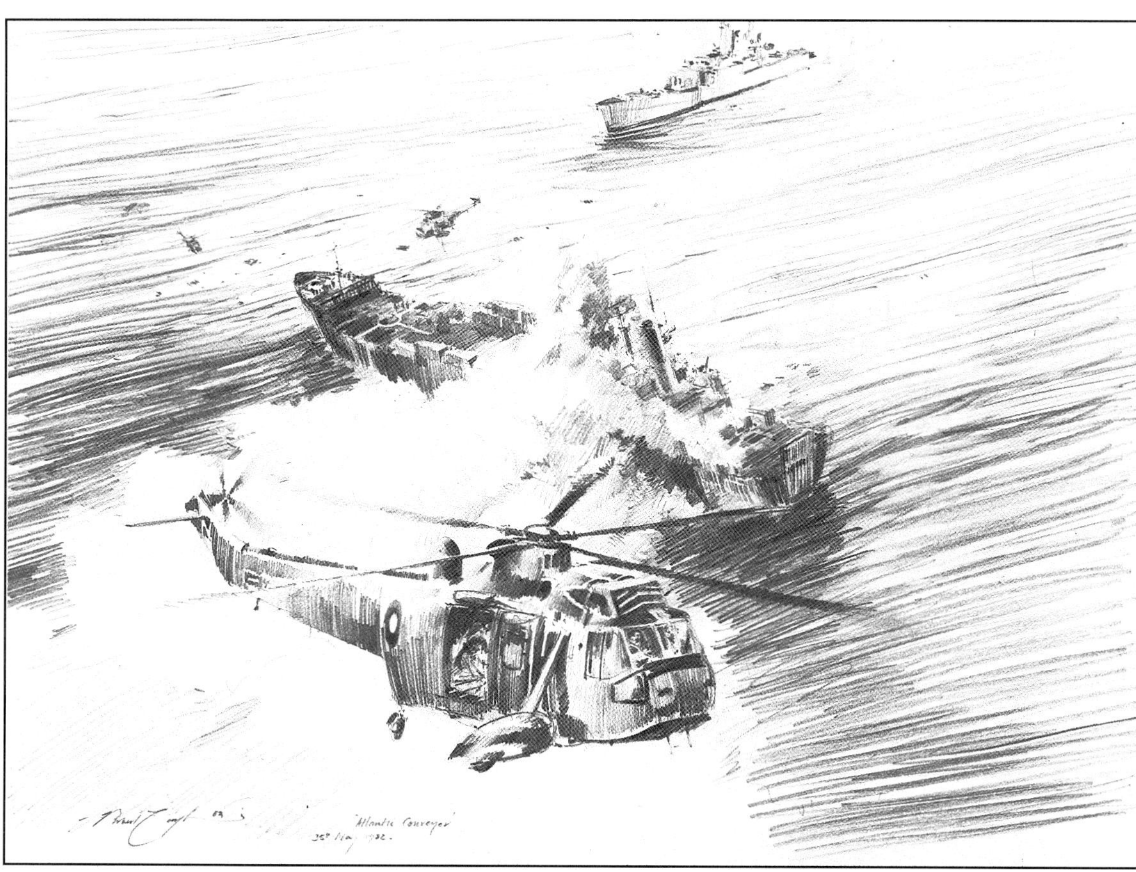

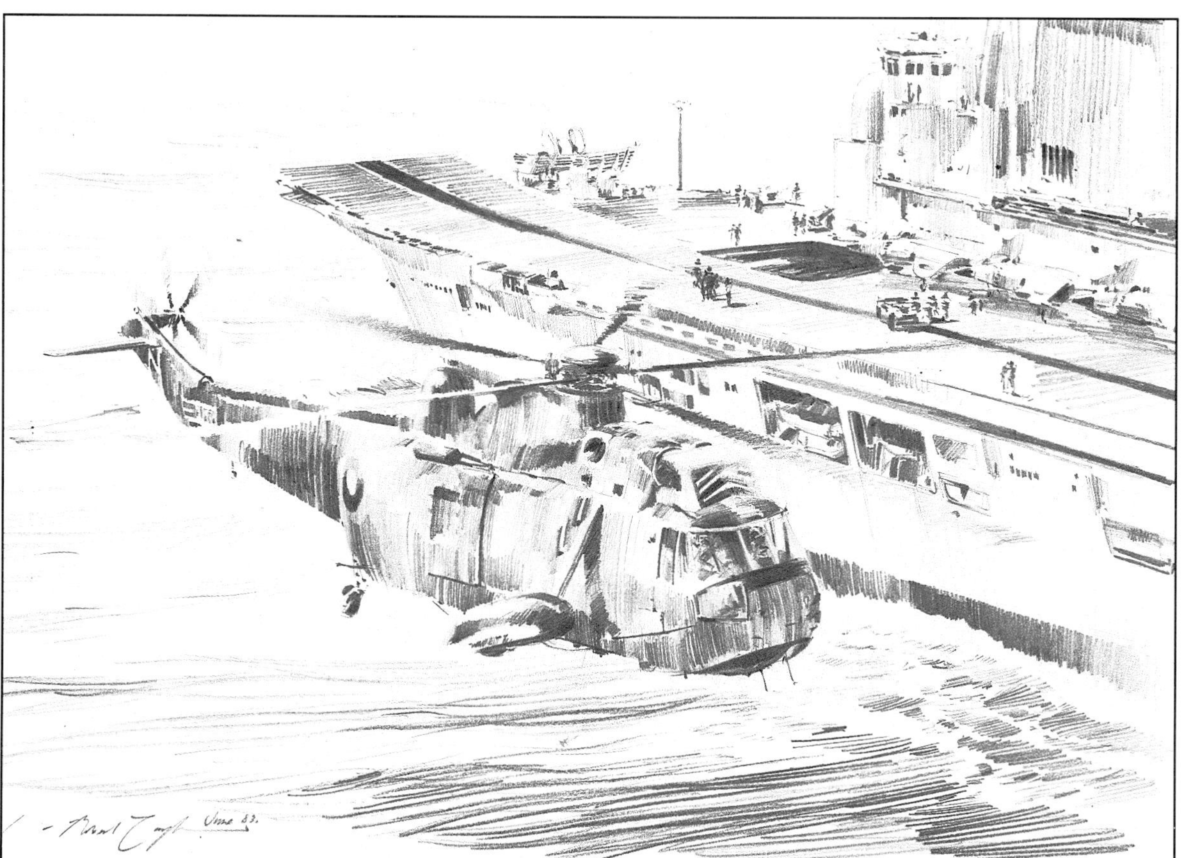

The composition below appeared to be much better, and the helicopter viewed from underneath in a climbing turn, provided a greater degree of movement. The life rafts shown in the drawing were removed at the request of His Royal Highness. They had been, in fact, on the other side of the ship!

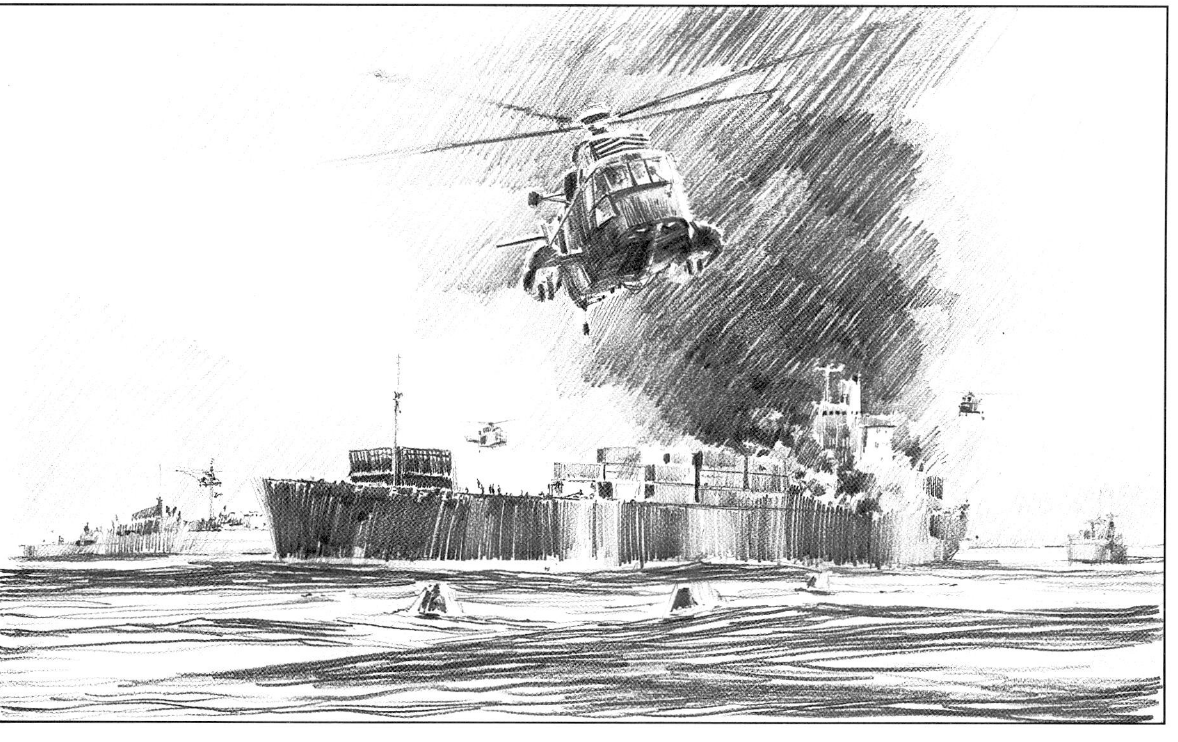

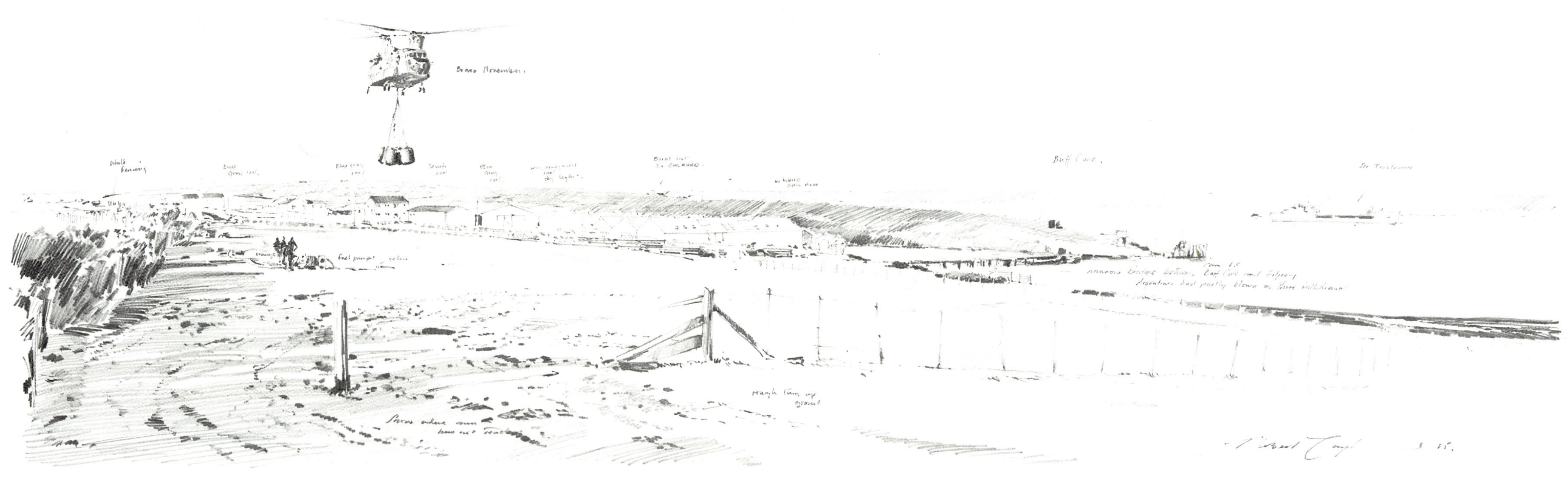

CORPORATE ACTION

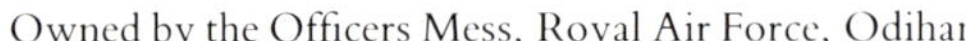
Owned by the Officers Mess, Royal Air Force, Odiham

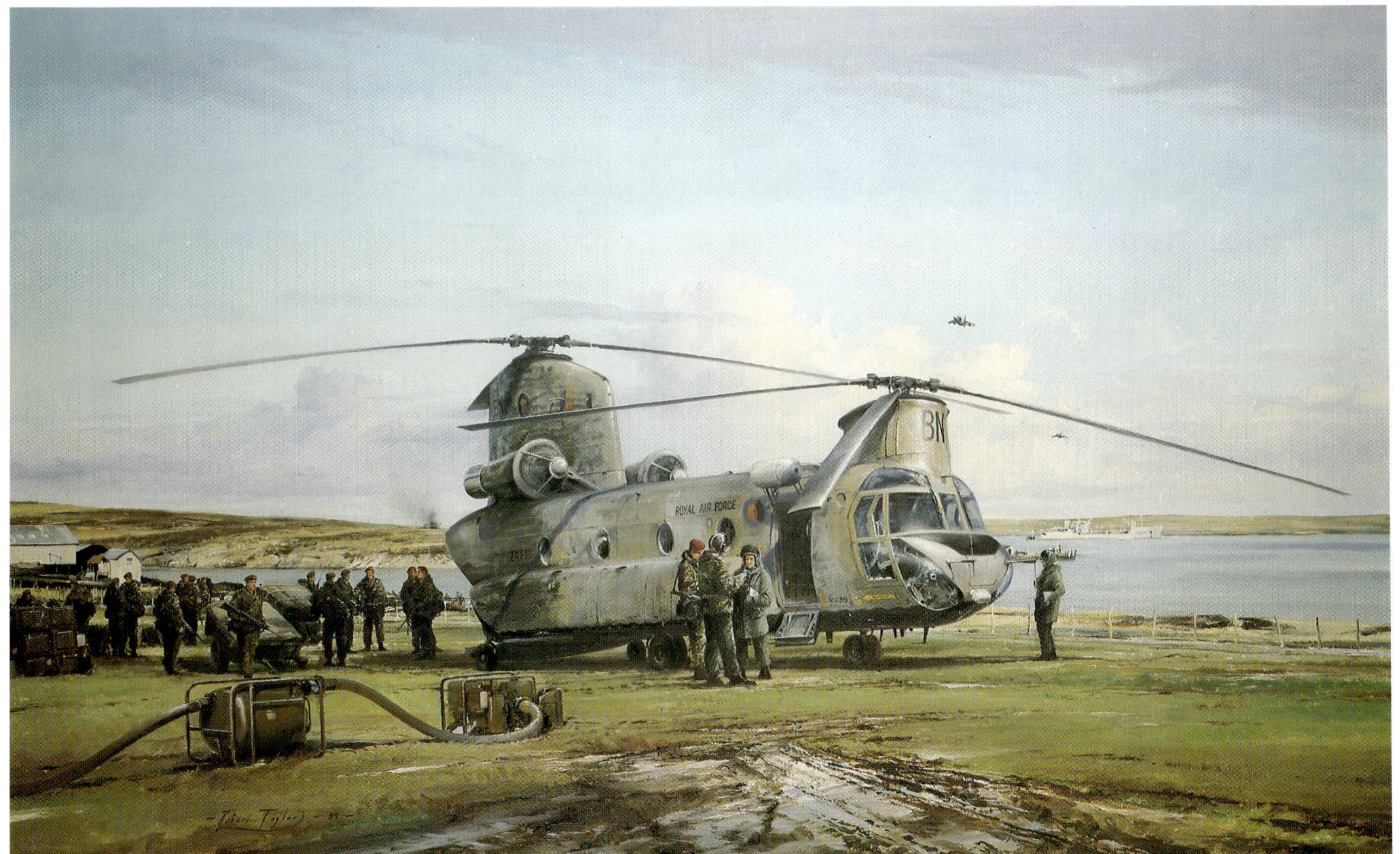

By their very nature helicopters are ungainly beasts, and few have graceful lines. In fact, the only people I have met who think of helicopters as beautiful are the aircrew who fly them. From the artist's point of view they are wonderful aircraft to paint, mainly because one can actually see so much of what makes them 'tick'. Being purely functional aircraft which are not designed to fly at any great speed, aerodynamics are not of paramount importance and as a result they nearly all have an outwardly workmanlike appearance. The Westland Sea King is a good example.

The Chinook is an amazing flying device. Aside from its size and the fact that it lifts itself and such enormous loads vertically, the idea of the two huge rotor blades meshing with each other at such high speed is difficult to comprehend.

I was commissioned by RAF Odiham to paint the Chinook 'Bravo November' – the only one to get off the ill-fated *Atlantic Conveyor* before she was sunk (three others went down with the ship). I prepared the drawing above whilst working on the locational background required for the painting. In the painting which is illustrated at left, I was asked to include certain recognisable aircrew briefing for a sortie over Fitzroy and about to embark members of 2 Para during 'Operation Corporate'. On one sortie, Bravo November lifted eighty-one troops which is about fifty more than the norm! The keen-eyed will spot two RAF GR3 Harriers heading out on a strike mission.

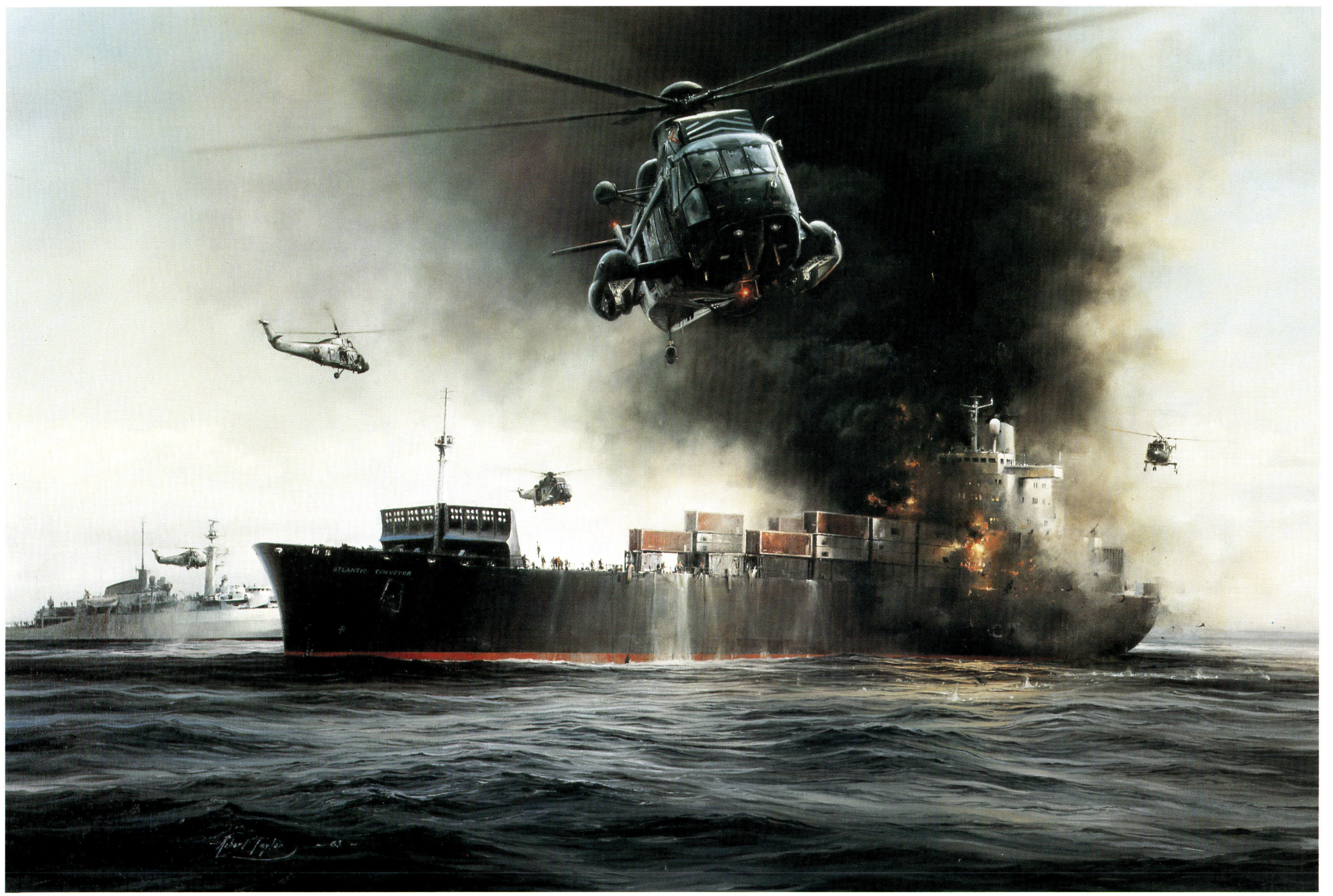

SEA KING RESCUE

In the collection of The Fleet Air Arm Museum, Yeovilton

FIRST OF MANY

The title *First of Many* relates to a specific combat early in the Battle of Britain. The sortie was flown by a single pilot – the Commanding Officer of No 242 Fighter Squadron – and it culminated in the first air victory for the squadron during World War II.

At about 7 o'clock in the morning, shortly after he had taken command of No 242 Squadron, Douglas Bader picked up the telephone in the dispersal hut the moment it began to ring:

'There's a bandit flying up the coast towards Cromer. Can you get a section off?'

The weather outside was appalling. Douglas looked out of the window and promptly replied: 'No! The weather is too bad. I'll have to go by myself. I shall be out of radio touch almost as soon as I leave the airfield, so I'll fly straight to the coast, turn left and fly as far as Cromer. If I don't see anything I'll come back.'

He took off in his new Hurricane alone and went in search of the controller's 'bandit' – the term used for a lone enemy aircraft.

Conditions were indeed very bad. The cloud cover over the airfield was down at 600 or 700 feet. On reaching the coast, Douglas discovered that the cloud base had lifted to 1,000 feet. He made his turn up the coast and, suddenly, there was the enemy aircraft. It was a Dornier 17. He approached it, at first unnoticed. As he drew nearer, he was spotted by the Dornier's rear-gunner who opened fire immediately.

Listening to the events described by Sir Douglas during my research for this painting, I was enthralled. He had a way of describing occasions like this which made them sound about as traumatic as a trip to the local supermarket. A couple of his quotations illustrate my point:

'I remember thinking to myself as the Dornier gunner opened fire on me: I've got a bullet-proof windscreen in front of my face, a twelve-cylinder engine in front of my body and tin legs beneath me, what harm could I possibly come to? I was totally relaxed.' And, from his book *Fight for the Sky*: *'Now, one of the defects of the German twin-engined bombers of that period was their lack of effective defensive firepower. The Heinkel 111, the Junkers 88, the Dornier 17, and indeed the Messerschmitt 110 twin fighter (after the Junkers 87 dive bomber, the easiest to shoot down) were all equally ineffective. The rear-gunner had but one (sometimes two bracketed together) machine gun which fired over the tail as defence against attack from behind. Worse still, the wretched gunner had to manhandle his gun, aim it, and fire it in a 200 mph (or more) slipstream unless his pilot had the nerve to continue flying straight and level with a fighter on his tail.'*

So Douglas engaged his Do 17 and, having closed on it and re-set his reflector sight, fired a few bursts. The Dornier banked steeply to the left and began to climb into the cloud. After a couple more bursts of fire at the disappearing enemy aircraft, Douglas headed for home, cursing at not having had a better opportunity to destroy the Dornier, and in doubt as what damage he had been able to inflict. Shortly after he reported uncertainty as to whether he had shot down the 'bandit', Douglas received a confirmation call from the controller to tell him that a Home Guard observation post had reported a Dornier crashing into the sea at precisely the time and place of his engagement.

This air victory was the first of the war for No 242 Squadron, and was to be the 'First of Many' successes of the squadron during the war. It was appropriate that it should have been achieved by its famous Commanding Officer, and typical of the man that it took place under flying conditions so appalling that he would not allow his other squadron pilots to take off.

All pilots have a flying log book in which they record, usually in cryptic fashion, the basic details of every flight made. Today they are valuable collectors' items and, on the rare occasions when they become available at auction, they realise substantial sums.

I have found reference to pilots' log books useful for checking dates, aircraft types and so on but the Combat Reports, which are now available under the '30-year rule', are much more descriptive and therefore more informative. Below is a page of Douglas Bader's flying log book showing the entry he made on the date featured in *First of Many*.

Year 1940		Aircraft		Pilot, or 1st Pilot	2nd Pilot, Pupil or Passenger	Duty (Including Results and Remarks)
Month	Date	Type	No.			
						Totals Brought Forward
July.	9th	Hurricane	D.	Self	—	To Newmarket.
	—	Hurricane.	D.	Self.	—	To Coltishall.
	—	Hurricane	D.	Self	—	Formation.
	8th	Hurricane	D.	Self.	—	Defence practice.
	10th	Hurricane.	D.	Self.	—	To [illegible]
	—	Hurricane.	D.	Self.	—	Formation.
*	11th	Hurricane.	D.	Self.	—	Attacked & destroyed one Dornier 17 off Cromer (confirmed)
	—	Hurricane.	D.	Self.	—	Weather test.
	13th	Hurricane	D.	Self.	—	Attempted interception of [illegible] Never saw it.
	—	[crossed out]				
	—	Hurricane	D.	Self.	—	Investigate X-raid [illegible]
	16th	Hurricane.	D.	Self.	—	Local flying.
	—	Hurricane.	D.	Self.	—	Local flying.
	17th	Hurricane	D.	Self	—	Weather test.
	—	Hurricane	D.	Self	—	Local flying
	—	Hurricane	D.	Self.	—	Local flying
	18th	Hurricane	D.	Self	—	Formation practice.
	19th	Hurricane	D.	Self.	—	To & from Hendon
	20th	Hurricane	D.	Self.	—	To [illegible]
	21st	Hurricane.	D.	Self	—	Formation
	—	Hurricane	D.	Self.	—	[illegible] out.
	—	Hurricane.	D.	Self.	—	Convoy patrol
	22nd	Hurricane	D.	Self.	—	Formation attacks.

Grand Total [Cols. (1) to (10)] 326 Hrs. 0-0 Mins. Totals Carried Forward

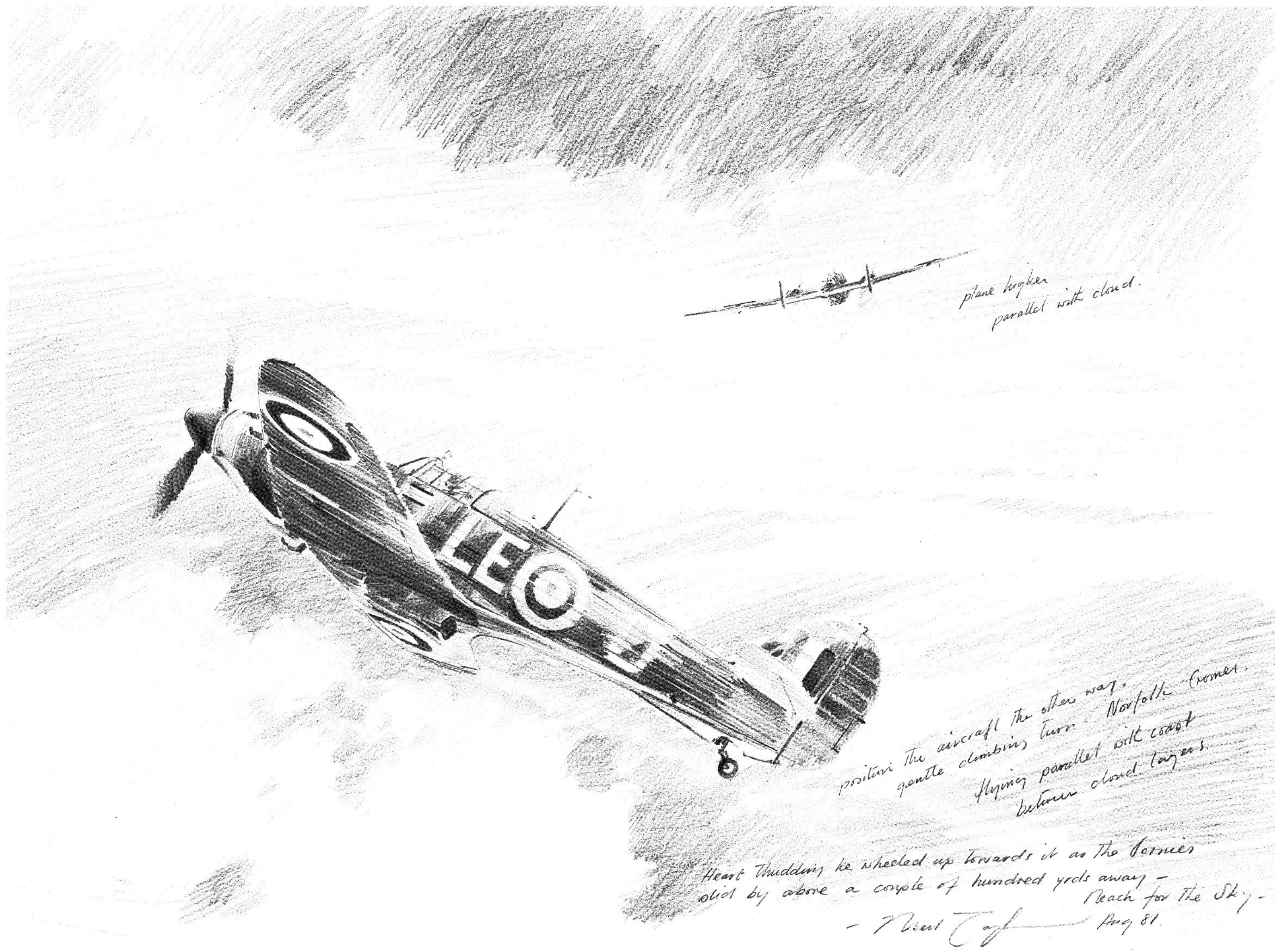

The first drawing made for this painting is illustrated above. Both aircraft were drawn from memory and as a result there are a few inaccuracies in the drawing. I usually like to have some reference in front of me, even when I am doing preliminary drawings, because unless the subject is drawn reasonably accurately it can upset the balance of the drawing. I have noticed this on a number of occasions where I used no reference for my drawing, and as a result sometimes did not like the composition. When taking more care with the accuracy of drawing, I have discovered this helps me to evaluate better the construction of the picture.

In this particular case it didn't matter because when I showed this first concept to Sir Douglas he told me I had him flying in the wrong direction! I redrew it showing the moment when he broke between the layers of cloud, first sighting the Dornier, and this I decided looked much better. This drawing is below.

There were two main problems with the picture. The first was the overall colouring – the combat having taken place on a filthy day where just about all that was around was solid grey cloud. It was obviously important to record the event as accurately as possible so I was stuck with fairly sombre greys, but used the brighter area of light between the two layers of cloud to get a little warmth into the picture. I had great difficulty painting the right effect into the clouds but Sir Douglas seemed very pleased with my attempt and in the event told me it had worked well. Certainly I could not be accused of using much 'artist's licence' on this occasion.

The second problem was the distance between the two aircraft. In the first drawing the Dornier was sketched in at about the size I wanted it, but when Douglas Bader saw it he said it was too close. The further away it was moved the less recognisable it became, and I certainly did not want it to appear as a blob on the horizon! In the event Sir Douglas agreed with the position in the second drawing as being about right, which was a relief.

The Hurricane is a beautiful aircraft to draw and paint. Though it lacked perhaps some of the pure elegance of the Spitfire, to me the Hurricane was a wonderful-looking aeroplane. Full of character, its fuselage is a gift to artists, with its prominent ribcage and canvas covering. The Spitfire became the symbol of the Battle of Britain, but in fact four out of every five enemy aircraft shot down during the battle succumbed to the Hurricanes' guns.

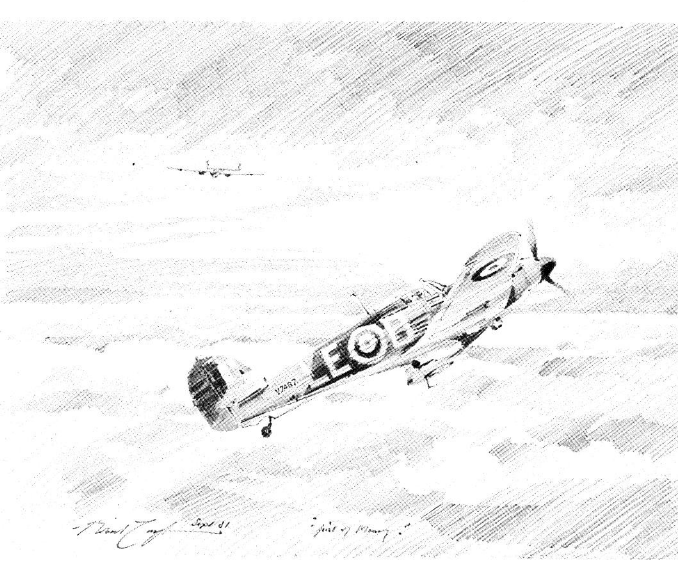

For the painting *Reach For The Skies*, featured below, I wanted to get the impression of height and solitude, and decided to put the aircraft against a huge 'thunderhead' – a cumulo-nimbus cloud with a further layer of cloud below. These are typical of the summer storm clouds and are the mightiest of all, sometimes reaching up to 30,000 feet and above. To fly through one in a small aircraft would be extremely dangerous, for the turbulence in the centre can be ferocious. They are, however, the most spectacular of cloud formations and magnificent to paint. On the subject of clouds, I think it is vital for an aviation artist to understand both cloud formations and the concomitant weather conditions. I find cloud formations utterly fascinating and totally absorbing.

I painted *Reach For the Skies* just before Sir Douglas Bader died. It was to have been issued as a limited edition print, carrying his signature. It depicts no special event. I felt I wanted to paint a picture of this quixotic fighter pilot, in his beloved Spitfire Mk Va, high in his element. Douglas Bader had been a wonderful friend and, in some ways, a mentor during my early days as a professional painter of aviation subjects and I felt particularly moved when I did the painting. Sir Douglas never saw it. Had he done so he would probably have said: 'Can't you put a couple of Me 109's into the picture Robert, and liven it up a bit?'

REACH FOR THE SKIES

In the collection of The Military Gallery

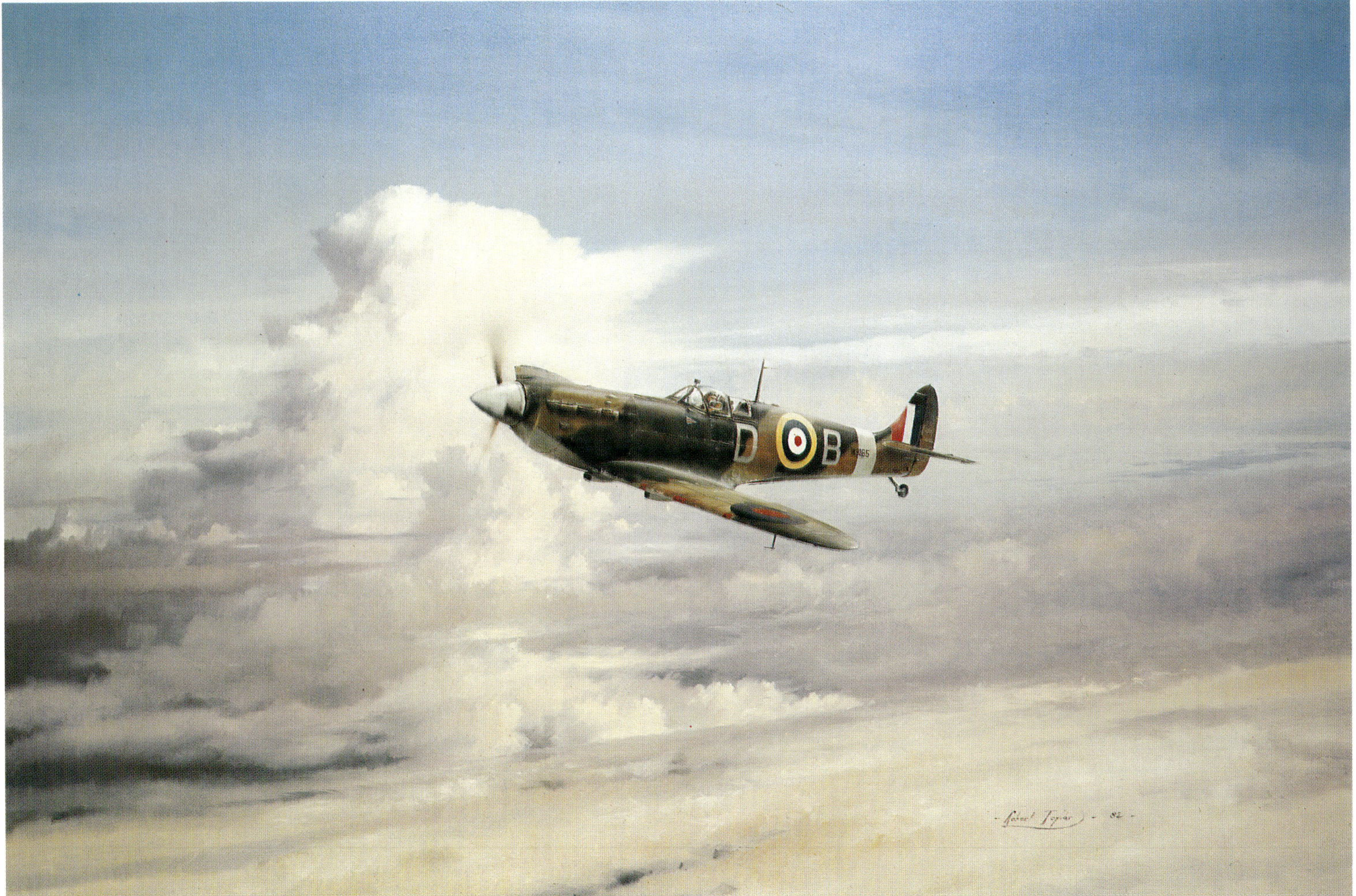

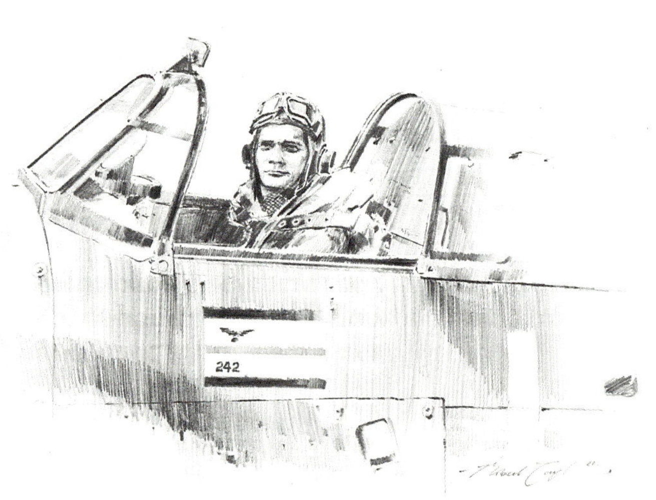

SIR DOUGLAS BADER, CBE, DSO, DFC

Probably the most well-known fighter pilot in aviation history, the name of the late Sir Douglas Bader still today inspires one with a feeling that nothing is impossible. Having lost both his legs in an air accident as early as 1931, the rest of his life, to others that is, seemed destined to remain securely tied to the ground. Bader felt differently. He refused to fall in with the view that tin legs could prevent him from flying.

When war looked a grim possibility, he badgered the Air Ministry to consider him for the active list once again, pointing out that experienced pilots, legless or otherwise, were going to be in great demand!

Bader soon found himself back on active service, on Spitfires, at Duxford. His experience quickly began to show and, despite his years out of the cockpit and the huge differences between the sleek, new fighter aircraft of 1940 and those he had flown previously, he very quickly proved that he was a born leader – by example.

Bader's wartime career is legendary. Nothing short of Colditz could keep him down. His inspirational leadership and charismatic presence enabled him to extract the best from the pilots he led. In later life, he employed those same characteristics in both a successful business career and as a shining example to other disabled people, through his vigorous work on their behalf, to prove that, given the right attitude, anything can be achieved.

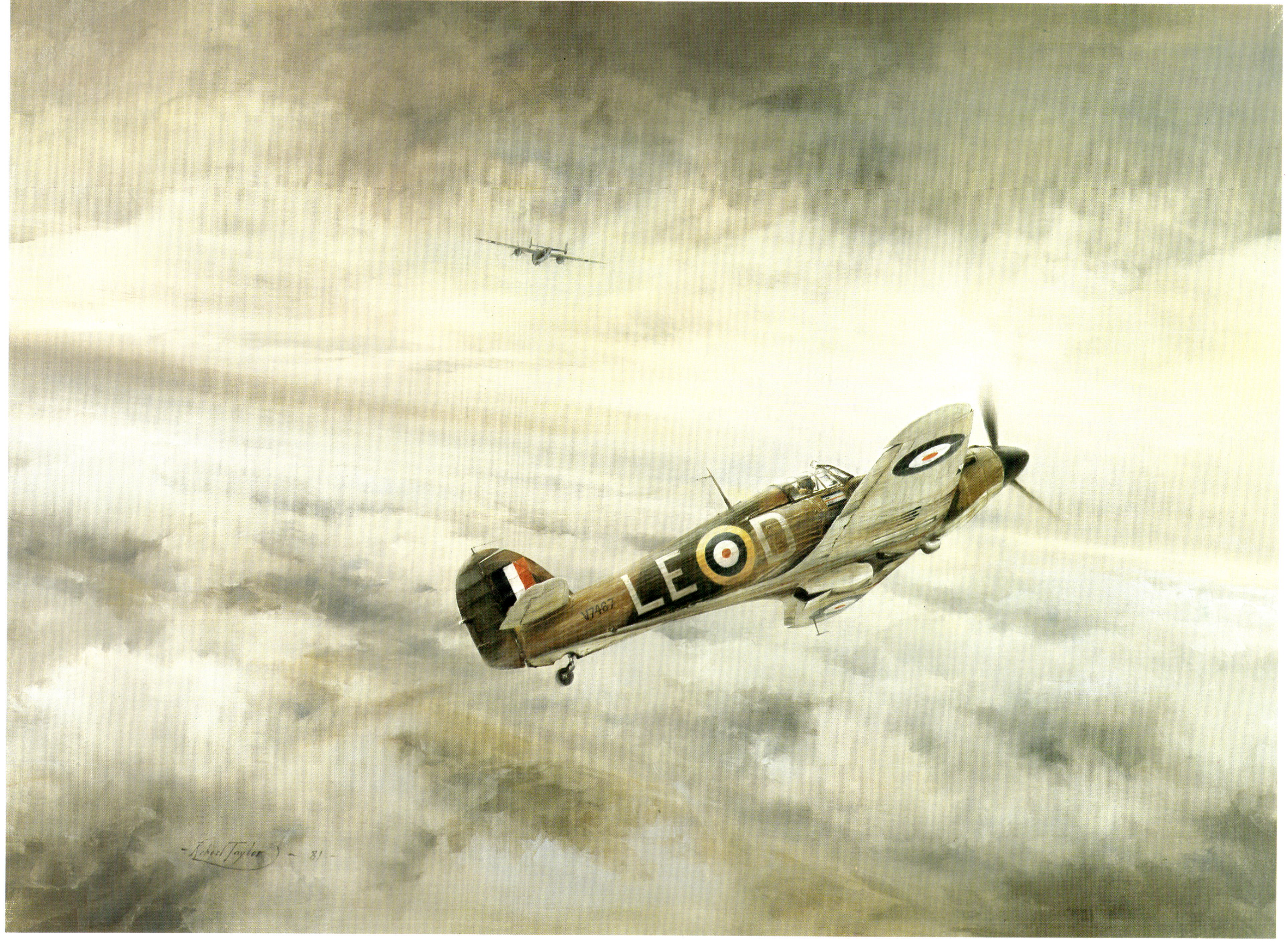

FIRST OF MANY
Artist's Collection

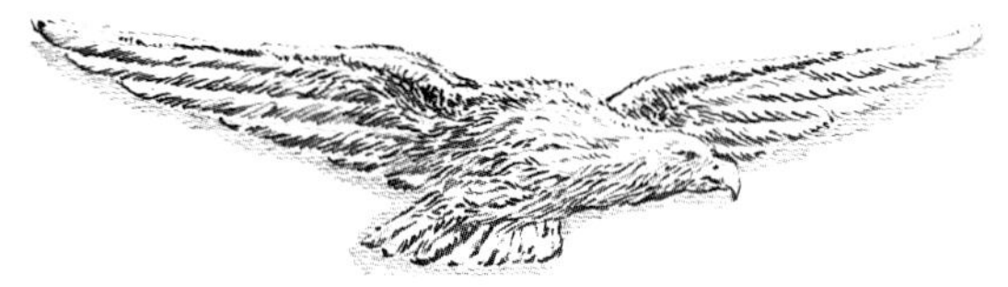

BOMBER'S MOON

There has always been widespread admiration for the men of the Pathfinder Force (PFF). They were all volunteers and had, in addition to their undoubted courage, great flying and navigating skills. Many had already served more than their fair share of tours when they joined the Force, and a high percentage lost their lives serving with the Pathfinders.

When commissioned to paint a picture featuring the Force, I was given a completely free hand to decide how best to portray a Pathfinders scene. The great Donald Bennett, founder of the PFF, was to sign the prints which would follow. I had already met Don Bennett some years earlier, and I knew him to be a perfectionist!

I considered a number of approaches to the composition, but kept coming back to an airfield scene, depicting those poignant moments just before take-off. Unusually, the title became clear in my mind even before working out the general composition – *Bomber's Moon*.

I remember reading that during the war a clear moonlit night was always referred to as a 'Bomber's Moon' and I had often thought this would make a good title for a picture. The subject and the title obviously meant painting a moonlit scene, and this presents a whole set of problems, particularly when the painting is to be reproduced as a print. A fair amount of artist's licence would need to be used in order to get enough light into the picture.

Wanting to include a number of both air and ground crews in the picture, I set about drawing a number of ideas, but none of these seemed to work. One day whilst idly sketching the front turret and bomb aimer's dome of a Lancaster, daydreaming more than concentrating, I suddenly stopped and looked at what I had sketched. The idea for the painting came to me in a flash. The cockpit, front turret and dome of the Lancaster, with all that expanse of perspex would give me a wonderful area to work with, reflecting the light of the moon. I decided to dominate the picture with the front section of a Lancaster and paint two others standing off, using their cockpit areas also to pick up the light of the moon. After some preliminary sketches the final drawing was started.

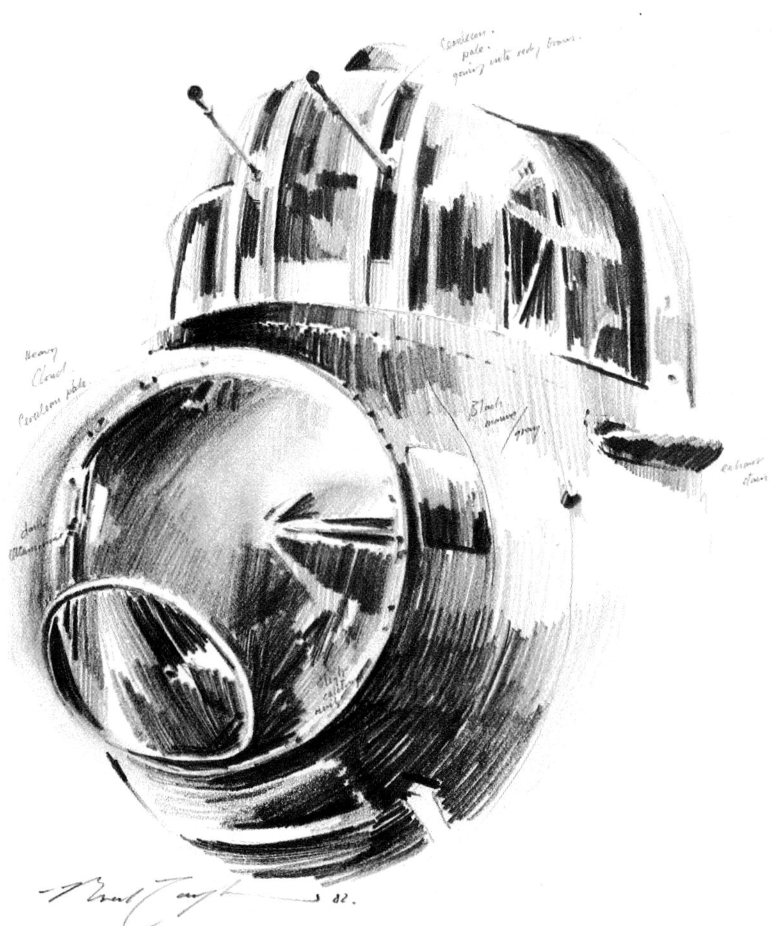

THE PATHFINDERS

By Group Captain Hamish Mahaddie, DSO, DFC, AFC, CZMC, C.Eng, FRAeS,

In his paintings of great bomber aircraft of World War II, Robert Taylor takes me back almost half a century, reminding me so vividly of operational tours on Whitleys and Stirlings, and of my involvement with the Pathfinder Force.

In late 1939, after taking heavy losses whilst achieving poor results, Bomber Command abandoned its daylight bombing tactics. With the mounting threat of invasion, the effective use of bombers by the RAF became an increasingly vital requirement but, with almost total absence of navigation aids, the night bombing offensive was producing no better results. A study of 600 photographs of targets confirmed the inescapable truth that we were wasting our bombs, and worse, we were squandering our seed-corn – the crews.

The first encounter I had with target location was in mid-June 1940. We had been briefed to attack German heavy armour concealed in a wooded area near Rotterdam. One of our junior officers had suggested, 'Why don't we make a timed run from the centre of Rotterdam's blazing docks, then fire a Very light and drop a flare?' 'Great idea, let's try it!' We did, but so inaccurate was our navigation that, at the debriefing, not a single crew reported sighting either a Very light or the flare. The 'sprog' officer had all our compasses reswung, airspeed indicators re-calibrated and, somehow, managed to get us special watches. During the following night's raid six or seven crews reported sighting the flares and Very lights, and a curtain of light flak signalled that we had indeed found our target. In this and other haphazard ways, crews were left to devise their own such rudimentary methods, in an effort to improve our pitifully poor results. With only a compass and airspeed indicator, in average weather conditions, it was virtually impossible to locate our targets in Germany.

As if our problems were not enough we had to contend with mounting enemy defences in the form of flak and fighters. Losses continued to rise as we impatiently awaited the development of new scientific devices that would assist navigators to get us to the target area. Help was at hand.

Early in 1942 Bomber Command got a new C-in-C,

Arthur Harris. Aware that the knives in Whitehall were out for his command, he immediately made his presence felt (both in Whitehall and in Germany) by mounting the first ever 1000-bomber raid.

Flushed with the success of the strategic bombing tactic, the Ministry pressed for the acceptance of a Target-Finding/Marking formation to lead main bomber forces. Initially Harris bitterly resisted the idea, but subseqently agreed, on two conditions: that the new formation should be known as the Pathfinder Force and that it should be led by one of his then squadron commanders, a young Australian, Wing Commander Don Bennett.

On 15 August 1942, the Pathfinder Force (PFF) was formed. The unenviable responsibility of PFF was to spearhead main bombing sorties and locate and mark the targets with brilliantly-coloured Target Indicators, thus enabling the main bomber stream to release their bomb-loads using the TI's as their aiming points. The objective was to ensure that more of the lifted weight reached the target.

At last the navigational aids became available; the first was known as H2S – a pulse device which scanned the ground electronically by two stations in the UK which could not be jammed. Finally came GeeH which was both a navigation aid and a release indicator.

Bennett was a mercurial leader. He had completed a full operational tour as a squadron commander and had already been decorated with a DSO for his attack on the Tirpitz. *He brought to the command, at the right moment, the knowledge, skills, and vast air experience of a highly professional airman, and commanded the incomparable respect of his crews by never asking them to do anything he had not already fully experienced himself.*

By late 1943, PFF was able to claim tremendous improvement in the marking of targets. By 1945 PFF, all volunteers, had flown over 50,000 sorties against thousands of targets, but the cost had been grievous: the odds against completing the 60-sortie tour of operations were terrifying. At least 3,720 aircrew were lost on ops, and hundreds more were wounded, accounting for a sixth of Bomber Command's losses throughout the war.

After the war a Luftwaffe Intelligence report came to light. It was dated March 1944 and concluded '. . . the success of the large scale night raids by the RAF is in increasing measure dependent upon the conscientious flying of the Pathfinder crews . . .' To this Harris is reputed to have replied: 'The customer is seldom wrong!'

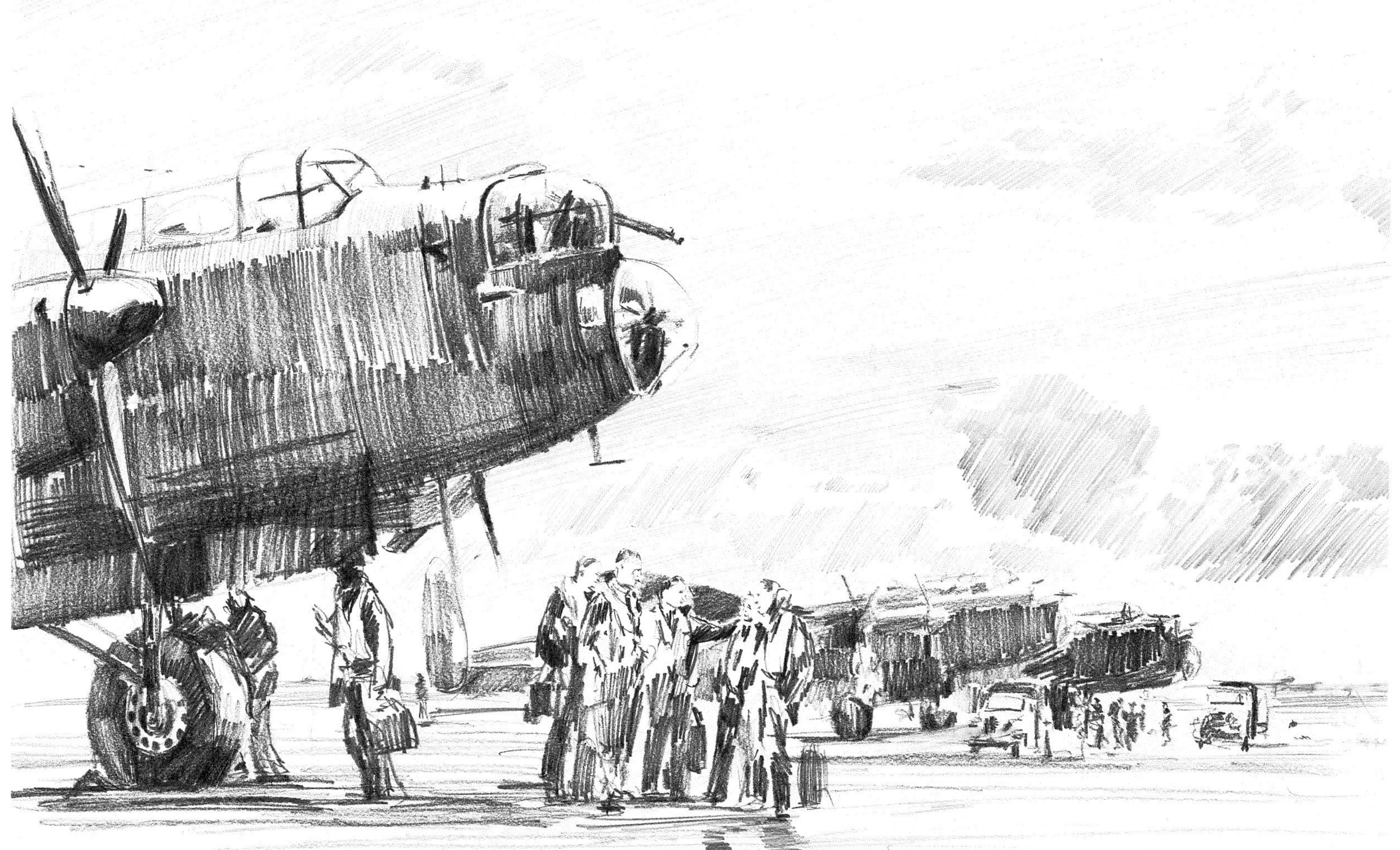

At first the composition of the final drawing (illustrated above) seemed satisfactory but, after looking at it for a while, I felt the aircraft were parked in too uniform a way. The picture looked too 'staged' for a busy air-base so I reorganised the secondary aircraft. In the event this helped not only to achieve a more realistic composition, but to get more light into the centre of the picture. When comparing the drawing above with the painting on the next page it will be seen that the figures in the foreground were also altered, in the cause of obtaining balance.

Working out the composition of a painting is an agreeable task. It is a constant challenge because a change in design often alters other facets – perhaps the mood changes, or the atmosphere; even the whole story. Lighting is critical in any picture. It controls everything else, and one is always conscious of where the light will come from, and where it will fall. How the lighting in a painting is achieved depends, to a significant degree, upon the composition yet so often the composition depends upon the lighting – an artist's 'Catch 22' situation!

On the subject of painting night time scenes, a naval flyer once suggested to me that the easiest painting of all must surely be that portraying a deck-landing at night, because, he told me, he could never see anything at all when he made one. In any case, he went on, all that would be required would be a tube of black paint!

It is hard to imagine anything more difficult or frightening than making a deck-landing at night but, in some ways, my friend's remarks have similarities with my feelings when talking about painting night-time scenes. To an artist they can also be difficult – and a little frightening!

Choosing the light for any painting represents a major part of the preliminary work, offering many alternatives and often posing many problems. These difficulties are compounded for the artist when he attempts a night-time picture, simply because of the lack of light. If the painting is to be reproduced as a print, which quite a number of mine are, the artist must take into consideration the problems which the printer will also encounter in his efforts to reproduce a dark painting.

It is generally accepted that the artist may use a little 'licence' in order to make his painting interesting, but in my area of representational painting one has to remain within the realm of reality. Thus plenty of planning is necessary in the early stages of each painting. I find it is best to back-light a night scene whenever it is practical. In *Bomber's Moon*, the moon is right in the centre of the picture. This provides most of the light but to provide some variation to the bluish light of the moon I have used the yellow light from the headlamps of the crew's van. The moonlight is reflected on the perspex canopies of the aircraft and from the moisture on the tarmac, following an earlier passing shower. The yellow light is highlighted on parts of the Lancaster and on the clothes of the crews in the foreground. This is aimed at bringing warmth to the picture and allows me to emphasise some interesting parts of the painting.

Painting night scenes is not easy but I enjoy them – which I suppose is fortunate because the aviation artist cannot avoid painting aircraft flying at night if he is to portray a balanced selection of the greatest events in the history of air combat.

NIGHT INTRUDER

In the collection of Empire Press, USA

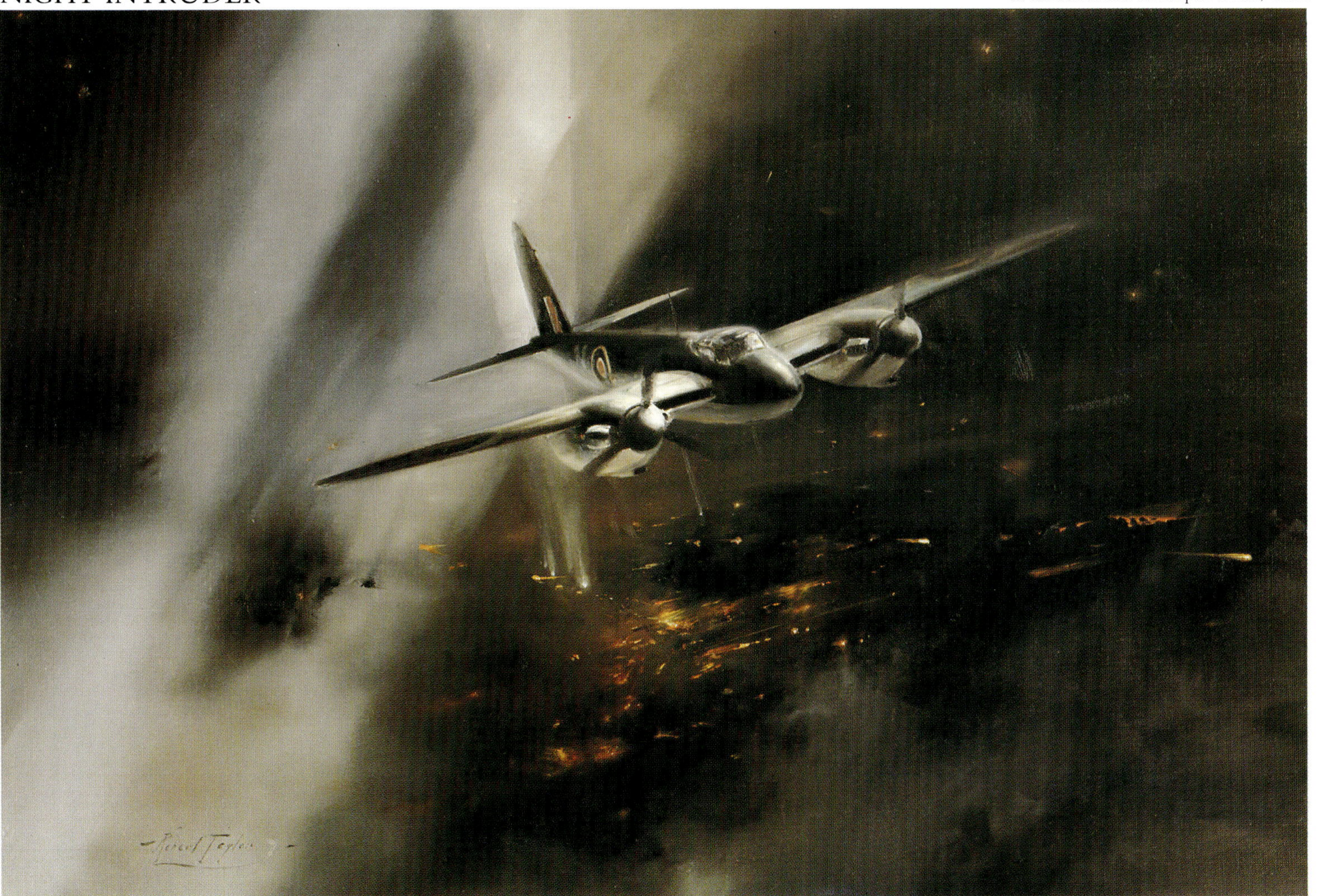

Another example of a night-time scene is *Night Intruder*. This painting, illustrated below, shows a Mosquito on a low-level attack. Searchlights provide most of the light and add atmosphere to the picture. Below the aircraft are some signs of fire which aim to give the aircraft its height. The tracer shells are to add authenticity and realism to the scene, and all of these combine to make the maximum possible use of the limited amount of available light.

The Mosquito was a wonderful aircraft which served in almost every role performed by the RAF during World War II. Its two Merlin engines made it, when introduced, the fastest aircraft in service. Its airframe was constructed entirely of wood. Many pilots who flew numerous types during the war remember the Mosquito fondly as their favourite aircraft. It achieved great success in all its various roles, which included many night activities, for which it was an ideal aircraft. The great bomber pilot Leonard Cheshire used the Mosquito to great effect in his daring low-level 'marker' bombing escapades.

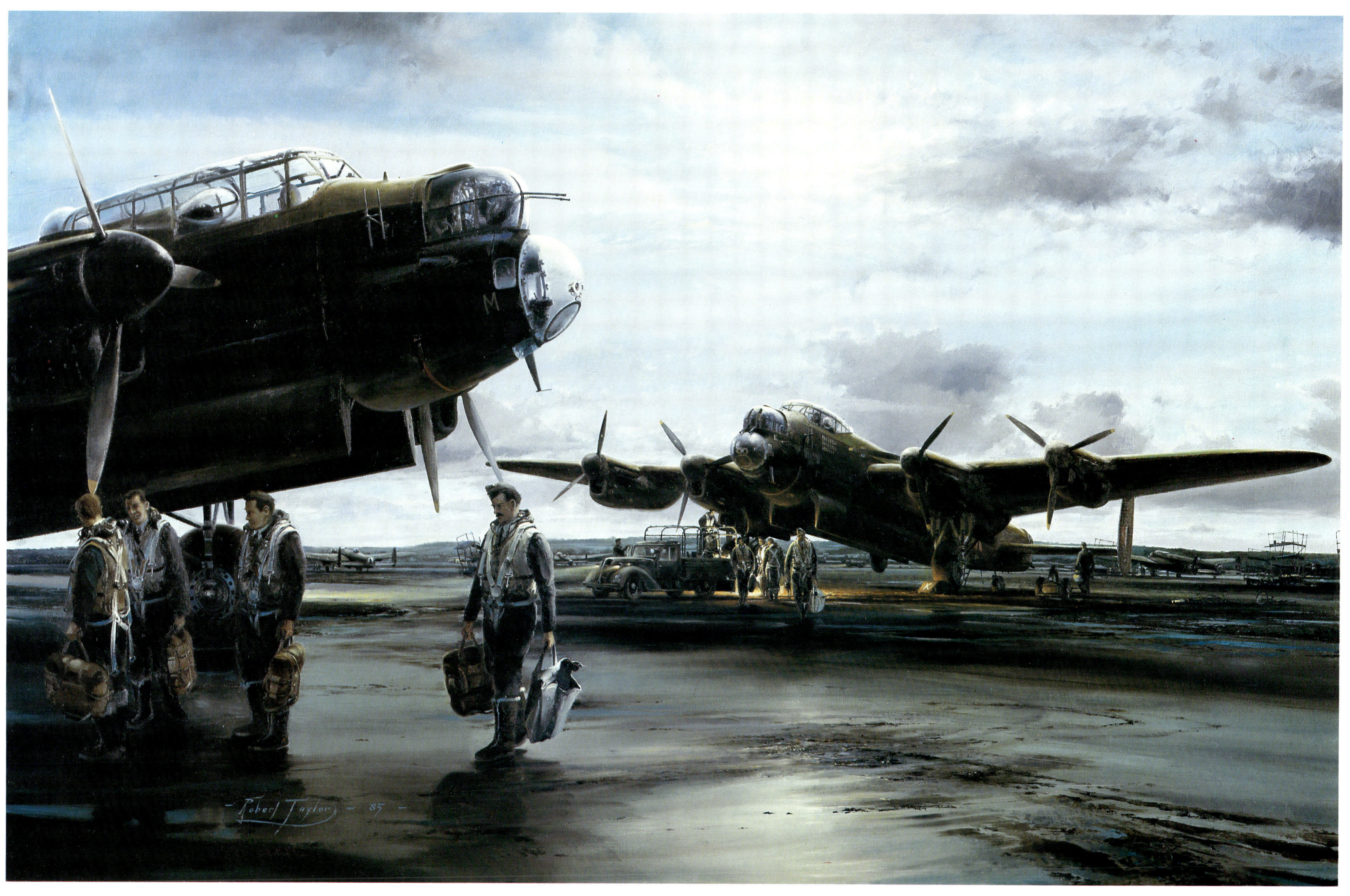

BOMBERS MOON
In the collection of The Military Gallery

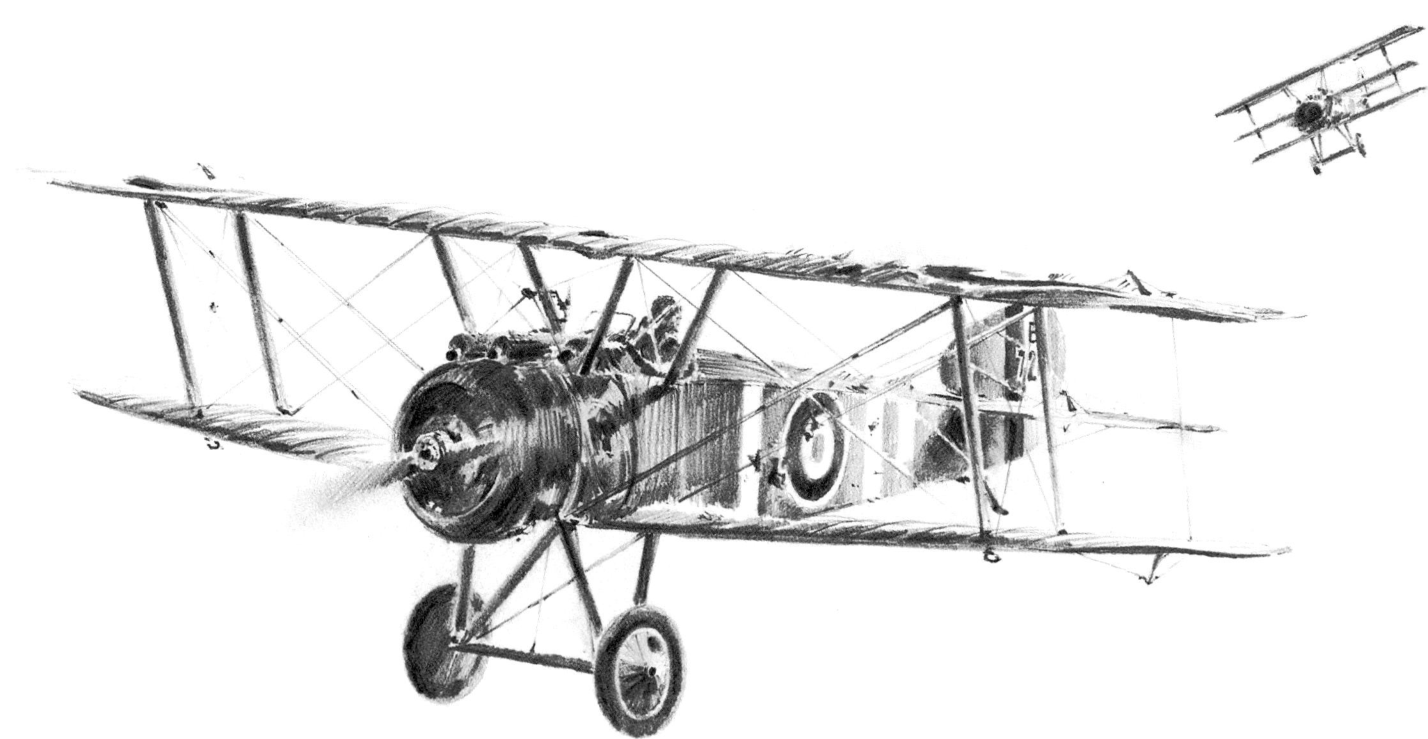

HIGH PATROL

For many years I nurtured a desire to paint the Sopwith Camel. It is a beautiful aircraft and, historically, a very important one. The opportunity did not arise for some time, since there always seemed to be so much commissioned work to complete. One day, however, after reading a particularly interesting article on the career of one of the Camel's most illustrious pilots, Captain A. R. Brown, DSC, I decided it had to be done and set about the necessary research work.

The Sopwith Camel, in the hands of the pilots of the RFC, RNAS and later the RAF, destroyed no fewer than 1,294 enemy aircraft between 1916 and 1918, yet it was in operational service less than two years during World War I. This superbly successful aircraft was, for experienced pilots, almost invincible at the mid-altitude levels. It was nimble and responsive and had a high rate of roll and a phenomenal rate of turn. With a top speed of 110 mph, armed with two Vickers machine guns and four 25lb bombs, it was the dream machine of the fighter pilots of that era. It was not, however, an aircraft for beginners. Compared with its predecessor, the Sopwith Pup, it was ruthlessly unforgiving of inexperienced or inattentive pilots. This was mainly due to the fact that the majority of its mass was concentrated in the front six or seven feet of the aircraft where the engine, guns, pilot, fuel and ammunition were positioned. There were very few instruments and, having no radio communication available in those days, most of the navigation was confined to map reading and good local knowledge. It took a considerable time for pilots to acquire all the skills and the confidence that were required to take full advantage of the capabilities of the Camel but for those who had done so she was supreme in the air.

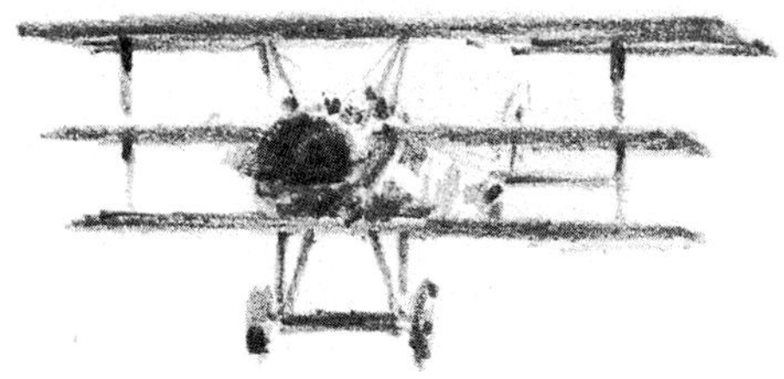

Full engine speed (for which there *was* an instrument) was used only in climbing. The engines used in the Sopwith Camel were the 150 hp Bentley, the 100 hp Gnome Monosoupage, the 110 hp Le Rhône or the 130 hp Clerget rotary engine. The Bentleys and Clergets had conventional throttles, unlike those in the Pup's Le Rhône and Gnome engines, which had only 'on' and 'off' positions. The ignition cut-out button, however, was always required for low-speed manoeuvres such as landing, since the throttle range only enabled a pilot to reduce the engine speed from the full-rate 1,100 rpm to around 750 rpm. Thus many inexperienced pilots met with disaster through the lack of understanding of just when to cut the ignition.

On a happier note, those who did master the Camel were able to perform apparently impossible feats. One of the most accomplished and well known of this group being of course Captain Brown, whose Camel is featured in the painting, leading his fighters, high over the trenches, during 1918. It was Captain Brown who despatched the most famous of Germany's World War I Aces, Baron Manfred von Richthofen, on 21 April of that year. This was a considerable achievement since the 'Red Baron' was a formidable fighter pilot and was flying one of the very few German aircraft which could compete with the great Sopwith Camel, the Fokker Dr 1 (so named because it was the first *Dreidecker* – triplane)

Reading descriptions by World War I pilots of aerial warfare at that time, it all seems like a very gentlemanly affair. This in many ways I am sure it was. There is a long tradition of mutual respect amongst fighter pilots which still exists today, and this stems directly from the attitudes of these World War I pilots. Nonetheless, conditions were sometimes awful and, irrespective of the ethics the pilots may have displayed, one can never forget that in their combats they were involved in a life-and-death struggle. One of von Richthofen's combat reports encountered during my research for *High Patrol* illustrates the point graphically:

'Flying my triplane for the first time, I and four of my gentlemen attacked a very courageously-flown British artillery aircraft. I approached and fired 20 rounds from a distance of 50 metres, after which the Englishman plunged to the ground and crashed near Zonnebeke. It is most likely that the British pilot mistook me for a British triplane because the observer was standing upright in his aeroplane and watched my approach without using his machine gun.'

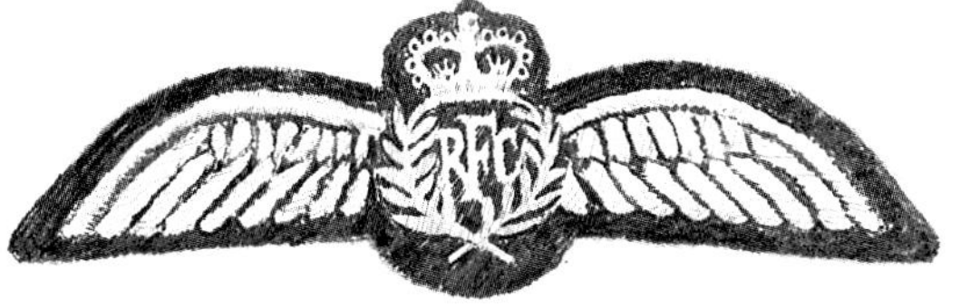

While the wretched people on both sides were experiencing the agonies and horrors of trench warfare thousands of feet below, these men were, despite the deadly nature of their business, engaged in cleanly-fought, exhilarating duels – dipping and climbing, diving and turning in the clear bright sky.

While researching for *High Patrol* I encountered a number of the frail-looking yet beautiful aircraft which flew early in this century. One which struck me very forcibly was the SE5A. I could not resist producing the sketch below, even though these aircraft were not to feature anywhere in my final painting. A robust aeroplane with no vices, the SE5A was popular with her World War I pilots and was flown by many of the leading Aces of the day: Bishop, Ball, Mannock, McCudden and many more. I hope, one day, to feature this classic machine in a full-size oil painting. I know I shall enjoy the research.

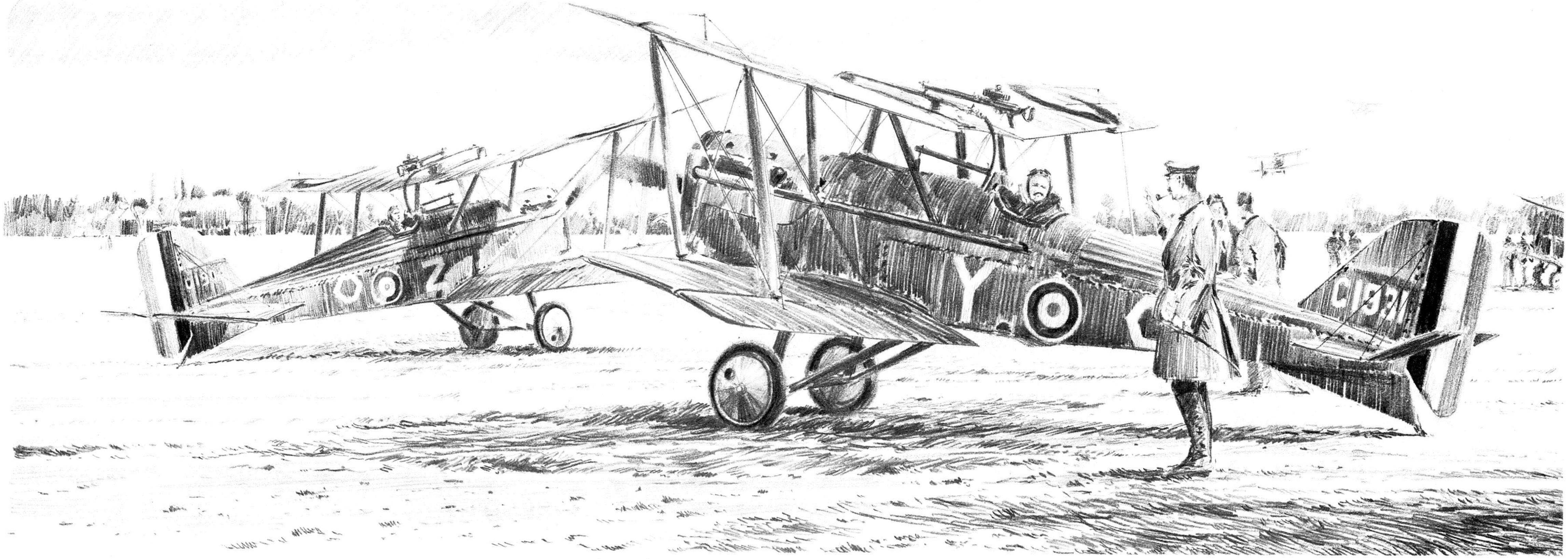

S.E.5A Scouts of 85 Squadron leaving the airfield at St Omer, France June 1918.

The classic biplanes contain many of the same elements which fascinate me so much about the old sailing ships. Their rigging is one example. In the same way as it is important to understand the function of rigging in a sailing ship, so it is with the old biplanes. As I painted I remembered a conversation I had had with Peter Townsend, who flew bi-planes before moving on to Hurricanes. He recounted a flight when a rigging wire had snapped with a sharp 'ping', leaving him apprehensively wondering all the way back to base how this might have weakened the geometry and if so which would be the next to go! Biplanes all had fascinating and distinctive shapes, and lovely intricate rigging arrangements which often extended beyond the wings to the tailplane, and even the undercarriage. The detail below from my painting highlights, perhaps, this intricacy.

With the march of time there seems to have been a merging of identity in aircraft design resulting, perhaps, in a little loss in character. This is probably my nostalgic emotion speaking. Today's Tornado and Tomcat pilots will, I am sure, look back fondly thirty years hence and say 'Ah, they don't make them like that anymore!'

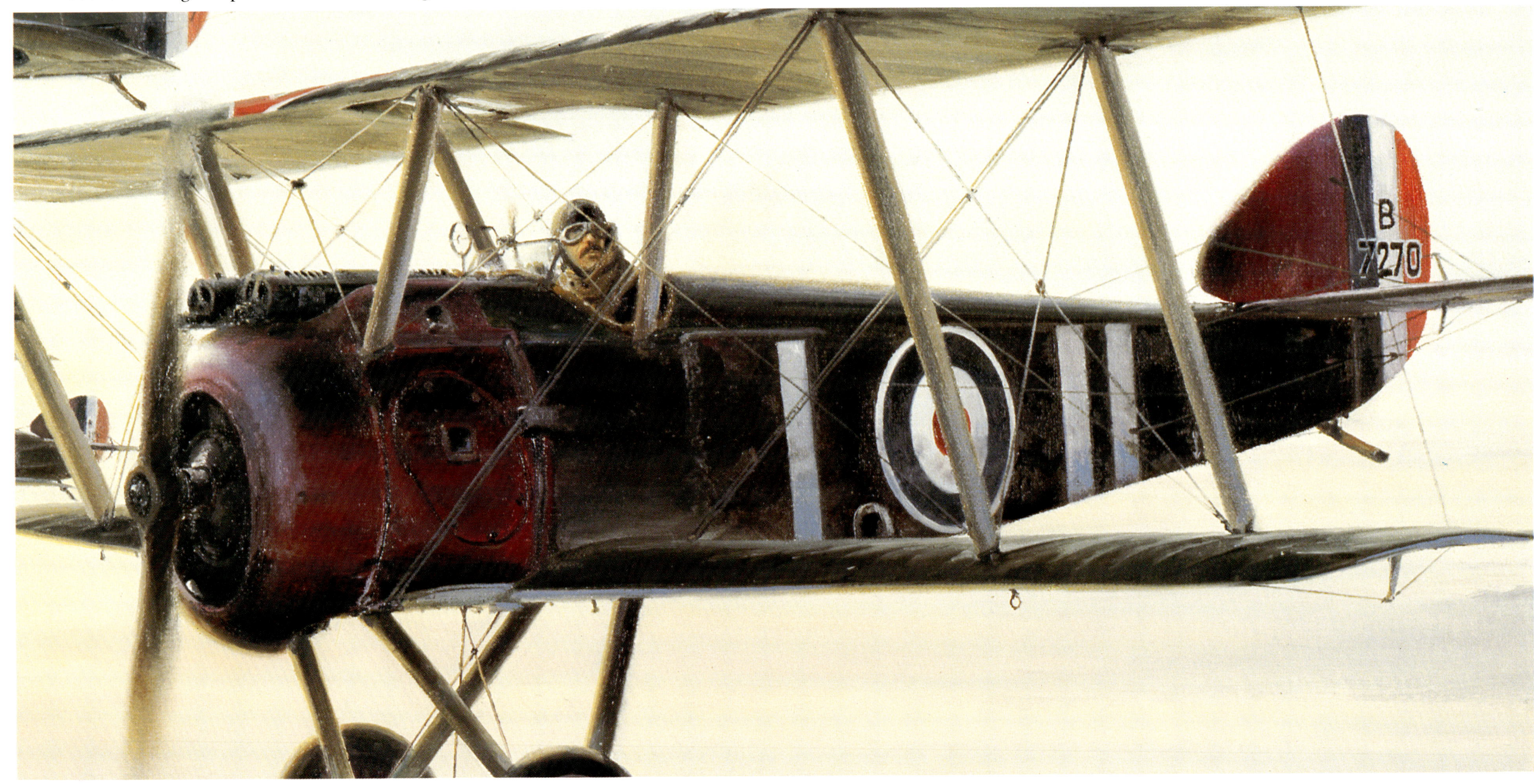

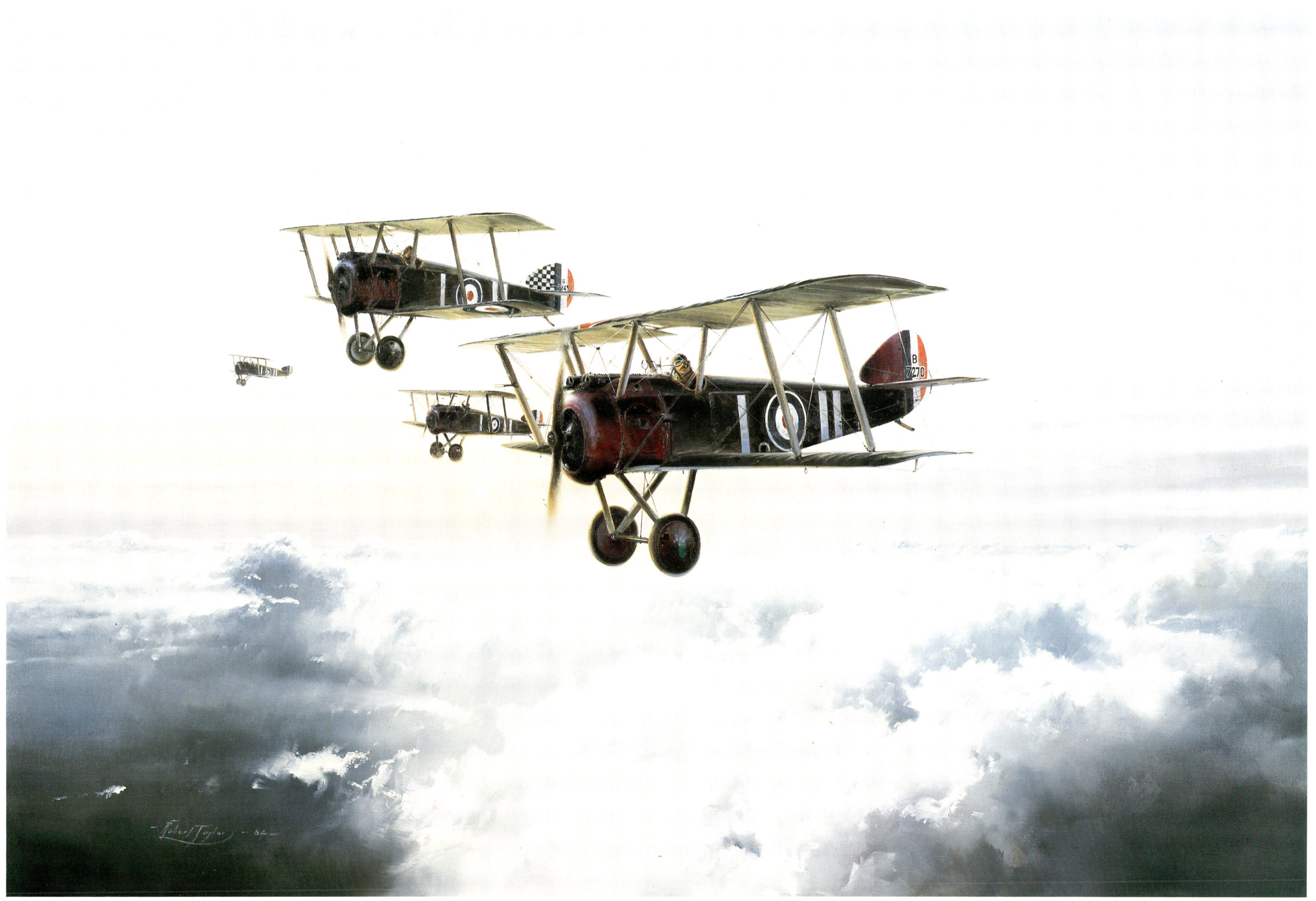

HIGH PATROL
Artist's Collection

VICTORY OVER DUNKIRK

I believe it is true that there is only one fighter pilot who accounted for three enemy aircraft destroyed on his first day in combat – and that is Wing Commander Bob Stanford-Tuck. Adding credit to this amazing feat, the combat took place during the early part of the war, when most of the time the RAF pilots were heavily outnumbered.

Bob Stanford-Tuck was a legend before I was born. His photograph and accounts of his exploits in the air have been well documented in books, press articles and on film, and he is recognised as being one of the greatest of the RAF's Battle of Britain fighter pilots.

I was excited when asked to paint one of his first air victories and wanted to attempt a difficult exercise – to portray the event looking straight down. It seemed that if this worked it would provide a dramatic spectacle, which the occasion certainly deserved.

A number of preliminary sketches were made in order to get the composition right. Having no horizon in the picture changes the whole complexion of an aviation painting and great care is needed with the perspective. The painting was to feature the coastline and the small French port of Dunkirk, with the land behind, looking almost vertically down upon them. Bob's Spitfire, in a steep banking turn, would occupy a large part of the canvas and below this I wanted to show on its way down the Me 110 he had just despatched. In the event I placed this just above Bob's head in the picture, although it is actually several hundred feet below him. To help with the perspective, and to give a feeling of height, I included another Spitfire below Bob, diving on the tail of another Me 110. A lot of thought went into where the coastline would run through the picture, and also how to use cloud to help the overall composition. The pencil sketch on the opposite page was the final drawing. I was happy with my painting when completed and flattered when Bob Stanford-Tuck was kind enough to remark that I had depicted the event 'Just as it was'.

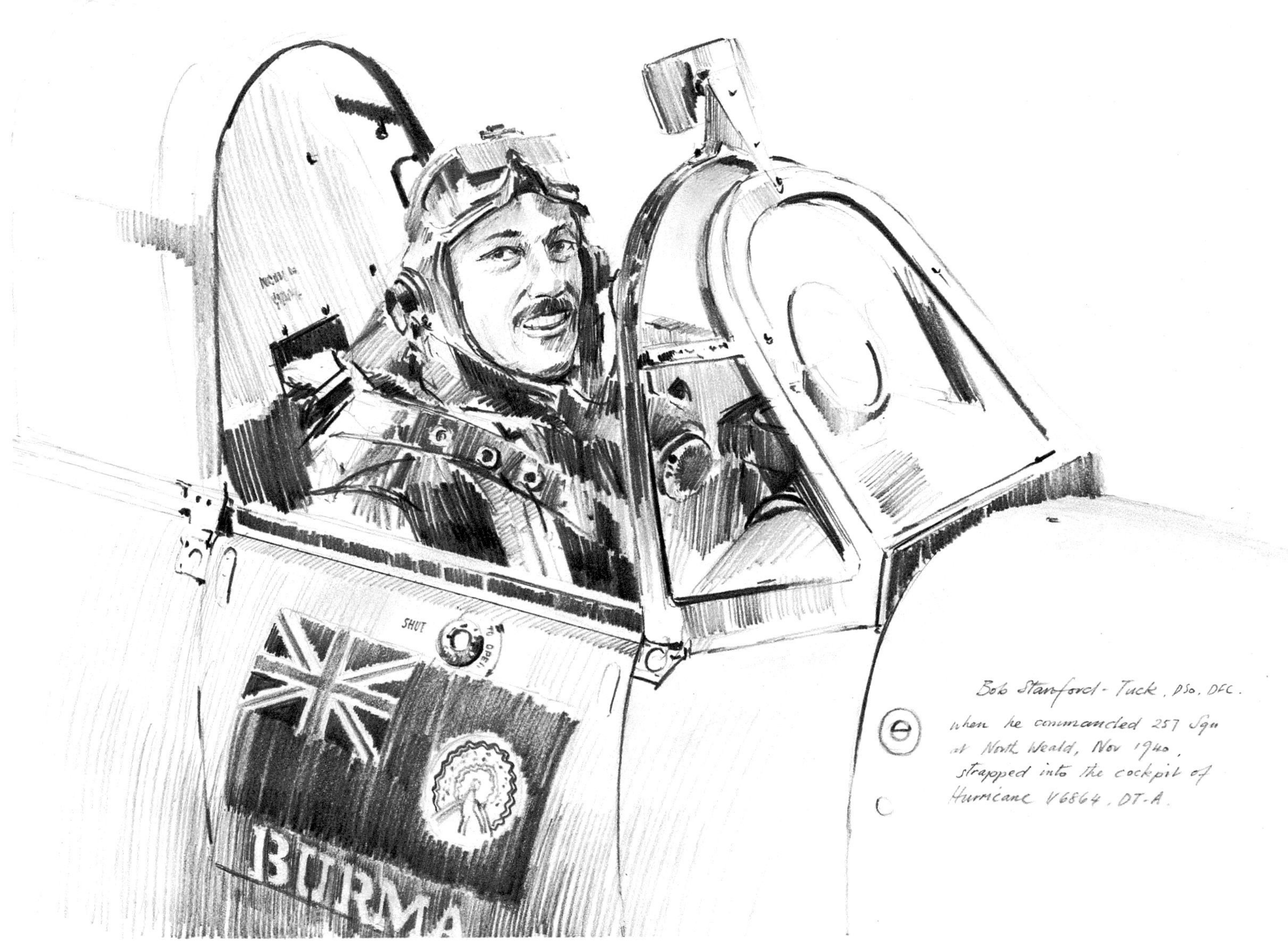

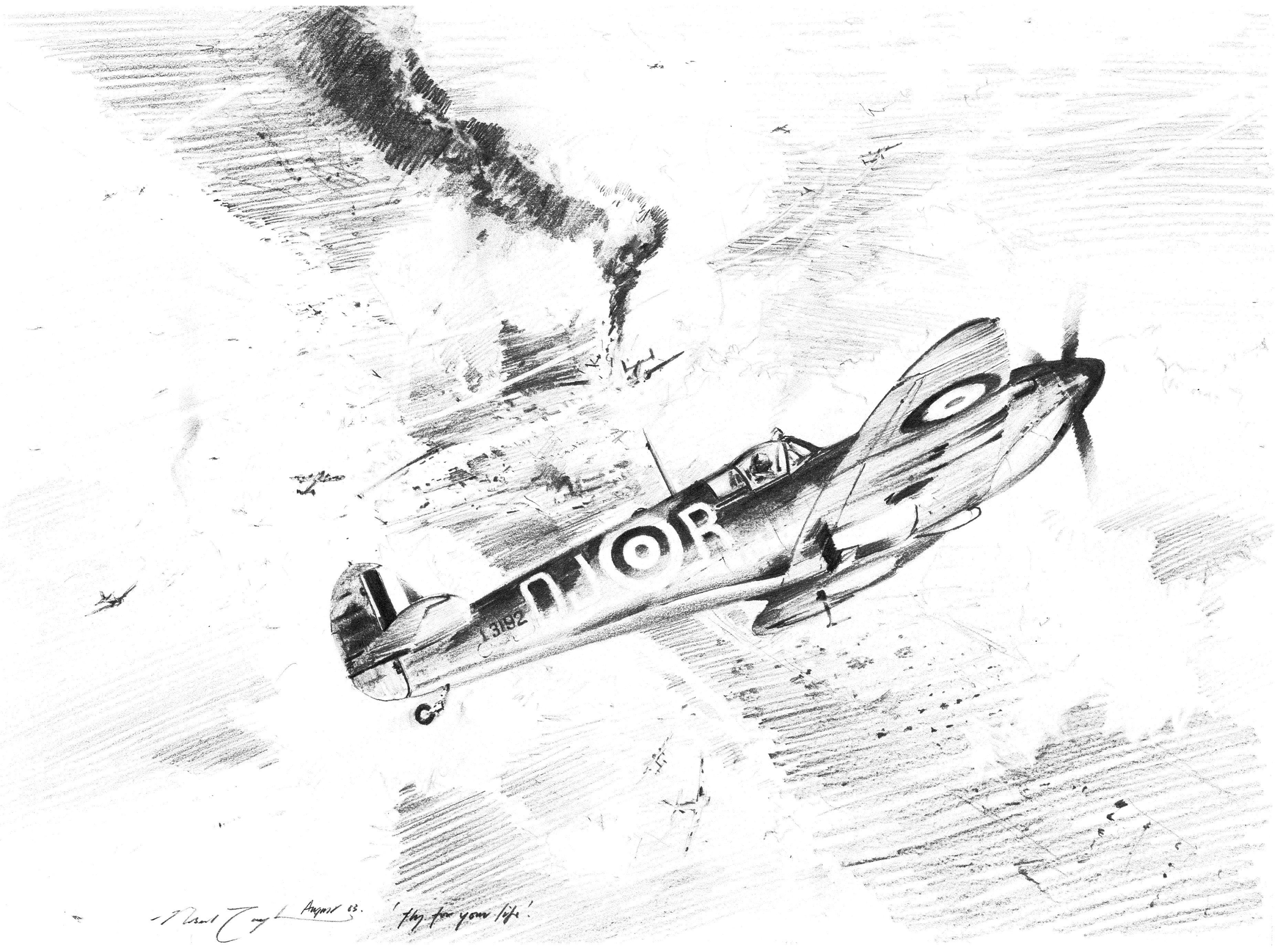

L3192
August 03.
'Fly for your life'

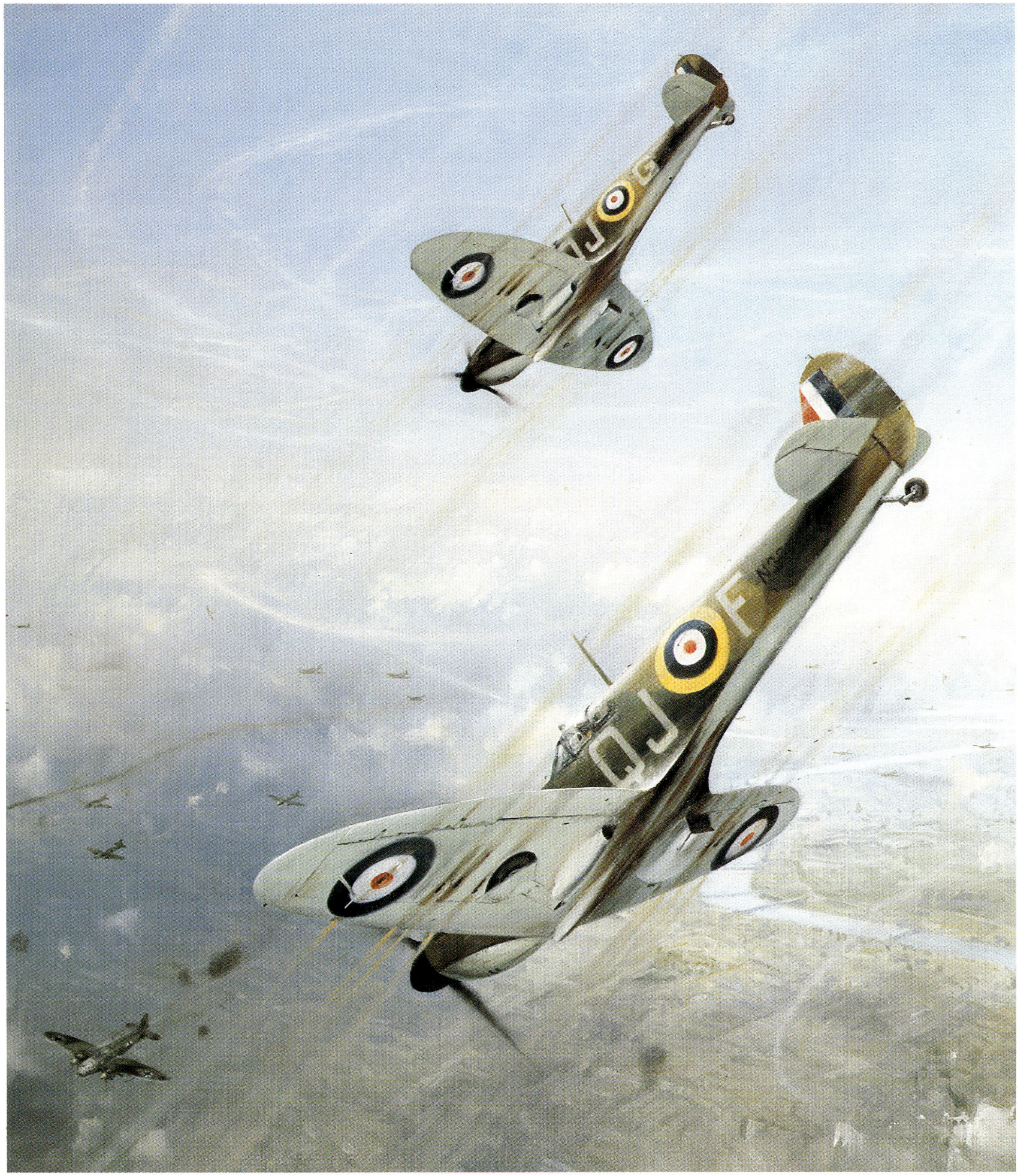

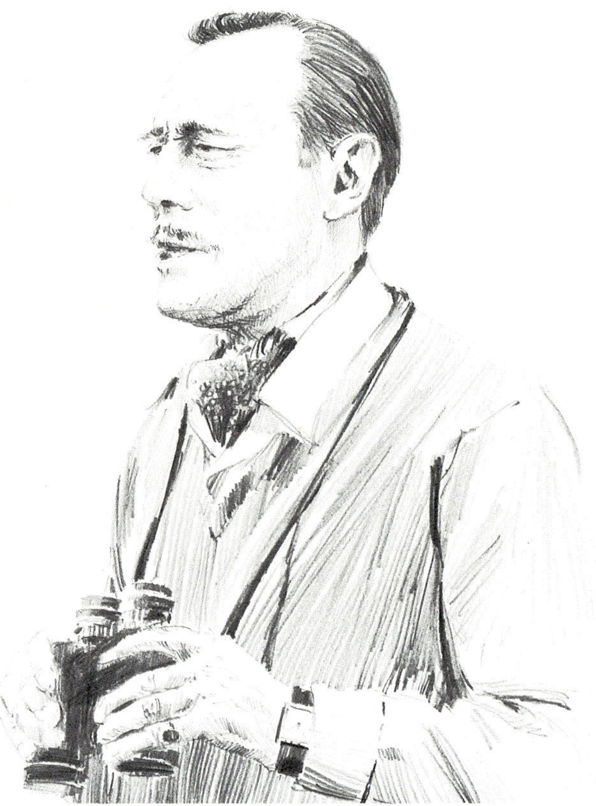

Wing Commander
BOB STANFORD-TUCK, DSO, DFC

The late Bob Stanford-Tuck was an exuberant character. He joined the RAF in 1935 and, after training at Grantham on Tutors, Harts, Furies and Bulldogs, he gained his wings with the rating 'exceptional'. In 1936 he joined No 65 Squadron, first flying Demons, followed by Gauntlets, Gladiators and then, in 1938, Spitfires. When war broke out he had already flown several hundred hours on Spitfires.

Bob flew his first combat on 23 May 1940, during the Battle of Dunkirk. Flying a Spitfire with No 92 Squadron, he destroyed an Me 109 in the morning and two Me 110s later the same day. He fought in all the great air battles over Dunkirk and the Channel during the build up to the Battle of Britain. During the Battle he was posted to command No 257 Hurricane Squadron, which had suffered heavy casualties – a post he held until mid-1941, when he took command of the Duxford Fighter Wing. After a brief period in the USA he assumed command of the Biggin Hill Wing consisting of four Spitfire squadrons. In January 1942 he was shot down by ground fire during a low-level attack over Northern France, by which time he had scored 29 air victories.

A detail from Tally Ho! shows Spitfires of No 92 Squadron diving in to attack He 111s over London during the Battle of Britain. In the collection of Dr Steve Moseley.

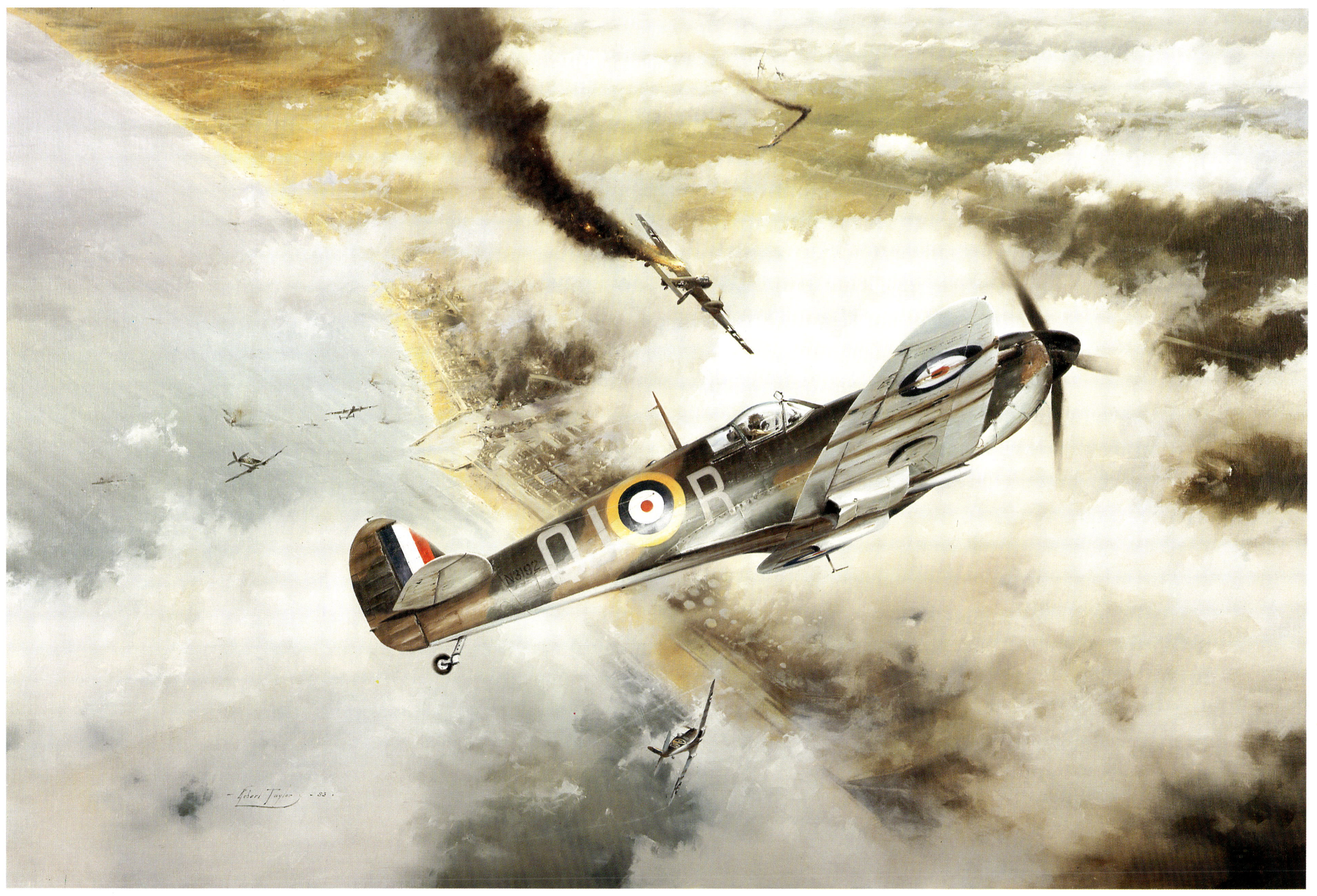

VICTORY OVER DUNKIRK
In the collection of Mr and Mrs R A James

FLIGHT OF EAGLES

The fighter wings of the Luftwaffe were led mostly by pilots who had gained experience in the Spanish Civil War, and who were highly professional in their approach to aerial combat. One such typical Fighter Wing *(Jagdgeschwader)* was JG-26, based in Northern France and led by the mercurial Adolf Galland. Equipped with Me 109's, Galland and his pilots built a formidable reputation in the air, and their 'Aces' achieved unprecedented success in combat. Flying escort to the bombers during the Battle of Britain, the Me 109's had an endurance of only about 10 minutes over south-east England, yet they were a continual thorn in the side of the RAF. Later in 1941 when Britain turned to the offensive, the Me 109 pilots fought with distinction daily with the Spitfire and Hurricanes of the RAF and many lost their lives. Many became Aces – Adolf Galland was one, leading his wing from the Pas de Calais, he achieved 94 victories on the Western Front. Later on, this number increased to 104. He was quickly promoted and, at the age of 29, became General Inspector of the Fighter Arm and at 30 he was promoted to Major General. From July 1943 onwards he also became responsible for the Night Fighter Arm.

A natural leader, Galland had much in common with Douglas Bader. Both insisted that a Wing Leader should have freedom of choice of action in the sky. He refused to allow his pilots to shoot at RAF crews parachuting from stricken aircraft – a tactic considered by the Luftwaffen-Supremo. And later when asked by Goering how to improve the bomber escort capability of his wing, Galland answered 'Please, Herr Reichsmarshall, equip my wing with Spitfires.' General Galland kindly wrote the following fascinating and helpful notes on the history of the Me 109. My painting *Flight of Eagles* depicts Galland leading his famous JG-26 Me 109's in an early morning patrol.

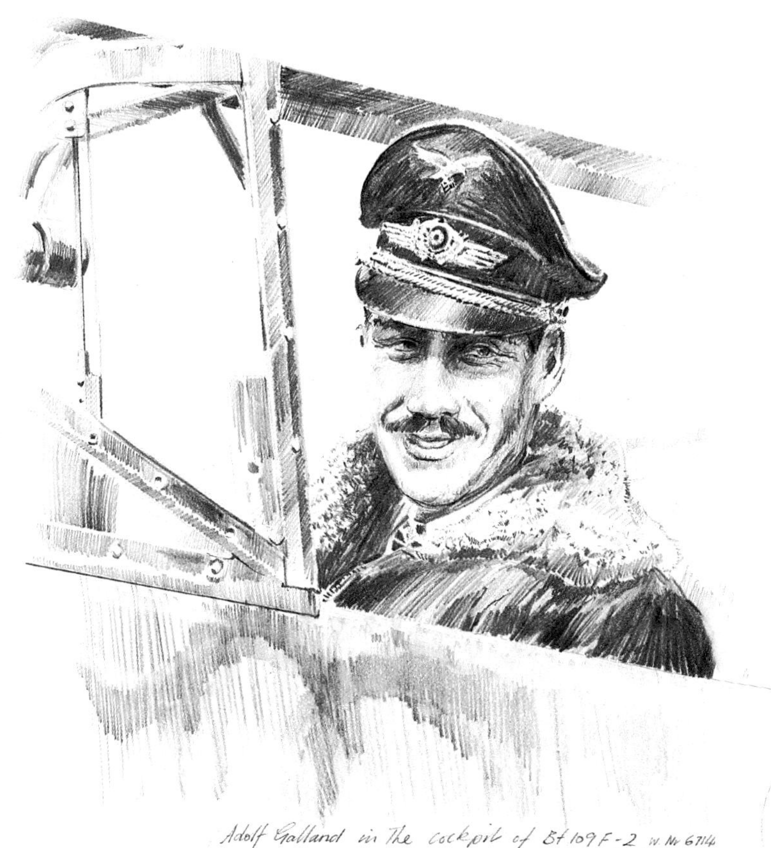

Adolf Galland in the cockpit of Bf 109 F-2 W. Nr 6714 April 1941

THE MESSERSCHMITT Me109
by General Adolf Galland

When the early prototype model of the Messerschmitt Me109 was announced we, the officers and young air force pilots had many discussions regarding the probable advantages and disadvantages of this new fighter – a new generation aircraft to be equipped with retractable gear, closed cockpit, steep ground angle, automatic wing leading edge slots, and high wing loading. The elder pilots with flight experience from WWI were sceptical and declared an open cockpit essential for smelling the enemy in the air before seeing him!

In the Spanish Civil War the He51 biplanes were outclassed by the Russian Polikarpov J 15 fighters. Berlin was alarmed and sent the three armed BF109 prototypes to Spain for combat evaluation. Very soon the 109's proved their superiority over all aircraft in the Spanish sky. I personally made my first three flights from the small airfield Llanes in Northern Spain in 1937. I was impressed by the performance, even though it was somewhat underpowered with its twin-blade fixed wooden propellor.

The He112 would probably have been the superior fighter prototype having a better development factor. However, there were difficulties with production and, although it undoubtedly had the advantage of a broader and stronger undercarriage, the Messerschmitt finally won the competition to become the new fighter aircraft of the Luftwaffe. Up to the end of WWII a total of about 33,000 Me109s in more than 50 various versions had been built, with both Daimler-Benz and Junkers engines, improving gradually from 600 to 1,700 hp during that period.

All the different versions had the narrow undercarriage

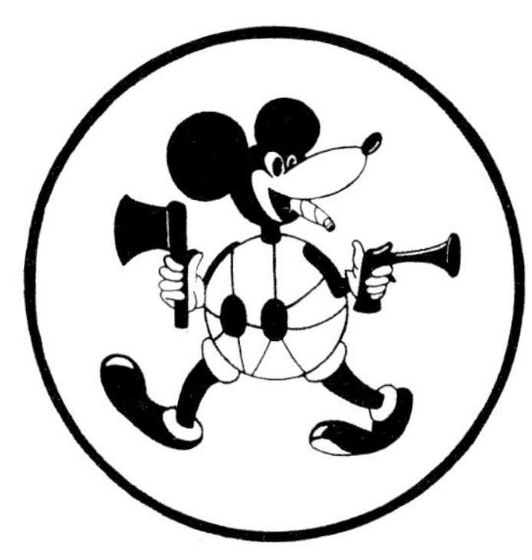

which was mounted on the fuselage and retracted into the wings. Take-off and landing all variants of the Me109 needed careful judgement and was never easy. The aircraft presented a tendency to 'break out' from the desired direction and finally to ground loop. The aircraft's bad habit was increased by cross and tailwinds – landing on rough strips only added to the pilot's problems. By avoiding all mistakes, experienced pilots could avoid accidents, however during both training and combat operations thousands of Me109s were damaged or destroyed, owing to the problems originated by the narrow gear.

I have described a typical incident which my wing-man First Lt. Rödel and myself experienced in the first days when the German troops entered France near Sedan, in 1940, in my book 'The First and the Last'.

On another occasion I had to land with a flat main undercarriage tyre. During the Battle of Britain in 1940, when flying over Kent, I was fired on by a Spitfire at long range and from an angle of 90°. I received hits in the rear part of my fuselage. The cable to my rudder was destroyed and one tyre of my landing gear had also been hit. Fortunately I was able to make a flight back to my coastal airfield and managed to land my Me109 without further damage.

More powerful engines, additional armament, extended coolers and radiators, windscreen and canopy modifications, sand filter, drop tank, and bomb racks were added during the course of the war. For each new addition a new 'bump' appeared. The Me109 finally had so many of them that pilots and mechanics nicknamed the plane 'The Bump'.

The performance of the Me109 became less competitive as the Spitfire was developed with more powerful engines, and later when the P51 Mustang was introduced by the RAF and USAAF. A single Me109 in combat on a one-to-one basis with a Spitfire or P51 Mustang was not too bad but a single Me109 against 10 or 20 enemy fighters, as was often the case later in the war, were terrible odds. Switching production to the more competitive FW190, TA152 and Me209 or Me309 was not feasible taking into account their much lower production capacity. By that time we needed fighters in quantity! With the advent of the Me262 we took the quantum leap forward in fighter design, but the Me262 is another story . . .

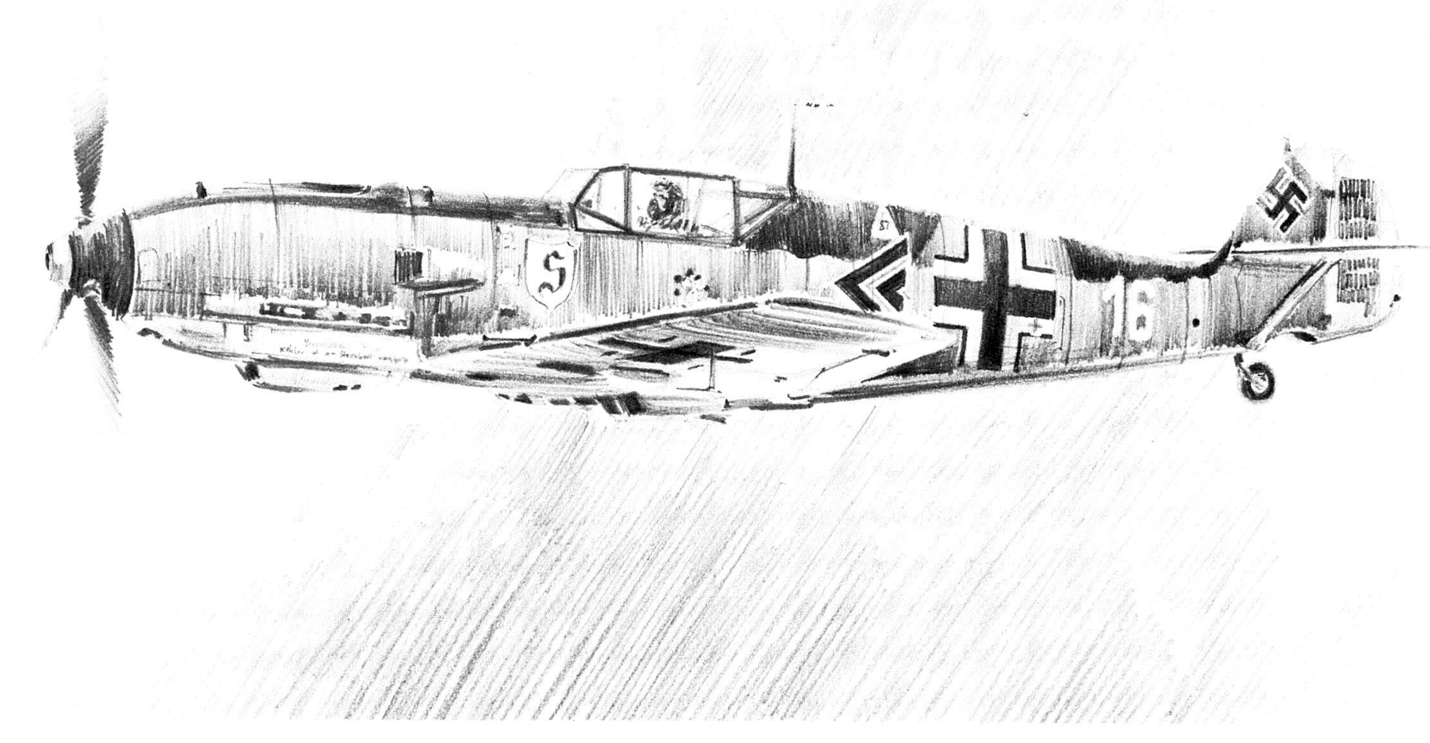

OUT OF THE SUN

In the collection of Mr A Parker

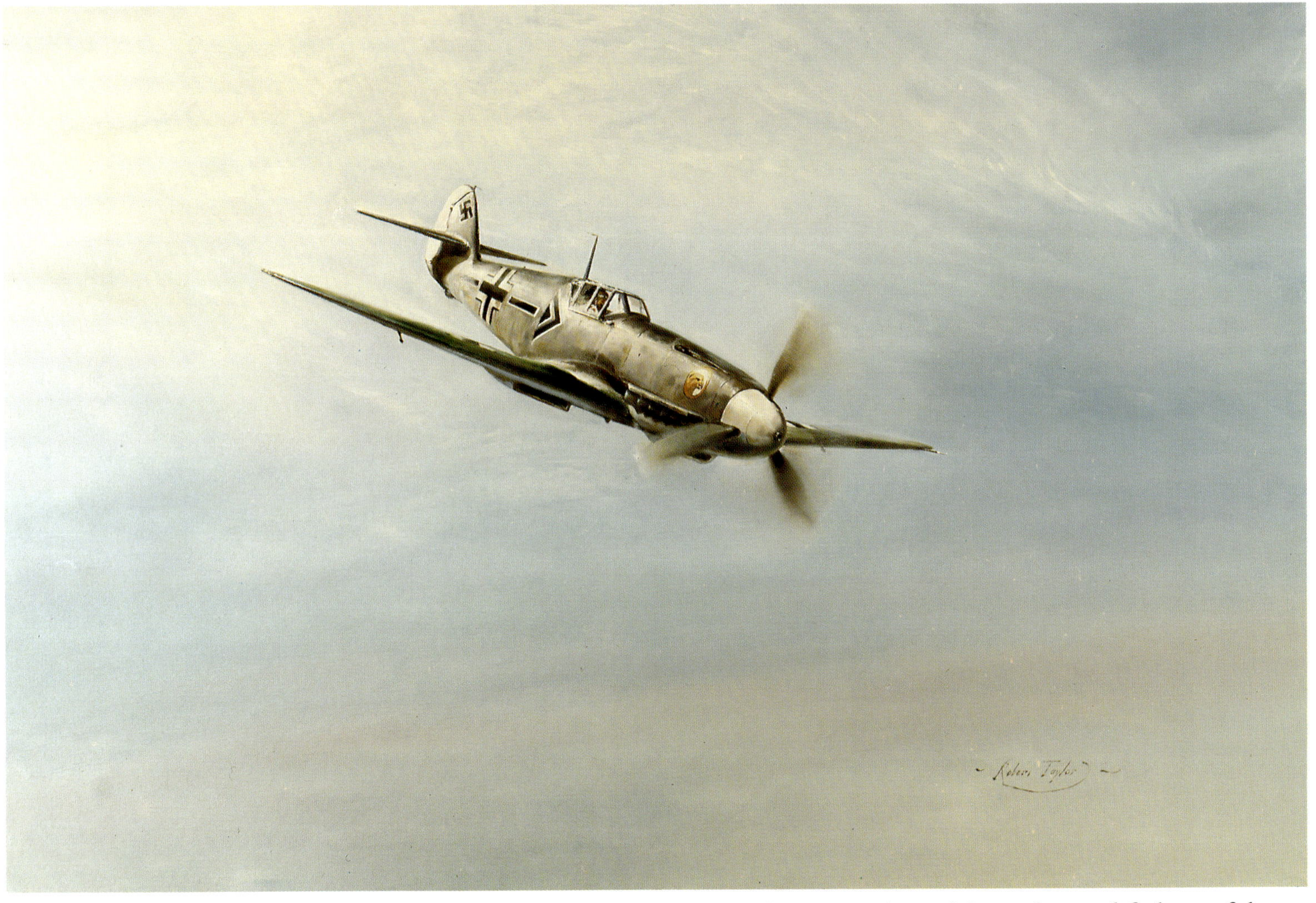

The Me109 was the outstanding fighter of the Luftwaffe during World War II. It was in service at the beginning of the war and, like the Spitfire, went through a succession of improvements and was still a highly competitive fighter when the hostilities ended. Most Luftwaffe Aces who flew throughout the war remember the Me109 with affection. Even those who flew the later FW190s and the Me262 jet, will still say the Me109 was their favourite aircraft.

Its shape was that of the archetypal fighter of the day: long nose, housing a powerful engine, sleek fuselage, slim wings with a suspicion of dihedral, small cockpit – beautiful lines and wonderful to paint.

The painting above is of the Messerschmitt Me109 (f) flown by the Luftwaffe Ace Werner Molders, and depicts a typical attacking manoeuvre diving *Out of the Sun* – the title of the picture. It was painted in 1980.

When *Flight of Eagles* was commissioned I knew that General Adolf Galland was to sign the prints which would result from the painting. I had read a great deal about the Fighter Wing he commanded during the early part of the war – the famous JG-26, *'Schlageter' Geschwader*, with its nine squadrons of Messerschmitts, based at various airfields in the Abbeville area of Northern France. I knew that Adolf Galland was well respected by the fighter pilots on both sides. Johnnie Johnson had said in his excellent book *Wing Leader*: 'After the war we were greatly impressed by the man's quiet dignity and unshakeable confidence in his own tactics and theories'.

Adolf Galland was unquestionably the greatest fighter leader of the Luftwaffe, and any painting featuring his famous Me 109's had to portray those leadership qualities in some way, yet at the same time convey the threat that he and his pilots of JG-26 posed daily to the Allied pilots. I decided that a *schwarm* of Me 109s with Galland leading, climbing out to battle height would make a suitable setting.

Fighter pilots have always been early birds. The earliest patrols of the day were usually flown at first light and it was commonplace for the fighter pilots to be in the air as the dawn came up. Though few had the time to appreciate the morning glory at the time, they frequently witnessed the magnificence of the sunrise from their world above the clouds. For some time I had wanted to paint a picture showing these magic moments and this, I decided, would be the one. The picture must have existed clearly in my subconscious, for I needed to make only a single pencil drawing. It worked first time!

I wanted to capture the delicate pastel shades of colour as the sun emerges above the horizon – orange turning to yellow and then azure blue. Below the clouds the rest of the world had yet to awake, yet up here was all the splendour of the dawn; and witnessing the morning glory – a *Flight of Eagles*.

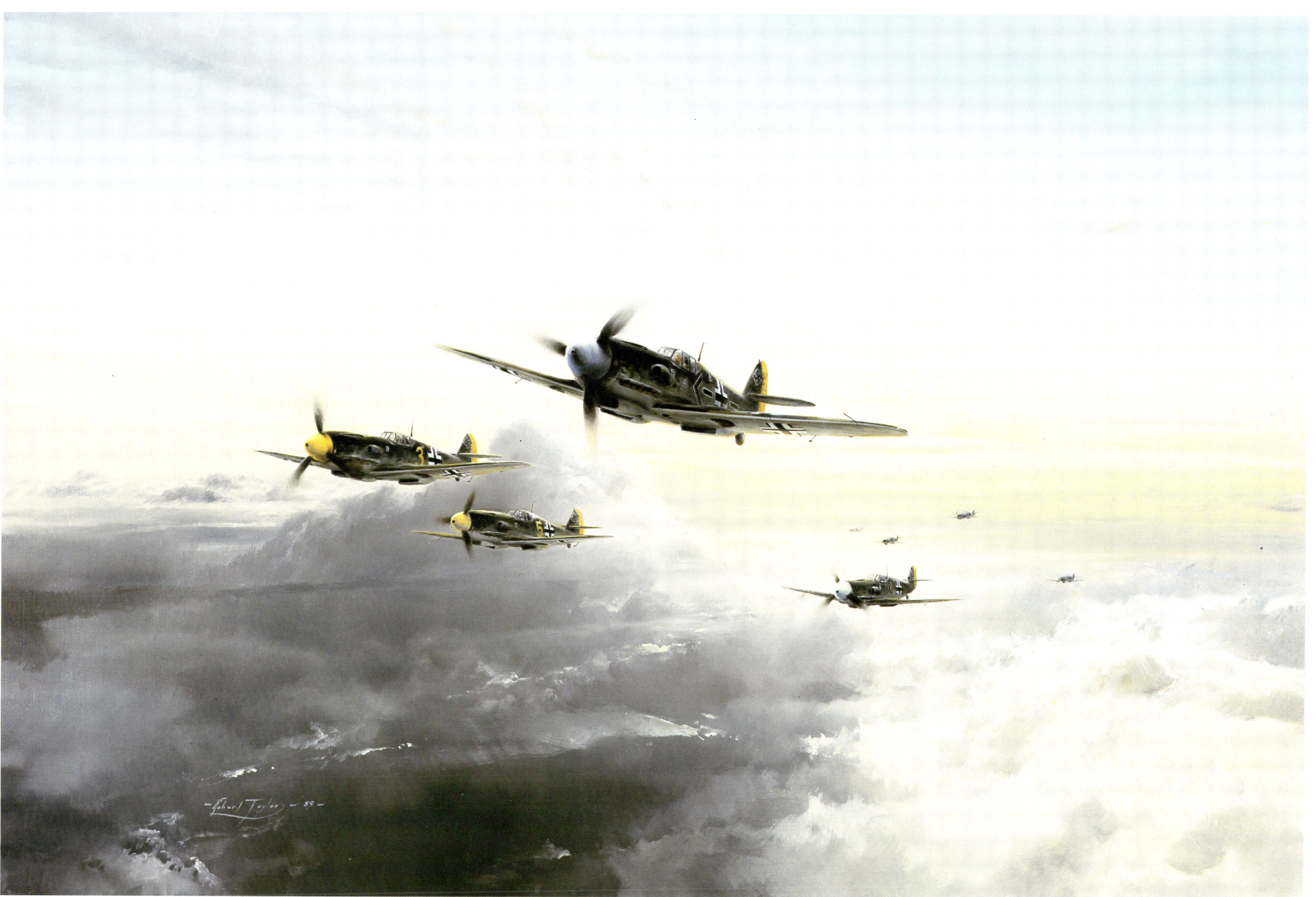

FLIGHT OF EAGLES

In the collection of Mr E Leicher

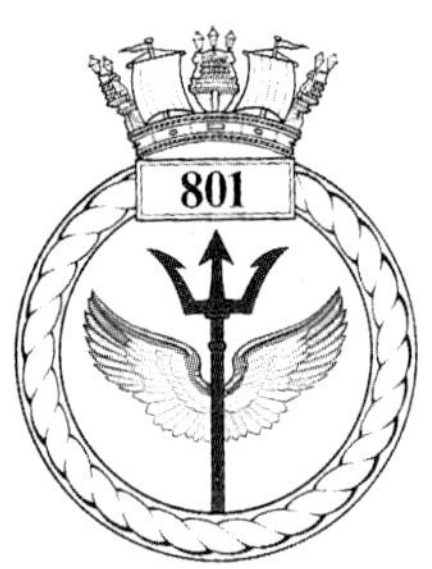

AIRSTRIKE OVER WEST FALKLAND

I had known Nigel 'Sharkey' Ward since he took command of 700 Alpha Naval Air Squadron – the very first squadron to be equipped with the Sea Harrier. 'Sharkey', as he is known to all, was responsible for the aircraft's initial flying trials in the Service, and he took command of the first operational Sea Harrier Squadron. It was therefore fitting that he should be in command of 801 Squadron, flying Sea Harriers, when the squadron took their new aircraft into combat in the South Atlantic during the Falklands War of 1982.

Sharkey was one of the most experienced fast jet pilots in the Navy, having flown Buccaneers and Phantoms previously and, following the phenomenal success of the Harrier and its pilots in the South Atlantic, I was fortunate to be able to spend time discussing events with him when commissioned to paint a Sea Harrier combat scene. Unlike many other discussions with pilots about their combat experiences, most of which were recalled over a period of forty years or more, this one was 'hot off the press'. This had its difficulties because Sharkey was not always at liberty to tell me everything, the aircraft being a front-line fighter and still obviously subject to a degree of secrecy, particularly concerning certain aspects of tactics and firepower performance. We were able to circumnavigate successfully the Official Secrets Act, and Sharkey provided all the detail necessary to paint the picture.

Talking at length to Sharkey I decided to paint a particular combat which he and his wingman, Steve Thomas, had fought on 21 May 1982 – the day that the air battles over the Falklands reached their peak. Some thirty Sea Harrier pilots destroyed nineteen of the Argentinian jet fighters during this day of seemingly incessant attacks by Mirage, Dagger and Pucarra aircraft.

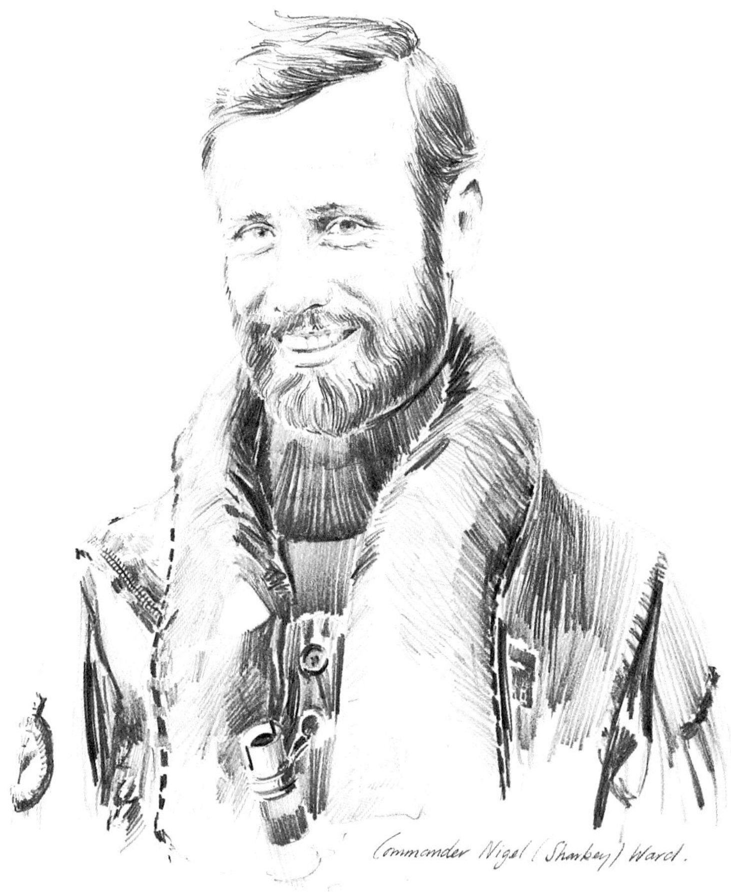

FLYING THE SEA HARRIER IN COMBAT
by Commander 'Sharkey' Ward, DSC, AFC, RN.

The Falklands War gave a small group of Fleet Air Arm pilots the chance to live up to the expectations of their illustrious predecessors. During the passage to the South Atlantic there was time to prepare for action and time to be grateful to all those fighter pilots of previous wars, who, through sacrifice and achievement, had set the standard for British aviators in action.

Since the 1939–45 war, the Royal Navy's Carrier Force had shrunk from over eighty flat-tops to just two: the Invincible *and the* Hermes. *These two warships carried twenty Sea Harriers and about twenty-eight pilots. The aircraft was a multi-rôle, single-seat, all-weather fighter, reconnaissance and strike aircraft. The pilots represented an accumulation of air warfare expertise that had been passed on by word of mouth and by example from previous generations of Fleet Air Arm pilots.*

Since World War II, hundreds of naval aviators had been lost at sea during endless exercises whose aim had been to maintain a war-fighting capability for use in emergency. The air defence of the Task Force rested on the ability of the Sea Harrier aircrew to live up to their hard-won pedigree.

Many pundits forecast disaster. Physical odds were ten to one against. The Argentine had Mirage IIIs, Vs, Skyhawks, Canberras and Etendards, not to mention the Pucarras which were to plague our ground forces.

Fortunately, fighter pilots have to be, by the very nature of their trade, extroverts with a jingoistic self-confidence that does not recognise great odds. We were used to our close colleagues dying in peace-time accidents and were not therefore unduly perturbed at the thought of losses in war. Instead of counting the danger, we were keen to do the job required of us. It was a privilege to fight for our country and the only difficulty facing us was how to fight to our own advantage with better tactics and better skills in the air.

Fortunately, we had enormous faith in our 'Jump-jet' fighter. It was a faith based on consistent achievement at sea and on land against a whole selection of the best air-superiority fighters that the West could provide. Our peace-time, combat-proving exercises had been conducted against the cream of the UK and US Air Forces and the US Navy. In these exercises we had achieved a 3 to 1 kill ratio against the F-15 Eagle, over 10 to 1 against the F-14 Tomcat and well in excess of these ratios against the F-4 Phantom and other jets.

On the balance of this experience, therefore, we were confident of at least a 10 to 1 kill ratio in action against the Argentine pilots.

Flying conditions in the South Atlantic varied from perfect to atrocious and it was in the bad weather that the Sea Harrier came into its own. We flew when conventional aircraft could not have operated from a deck at sea. Day or night, fog, snow or gale; it made no difference. The aircraft has an amazing capability to cope with dreadful weather conditions and we had a job to do: protect the Fleet and protect our troops inshore.

Patrolling over West Falkland looking for enemy aircraft was a most visually satisfying experience. On occasion, one could see for eighty miles and the terrain below had a beauty far beyond expectation. All the tints, hues, purples and browns of Scotland were there and, for much of the time, this compensated for the relative 'boredom' of some patrols. Robert Taylor captured the scene extraordinarily well in his painting 'Airstrike'.

We flew in pairs with each man watching the other's vulnerable six o'clock area, always scanning for the little dots that would grow into excitement, challenge and combat.

There was pressure on us all from fuel considerations. At times our carrier could be in excess of three hundred nautical miles away. On the one hand we needed to remain on task protecting our troops in San Carlos for as long as possible. On the other, we did not want the ignominy of running out of fuel before we got 'home'. We had too few aircraft to

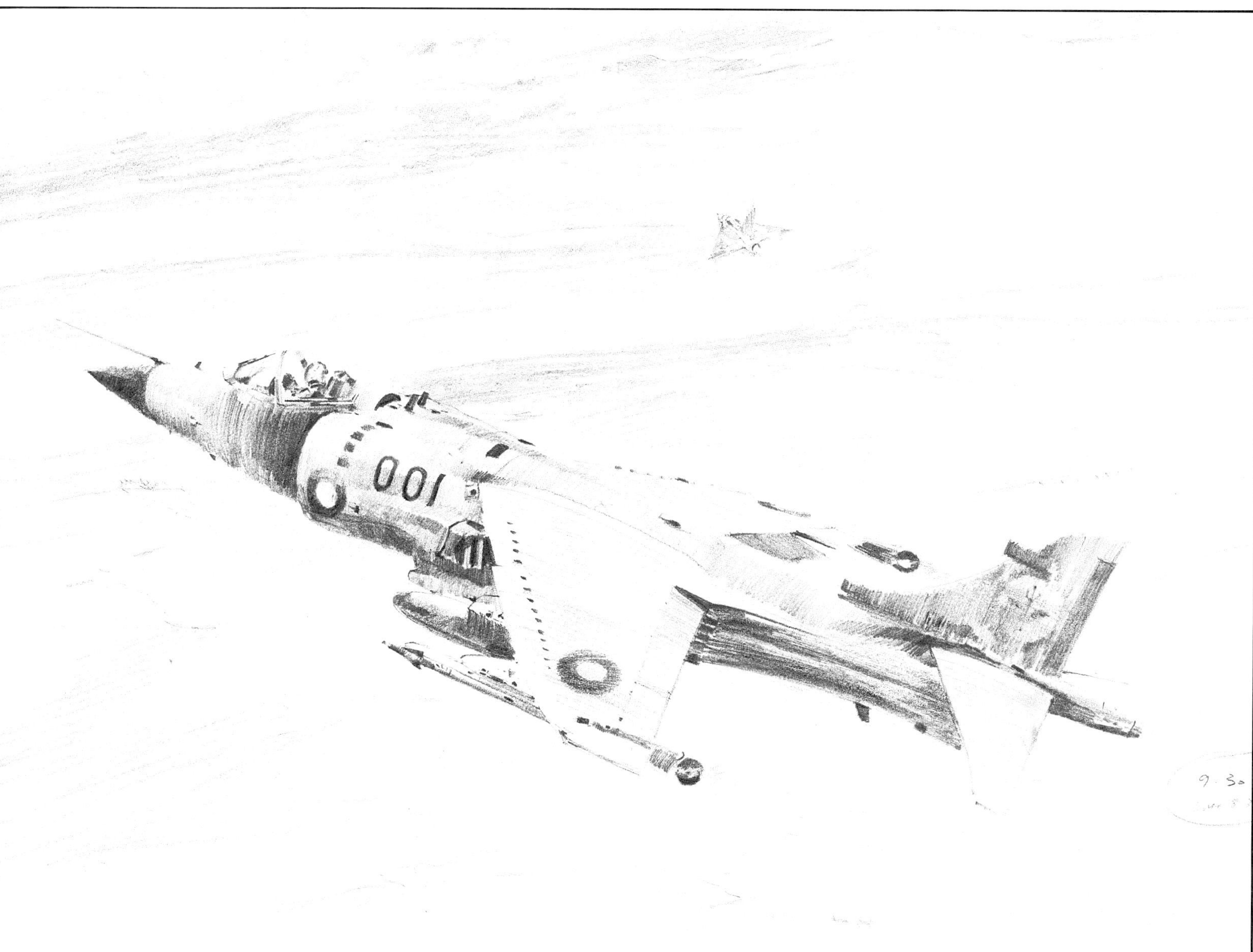

Sharkey Ward had decribed this particular combat to me in great detail and one thing that left a lasting impression upon me was the speed with which events had taken place. As usual, several different formats were contemplated for the painting. There is an old problem that all aviation artists have when depicting one aircraft shooting down another: because of the usual distance between the two opposing airplanes one has to view either from in front or behind. If one views from in front the vanquished forms the main subject, and the victor is seen in the distance. If one reverses the positions, the vanquished is seen in the distance, which is all right, but one is faced with looking at the victor from behind which is not always ideal. I had managed to get a good look at the Sea Harrier from above and behind (although not in the air) some months earlier at Yeovilton when 700A Naval Air Squadron had kindly loaned me one of their aircraft and a hydraulic lift truck! Whilst this rear view seemed promising, I wanted first to try a particular moment in the combat as described by Sharkey. The above drawing depicts this moment. The Argentinian Dagger aircraft had passed under Sharkey's Sea Harrier, with reheat in, at high speed. Sharkey has already moved his controls and his aircraft is just starting its savage turn to starboard. In a few seconds he would bring to bear and release his Sidewinder missile with due effect.

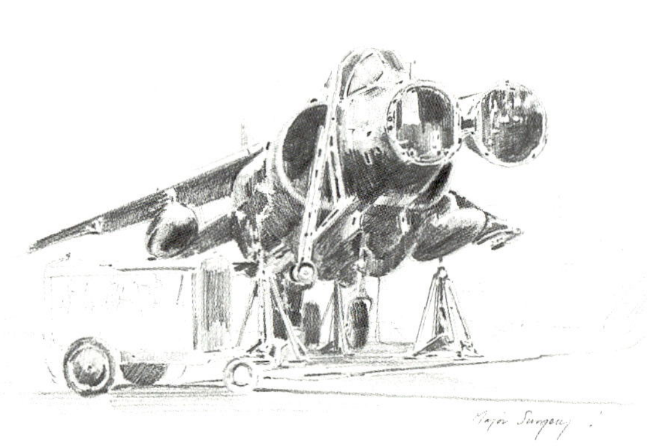

throw them away! Without Sea Harriers, the Task Force would have been helpless. There was no choice but to 'get it right'.

Fatigue and stress took its toll but was always forgotten when the opportunity to fight arose.

I and my wingman, Steve Thomas, were more than fortunate. We were involved in actions which resulted in twelve kills and we claimed six of these for ourselves. There can be little in life more exciting than a fight to the death and, at no time when involved in a combat situation, would I have swapped my Sea Harrier for another jet.

The Jump-jet is slower and does not turn as well as some: but it has other attributes which more than make up for this. In combat it will always run the opposition out of fuel and, in a one-against-one situation, it has an ability to point at an adversary that is unmatched. In a slow speed fight, it should always win.

Of course, the aircraft is just a tool. It is a weapons platform which must be used to best effect if it is going to be a success. Prior to the war, I had been lucky enough to be in charge of the operational development of tactics and the training of all Sea Harrier aircrew. My policy had been to concentrate on air combat skills because this is undoubtedly the most demanding form of flying. It demands 100 per cent effort, concentration and aggression. The pilot must think of a dozen things at once. If he can cope with the combat task, the rest of the operational rôles fall easily into place.

Fulfilling these several rôles in the Sea Harrier is hardly 'a swan' but it is very rewarding and I could not ask for a more enjoyable and reliable steed.

After considering the drawing shown, on the previous page, I decided it did not portray the event clearly enough. It also seemed better to show the Sidewinder in action, as it was obviously highly significant. I needed to paint the Sea Harrier from behind, so I reverted to the sketches of the 700A Squadron Sea Harrier which I had made at RNAS Yeovilton. Depicting Sharkey's aircraft a few seconds later in the combat meant painting land beneath, rather than water. This was difficult from the reference point of view and the hilly countryside was somewhat colourless – but that is how it was! The painting on the right hand page resulted, and now hangs in the Fleet Air Arm Museum at Yeovilton.

The oil sketch *Bluff Cove Sortie*, illustrated below, was painted as part of my programme for *Airstrike*. It shows a Sea Harrier of 801 Squadron at about 12,000 feet over the Falklands, and was a useful exercise within the project. From most angles the Sea Harrier is an enjoyable aircraft to paint. Its configuration seems to convey a very 'waspish' impression; not a fighter to annoy too much – it could get very nasty!

The oil sketch, which measures 14 by 10 inches, was exhibited at the Guild of Aviation Artists' exhibition in London in 1982.

BLUFF COVE SORTIE

Private Collection

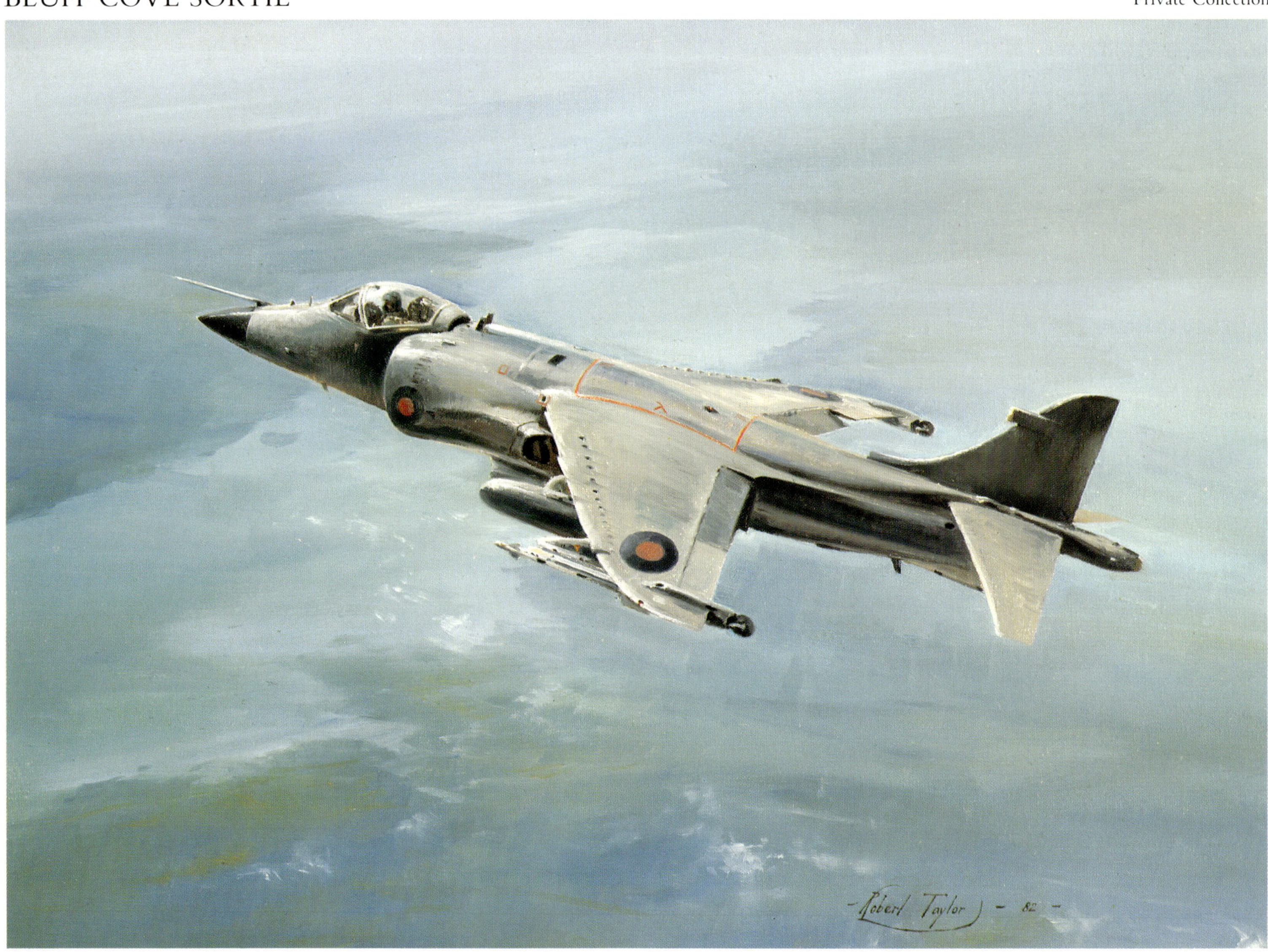

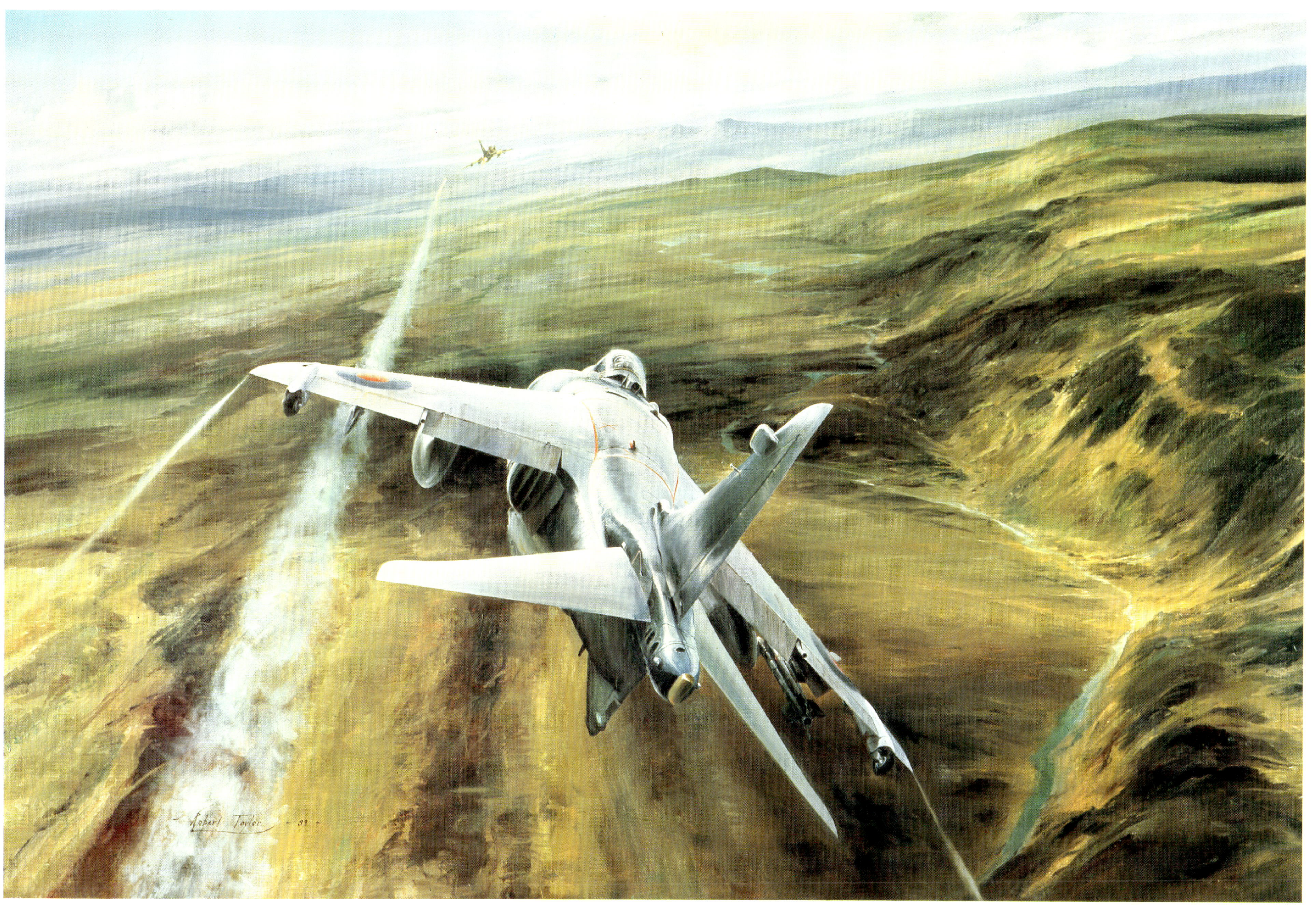

AIR STRIKE OVER WEST FALKLAND
In the collection of The Fleet Air Arm Museum, Yeovilton

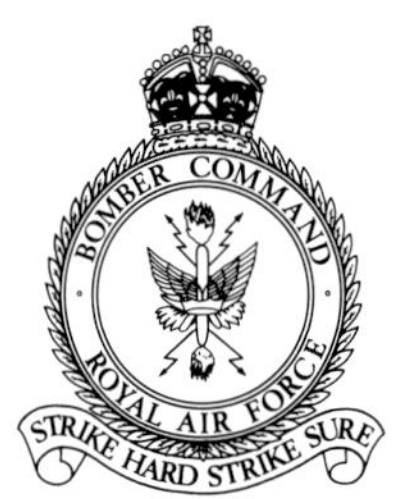

LAST FLIGHT HOME

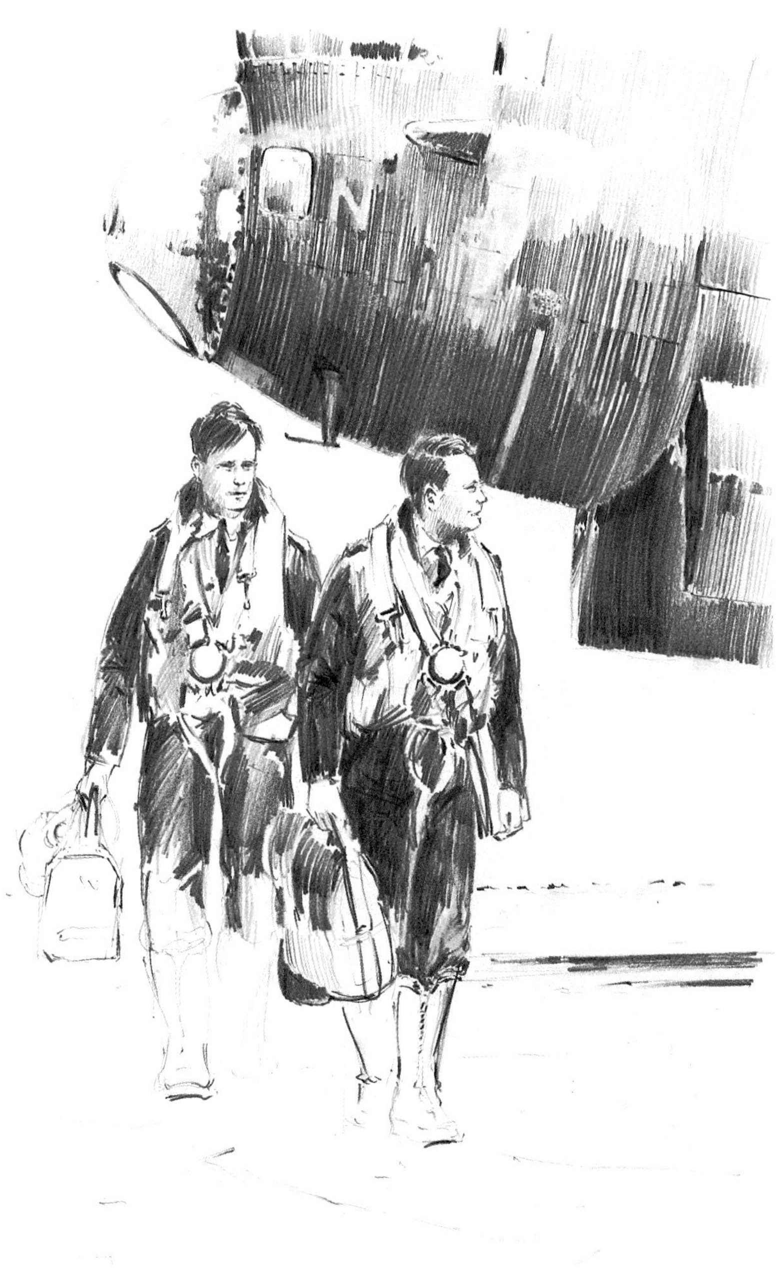

In 1985 the Royal Air Force commemorated the fifitieth anniversary of the formation of Bomber Command. When commissioned to paint a picture to mark the occasion, my mind went back to the dark war years, when the Command played a vital role and paid such a heavy price. How was I to convey, in one picture, the importance of all that this famous Command was to the RAF, and indeed to Britain? Literally dozens of ideas appeared in my mind but I kept coming back to one theme.

With the passing of time, thankfully, we tend to remember only the better things and I wanted this philosophy somehow to permeate through to the painting. I wanted to paint a picture which would remind people, if possible, of the men as much as the machines, and at the same time perhaps to indicate in some way that 'at last it was all over'.

Bomber Command's offensive against Germany during the bleak years of World War II was one of the most remarkable passages in the history of arms. When England stood alone in 1940, and Winston Churchill could see no other road to victory, the famous Command began what was later described by the official history as '. . . the most continuous and most gruelling operation of the war ever carried out'. For four long years it served as the only effective means of waging war against Hitler's European Fortress. It cost the lives of 55,753 of the finest and most highly-trained men in the Allied forces.

When World War II broke out there was a popular misconception that in any future large-scale hostilities it would be the bomber which would decide the outcome. Huge armadas of bomber aircraft, went the story, would drop vast quantities of explosives and, worse still, poisonous gas on civilian populations. In fact, as it turned out, bombers did prove to be one of the most effective weapons available to both sides during the World War II but a force neither so devastating nor so easily-operated as was generally believed. It took several years and many hard-learned lessons before Bomber Command was able to function effectively as a decisive factor in modern warfare. Accuracy was the greatest problem and the key to the success or failure of any bomber offensive. Probably the greatest advantage achieved during this time was the development, by the Allies, of superior electronic targeting devices and a target marking force – the 'Pathfinders'. With these fearless teams flying ahead of the main group of bombers, dropping marker flares on the targets with pinpoint accuracy, and devices such as 'Gee', 'Oboe' and 'H2S' the Allies were able to turn the tide and the Axis powers began to suffer a decline in their fortunes. Those targeting devices the latter employed were easily jammed by the Allies while their own equipment enabled them to make a success of a much higher proportion of raids.

Despite the Allies' technical superiority in this area, bombing operations were by no means a comfortable task. The odds against survival were measured in mere nights and those who volunteered to serve with Bomber Command were among the most courageous, tireless and determined who ever bore arms for their country. It is to those men that *Last Flight Home* is dedicated.

Many aircraft served the Command since it was formed in 1935, but to me there was only one which could feature in this particular painting, for the Lancaster became the backbone of the Command during the period of its greatest activity.

The idea of painting a flight of three Lancasters returning home appealed to me, and whilst I am aware that most such homecomings were at the dead of night or, stretching it, at dawn, on this occasion I used a little licence. After all it was an important occasion – I brought these three Lancasters home on a summer day, with the sun on high!

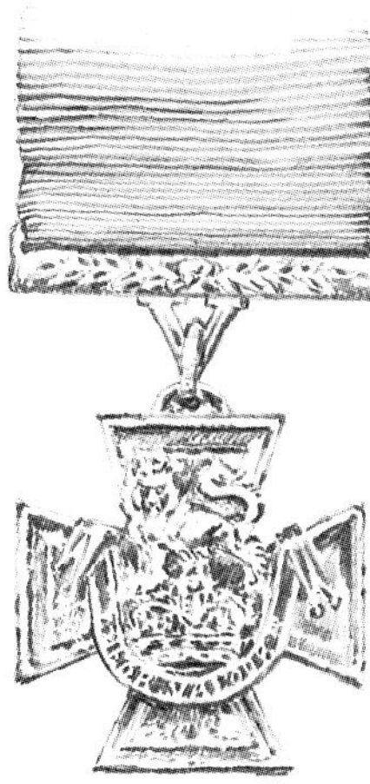

THE VICTORIA CROSS

During the mid-1850s, at the height of the Crimean War, it became very evident both to Britain's leaders and, through accurate newspaper reporting from the front, to the public, that there was a need for a decoration acknowledging great gallantry on the part of individuals in the firing line. An award was called for which would demonstrate the nation's gratitude and respect for those people whose selfless heroism goes far in maintaining the country's morale and indeed ensuring its survival in such times of strife.

The Victoria Cross (VC) is the highest British decoration for conspicuous bravery or devotion to the country in the presence of the enemy. It was founded by Queen Victoria towards the end of the war in 1856 and the medals have always been cast from the metal of Russian guns taken at Sevastopol, save for brief periods during the two world wars. It consists of a Maltese Cross made of bronze, bearing in the centre the royal crown surmounted by a lion, and with the scroll superscribed 'For Valour'.

The winning of the VC carries with it a tax-free annuity of £100. A Royal Warrant of 1920 extends eligibility to women of military nursing services and to civilians of either sex when serving under naval, military or air authorities. Since its inception over one hundred years ago less than 1,400 VCs have been awarded. During World War II a total of 182 were awarded, of which 23 were to members of Bomber Command.

'FOR VALOUR'

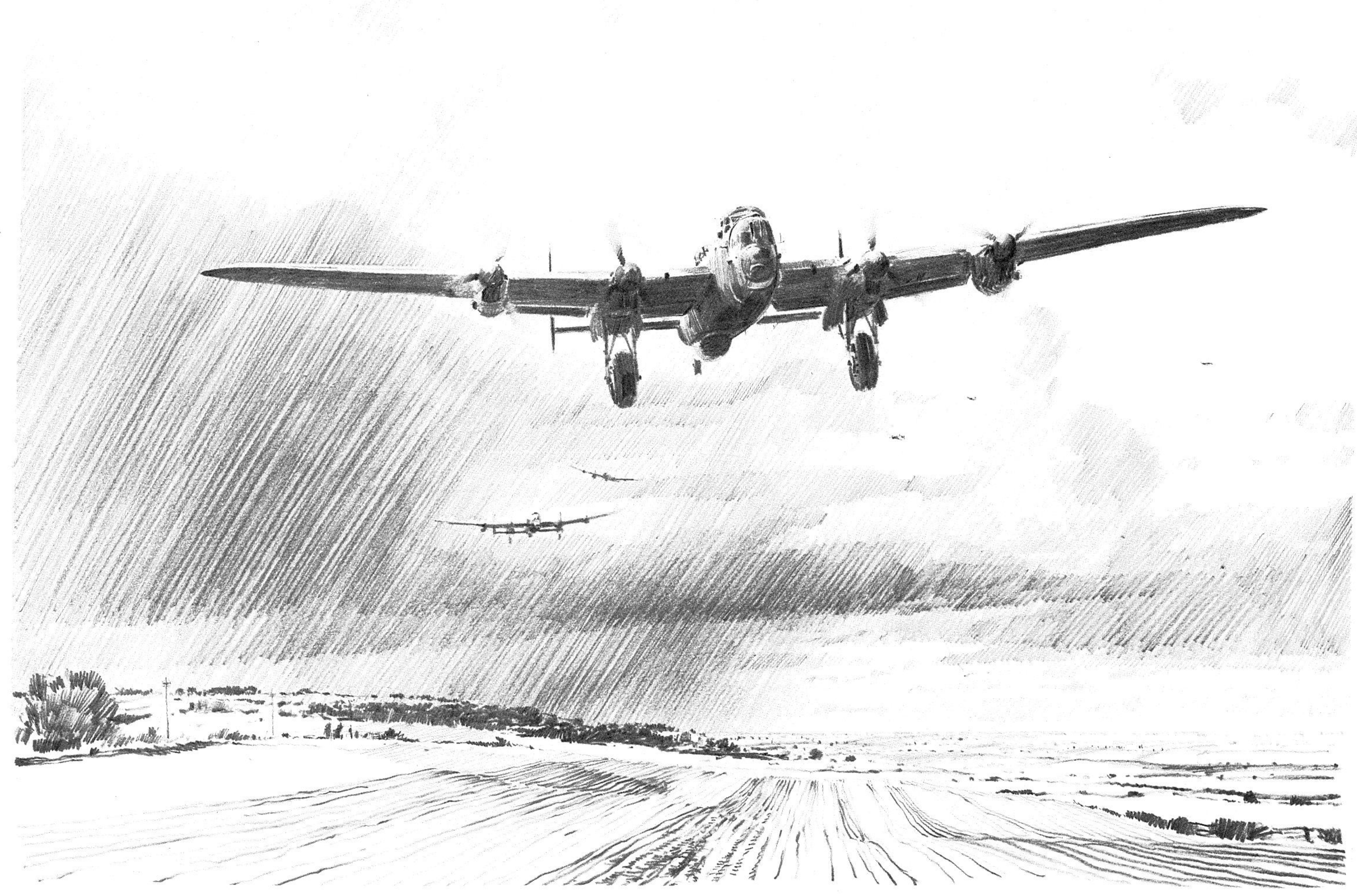

The above pencil sketch was the penultimate drawing for *Last Flight Home*. Originally I had intended to show a rolling and mostly distant landscape beneath the incoming Lancasters but after studying the drawing for some time I felt that the composition lacked some interest in the foreground, particularly in the fairly large expanse of canvas below the main Lancaster. By choosing the right subject for this 'interest' the atmosphere of the painting could be substantially added to. A comparison between the above sketch and the final painting will, perhaps, demonstrate my point.

The idea of a haymaking scene appealed to me for two reasons. The first was that it would create nicely the activity required in the area of the painting. The second was that it would act as a reminder of the importance of the people who worked at home and in the countryside, and would at the same time provide, perhaps, a hint of peace to come.

As the painting was to commemorate fifty years of Bomber Command I thought it would be nice to try to invoke some of the best memories of the war era, if possible, and the title was intended to help imply that perhaps now, at least, it was almost all over.

I have always been interested by the detail which some of the Old Masters brought into the backgrounds of their paintings. It was this attention to detail that attracted me to the work of certain painters and, during my years as an art restorer, I used to study their various techniques. The enormous amount of interest, additional to the main theme of a picture, that was created by all the detailed 'secondary' work in their paintings always impressed me.

This influence has been with me a long time and today I take great delight in working on the 'background interest' in my own paintings, be it cloud formations, or a haymaking scene.

The section of my painting below shows the detailed work in the haymaking area of the painting and some of the landscape beyond. The position of the farm workers was carefully planned in an endeavour to concentrate attention back to the main Lancaster aircraft. The hedge in the foreground was added to stop the field falling into the rebate of the frame!

During my research concerning the hay elevator, positioned by the haystack, I came across all sorts of wonderful examples of old farm machinery which I would like to paint one day!

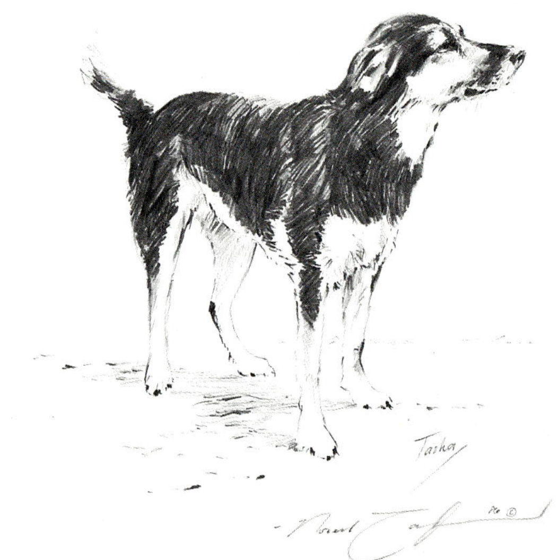

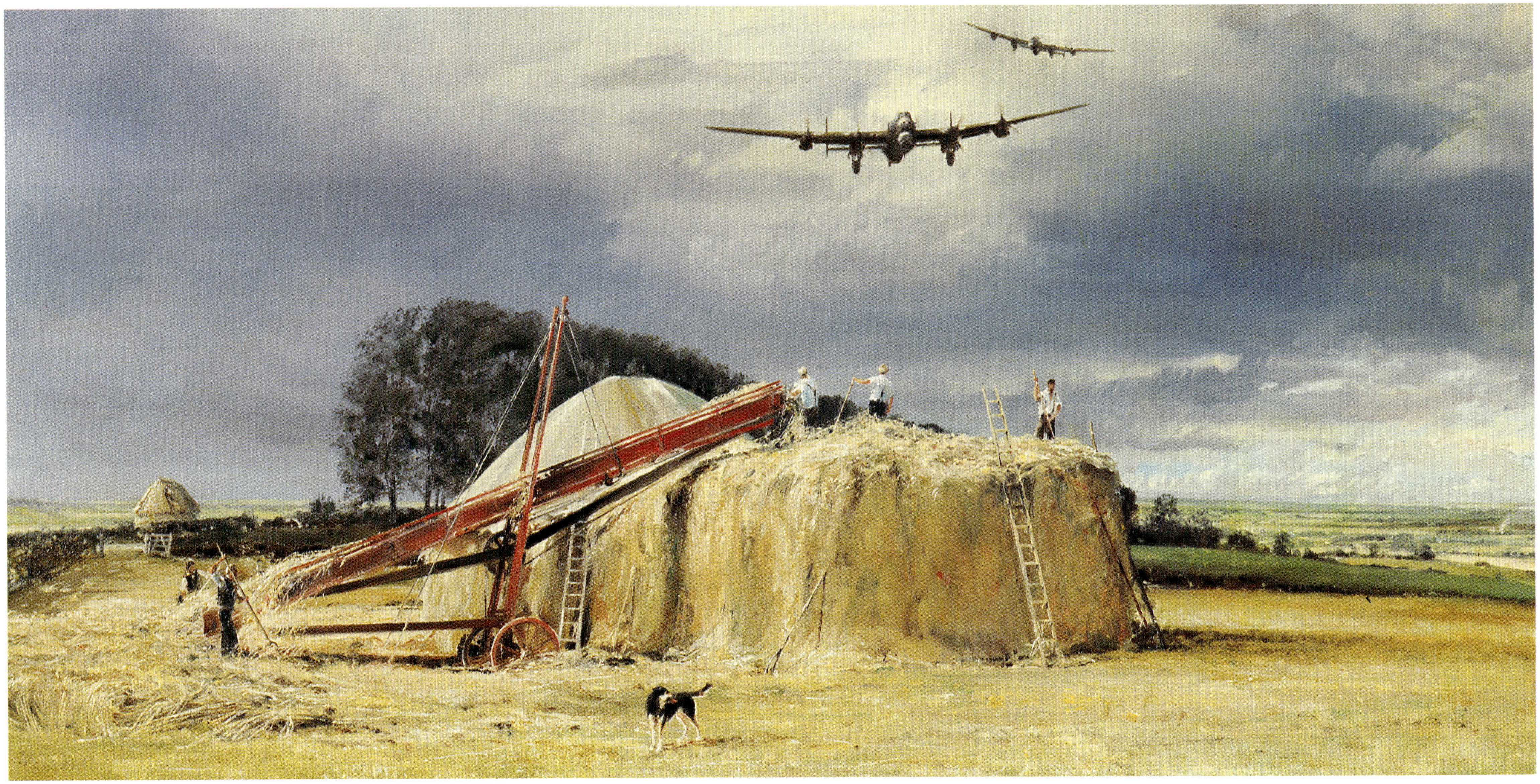

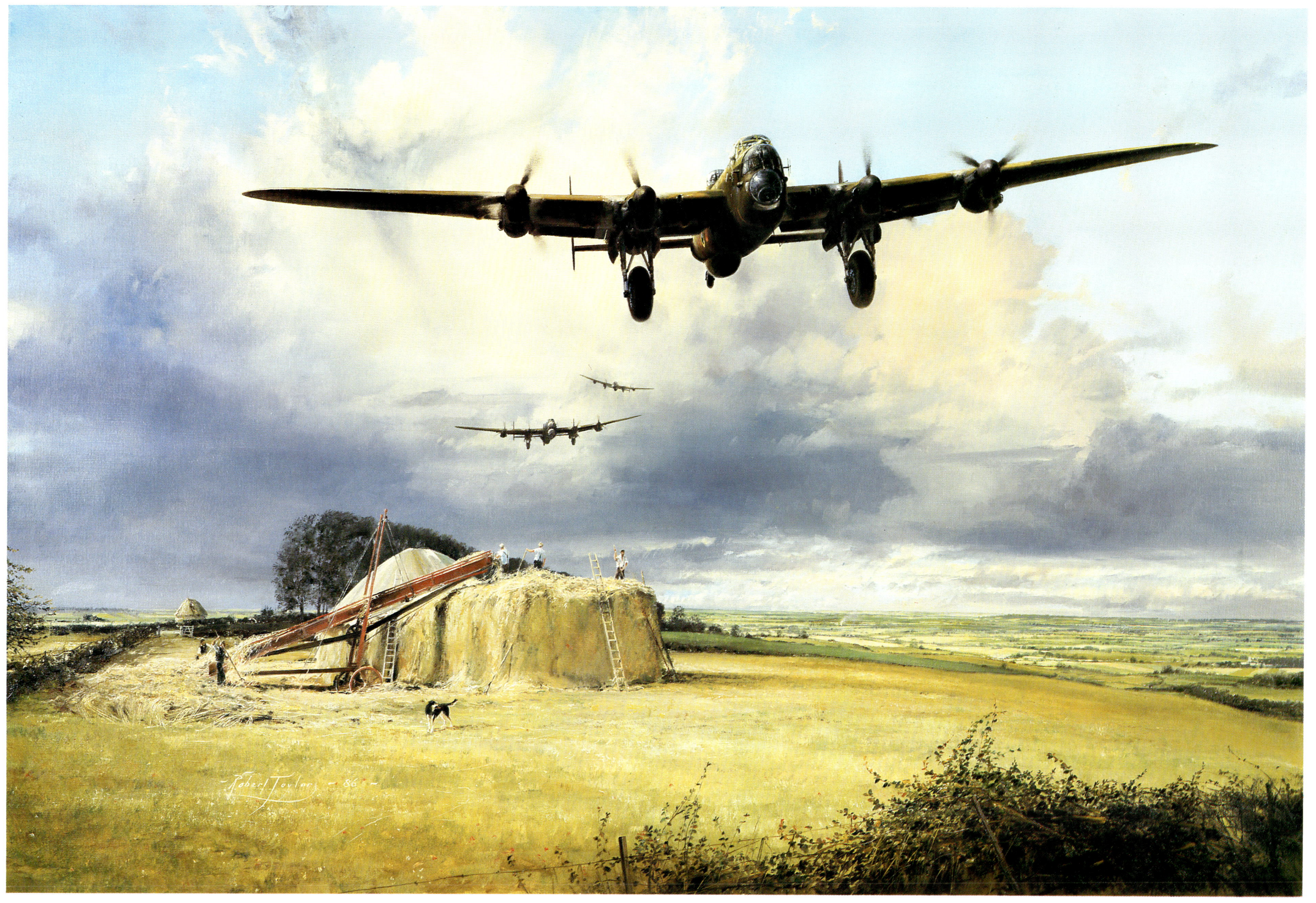

LAST FLIGHT HOME
In the collection of Mr Tom Greenham

TYPHOON ATTACK

I have always thought that the Typhoon was a truly aggressive-looking fighter aircraft and remember often drawing it as a boy. I think it was the large airscoop and radiator below the engine that did it! I also remember reading that the Typhoon went through a traumatic early existence, one of its problems being that the entire tail section would part company with the rest of the aircraft from time to time!

Liking the look of the Typhoon, I was pleased to have the opportunity to paint a full-scale canvas featuring the aircraft in action but what was most exciting was that it had been arranged for me to collaborate with Wing Commander Roland Beamont for the research on the painting. 'Bee' Beamont had flown in the Battle of Britain and, between operational tours, was detached to the Hawker Company where he made over 400 test flights on the Hurricane. During the Typhoon's development Bee Beamont played a large part in its test-flying programme, when, incidentally, he had to help solve the problem of the tail falling off! When the Typhoon's teething problems had been resolved, in no small measure due to Bee's flair as a young test pilot, he took the aircraft to war, commanding a Typhoon squadron with great distinction. Before meeting Bee I knew of course that he had been first to fly the Canberra, the ill-fated TSR2, and the Lightning, and he had been much involved in the early development work on the Tornado. I also knew that, since he had retired from flying, he had become a successful writer on aeronautical subjects, so I was very much looking forward to meeting this extraordinary aviator. I was not disappointed. Bee immediately gave me the benefit of his tremendous knowledge about the Typhoon and, even more important perhaps, his wholehearted enthusiasm for the project.

The Typhoon distinguished itself in the low-level attack role and so the painting would obviously need to feature this aspect of the aircraft. I favoured a shipping strike rather than a ground attack scene and Bee recalled a particular combat which, when he described it to me, sounded perfect for the painting. His Squadron had been returning from escorting a bomber raid on the Abbeville Marshalling Yards when they were vectored to make an attack on a group of armed R-boats escorted by a heavily-armed flak ship. Bee and his Typhoon pilots had encountered a heavy barrage of fire during their attack – a successful strike which left the majority of the enemy craft damaged and burning.

I am indebted to Bee Beamont for his help with my research for the painting and also for the fascinating notes he has penned for me concerning his experiences testing the heavy fighters, which are reproduced following.

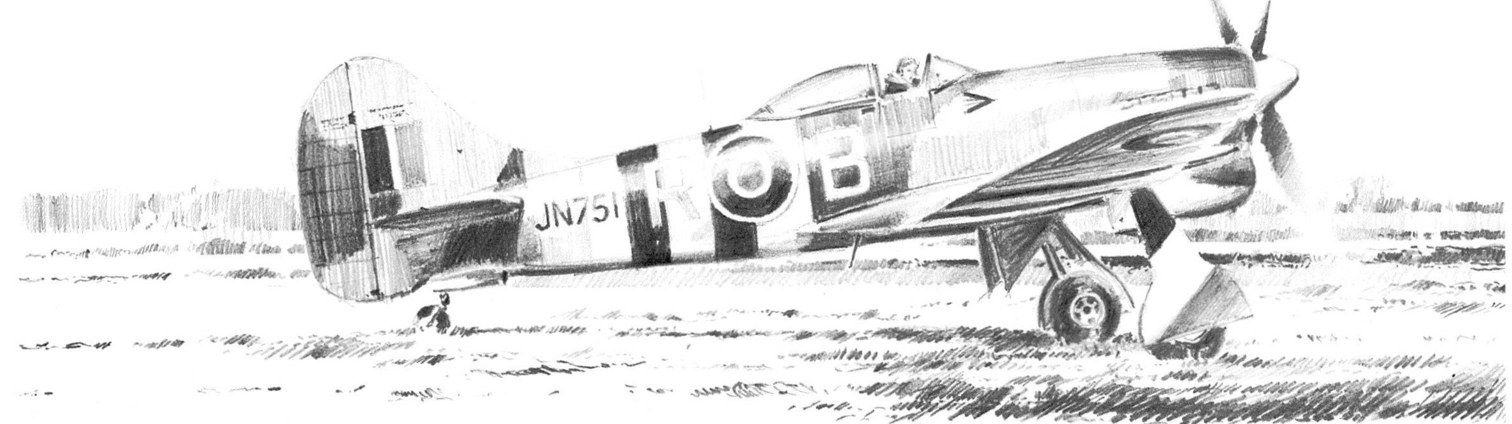

Wing Commander 'Bee' Beamont's Tempest JN751 in D-Day invasion stripes Newchurch June 44.

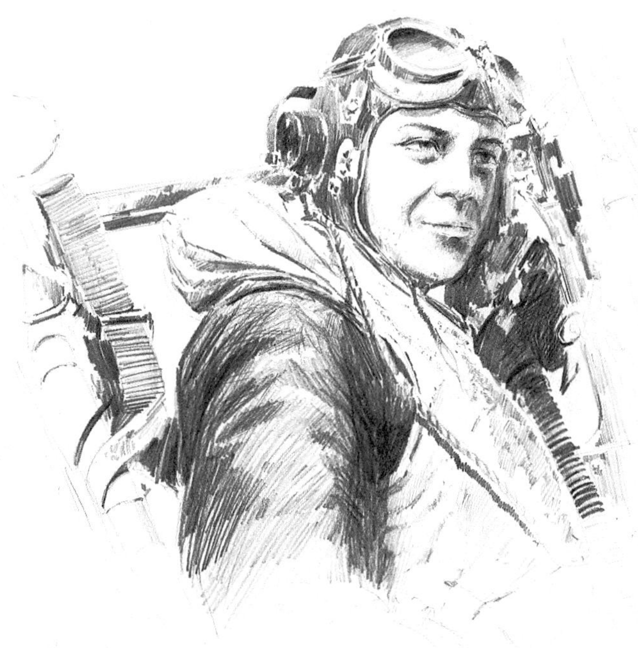
Wing Commander 'Bee' Beamont CBE, DSO, DFC

TESTING THE HEAVY FIGHTERS

By Wing Commander 'Bee' Beamont, CBE, DSO, DFC, DL

In the winter of 1942, following an exciting eighteen months with No 87 (F) Squadron on Hurricanes throughout the Battles of France and Britain, I was posted for a 'rest period', to the Hawker factory at Langley near Slough, to test the new Hurricanes which were rolling off the production line at more than 200 per month.

Test-flying Hurricanes at the factory was a very different matter from flying them on a squadron where, under hard combat conditions, pilots had quickly become accustomed to the idea of 'when in trouble, bale out', but at Langley the opposite philosophy was the rule, 'when in trouble, bring it back!' This, coupled with the heavy pressure of the times to get vital replacements out to the squadrons which called for up to ten or more test flights per day from each of the five 'production' test pilots, soon inculcated into the newcomer a sense of urgency and of the need for an analytical approach. It was no longer adequate to tell the ground staff 'it doesn't work'; now one had to understand why.

At the south end of the tarmac at Langley, beyond the pilots' office and behind a security barrier, was the 'Experimental Shop', and from this area occasionally emerged a large, brutal-looking, single-seater fighter with what then seemed to be an enormous engine driving a great four-bladed propeller. Four 20mm cannons projected well out from the wings' leading edges and when on engine runs the din drowned all the Merlin engines of the Hurricanes. It was the prototype of the new Hawker Tornado which was still under test and development as a replacement for the Hurricane, and which had been experiencing a long period of technical problems.

Philip Lucas, Hawker's acting Chief Test Pilot, had only recently landed back safely after a severe flutter incident which had nearly severed the rear fuselage behind the cockpit – a feat for which he was awarded the only George Medal ever granted to a test pilot – and it was not long before I persuaded him to allow me to join in the testing of these ominous-looking but potent new fighters, the Rolls-Royce Vulture-engined Tornado and its ultimately more successful development, the Napier Sabre-engined Typhoon.

Part of my argument for being allowed to fly them was a strong criticism that I made as a fighter pilot of the severely limited vision from the cockpit, due to very heavy windscreen and canopy frames, and to no rearward transparancies at all: I said that unless these aeroplanes had some other remarkable qualities they would be useless as air-combat fighters and that, in any case, drastic improvement in vision would be essential.

Lucas seemed impressed with this outburst from a 22 year-old Flight Lieutenant and said, 'Well you'd better fly it and tell us what you think!'

My first Typhoon flight took place from Langley in March 1942, and, like all Typhoon flights, it was impressive from the word go! Bill Humble, the senior experimental test pilot, had briefed me on the very strong swing on take-off that had to be corrected by setting full rudder trim bias in the opposite direction to the swing – but somehow I got it wrong and this roaring monster swung away at least 45° to the right during take-off and headed straight for the factory buildings! With no available alternative I just managed to pull it up and over the roof-tops and then, in clear air, reached down and re-set the rudder trimmer in the opposite direction, which brought the situation back under control!

From then on the Typhoon was tremendously impressive. At full throttle it showed more than 400 mph on the ASI at low level, and at 500 mph reached in only a shallow dive, it was still adequately controllable and stable, although extremely raucous. At more modest speeds it was very pleasantly manoeuvrable, and in particular it showed exceptionally steady gun-aiming qualities in simulated attacks on ground-targets.

Testing these prototypes as often as I could during the next few months I became convinced that, while their poor high-altitude performance and the appalling vision properties would make them quite unsuitable to replace Hurricanes and Spitfires in the air-fighting role, the Typhoons could be of great value at low level as interceptors and ground attack fighters and I made recommendations to this effect.

This led to my posting to command No 609 (WR) Squadron with the new Typhoons at Manston with a brief from the AOC of 11 Group Fighter Command, 'Dingbat' Saunders, to try out the Typhoons in action in any way we thought practical, subject to HQ approval of course!

In wide-ranging operations in 1942–3, 609 proved the Typhoons to be exceptional ground attack aircraft on targets such as trains, military vehicles, barges, airfields, coastal shipping and light naval vessels; as a result the Typhoon was reprieved and ultimately formed the major part of the brilliantly successful ground attack/close support element of the RAF's 2nd Tactical Air Force for the D-Day invasion and the battles for Europe in 1944. One of 609 Squadron's successful actions is impressively captured in Robert Taylor's painting Typhoon Attack.

As a direct result of the Typhoon trials, Hawkers were able to incorporate significant improvements in a Typhoon 2 development, later named Tempest, and in late 1943 I was posted back to the factory to test this new version with the thinner wing, more fuel, improved 'spring-tab' ailerons for high-rolling power at the increased dive speed of 545 mph and, most impressively, a completely redesigned windscreen and all-round 'rear vision' canopy. This proved to be the finest general-purpose fighter for the low-altitude war of 1944, and, after an exciting five months of testing the Tempest at the Langley factory, I was again privileged to take this new fighter into action for the first time, in No 150 Wing at Newchurch from May 1944 onwards.

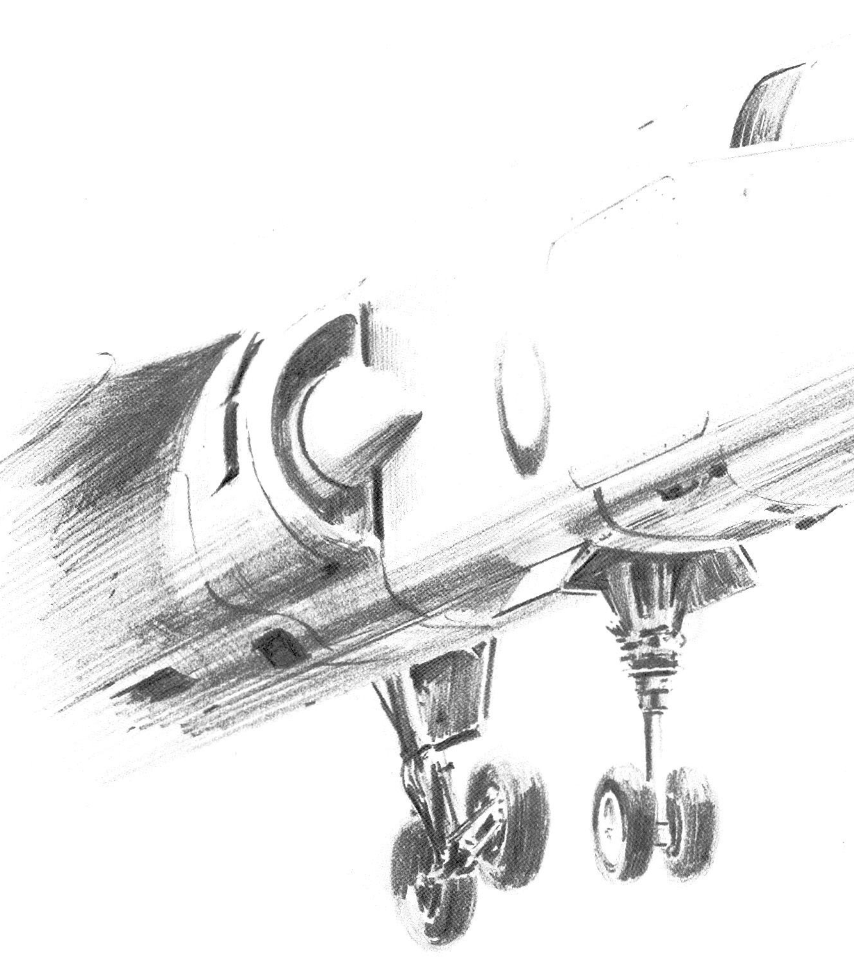

TSR2 . XR219 . lifts off from Warton 64

We scored the Tempests' first ground-attack successes in the softening-up period prior to D-Day in June and shot down the first enemy aircraft by Tempests, some Me 109 G6s, over Rouen two days after D-Day.

In June–August the Tempest Wing at Newchurch shot down no less than 632 V1 flying bombs that were on their way to London, and went on to major successes in the air-superiority and ground-attack roles through Belgium, Holland and Germany until finally flying in to Copenhagen Kastrup to accept the surrender of the enemy forces there in May 1945.

This experience of the practical development of strike-fighters was to prove invaluable post-war when I was responsible for the testing and development of some of the early transonic jets and the Canberra jet bomber; then the first British supersonic fighters, the P1 and Lightning and, later, the TSR2 supersonic strike and reconnaissance bomber. But the test-flying of these aircraft was quite another story.

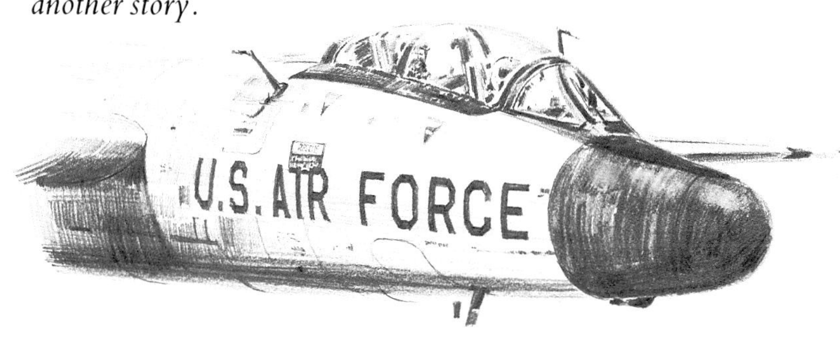

B-57 American variant of the English Electric Canberra.

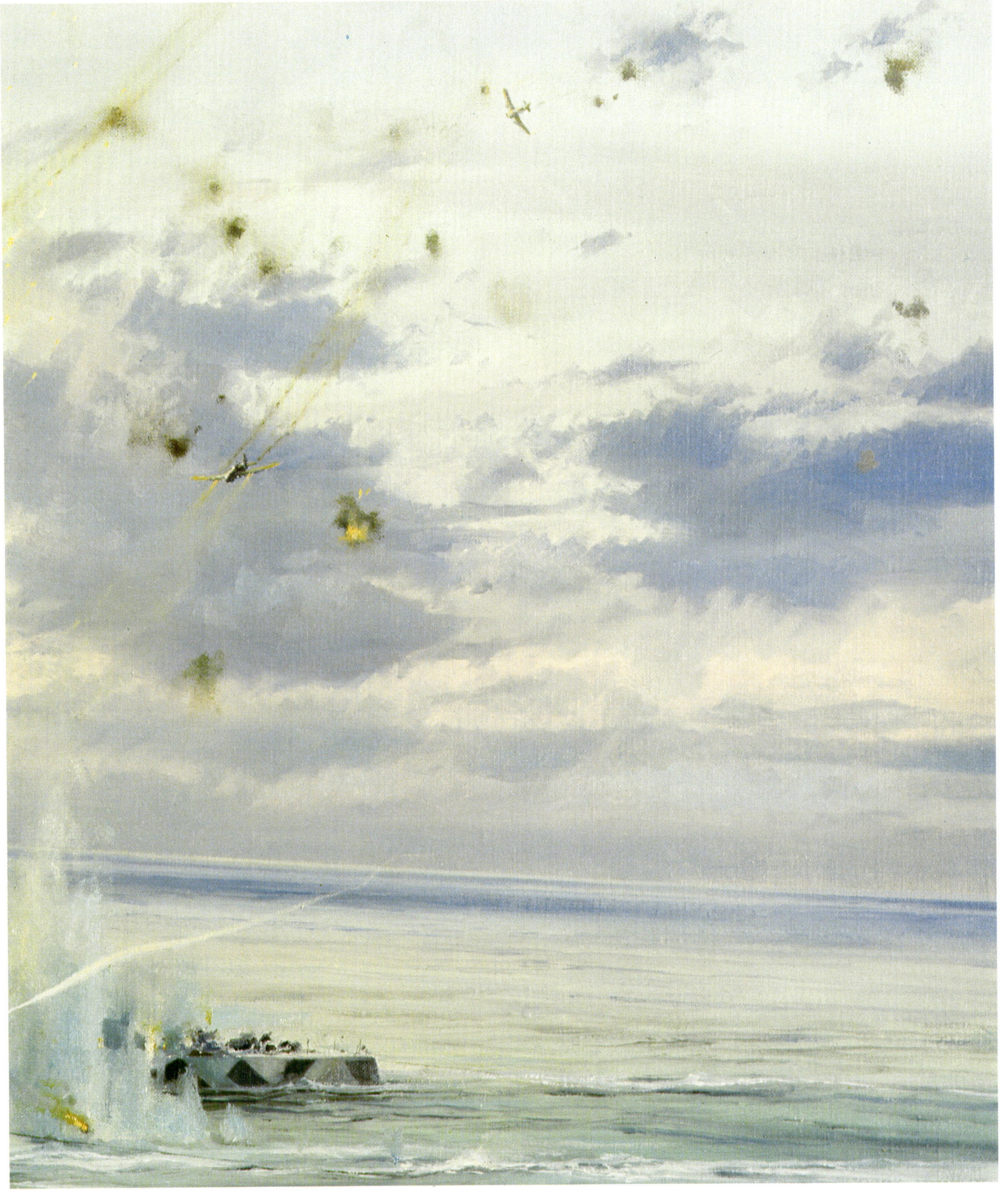

This detail from *Typhoon Attack* illustrates quite well a couple of aspects of my work which are very important. The first concerns research and the value of being able to talk to eye-witnesses, in this case pilots, who took part in the action being depicted. The second is the careful planning of background and the value this can have in a painting. After research is completed and painting begins, important points often come to light which initially had not been evident or in some cases had been completely overlooked.

I talked with 'Bee' Beamont on a number of occasions both before and during the work on this picture. During these discussions several things came to light: Bee had led his Typhoons into the attack depicted and the painting showed three more Typhoons coming in – two of them with their cannons blazing. Bee explained that these cannons always left a trail of quite dense smoke behind the aircraft, and I had overlooked this until he pointed it out. A further point of interest was the wide V-shaped wake caused by the mine cable-cutting hawsers which trailed out behind the ships, though only just visibly. Thanks to the sharp technical memory and the eagle eye of the Wing Commander, these points were included in the picture.

The two features of the backgrounds of my paintings which are important to me relate to their construction and colour. Careful construction of the background (in this case the sky and sea) can help considerably with the overall effect of the painting. The clouds behind the incoming Typhoons are constructed to help give the aircraft a certain 'height' and they run away to the horizon in an endeavour to give the picture as much 'distance' as possible.

The colours not only denote the time of day but help to create the atmosphere. This particular attack took place in the evening which gave plenty of scope for contrasting the hectic action with a peaceful sea and sky, painted in gentle colours.

Where it is practical I often set myself a little test when a painting is approaching completion : I find a way of obscuring the main subjects (aircraft or ships) from the painting, and, looking at what's left, I ask myself 'Have I painted a nicely-proportioned and balanced picture?'

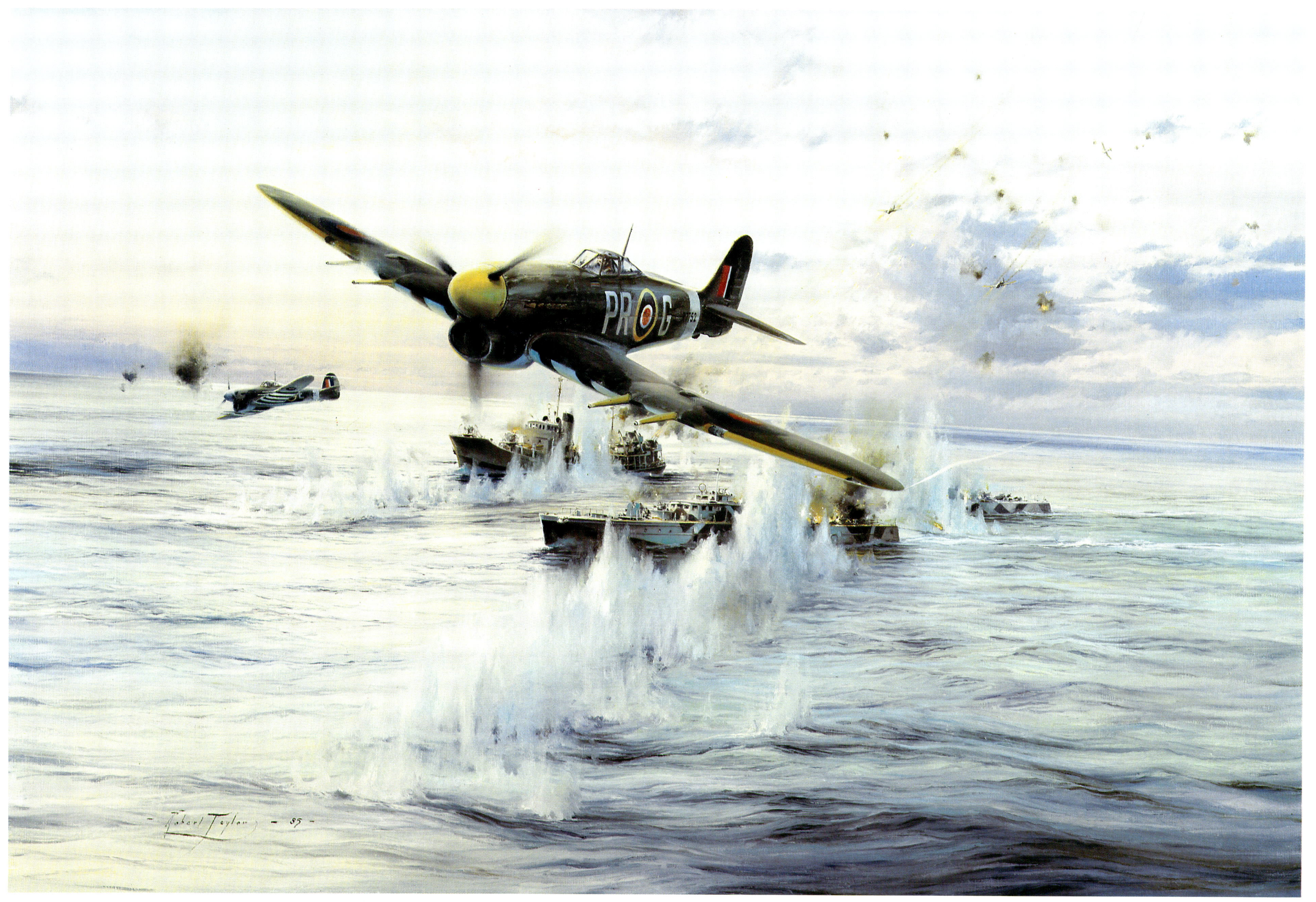

TYPHOON ATTACK
In the collection of Mr J Tait

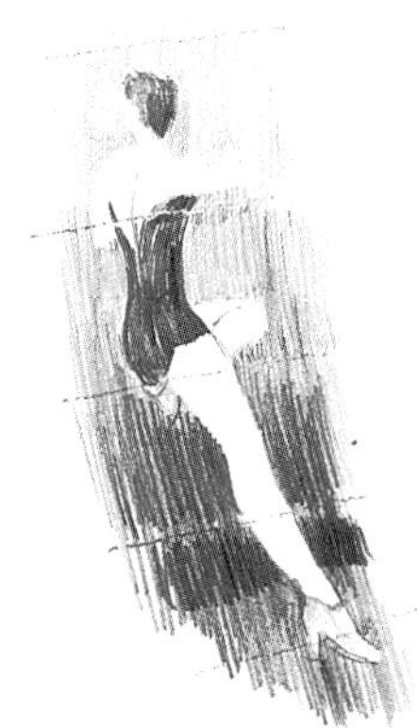

THE MEMPHIS BELLE

There have been some stirring films made in Hollywood featuring the famous B-17 Flying Fortress, but none was more dramatic than the one made about the *Memphis Belle*. All the footage was shot 'live'. Cameras were taken on a raid over Germany and these produced some of the best combat footage in colour ever seen. The film primarily features the 'Belle' but includes many dramatic shots of other B-17s and crews of the American 8th Air Force in action.

The Captain and pilot of the *Memphis Belle* on all twenty-five of her operational missions was Colonel Robert Morgan and I had the opportunity to meet him when he came to England in 1980. To see him one moment on my video screen, flying the Memphis Belle through a barrage of flak almost forty years previously and talk to him in person the next, was an unusual experience indeed.

Bob's features had not changed a great deal with the passing years. He has a cool, relaxed manner and cheerful personality and it was not difficult for me to imagine him holding a steady course whilst confusion reigned around him in the air.

After her operational contribution to the war effort, the *Memphis Belle* returned to the USA, where she toured as part of a recruiting exercise. Like most of the wartime aircraft she languished unwanted for forty years but, happily, is today in the process of restoration.

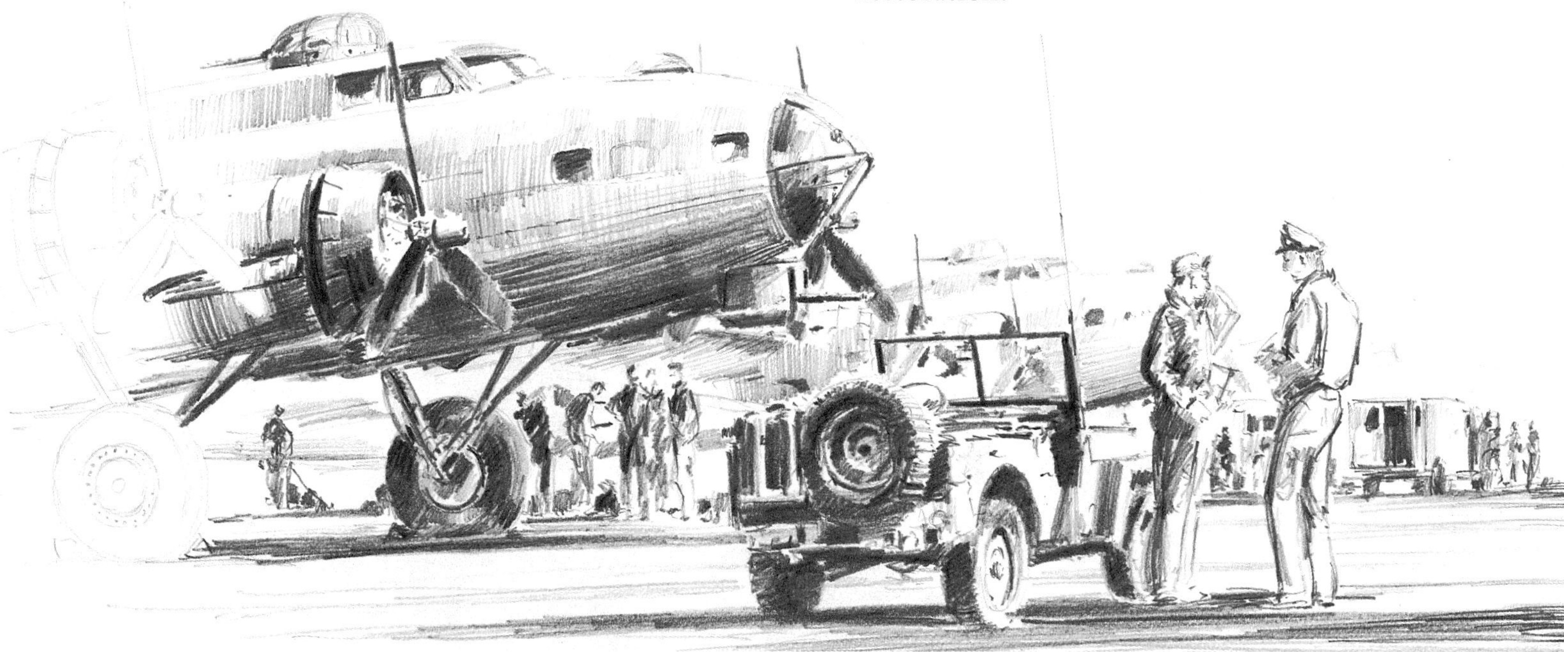

THE EIGHTH AMERICAN AIR FORCE

The entry of the American Forces into World War II came as an enormous boost to the Allies' morale. Though Bomber Command's campaign to break the German's war industry was achieving significant success, the consequent losses were horrifying. To match the RAF's enormous upsurge in night-bombing raids, the Luftwaffe had reinforced its night-fighter arm which resulted in a protracted struggle to achieve superiority in technological development, both sides suffering heavy losses.

The American Air Force had different ideas and maintained that daylight bombing raids against essential small targets would be more effective in curtailing the war. They went into action in tightly-packed 'boxes' of B-17 and B-24 bombers, all carrying substantial armour and loaded with heavy machine guns for self-defence.

German day-fighter production was stepped up at the expense of the night-fighter arm. American bombers, not expecting such a concentrated defensive force, were shot down in great numbers in the head-on attacks mounted by the Luftwaffe. At this time it was decided that fighter escorts should accompany the bomber forces. With the introduction of the new long-range fighter, the P-51 Mustang, deep-penetration daylight raids became a realistic proposition once again and in 'Big Week' the Eighth AAF flew no less than 3,800 sorties against 26 German aircraft factories, causing a serious undermining of their production capacity.

For the rest of World War II the USAAF continued to make a critical contribution to the further weakening of Germany's defensive forces until eventually they were broken completely and peace was restored.

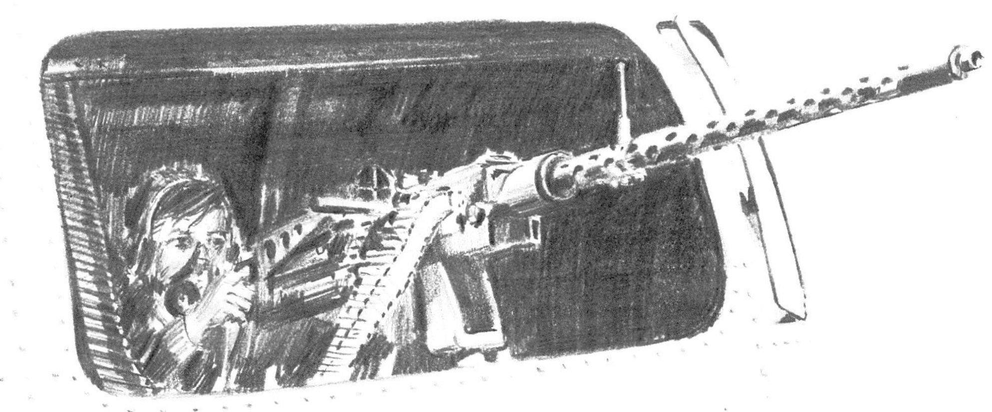

Starboard waist gunner B17

The B-17 was designed to fly in large formations, without fighter escort, defending itself by its own firepower, combined with that of the rest of the formation. Whilst to some extent the principle worked, a great number of aircraft were lost to the enemy fighters. The B-17 literally bristled with guns, and whilst preparing for the painting I drew many sketches relating to the aircraft's armament. Above is the waist-gun position. Though in some later models of the B-17 this gun position became enclosed, in the earlier models such as the *Memphis Belle*, the waist-gun position was open to the elements – not very comfortable at the sub-zero temperatures of 25,000 feet with an FW190 bearing down on you!

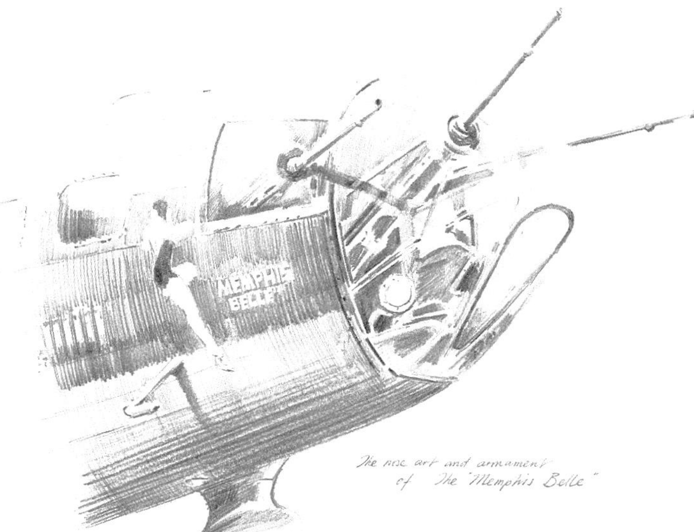

The nose art and armament of "The Memphis Belle"

The American Aircrews had a flamboyant and cavalier approach to their dangerous lifestyle. Whilst lacking nothing in professionalism, their fun-loving personalities were apparent in many ways. One such was the 'personalisation' of their aircraft. Each one was 'christened' with a name and sported a graphic interpretation somewhere on the nose of the aircraft. In the case of Robert Morgan's B-17 the *Memphis Belle* in question was a certain lady who was later to become Mrs Morgan. The lady was sketched from photographs of the aircraft, I hasten to add!

The drawing below carries my notes relating to some of the important features of the B-17, which was the most heavily-armed bomber of the war. The B-17 was designed as a high-altitude heavy bomber which could carry up to 17,500 lb of lifted weight, and cruise at 165 mph. Its maximum speed at 25,000 feet was 300 mph. In fact it could climb to 35,000 feet which for an aircraft of its type in those days was quite remarkable. Armament consisted of thirteen ·5 inch Browning machine guns. These were located in the cheek and chin (also see drawing at left), ventral, dorsal and waist positions (see drawing at top), and of course in the tail. The ventral turret could be jettisoned in case of an emergency belly landing. The B-17 had a crew of ten which included both a pilot and co-pilot – unlike the British bombers, none of which had a second pilot on board.

The drawing was made when I was trying to decide the angle at which to portray the B-17s in the painting. After deciding to view the formation from the front, the drawing was 'relegated', and I started writing working notes all over it!

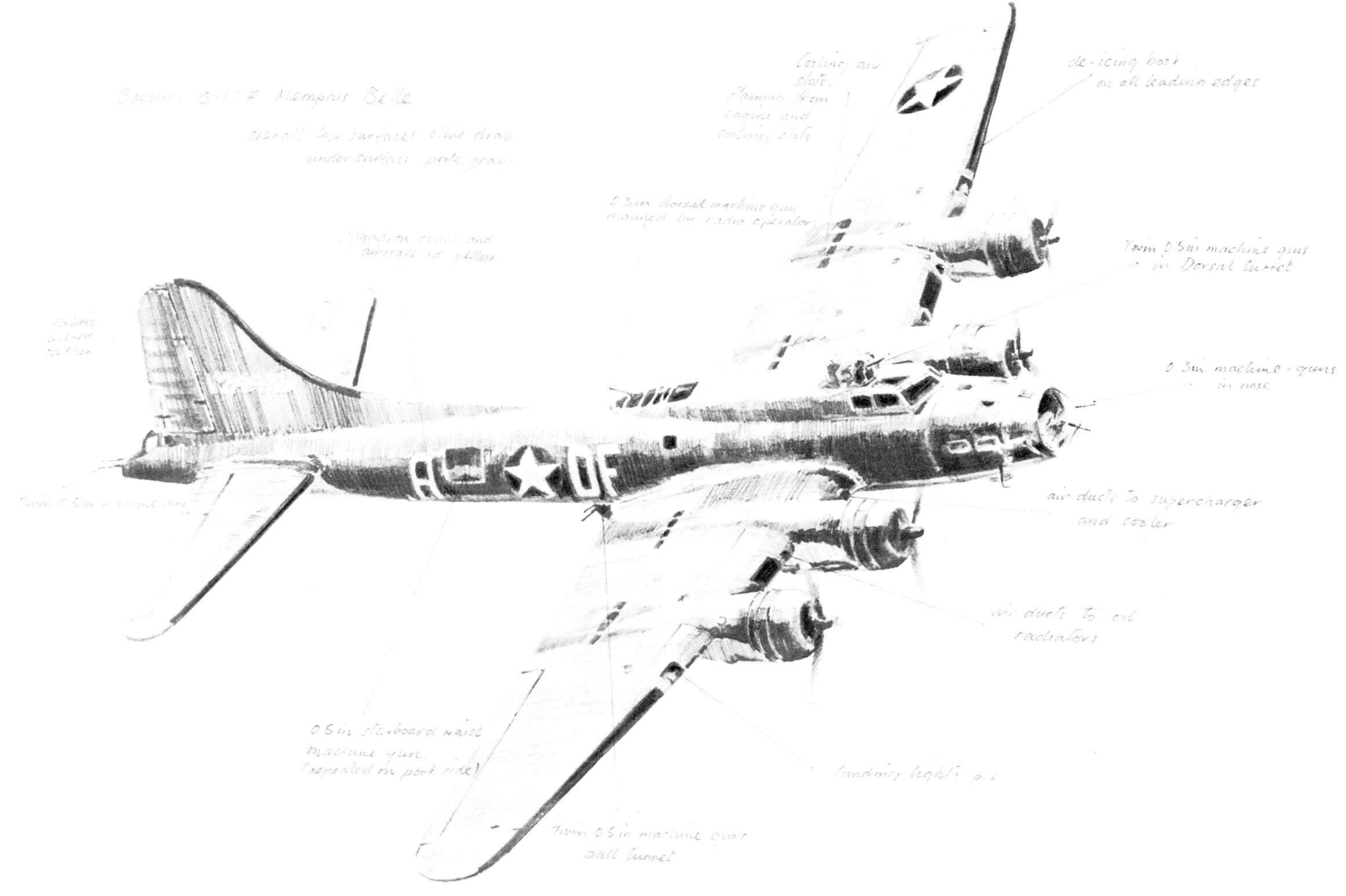

Flying the tortuous daylight raids, the B-17s flew in carefully-constructed 'boxes' so as to maximise their fire-power and therefore defence. The painting shows a group of B-17's on the outer 'box' of a large formation, at about 25,000 feet. The *Memphis Belle* is in the foreground, just ahead of the aircraft on the very outside of the formation, on the starboard side. I had thought of depicting a combat scene, with flak and attacking FW190's or Me109's, but eventually decided to make the picture a study of the aircraft.

Below is a detail from the painting showing a close-up of the *Belle*.

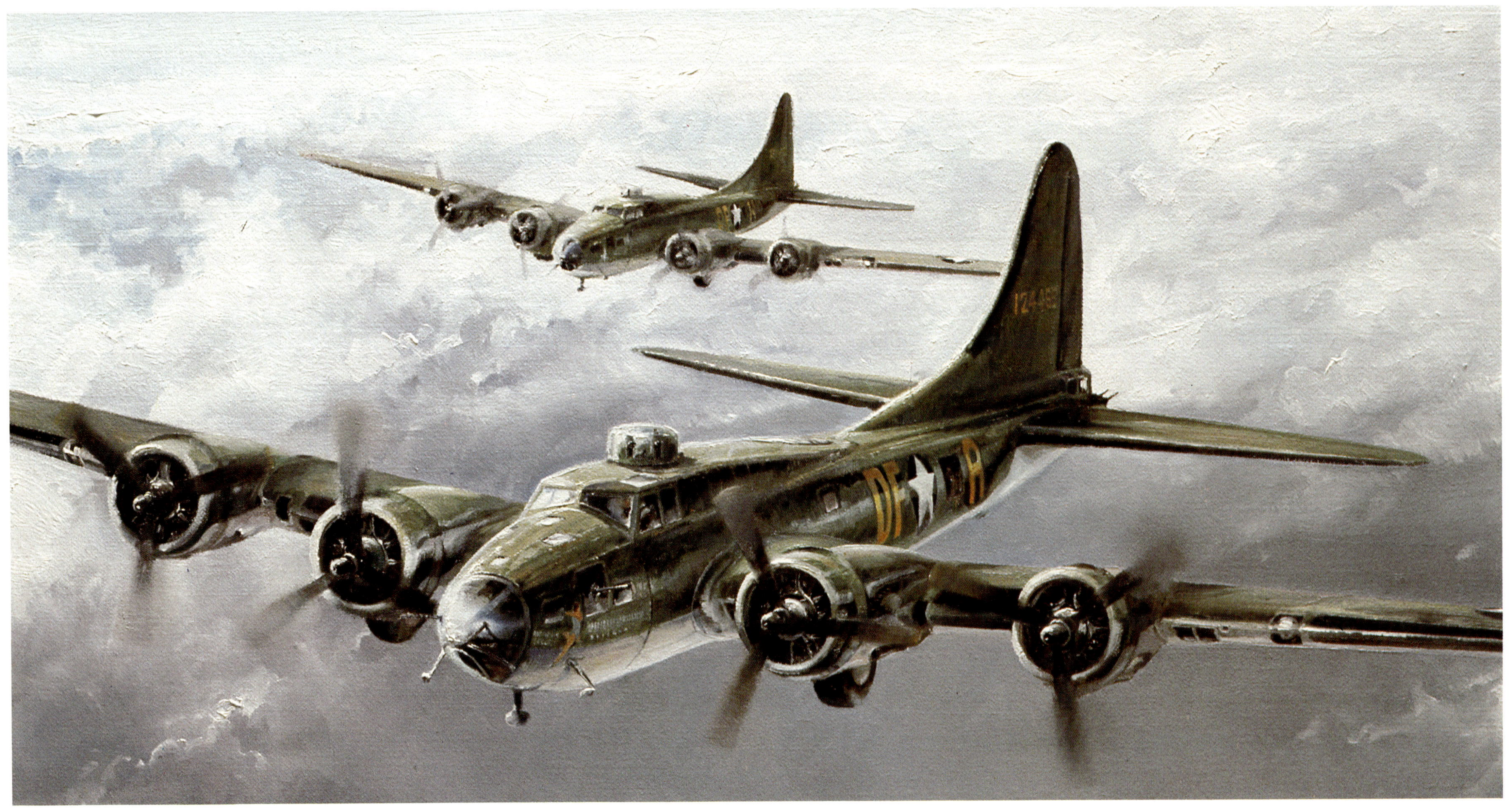

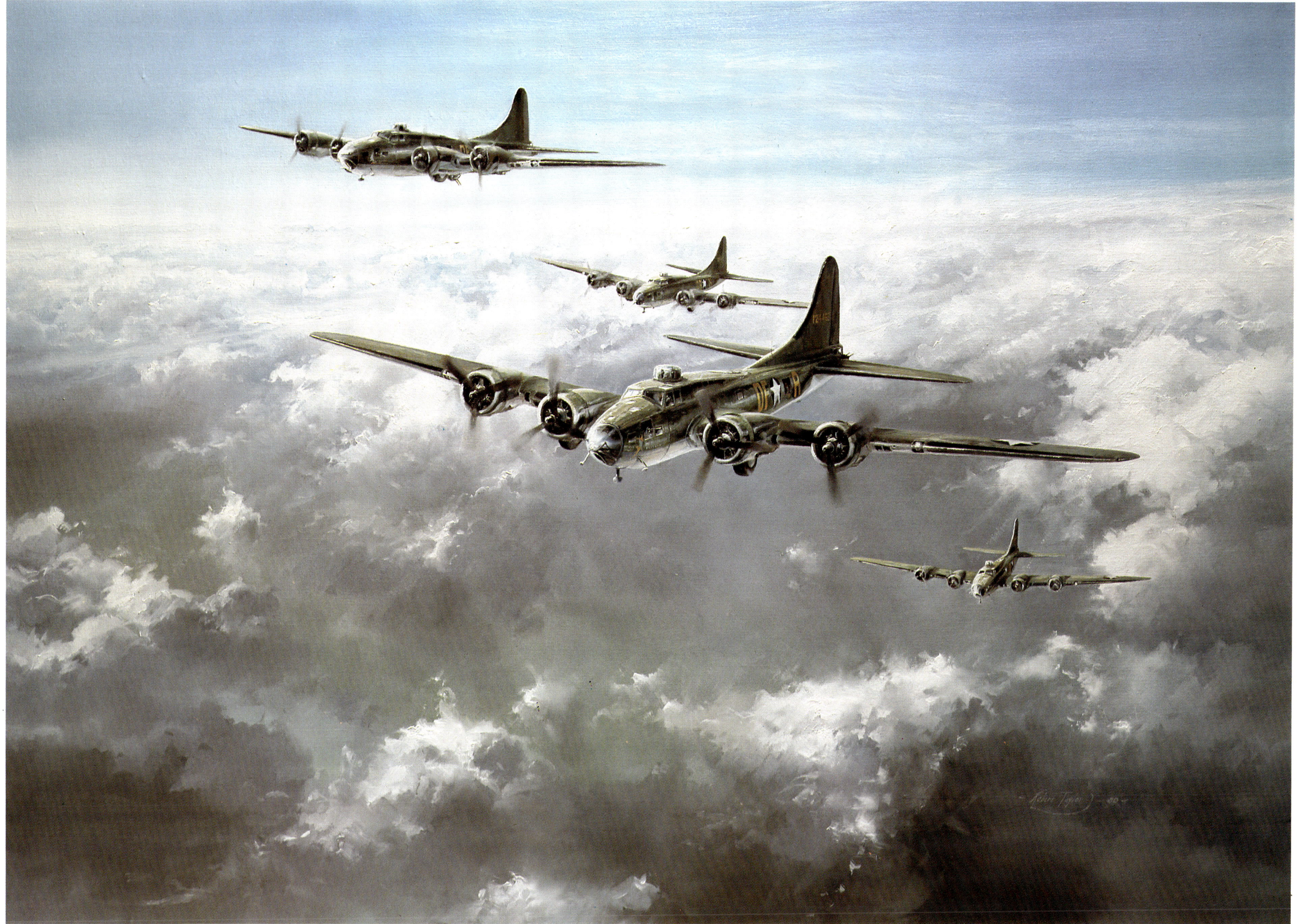

MEMPHIS BELLE
In the collection of Mr and Mrs James Verinis

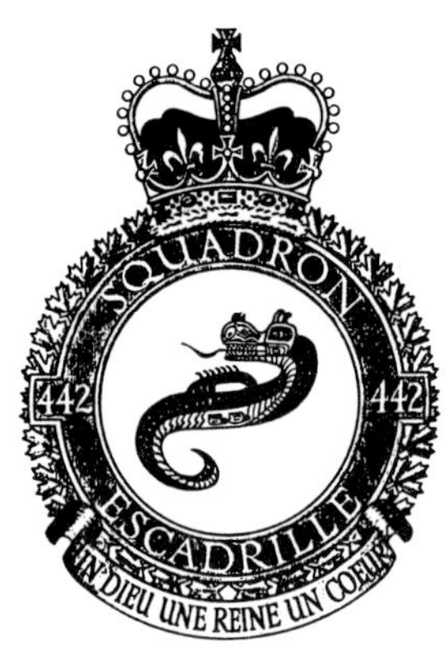

CANADIAN WING

Johnnie Johnson flew Spitfires virtually throughout the war. Johnnie was one of Douglas Bader's proteges, quickly making a name for himself as an aggressive fighter pilot and subsequently a dynamic Wing Leader.

His first command at that rank was at Kenley: Numbers 403 and 416 Squadrons, consisting of some seventy Canadian Pilots, equipped with the new Spitfire 9's. By September 1943 Johnnie Johnson had been flying operationally for over three years. He had led his Kenley Canadian Wing on 120 operations with great distinction and was due for a rest. After a short break he was back in action early in the New Year, this time at Digby, leading the new 144 Wing's Spitfire squadrons – again Canadian pilots. At the time of the Allied invasion of Normandy on June 6th that year, Johnnie Johnson had welded his new wing into a formidable fighting force.

On this historic day Johnnie recalls that flying conditions were 'reasonable' – better than had been forecast – with a cloudbase of around 2000 feet and visibility of five to six miles. Four times that day they made their way across the Channel to fly patrol over their designated area of the beaches, but during the entire day did not encounter a single aircraft. It was indicative of the fighting spirit of these Canadian pilots that, at the end of the day,.tired and drained, they were all bitterly disappointed with the Luftwaffe's failure to appear.

Within two days their Spitfires were on French soil, and before the month was out they were meeting and fighting the Luftwaffe every day over the Normandy countryside.

When first asked to paint Johnnie Johnson's Canadian Wing over the Normandy beaches on D-Day I was disappointed that I could not for the sake of accuracy portray a combat scene – an action scene somehow seemed more appropriate for that particular day in our history. However, having read Johnnie Johnson's account of his activity that day in his excellent book *Wing Leader*, and after talking to him about the day's events, those leading up to it, and those that followed, I began to think how significant were those patrols, flown by Johnnie's Canadians and all the other Allied pilots that day. If they had not controlled the skies on June the 6th what carnage might the Luftwaffe have dealt out to the landing forces below during those first vulnerable hours? The drawing opposite, which includes the Wing Leader's own personal graphics, (see top right!) was my final composition. In the painting I attempted to convey a feeling of dominance of the air which prevailed as the Spitfires protected their sector of the beaches, being fought for so doggedly below.

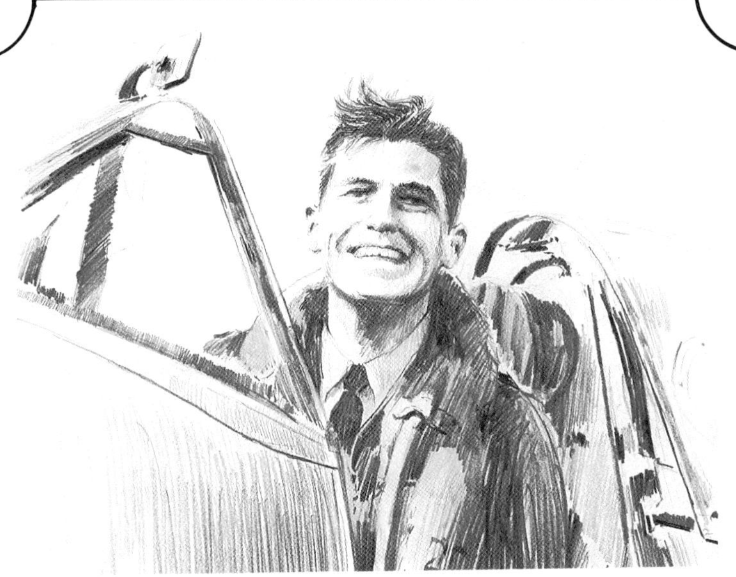

Air Vice Marshal
JOHNNIE JOHNSON, CB, CBE, DSO, DFC

Johnnie Johnson joined the R.A.F. Volunteer Reserve when it was expanded. After initial training he was posted to 616 Squadron at Kenley, however, the squadron was quickly moved to Coltishall after the loss of six pilots killed and five wounded. His eagerness to prove himself was soon satisfied, when another move occurred: Johnnie always describes his time at Tangmere as "the most exciting time in my air fighting career". Under Douglas Bader, he learned every aspect of the intricate art of the fighter pilot.

In the summer of 1942, having achieved great personal success, he was given his first command with 610 (County of Chester) Squadron. Less than a year later, with eight aerial victories to his credit, he was promoted Wing Commander and led his first Canadian Spitfire Wing at Kenley. During the following spring and summer he led his aggressive team on 140 missions over North-West Europe and together they shot down over 100 enemy aircraft.

In March 1944, after a short rest, was posted to lead another Canadian Spitfire Wing – 144 – and they flew four missions over the beaches on D-Day. The following weeks saw him and his Canadians begin their "exhilarating, buccaneering trek across France" as they moved further inland.

Johnnie Johnson ended the war as Group Captain commanding 125 Wing, and with 38 aerial victories, the highest scoring fighter pilot of the Allied air forces.

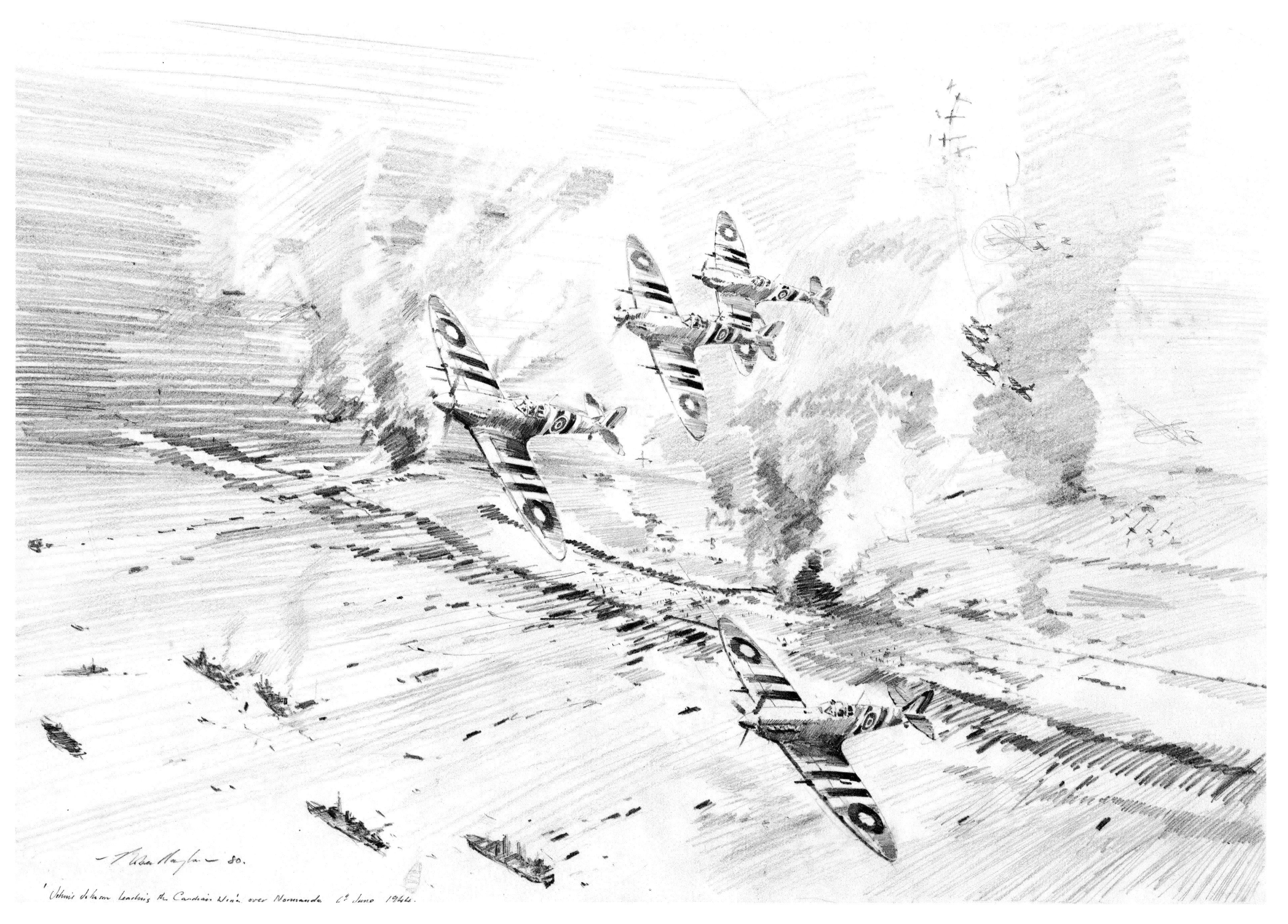
'Johnnie Johnson Leading the Canadian Wing over Normandy 6th June 1944.

I have talked elsewhere about the difficulties of portraying aircraft in close combat. Below are two sketches I made for a painting depicting one of Johnnie Johnson's air victories over Northern France on an entirely separate sortie which occured sometime after D-Day. The lower shows my first interpretation; the one above it was my final drawing. The various lines show the angles of deflection, and the handwriting are notes added to my drawing by Johnnie. At top left is a detail from the finished painting entitled *Ramrod 692*.

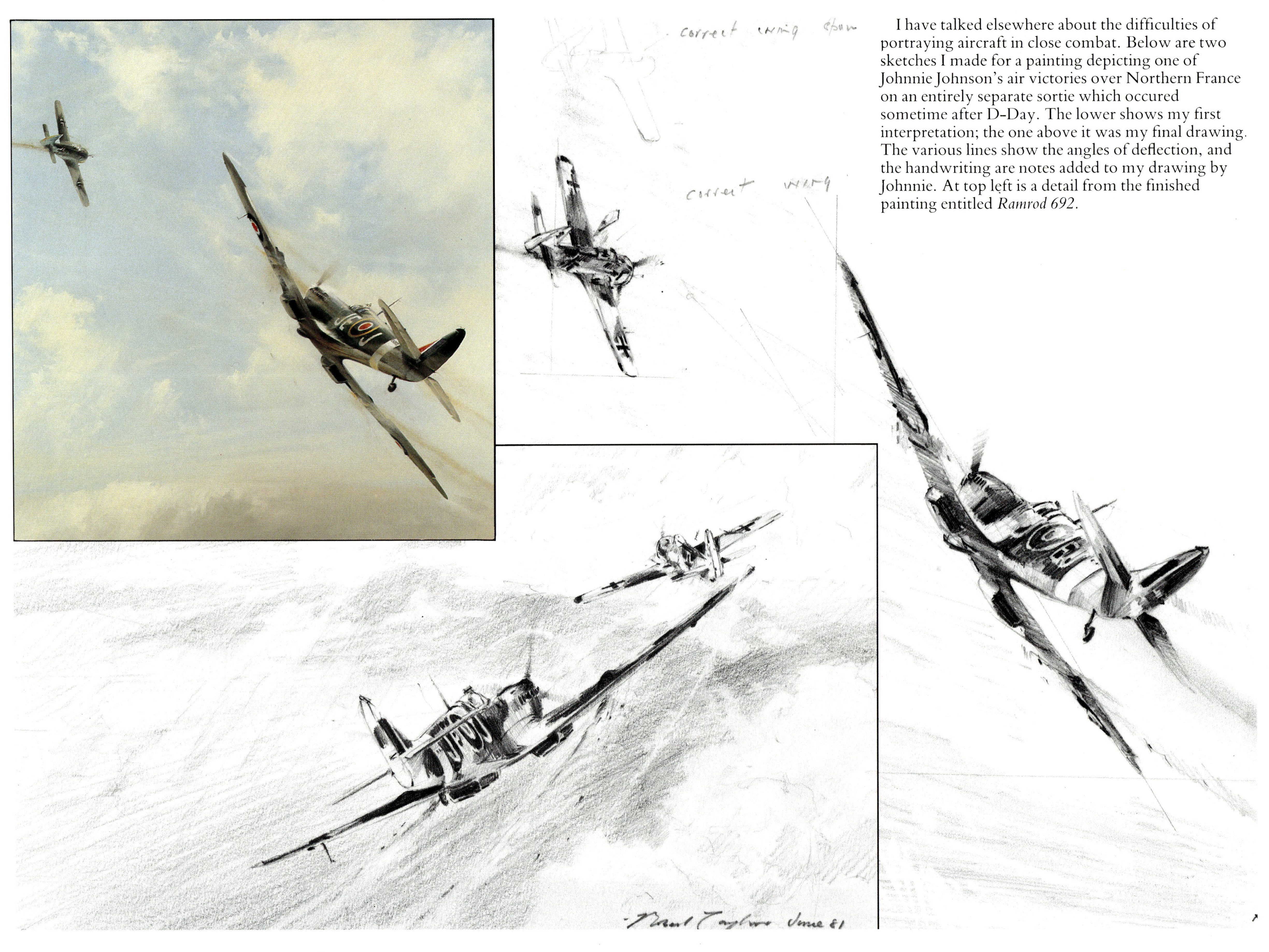

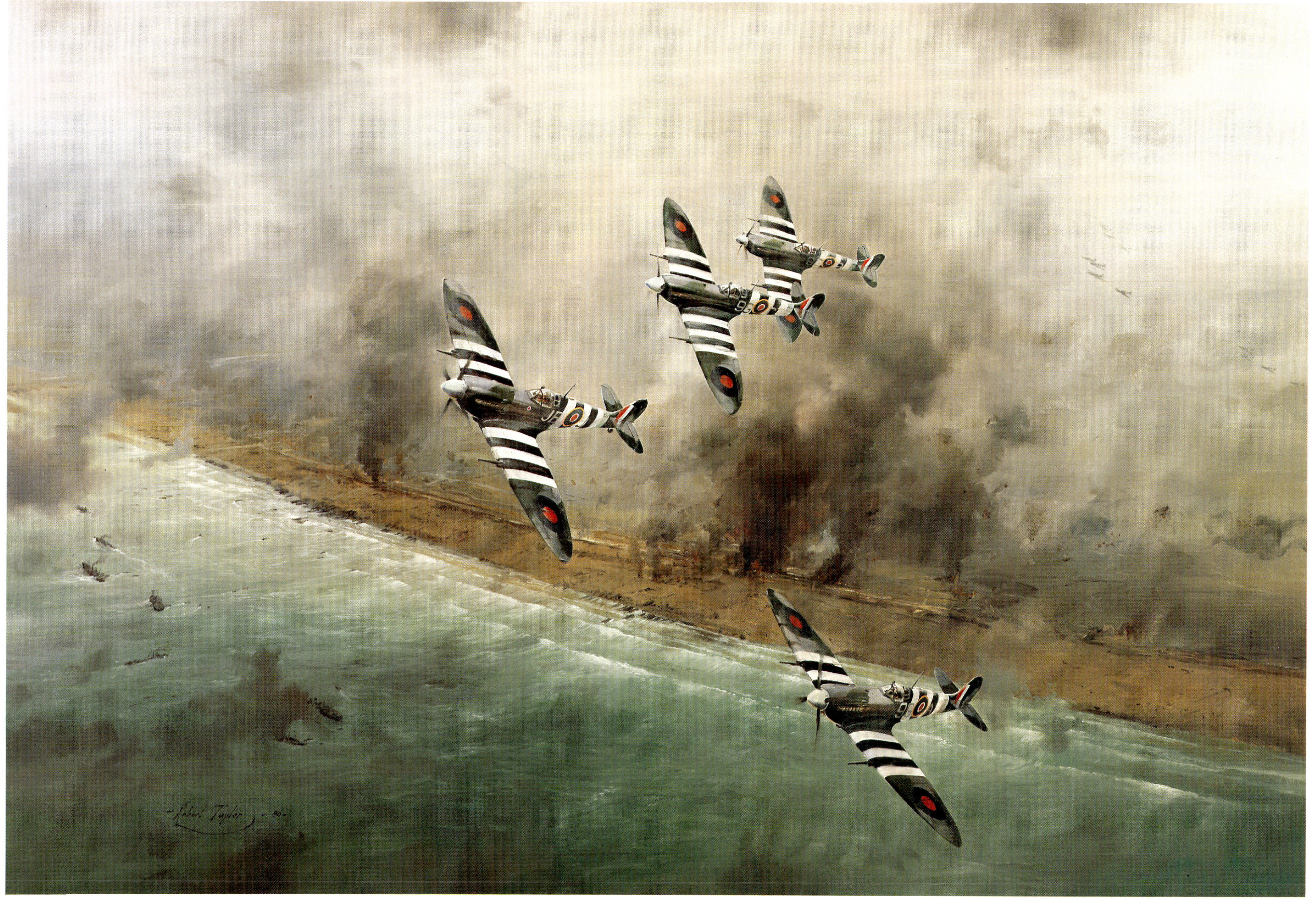

CANADIAN WING
In the collection of Mr Tom Greenham

BEKAA VALLEY GUNFIGHT

The General Dynamics F-16 Fighting Falcon must surely be one of the most beautiful-looking modern jets ever built. It has wonderful aerodynamic lines, and if ever the old pilot's adage 'If it looks good it flies good' was applicable to a modern jet fighter, it would surely apply to the F-16. With a top speed of 1,300 mph and outstanding manoeuvrability in the air, it is undoubtedly a modern fighter pilot's dream airplane.

Air Vice-Marshal Johnnie Johnson had asked me to do some drawings for his book, *The Story of Air Fighting*. These required me to portray some modern jets to illustrate chapters on more recent air combats, including those of the Middle Eastern Wars. Although those I drew for Johnnie's book were done in pen and ink, I had sketched in pencil most of the aircraft which had taken part in the Israeli–Syrian air battles. Whilst working on these drawings I had access to much information regarding a number of particular air combats fought over the Bekaa Valley, including some excellent gun camera film. One such combat took place on 9 June 1981: a strike force of sixty Falcons, Eagles and Kfirs launched an attack on the Syrian SA-6 missile launch sites in the Bekaa Valley. Alerted to the attack, the Syrians put up sixty Russian-built MiG 21s to defend the SAM sites. By the end of the day the Israeli jets had brought down almost half of the Syrian jets and destroyed sixty missile launchers – almost all the SAMs sited in the valley. In the air battles that ensued over the valley during this and the following two days, the Israeli jets brought down over eighty Syrian aircraft, without loss to their own force.

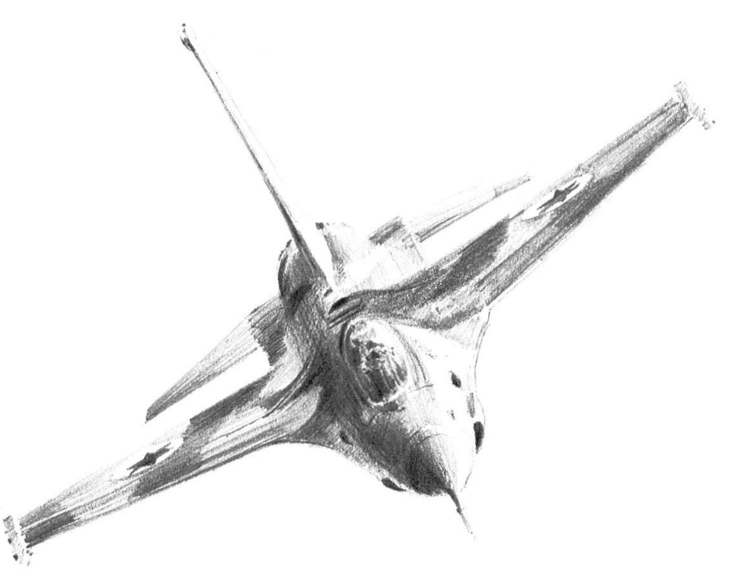

Bekaa Valley Gunfight depicts a combat between an F-16 Falcon and a MiG-21 (NATO code name – 'Fishbed'). The F-16, with its superior manoeuvrability, has turned inside the MiG and is firing his 20mm cannon directly into the Russian-built jet. The pencil sketch at right is a detail from the final drawing where it can be noted that the horizon is tilted by several degrees to help emphasise the rate at which both aircraft are turning.

When studying the various shapes of modern aircraft I often wonder why one can be so beautiful and another so ugly. I suppose it is largely due to performance requirements, and the results of wind-tunnel testing. It is said that computers design the shapes of aircraft today, but I am sure the F-16 was designed by an artist!

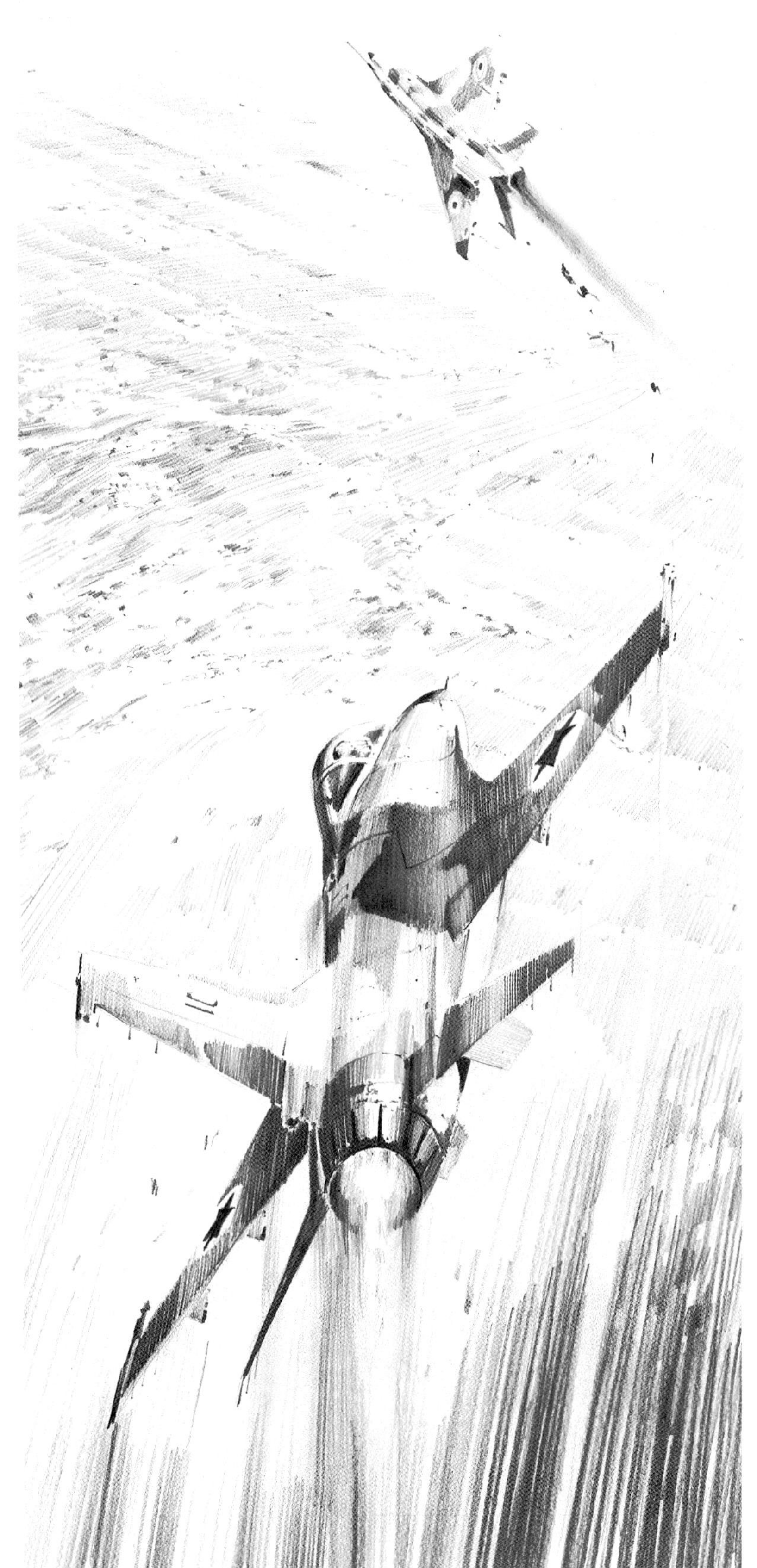

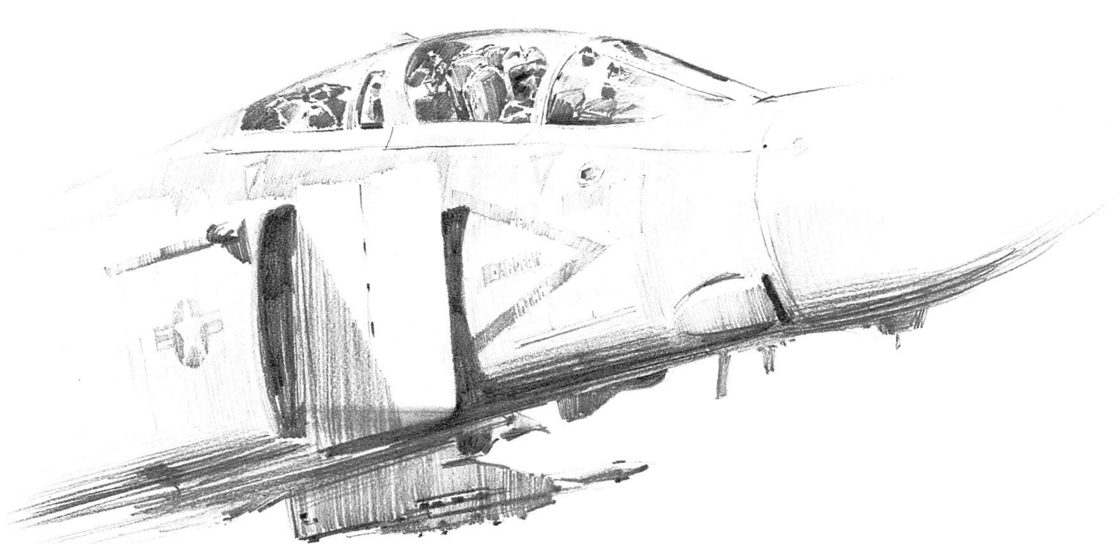

I am often asked which I prefer painting most: modern aircraft or the older types. The answer is both! I enjoy painting all types of aircraft, and am thankful that during the eighty years or so since the first powered flight there has been so much variety in design. This in itself presents an ever-changing challenge to the artist.

The older the aircraft, usually, the more difficult is the research. I have to admit, though, that I enjoy the work involved in research. Talking to the 'old timers', listening to their graphic accounts of epic flights and combats won and lost is often absorbing. Gathering information for painting modern aircraft is usually easier as one can simply go and look at them, climb into them, even, if one is lucky, get a flight in them. The aerodynamically efficient aircraft of today have graceful lines and far fewer appendages than the old airplanes and, painting these streamlined shapes, it is much easier to convey a feeling of speed.

In terms of difficulty, there is not much to choose between painting the new and the old. One needs considerable patience to paint, in accurate perspective, all the appendages on the earlier aircraft – sometimes four engines and four turrets on one fuselage, to say nothing of the number of propellers and guns pointing in all directions. On the other hand, the often subtle wing surface shapes of the modern aircraft can be very difficult to depict accurately. Concorde is a good example, having a very complex wing surface. I am currently researching for a painting of this incredibly beautiful supersonic airliner and will have to draw its undulating wing from every angle before I shall be ready to start painting.

There appears to be considerable interest in paintings of modern aircraft today. I am often commissioned by companies in the aeronautical and defence industries to portray aircraft which they either build, operate, or are otherwise concerned with in manufacture. Happily for the aviation artist, the portrait of the company chairman or president is being replaced more and more today by a painting of the company's product!

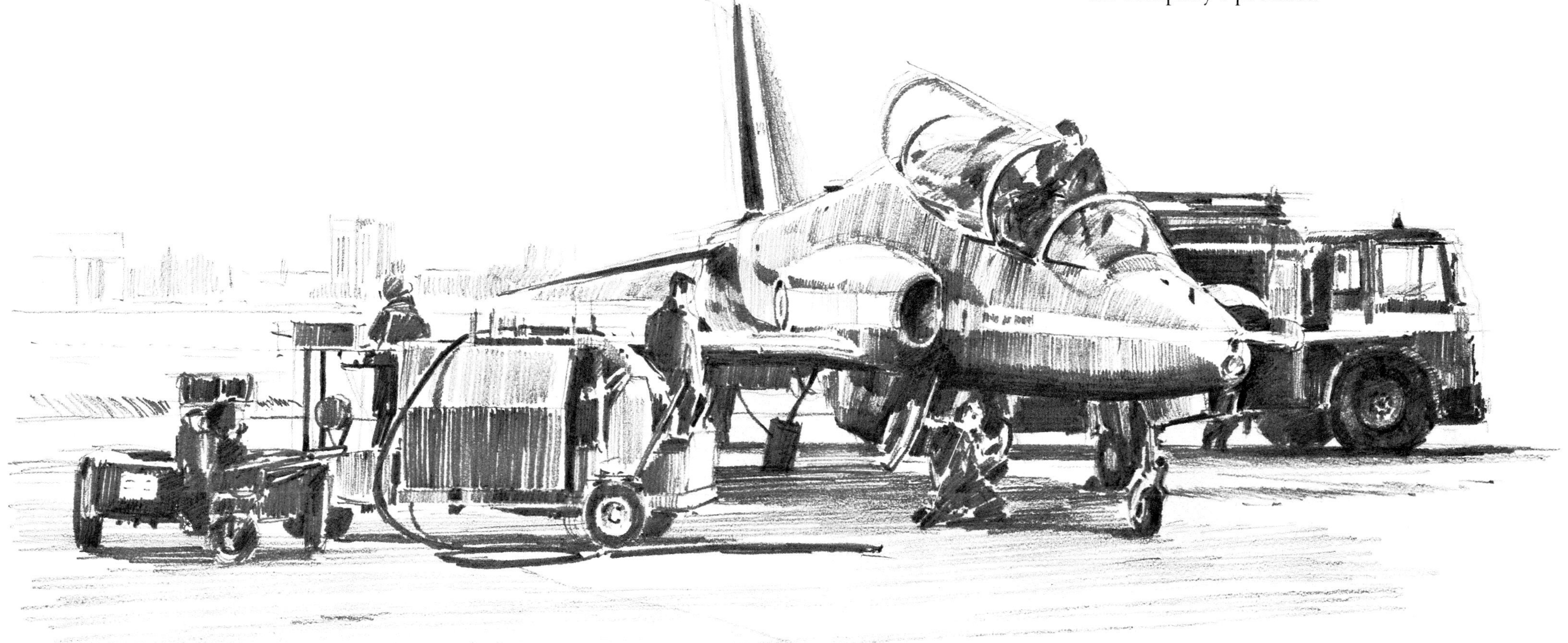

The painting below is an example of the type of work which I am regularly commissioned to paint by companies involved in the defence and aerospace industry. I enjoy these commissions and certainly learn a good deal about modern aircraft whilst painting them. Often the client is involved in manufacturing some highly technical but rather obscure system for the aircraft, vital to its performance but buried deep inside the airplane. In such cases it is not possible for me actually to show the parts in my painting, so it is important to portray the airplane in a role where the client's contribution to the aircraft is 'operational'. Such was the painting below where the client wished me to portray a pair of MkII Air Defence Tornados, in low-visibility grey livery. Both aircraft are carrying F4w Skyflash missiles.

The aircraft have wings swept, re-heat in, and are climbing out of some pretty murky weather. This emphasises the aircraft's interception role. For me the Tornado is a formidable-looking aircraft and, with its wings fully swept, has a degree of awe-inspiring beauty. Looking at the airplane from almost any angle in flight, it seems to be travelling at a vast speed!

TORNADO

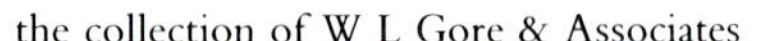
In the collection of W L Gore & Associates

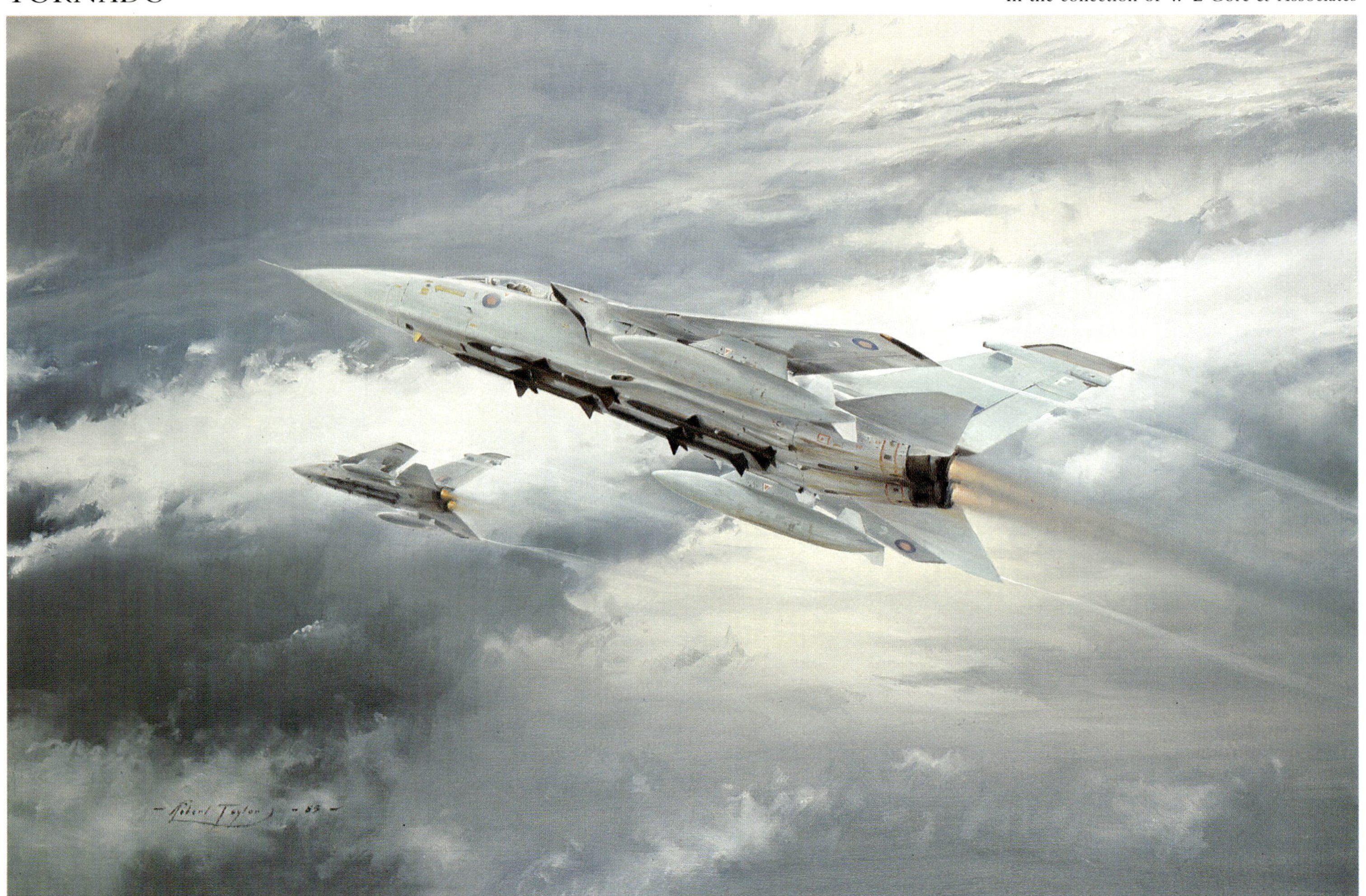

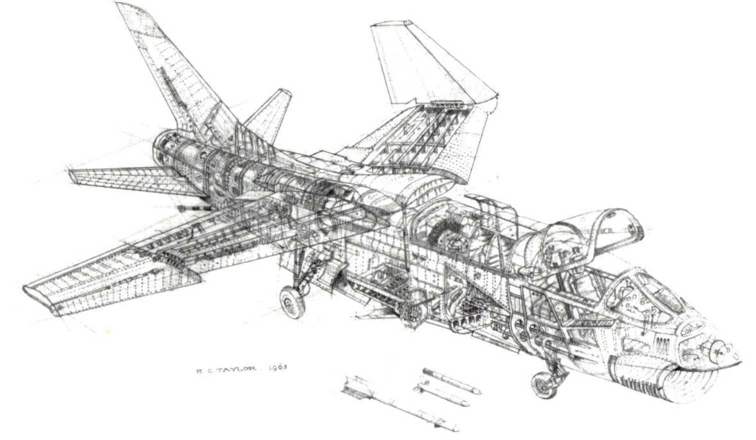

I made the above cut-away drawing when I was aged fifteen. Nowadays I rarely do any 'technical' drawing, though I find looking at the works of the top professional technical artists both interesting and useful. It is one thing to look at a modern 'variable-geometry' winged aircraft demonstrating this phenomenon in flight, but quite another to understand how all these wing movements actually work. Close inspection of a first-class technical drawing, such as those which appear in 'Flight' magazine, provides a useful insight into the workings of modern aircraft.

I have enjoyed making models since I was a small boy, and am fortunate to have been able to carry on with this hobby as part of my profession. I always make a large scale model of every aircraft I paint. Invariably this is placed on a simple wire plinth and displayed in a prominent position in my studio where it can be easily viewed as I paint. All models are made with great attention to detail, and usually painted in the colours, markings, and so on which are to be used for the painting.

Whilst I use photography a great deal as a means of recording and storing information, the use of models is far more important when it comes to the preparation of drawings. I enjoy sketching on location and, frankly, believe there is no substitute for it, but when preparing final drawings or actually painting in the studio I constantly check my model for accurate reference – and unlike those of a portrait painter, my models don't move!

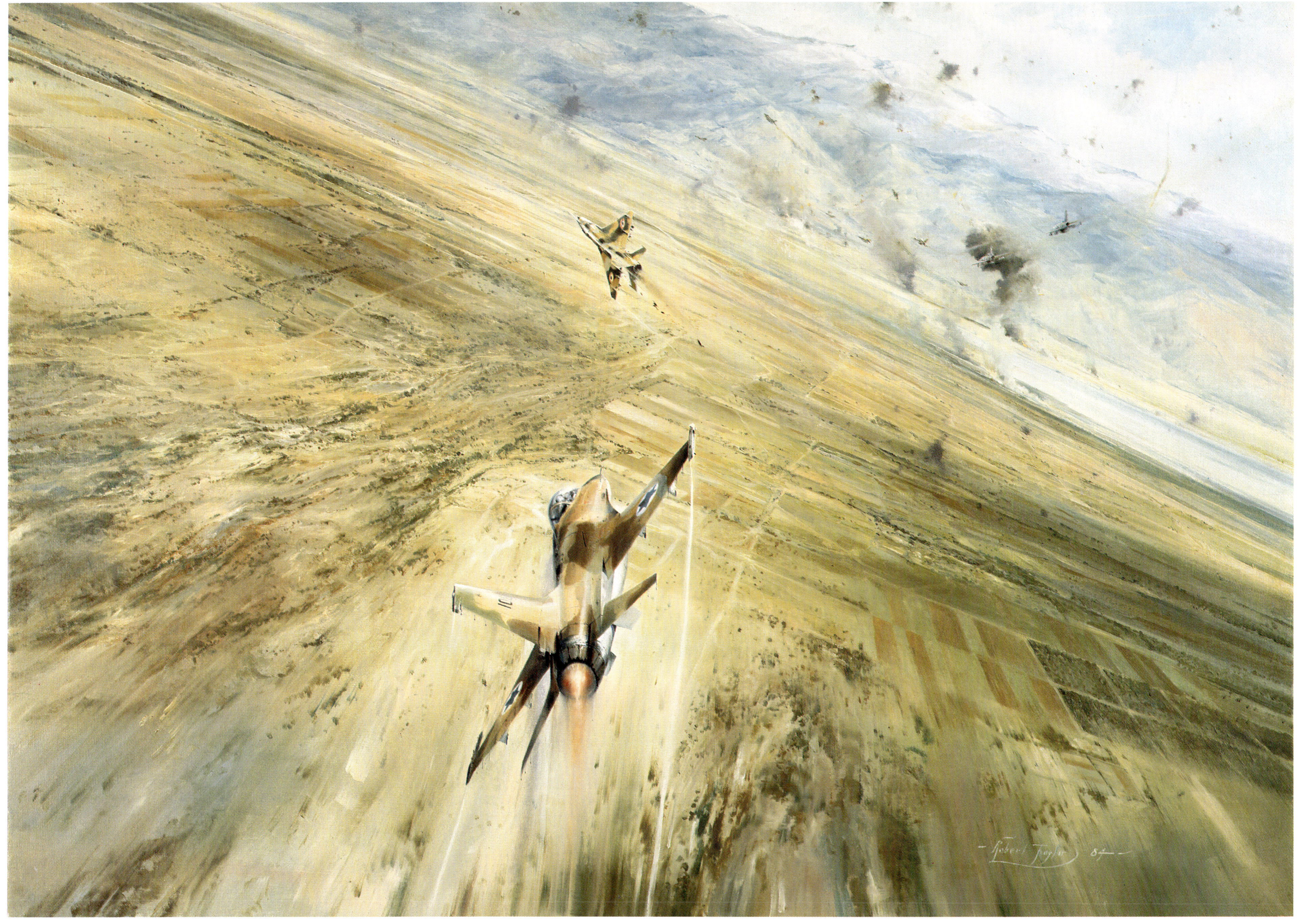

BEKAA VALLEY GUNFIGHT
In the collection of AVM Johnnie Johnson

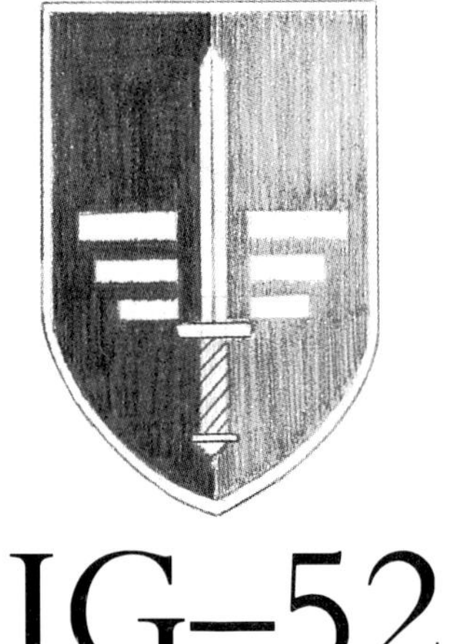

JG–52

Jagdgeschwader (Fighter Wing) 52

The Messerschmitt Me109 was a classic fighter aircraft. Its design made it a lovely airplane for an artist to work with and so I was eager to start when commissioned to paint *JG-52*.

Before work could commence on the canvas, however, a great deal of research was necessary. I knew that JG-52 had spawned some of the greatest Aces of the Luftwaffe but needed to know much more about this famous fighter wing. I was fortunate to obtain a wealth of information from General Walter Krupinski – JG-52's official historian, and himself one of the their leading Aces. The Jagdgeschwader or JG (Fighter Wing) consisted of three *Gruppen* (Groups). Each *Gruppe* had three *Staffelen* (Squadrons) and each *Staffel* had three *Schwarms*. A *Schwarm* consisted of four aircraft, and was in turn, divided into two *Rotten*. A *Rotte* of two aircraft formed the basic tactical element.

JG-52 was the most successful Fighter Wing of the Luftwaffe during World War II. Initially based in Germany, the Wing flew border patrols against the French, followed soon by becoming heavily involved in the offensive against Britain. Later moving to a base near Calais, the Wing took on the RAF Spitfires and Hurricanes in earnest during the battle for France and the Battle of Britain. During this intense period of airfighting the wing lost many pilots including its CO and two squadron commanders. In October, after the Battle of Britain was lost, it withdrew to rebuild after heavy losses of personnel and then transferred to Bucharest in Rumania. Its task here was the defence of oil refineries and after some months JG-52 was equipped with the Me 109e (having a new engine and rounded wing tips) and joined in the support of the attack on Crete. After the fall of Crete the Wing moved back to Rumania to continue flying missions against Russian bombers in defence of the oil installations. JG-52 then assumed the first fighter role in Southern Russia. It was on the Russian front that the Wing's greatest Aces notched up their substantial scores. Though conditions were often appalling, the pilots of JG-52 flew a tremendous number of missions. The Wing lost 678 of its pilots in achieving in the order of 10,000 aerial victories during the French campaign, the Battle of Britain, in Greece and on the Eastern Front. Sixy-seven pilots received the Knights Cross or higher decorations.

Armed with all this information, the detailed drawings were begun. The original idea had been to portray a *schwarm* of Me 109s in a diving attitude, attacking a group of British fighters below. I changed my mind and for a time worked on the idea of painting the four aircraft peeling off into the attack. The final concept involved going back a few moments earlier in the patrol, to the moment when the leader had just sighted the enemy below. The Me 109s are set against an evening scene so as to include cumulus cloud reflecting the hues of the warm-coloured light.

THE FIGHTER ACES OF THE LUFTWAFFE

Many of the fighter pilots of the Luftwaffe were men whose devotion to duty, courage and application were the equal of the greatest military heroes down the ages. Unlike their Allied counterparts they did not enjoy the benefits of 'tours of duty'. They flew without respite, while they were capable of doing so, throughout World War II. As one of the most successful of them, General Adolf Galland, so succinctly put it: 'Our fighter pilots fought until they were killed'.

The eventual downfall of the Luftwaffe airmen was due, in no small part, to over-commitment through a complete misunderstanding at the highest level of the extent of their superiority. Goering was convinced, and he, in turn, convinced Hitler, that they were invincible. The numbers of aerial victories scored by the aces of the Luftwaffe are far in excess of anything ever achieved by fighter pilots of any nation, before or since. In the early days of the war, due to their superiority, they achieved success in the air which, on paper, looked almost unbelievable. Later, despite substantial losses in the Battle of Britain, they notched up even greater strings of victories on the Eastern Front against the significantly inferior Russian pilots. Johannes Steinhoff, who himself ended the war with 176 confirmed victories, described the air warfare during 'Operation Barbarossa' as 'like shooting ducks'. Erich Hartmann, the highest-scoring ace of all time, achieved 345 of his 352 total of victories against the Red Air Force.

Probably the most unjust and tragic aspect of the war in the air for these Aces was the fact that, as the war progressed and the fortunes of the German forces went into decline, it was the Luftwaffe fighter pilots who were made scapegoats. Most significantly, the very man who built the Luftwaffe, Hermann Goering, denounced his own men, when things began to go seriously wrong, as the weak link in Germany's war effort. In fact, had German High Command listened to their comments and heeded the lessons to be learned from the Battle of Britain – the Luftwaffe's first major setback in their entire offensive – these courageous and devoted men may have re-written the history books.

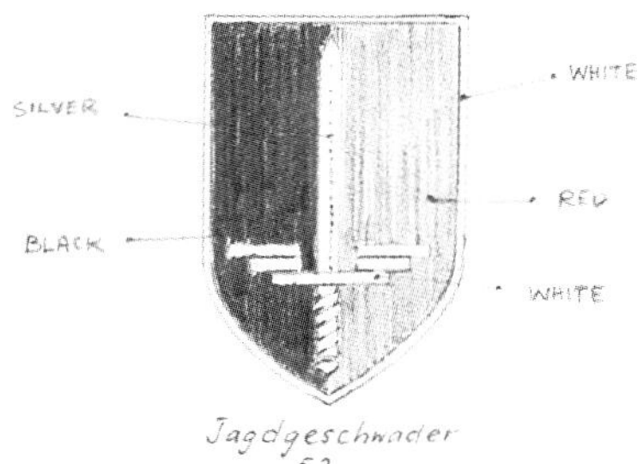

With the wealth of information that General Walter Krupinski had supplied, it became much easier to prepare detailed sketches relating to the Me 109, and individual markings needed for this painting. Some of these drawings are reproduced on this page.

Much of the reference material available for World War II subjects is in black and white. This presents a problem because it is important to be able to authenticate the colours used in a painting. Usually the pilots themselves cannot remember: I once asked Douglas Bader if his particular Spitfire had the often-used pale blue band painted around the fuselage, just in front of the tail. 'Hell, Robert, we used to fly them not paint them' he had replied, with his usual chuckle.

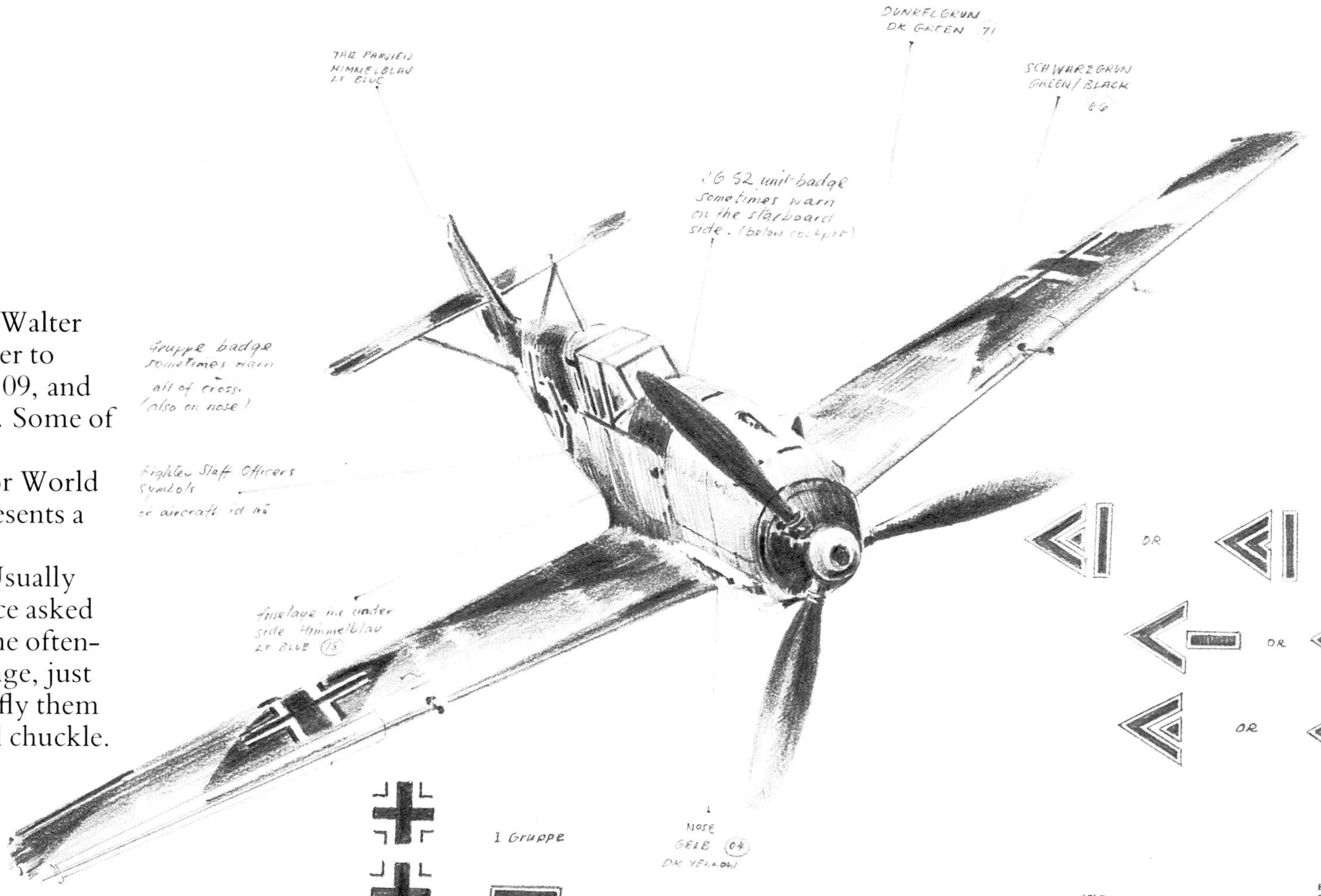

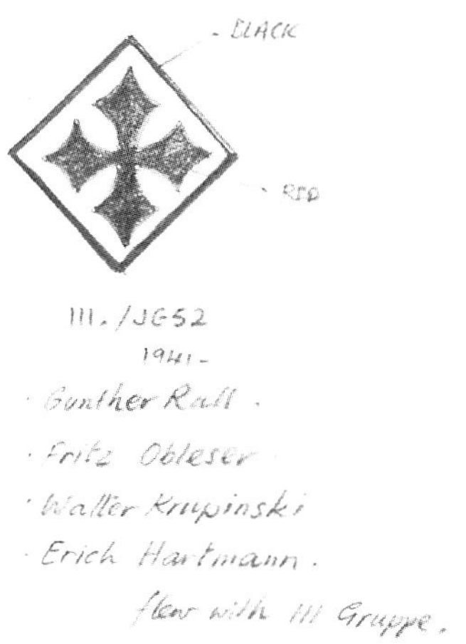

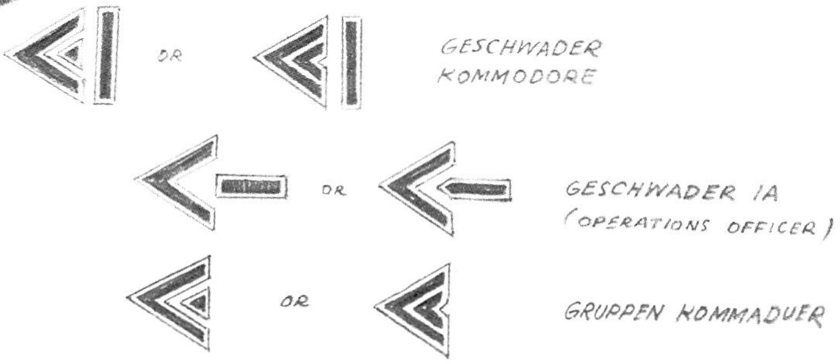

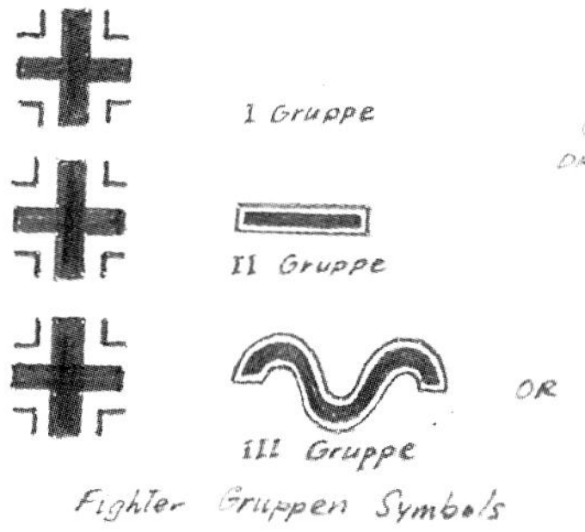

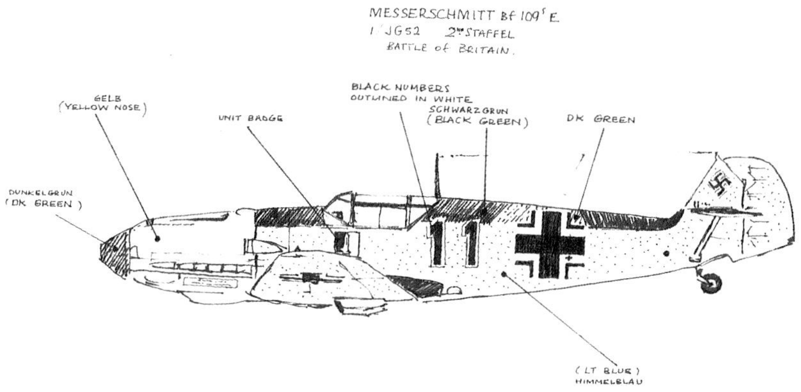

I have a vast collection of books, magazines, photographs, film, video, and other illustrative documents, made over the years, which provides a constant source of essential reference material. Modelling books and magazines are particularly useful when researching colour schemes, because modellers are such perfectionists. Luckily I have a number of friends who are professional researchers, writers and model makers with whom I am able to confer. Their friendly help is invaluable to me.

I constantly go back to previously made drawings for reference. Many of these drawings, particularly the preliminary ones, also carry notations made at the time, which are invaluable. In spite of the 'tidy' look of my studio in the press and publicity photographs, I have to admit that it is not the neatest room in the house. Nothing is ever thrown away!

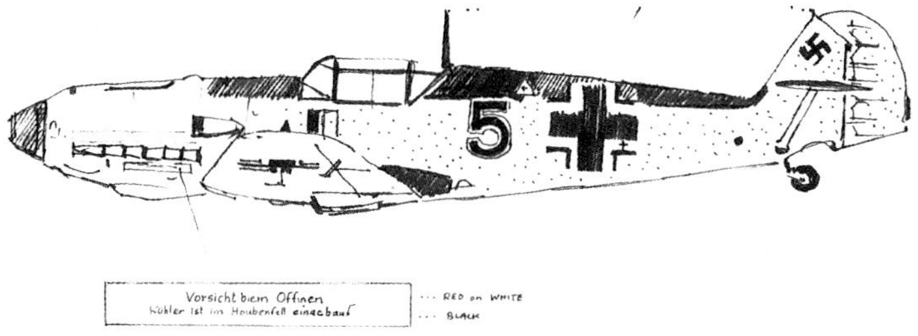

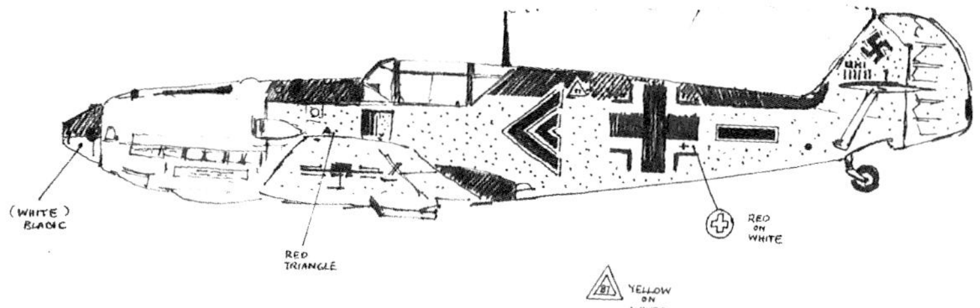

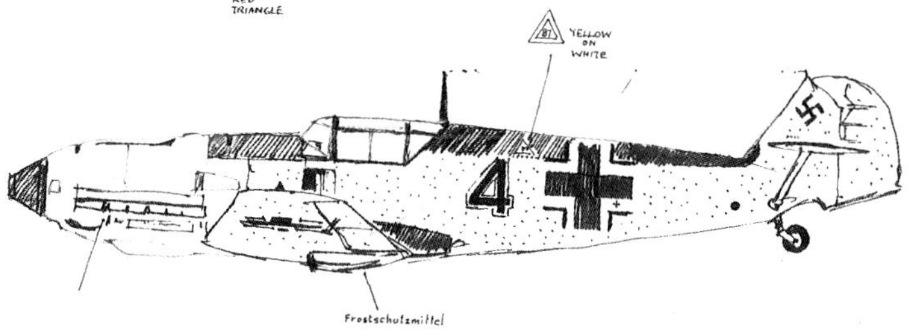

The Me 109s in *JG-52* represent only a small percentage of the total canvas area; however they are painted larger than one might perhaps imagine. The original painting of *JG-52* measures 42 by 28 inches, and the larger of the Me 109's measures 16 inches in length on the canvas. The detail below is reproduced a little smaller than in the actual painting.

It is important to include all the authentic insignia even when the size makes this difficult. It would be easy to portray an aircraft from the angle where critical markings would not be seen, thus avoiding considerable research, but it is preferable to avoid doing this. Sometimes obtaining the relevant information can delay the completion of a painting for weeks, but, for me anyway, deliberate shortcuts tend to remove much of the authenticity.

Occasionally, after weeks or even months consulting every possible authoritative source relating to a particular detail of reference, the information can remain inconclusive. Under such circumstances the artist is left to make his own arbitrary decision on the matter. Usually somebody appears the week after the work is published with every last bit of information available on the subject. There's a word for this law!

The detail below gives some idea of the amount of information an aviation artist needs concerning aircraft configuration, variations, colour schemes, insignia – even pilots' headgear!

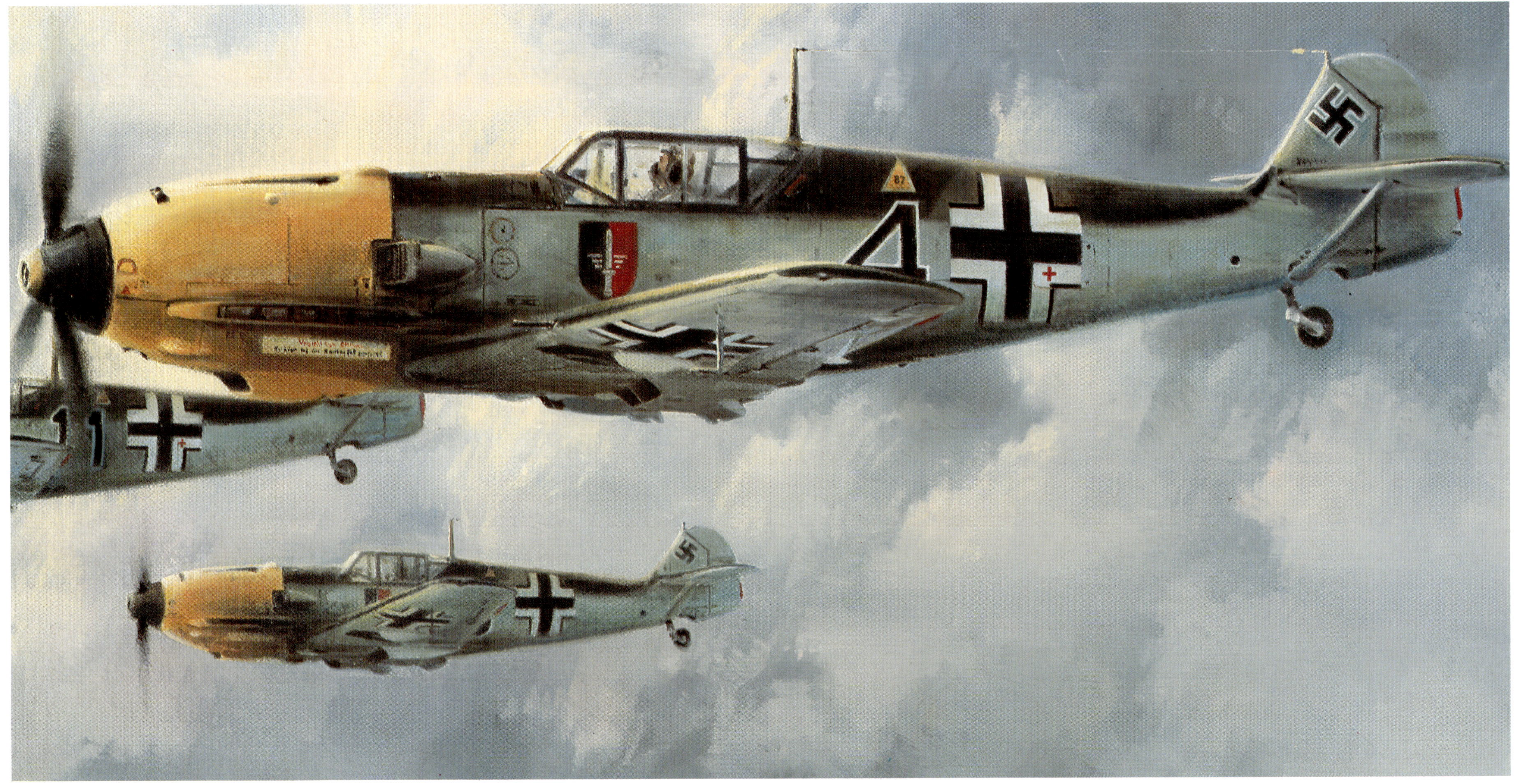

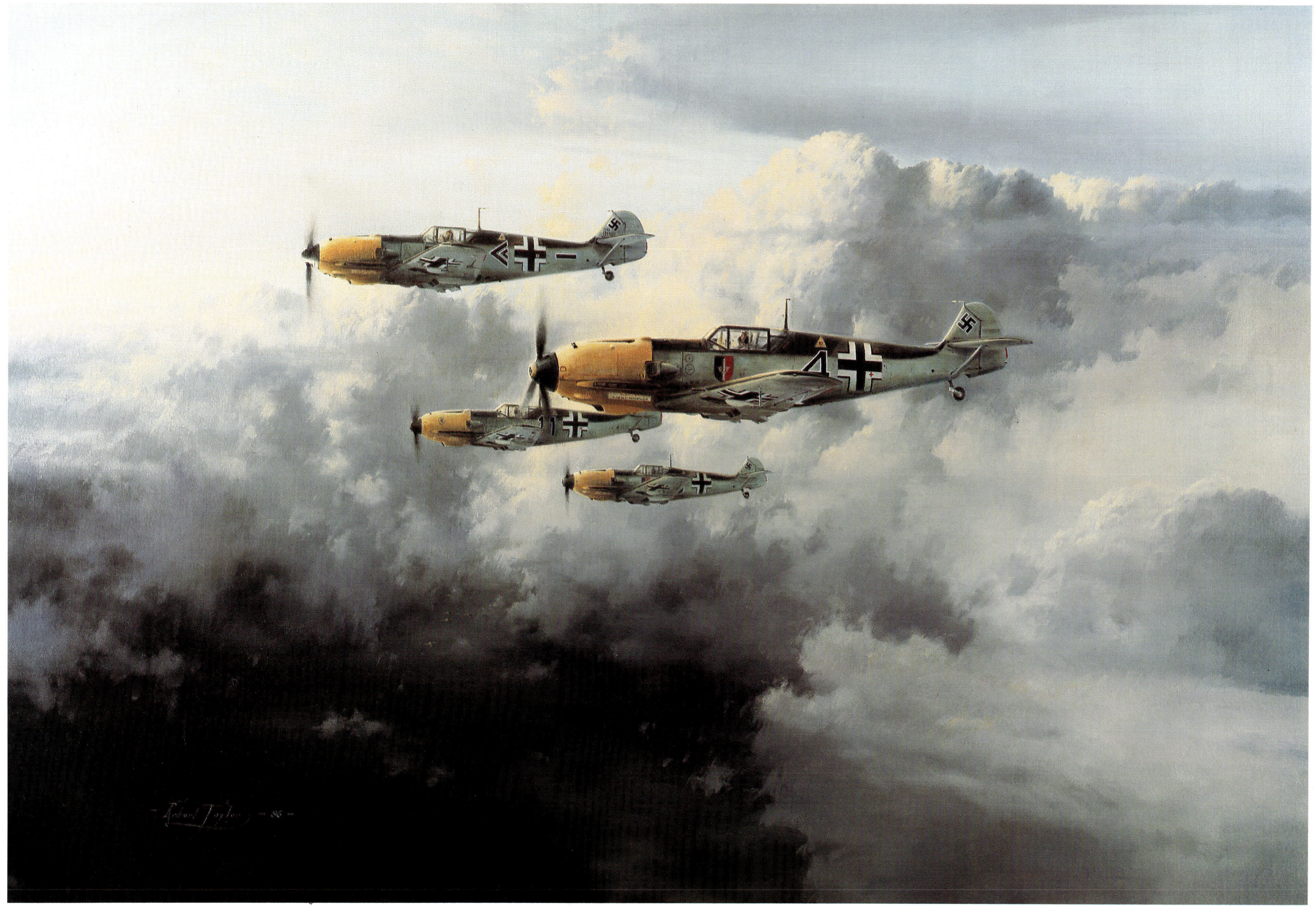

JG-52
In the collection of Mr N Maggos

BATTLE OF BRITAIN MEMORIAL FLIGHT

I have on many occasions seen the aircraft of the Battle of Britain Memorial Flight perform their emotive demonstrations at airshows and every time I watched these wonderful airplanes wheel and turn in the sky I had a strong urge to paint them.

Always flown by hand-picked RAF pilots with a special enthusiasm for these wonderful vintage airplanes, their flight demonstrations never fail to bring spectactors to their feet. When the opportunity came to paint the Memorial Flight I immediately set about obtaining some first-hand information. It was important to try to capture some of the emotion which the Flight never fails to evoke and some behind-the-scenes information might help in achieving this.

Winter maintenance on the Lancaster was, until recently, carried out at RAF Kemble. This was useful, as Kemble is located less than an hour's drive from Bath. I knew plenty of people at this station since at the time it was also home to the RAF aerobatic team, the Red Arrows. I telephoned one morning to arrange to visit the Lancaster: 'Good Morning, my name's Robert Taylor, can you connect me to the Maintenance Flight please? I would like to arrange to come and paint the Lancaster'.

'Thanks very much, old man, you'll be saving us no end of work!' came the immediate reply. I made a mental note to choose my words more carefully when again phoning that particular RAF Station!

The maintenance crew cheerfully invited me to go along to the base, where I was given willing assistance from this enthusiastic bunch of expert technicians. As so often before, I was given the run of the place, offered all kinds of 'artistic' advice, and was watched with a mixture of curiosity, and probably amazement, as I went about my investigation, clambering all over this magnificent old airplane.

Many sketches were made during my visits to RAF Kemble. The original intention was to use the concept shown in the large drawing on the opposite page for the painting, but in the event it was perhaps a little too 'busy'. Wanting to try to convey some of the emotion which so many people feel when they gaze upon these famous aircraft in flight, I ultimately painted the more serene picture, using a soft back-light, depicting the formation over the sea.

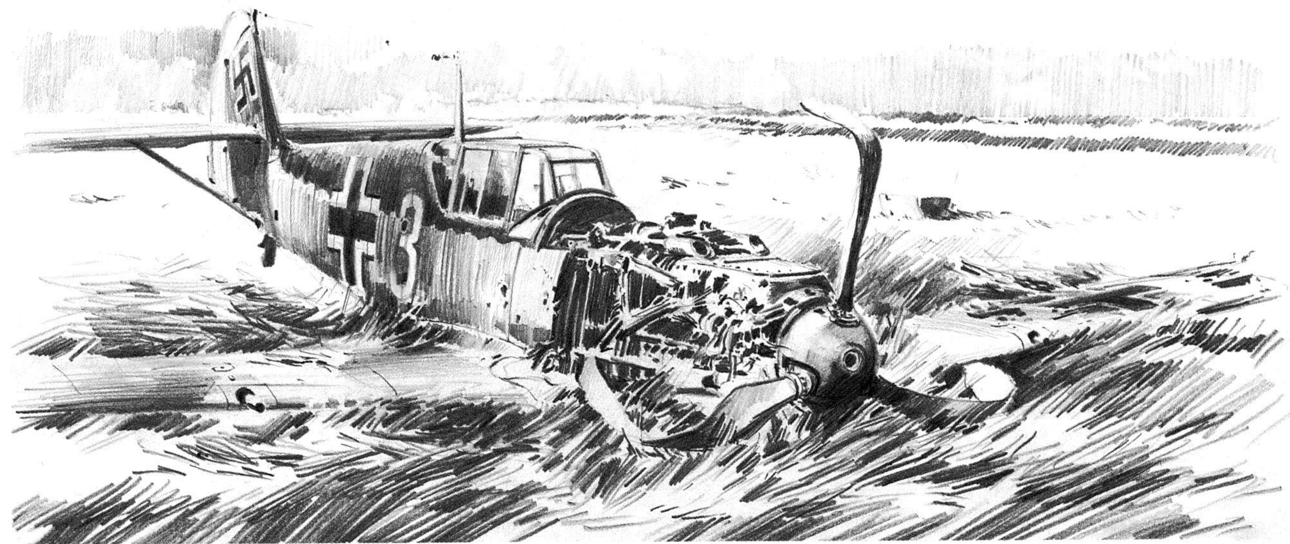

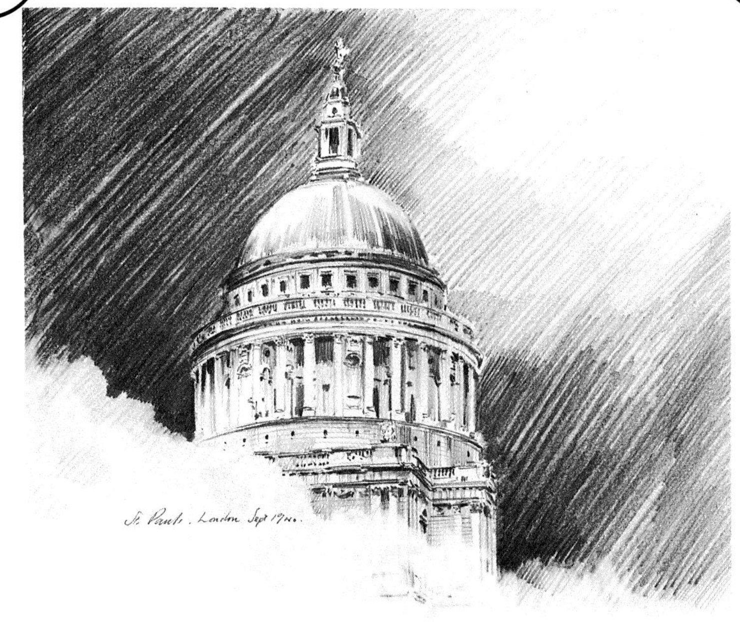

THE BATTLE OF BRITAIN

Fought during the latter half of 1940, and though preceding Allied victory by five long years, the Battle of Britain was one of the most significant turning points of World War II. Until this apocalyptic conflict, German forces had encountered no very substantial opposition in their speedy and decisive subjugation of vast areas of Europe. The defeat of the forces of Poland, Denmark, the Netherlands, Norway, and Belgium in 1939 and 1940 was achieved more quickly than such widespread devastation ever before in history.

When setting in motion the invasion of Britain, German authorities failed to pay due attention to several vital factors. Firstly, the Allied radar network, which was already, by August 1940, capable of pinpointing the German fighters as they took off from their continental bases.

Next the superbly efficient Allied ground control system, which was able to concentrate the numerically inferior RAF fighters in the most effective areas – and with precise timing.

The one less easily-defined and decisive factor, however, was the determination to win which existed among the fighter pilots of the RAF. Lacking this to the same degree, the Luftwaffe suffered severe, disproportionate losses. When Operation 'Sea Lion' was scrapped, a massive 1,733 German aircraft had been shot down for the loss of 915 of the RAF.

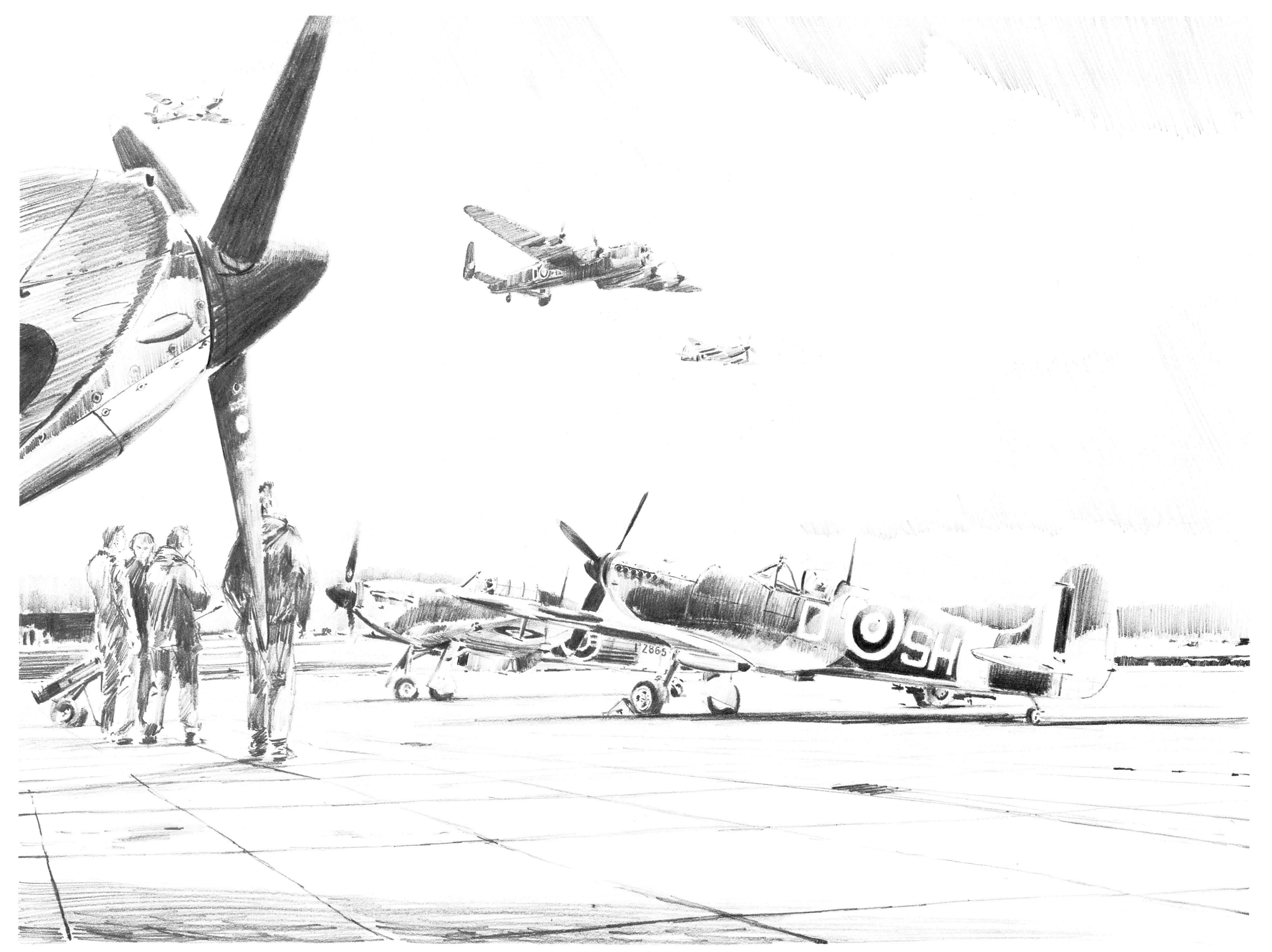

Battle of Britain Memorial Flight. R.A.F. Coningsby. 85.

The Battle of Britain Memorial Flight has an interesting history and the background to its present-day operation is fascinating to an aircraft enthusiast such as myself.

The Battle of Britain Flight was formed in 1957 at Biggin Hill to commemorate the greatest Battle Honour of the Royal Air Force. It performs a vital role in keeping alive for contemporary aviation enthusiasts the memory of three of the best known British aircraft which took part in World War II.

In its early days the Memorial Flight consisted of two Spitfire Mk XVIs, two Spitfire Mk XIXs and a single Hurricane. Tragically, the Mk XVIs were both lost in flying accidents but in 1965 the British Aircraft Corporation presented a Spitfire MkV to the Flight and, after being made airworthy for the film *Battle of Britain*, a Mk II joined in 1968. In 1972 a second Hurricane arrived, indeed it was the last Hurricane ever built, and was presented to the Flight by Hawker Siddeley. In 1972 the ranks of the Flight were swelled by the only airworthy Lancaster in the world. Although the Lancaster appeared after the Battle of Britain was won, by joining the Flight it provided a cogent reminder of the significant part played by the valiant crews of Bomber Command during World War II.

MERLIN OIL CHANGE

Artist's Collection

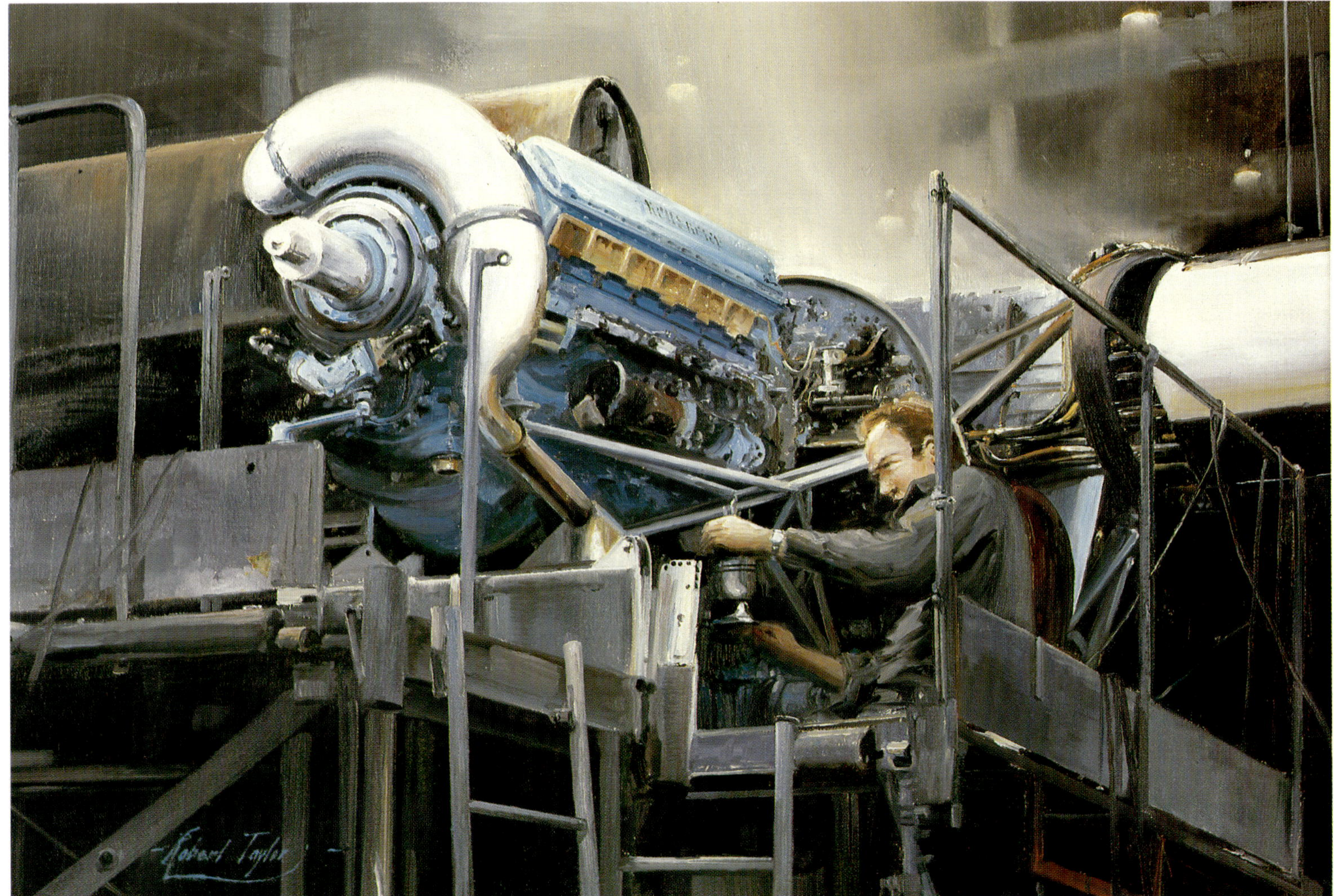

Lancaster P474 was built by Vickers Armstrong at Chester as a reconnaisance Bomber and modified for use with 'Tiger Force' against the Japanese in the later stages of World War II. In peacetime she flew photo-reconnaissance, a photographic survey in Africa, and then operated as a flying test-bed for newly-developed equipment. In October 1963 she moved to the Air Historical Branch and, nearly two years later, was flown from Henlow to Waddington for her well-deserved refurbishment, so ably completed by members of 44 Squadron and personnel of RAF Waddington. She now wears standard wartime Bomber Command camouflage and the code letters KM-B to represent the aircraft flown by Squadron Leader J. D. Nettleton, VC, of No 44 Squadron during the war.

The Spitfire I chose to portray was the Mk Vb AB910, which saw varied service (originally as a Mk I) with Squadrons 222 (Natal), 130 (Punjab), 133 (Eagle), 242 (Canadian) 416 and 402 (both RCAF), and 527.

The Hurricane LF363 (Mk 11c) in the picture flew with 63 Squadron for a large part of her wartime career and later entered 309 (Polish) and 26 Squadrons. LF363 subsequently had a very successful career as a film star! From time to time the Flight changes the colour schemes and markings of its aircraft. Today Hurricane LF363 carries the black colour scheme of 85 Squadron night fighters, whose story is so compellingly told by Group Captain Peter Townsend in his recent publication *Duel in the Dark*.

The oil sketch illustrated on this page was painted from a drawing made in the hangar of RAF Kemble. It shows a mechanic working on the port inner Merlin engine of Lancaster P474 during its winter maintenance. The sketch, which measures 18 by 12 inches, was fun to paint. Though it has no direct relationship to the final painting of the Memorial Flight, at the time I was working on the project it was quite a valuable exercise. Merlin engines were of course fitted to all three aircraft in the Flight.

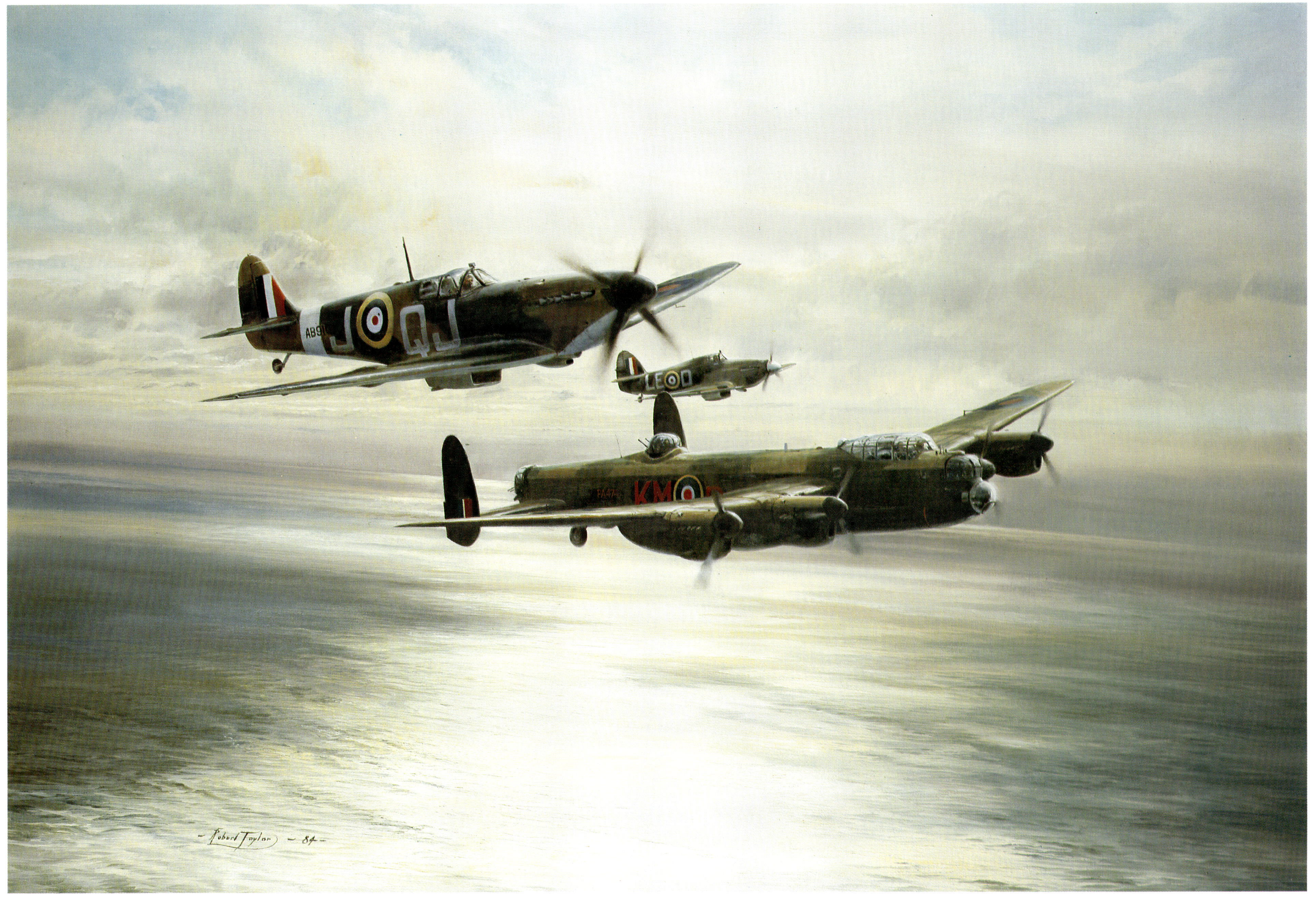

MEMORIAL FLIGHT

In the collection of James and Doris Francis

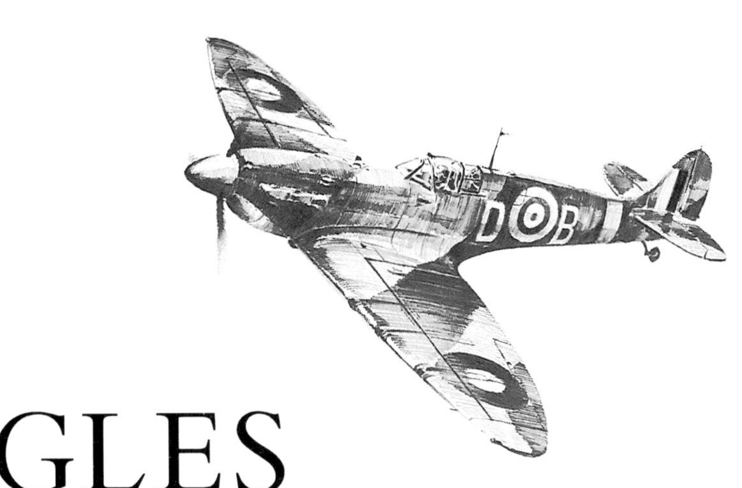

DUEL OF EAGLES

It would be difficult to imagine how an artist could have more fun painting a picture than I had with *Duel of Eagles*. Sir Douglas Bader was, as for many people of my age, a boyhood hero. When commissioned to paint this picture it was therefore with some trepidation that I first went to meet him to discuss the painting. I need not have worried.

Sir Douglas was an extraordinary person. Well into his sixties when I first met him, he always had a mischievous twinkle in his eye, and a ready wit. But it was his ability to lead and encourage others which set him apart from most. From the moment I first met him he enthused about the project and set about co-operating with huge gusto. In fact he became so involved that I think he would have painted the picture too, given the chance!

Composing the picture, however, was not without its problems. A special print edition was to be published, and each print was to be signed by both Sir Douglas and his old adversary from the Luftwaffe, General Adolf Galland. Both men had been Wing Leaders who often had very different ideas about what they wanted, and each was used to having his way! My brief was to paint a Spitfire and a Messerschmitt Me 109 in combat. How on earth was I to compose a painting in which both combatants would agree the concept? Which aircraft should have the advantage?

During 1941, when Douglas Bader commanded the famous Tangmere Wing, his squadrons were in almost daily combat with Adolf Galland's notorious JG-26 ('The Abbeville Boys'). Though no record ever showed that the two had come face to face in the air, neither could be sure that they had not. One thing both knew was that neither had ever gained the advantage over the other, and I was quite sure that somehow my picture would have to convey this – otherwise one of them might not wish to sign the prints.

Sir Douglas volunteered several suggestions and indeed prepared some diagrams for me, but I knew that none of these would work as a composition. I told him so, and why, and he accepted my point of view cheerfully. We agreed that I would prepare a series of sketches and return.

From talking to Sir Douglas, and many other World War II fighter pilots, it was clear that in skilled hands the Spitfires and the Me 109s were very much a match for each other. However, the Me 109s big advantage was that, with its fuel-injected carburettor, it could be nosed-over into a vertical dive without missing a beat. A pursuing Spitfire would, if put through the same manoeuvre, cough and splutter for a few seconds, the gravity feed of the fuel to the carburettor being momentarily interrupted. Thus the Me 109 could escape. On the other hand, the Spitfire could always out-turn the Me 109 – so well in experienced hands that it could, within a few turns, convert a defensive manoeuvre into one of attack. I was sure that the answer to my dilemma of advantage lay somewhere here, and my preliminary drawings were all based upon the Spitfire out-turning the Me109. I felt that with the Spitfire placed ahead of the Me109, at least General Galland would have the satisfaction of knowing he had made the surprise attack – or that at least it could be construed that way. The Spitfire could then be positioned turning inside the Me109, thus preventing the Me109 from bringing his guns to bear.

Happily, both of these two great fighter pilots accepted this final drawing and I was able to proceed. I painted the picture back in 1980 and years later Sir Douglas was kind enough to say that *Duel of Eagles* was his favourite Spitfire combat painting.

THE OLD ADVERSARIES

If Douglas Bader and Adolf Galland did not actually duel together in aerial combat in 1940–1, then certainly their respective wings did. They first met in person when Bader was brought down over France in August 1941, and again at Tangmere at the end of the war. It was the start of a lifetime friendship succinctly summed up by Bader in his foreword to Adolf Galland's excellent book, *A Pilot's Life in War and Peace*, 'Politicians cause wars and the ordinary decent citizen fights them. The true fighting man bears no animosity towards his opponent, in whom he recognises the same attitude of mind as his own.'

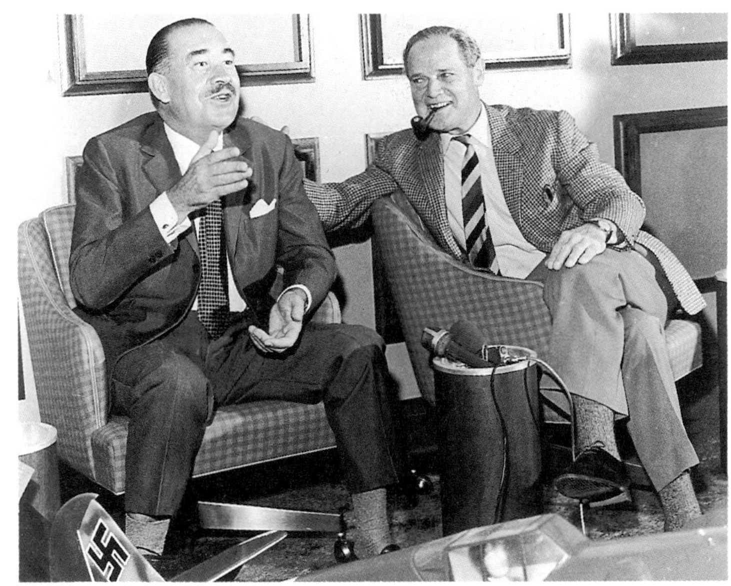

Galland and Bader discuss air tactics

I liked my first drawing because it showed off nicely the beautiful elliptical wing shape, unique to the Spitfire, but the overall composition seemed to lack something. The position of the aircraft relative to the viewer did not convey any great idea of speed, and there was not much feeling of the grace and beauty of these two wonderful fighter aircraft. Whilst these deficiencies could be compensated by careful construction of the background, a completely different approach seemed preferable. I nevertheless took it along for Sir Douglas to see.

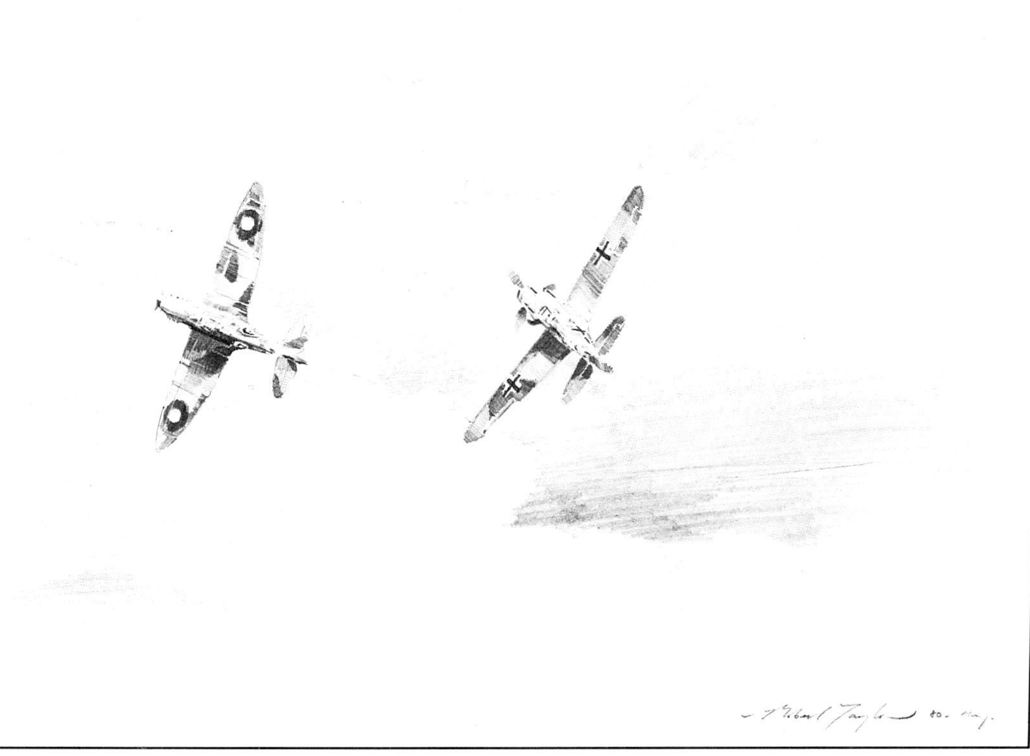

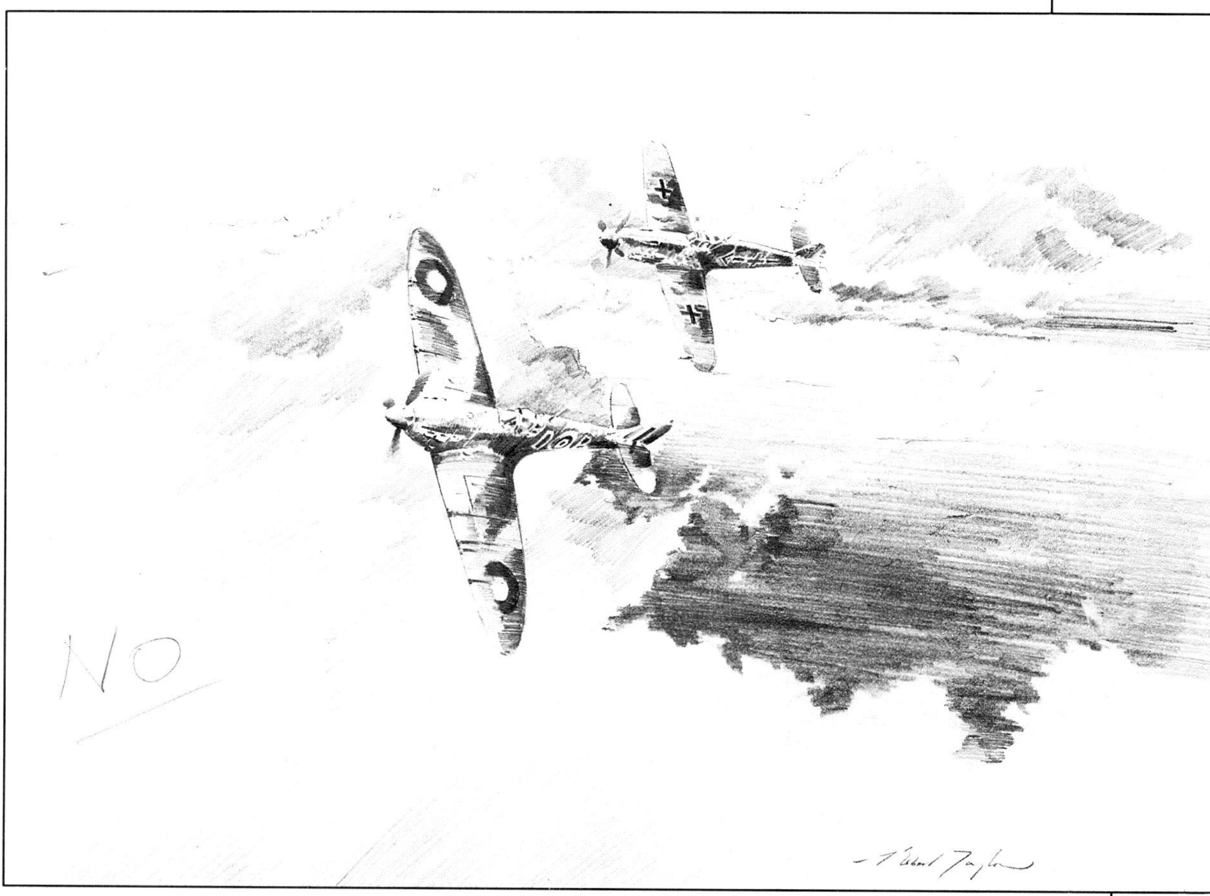

When I spread all the drawings on Sir Douglas's desk he immediately wrote a big 'No' in ballpoint pen right on my drawing number two (see above). 'Good Lord, old boy, we can't possibly use this one. It looks as if we're flying along in formation!' It was pointed out that he would already have turned well inside his opponent and thus achieved the advantage but the Group Captain was right. In fact the turning manoeuvre had been such a central theme that I had overlooked the possibility that perhaps not everybody else would see it my way!

'That one's perfect Robert. He'll never get a shot at me from there!' The third drawing was right! After General Galland had cast his critical eye over it, and given his approval. I was able to start painting.

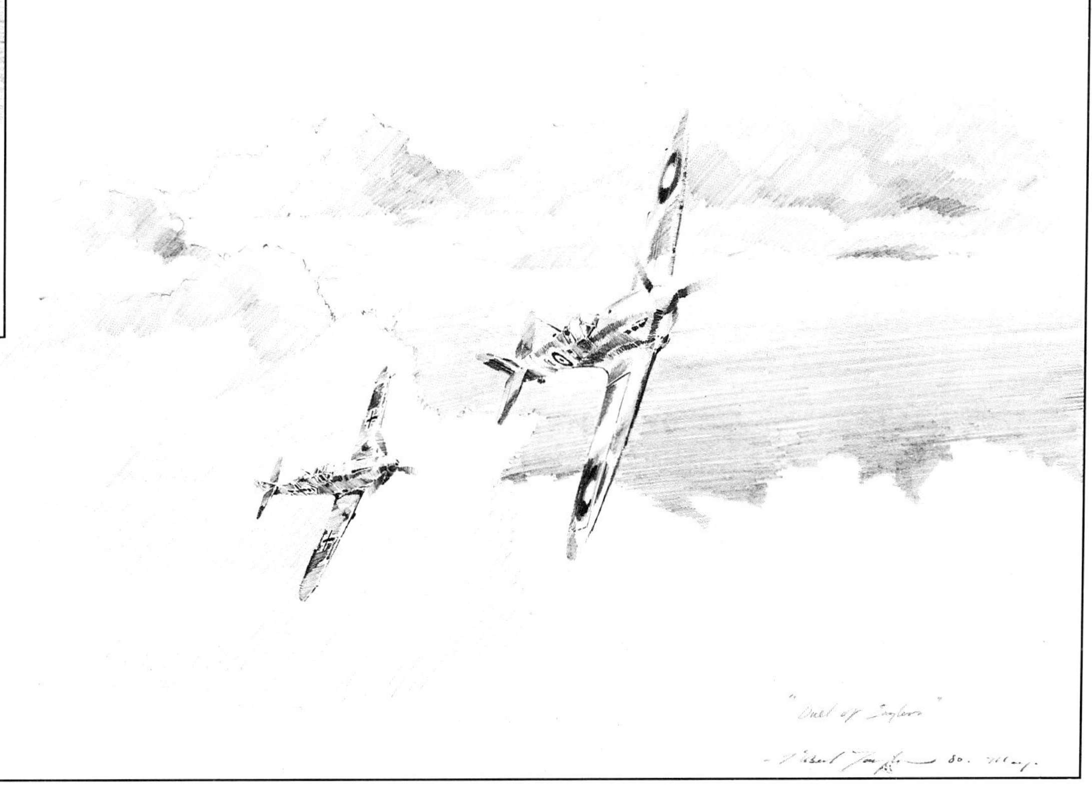

Duel of Eagles was reproduced as a print, which was sold out many years ago. The original painting was purchased quickly after completion. Its success led to another commission, featuring the great Tangmere Wing. This was reproduced as a private limited edition which was signed by Sir Douglas, who commanded the wing, and three of his fellow pilots – Johnnie Johnson, 'Cocky' Dundas, and Ken Holden. The painting, which is reproduced below, shows Wing Commander Douglas Bader leading his Spitfires over the South coast of Britain in 1941.

Bader flew the MkV Spitfire, preferring not to use the later Mk Vb – he was not an enthusiast of the cannons fitted to the Vb.

I had a number of meetings with Sir Douglas during the preparation of this painting. Always cheerful and full of enthusiasm, he continually encouraged me with my work, stressing how important it was for aviation artists of today to record the great aviation events of the era with accuracy. He used to say 'With us old codgers around you don't have any excuse for mistakes'.

TANGMERE WING

In the collection of Mr Tom Greenham

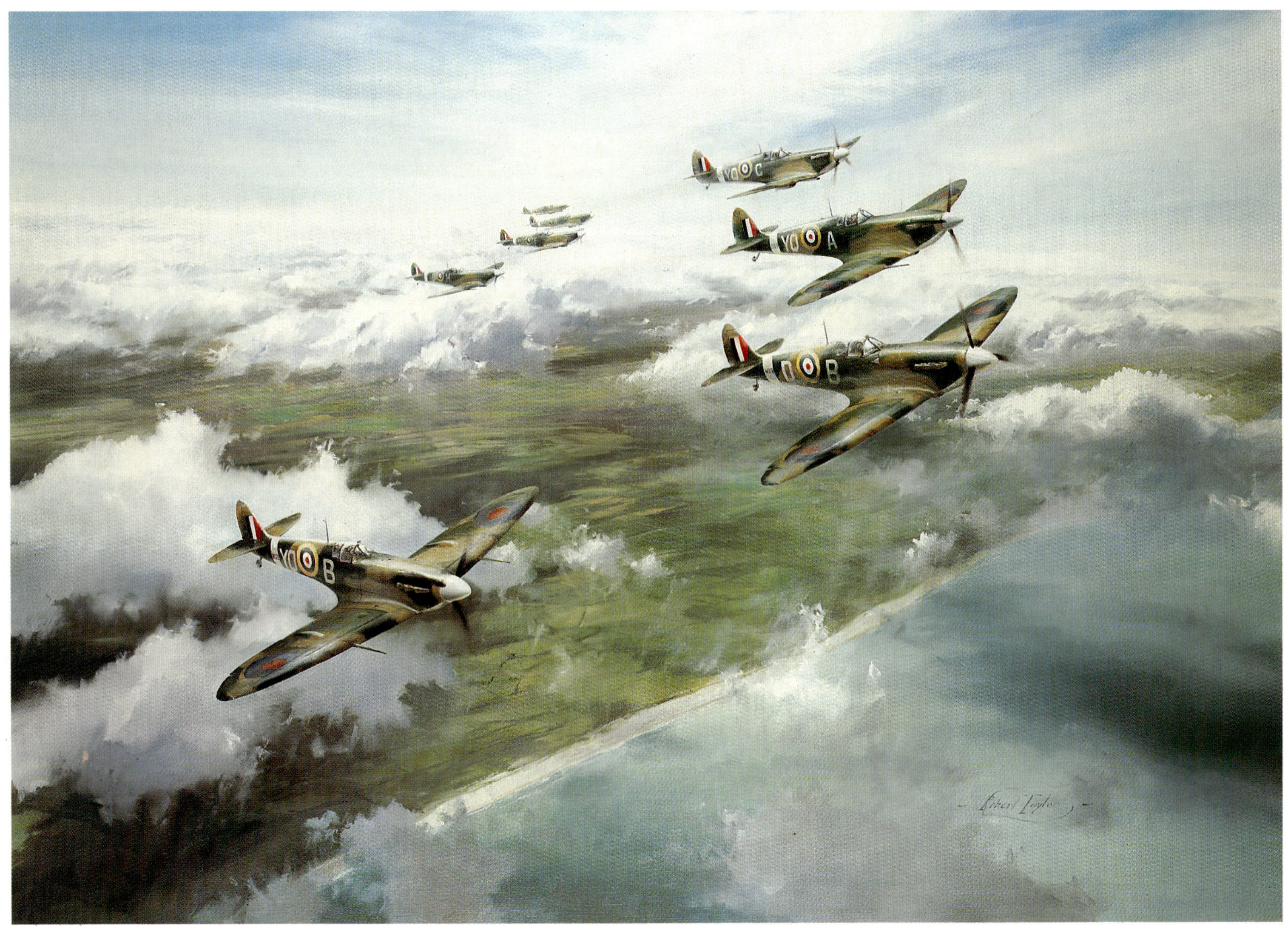

THE TANGMERE WING

Tangmere is a small village which lies at the foot of the South Downs near the coast, in the beautiful Sussex countryside. Today, in the centre of the village there is a pub called 'The Douglas Bader'. With the exception of a small military aviation museum housed in one of the few remaining original buildings, there is almost nothing left of what was once one of the most famous fighter stations in the history of the RAF.

First to make its home at Tangmere was 92 Squadron who, with their SE5 fighters, arrived in 1918. By the time World War II was declared, 605 Squadron was in residence with its Gloster Gladiators. It was not long before the geographical importance of Tangmere registered with Fighter Command and, during the Battles of France and Britain, Tangmere quickly became base for a number of the RAF's interception fighter squadrons.

During the Battle of Britain the station was bombed and badly damaged on a number of occasions yet remained operational throughout – in fact by the end of September 1940 its squadrons had claimed 275 enemy aircraft destroyed, 116 probable and 146 damaged. With the battle won, Fighter Command reorganised in preparation for the air offensive, and Tangmere became a base for a new wing of three Spitfire squadrons, to be led by a Wing Commander Flying. The first to fill this post was Douglas Bader.

The new Commander arrived in March 1941 and quickly stamped his personality on the Wing. Within no time his pilots were probing across the Channel into Northern France making attacks on enemy ground forces and clashing increasingly with the now-reinforced Luftwaffe fighter squadrons. One such was the famous JG-26 fighter wing based at the airfields around Abbeville, under the command of Adolf Galland. By high summer the Tangmere Wing, under the inspired leadership of Douglas Bader, was as fine an aerial fighting force as there had ever been. Their successes in the air were mounting all the time, and confidence abounded throughout this magnificent group of fighters.

The chapter closed on a beautiful summer's day in August when Bader failed to return from a hard fought battle over St Omer, having been taken prisoner of war. But the legend of the Tangmere Wing was already born.

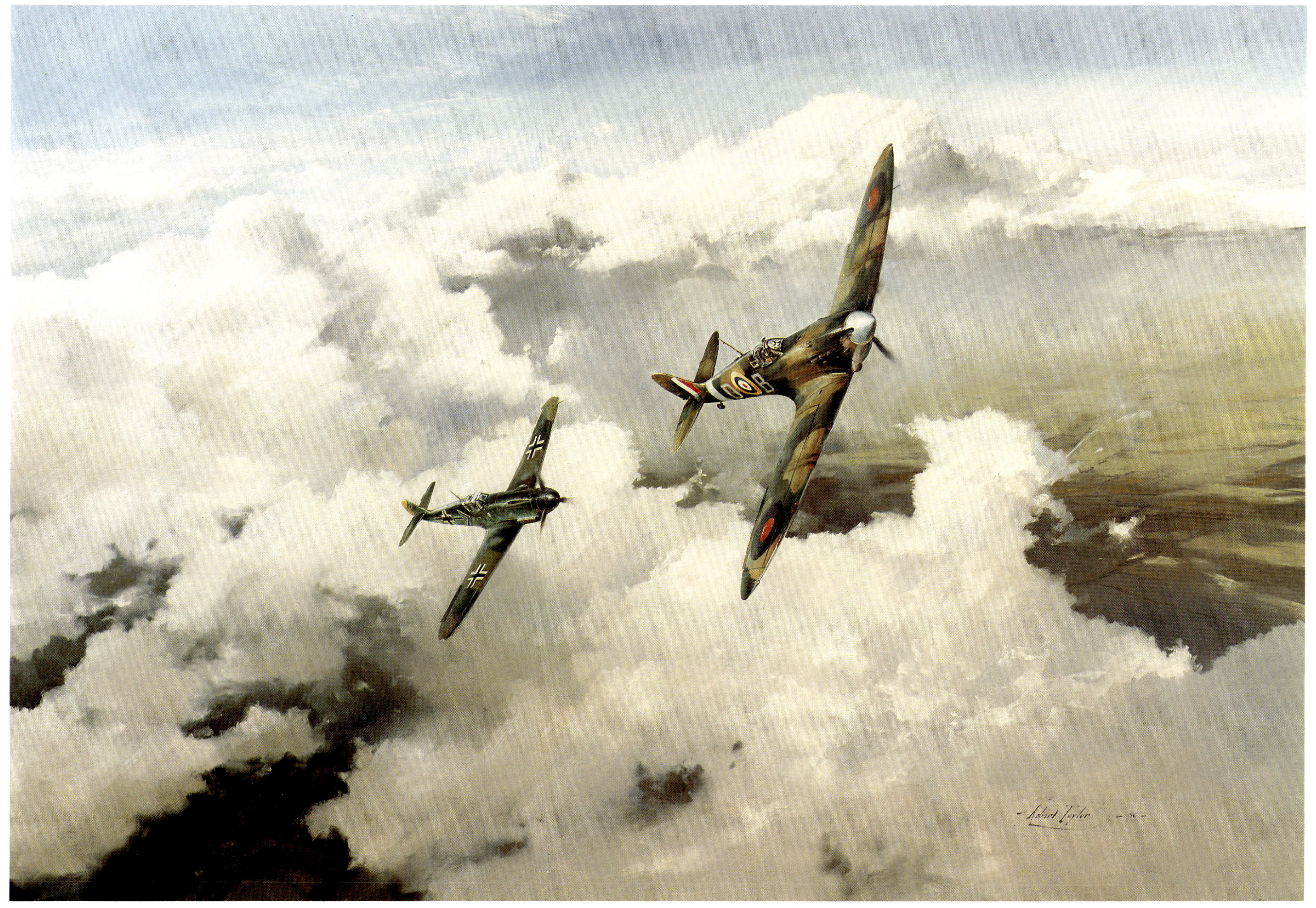

DUEL OF EAGLES
In the collection of Mr N Angel

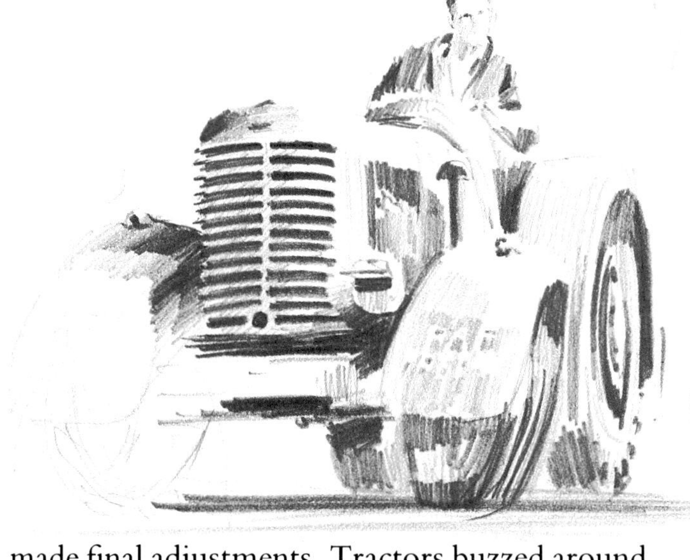

OPERATIONS ON

Ray Callow was an airgunner on Lancasters during World War II. An active member of both the Aircrew Association and the Bomber Command Association, Ray organises the popular Bomber Command Reunion every year. In 1982 Ray phoned me to ask if I would paint a picture which would be presented to Marshal of the RAF Sir Arthur Harris, to celebrate his ninetieth birthday. Sir Arthur had been Commander-in-Chief of Bomber Command from 1942–5, and the presentation was to be made by some of the aircrew who had served with him during this period – Sir Arthur used to call them his 'old lags'. Naturally, I was both flattered and honoured to receive this communication.

After talking to Ray and a number of others who knew Sir Arthur personally I quickly became aware of his strong and loyal feelings for all those who served in his command – both air and ground crews, and felt that somehow it would be important to portray this by including more than just aircrew in the painting. The four-engined Lancaster had become the backbone of Bomber Command during the years of Sir Arthur's leadership and so there was no hesitation in deciding that this should be the aircraft type for the painting. In order to include as many personnel of the Command as possible, the aircraft would need to be portrayed on the ground.

The weather in Europe, particularly in Britain, is highly upredictable. This played a large part in the decision as to whether a raid would take place or not, and often the decision would be in doubt for some hours before the announcement was made, 'Operations On!' As soon as the word went around, activity on the station quickly reached its peak. Whilst aircrews received their final briefing, the ground crews fuelled and armed the aircraft and the engineers made final adjustments. Tractors buzzed around, starter trolleys were hauled into position and people scurried around in a flurry of activity.

Operations On endeavours to capture all of this. Aircrew are about to board their aircraft and within minutes the whole airfield will echo with the sound of a hundred Merlin engines. For the ground crews, their part completed, there will be an agonising wait. The bombers will take off one by one, assemble into formations and head out into the night and towards untold dangers.

Painting the Lancaster is always a pleasant task. It is an aircraft with which I am very familiar and so I do not often meet with any great difficulty. The drawing on the opposite page was the final one. The painting only differs in that the position of the ground crews and airmen are changed somewhat, and the tractor is moved a little further forward. I also added an airman with a bicycle – a very popular mode of transport of the day – in the centre of the picture.

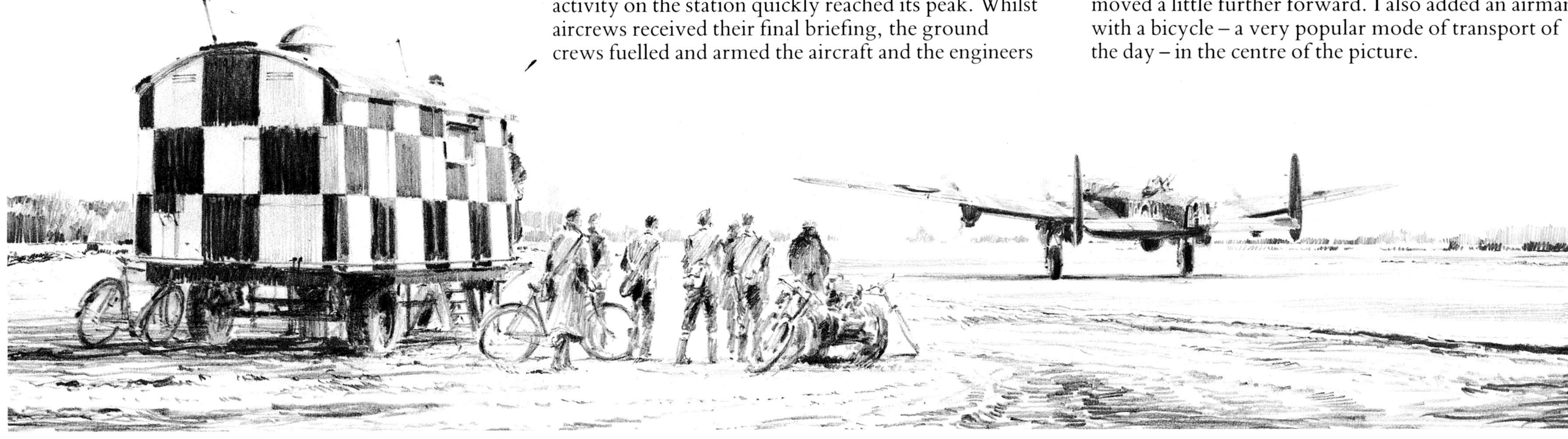

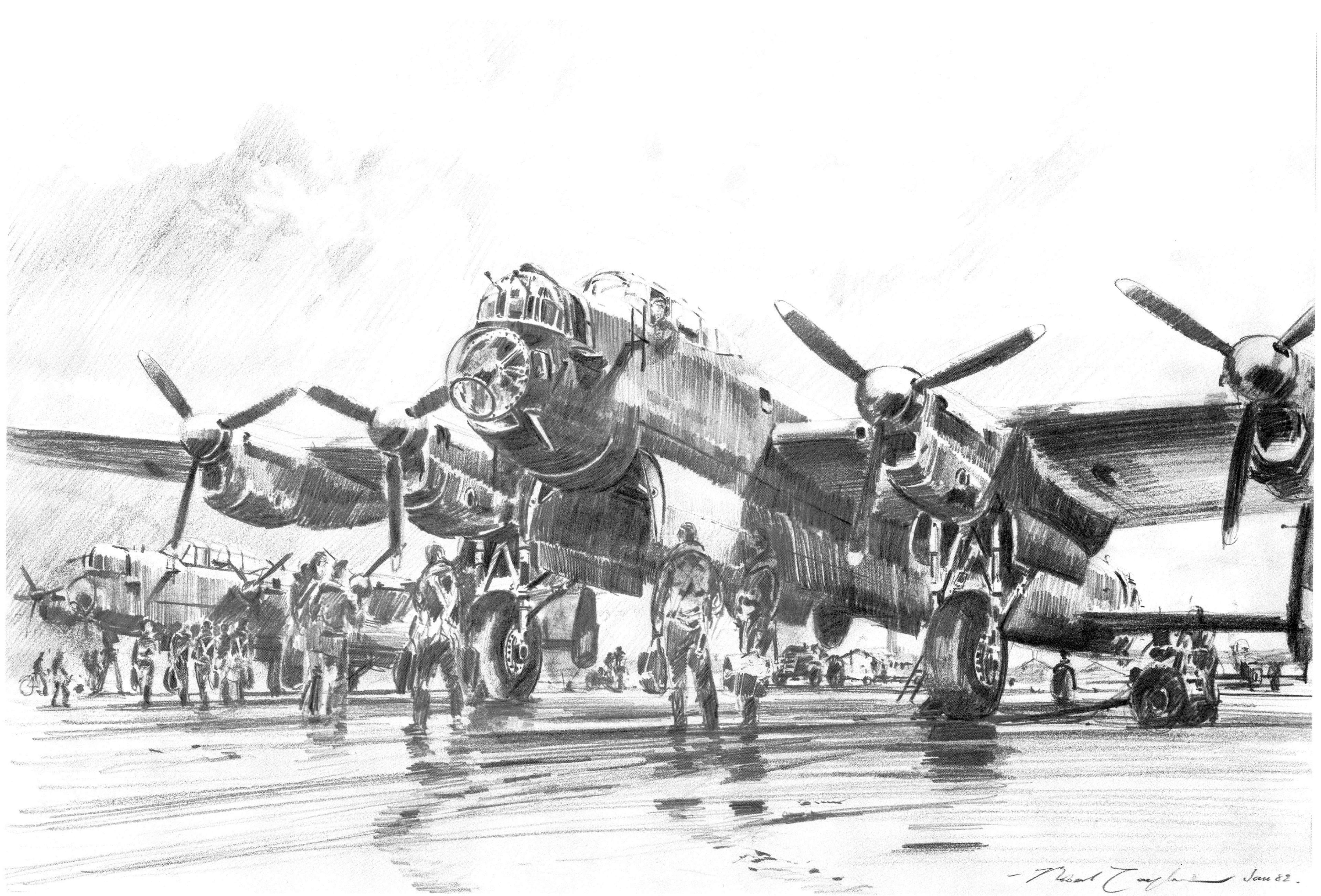
Jan 82.

After *Operations On* had been presented to Sir Arthur Harris, it was decided that a limited edition print should be published – though that had not been the intention originally. Sir Arthur generously consented to sign copies from the edition. My publishers therefore needed the painting for at least a couple of months while the complicated process of making fine art prints was accomplished. Sir Arthur had already 'moved things around a bit' at his home to accommodate his new painting which had, I was told, been given pride of place and he was already rather attached to it. I was asked if I could find a painting to fill the gap whilst *Operations On* was to be absent. Fortunately another painting of a Lancaster was available which I had painted a year or so previously. That painting was called *Limping Home* and is shown below.

A Lancaster, is returning from a raid, badly damaged by enemy anti-aircraft fire with its port outer engine stopped and its starboard outer overheating. As the morning sun rises the pilot is struggling to maintain height and make it to the English coast.

LIMPING HOME

In the collection of Mr Pat Barnard

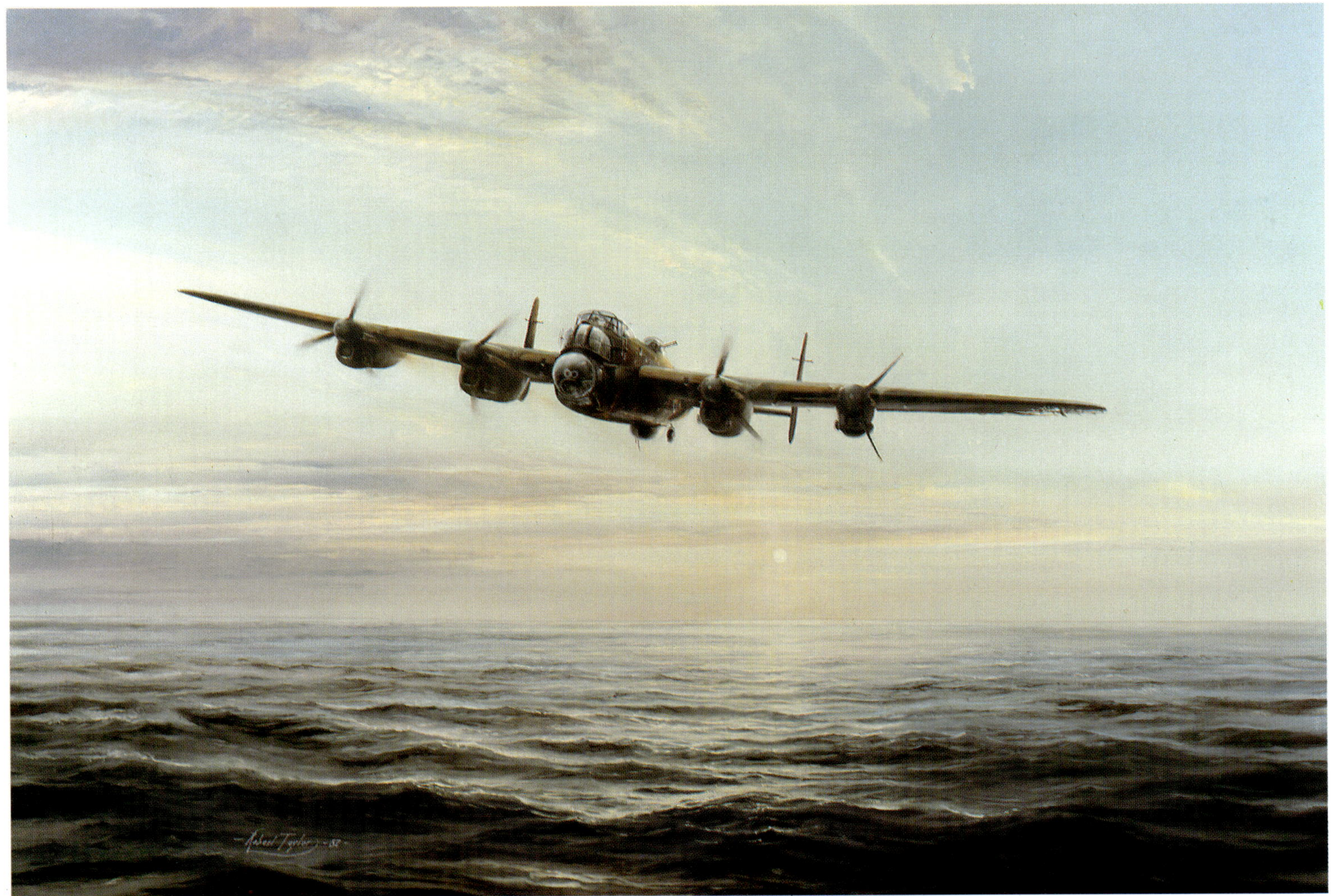

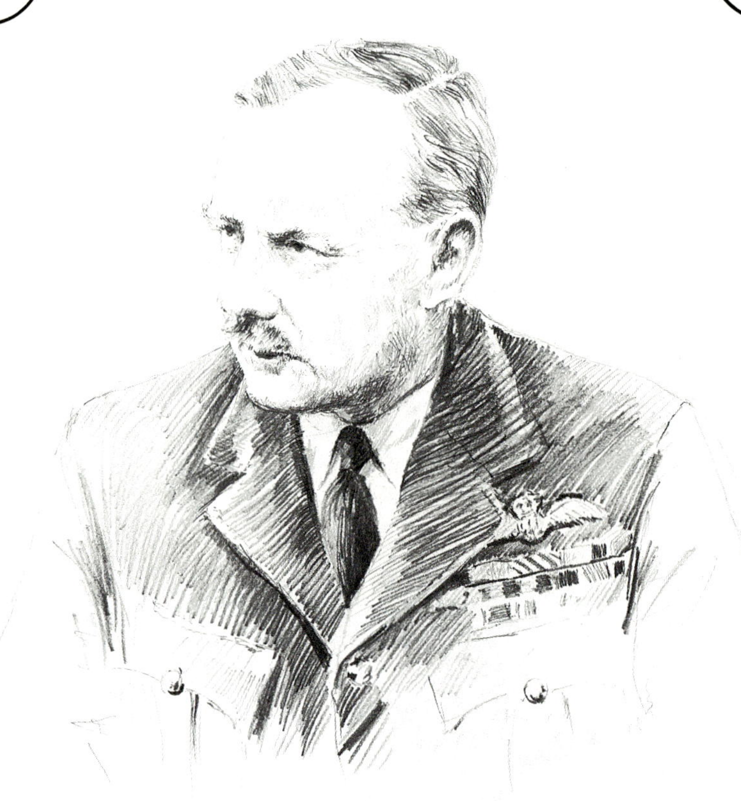

Marshal of the Royal Air Force
SIR ARTHUR HARRIS, BT, GCB, AFC, LLD

In mid-1940, when the Nazis had defeated the French and British armies, which led to Dunkirk, Winston Churchill sent an historic minute to Lord Beaverbrook. It said:

'When I look around to see how we can win this war there is only one sure power. We now have no army that can defeat the Nazi military power. Our sea blockade of Germany is broken and shortly Hitler will have the resources of Africa and Asia to draw from. Should he fail to invade the UK he will rebound eastward. There is only one thing that will stop him and that is devastating attacks on the Nazi homeland by very heavy bombers from this country, without which I do not see a way through.' Beaverbrook drew up production plans and Arthur Harris was made Commander-in-Chief of Bomber Command and ordered to implement Churchill's policy.

Unswerving leadership, determination and strategic skills made his bomber offensive one of the most significant factors in the ending of the Nazi threat.

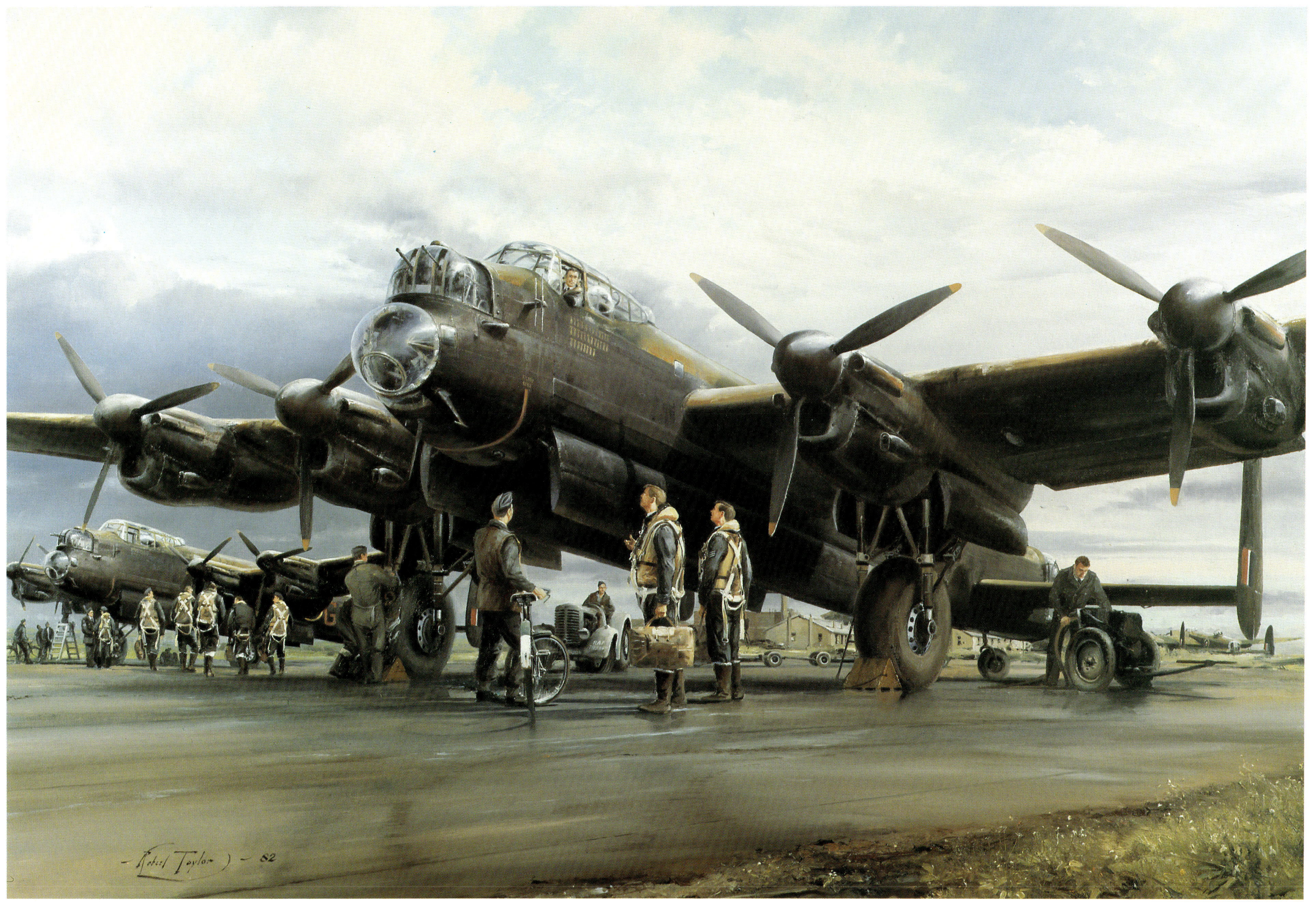

OPERATIONS ON
In the collection of Lady Harris

GATHERING OF EAGLES

This was a challenging commission. In 1985 the American Air Forces Association held their fortieth Anniversary Reunion, a major event, attended by over 5,000 people, in Las Vegas. Veterans from the Allied Airforces joined many of their old adversaries from the Luftwaffe in a gathering of aircrew the likes of which had never been seen before.

Virginia Bader, a cousin of the late Sir Douglas Bader, who runs a successful aviation art business in the USA, was to hold a symposium featuring British, American and German fighter pilots, and wanted to commission a limited edition print to commemorate the event. The problem I had was to come up with a composition that somehow conveyed the title of the event, a Gathering of Eagles, which would be an acceptable subject to all concerned. Seven different fighter aces were to sign the prints, representing three different World War II air forces.

Bearing in mind the light hearted remark of the great German Fighter Ace, General Gunther Rall, 'I usually seem to be asked to sign prints depicting Luftwaffe aircraft going down in flames', I felt I should at least try to avoid his having to do that in this case.

The aim was to compose a kind of gathering of eagles (combat pilots) in the air and from the outset there needed to be a lot going on in the painting. My immediate thought was to portray one of the great daylight raids showing P-51 Mustangs defending B-17 Flying Fortresses from marauding FW 190s. As two British fighter pilots were included in the project (Group Captain Peter Townsend and Wing Commander Geoffrey Page), it was obviously important somehow to include a British fighter aircraft. After some research it was revealed that on a number of occasions Spitfires had joined P-51s in the defence of B-17s, although this was a relatively rare practice. Finally, because the painting was to commemorate a friendly reunion, it was my aim to convey all the action of air combat whilst suggesting that everyone got home that day!

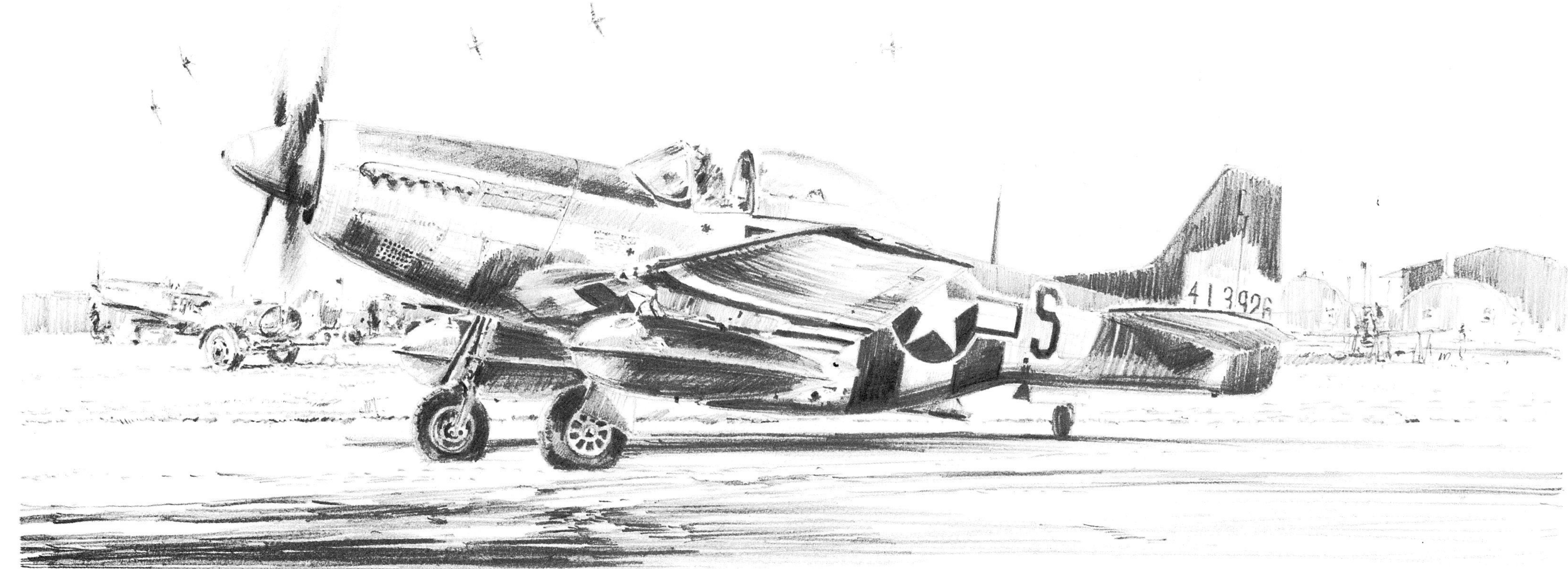

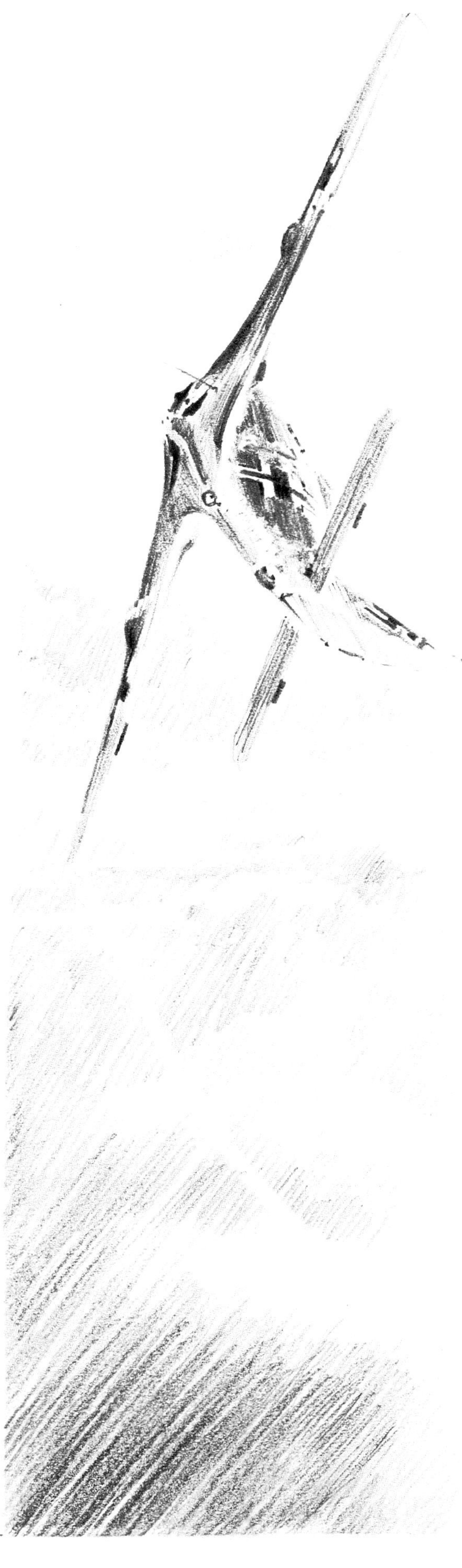

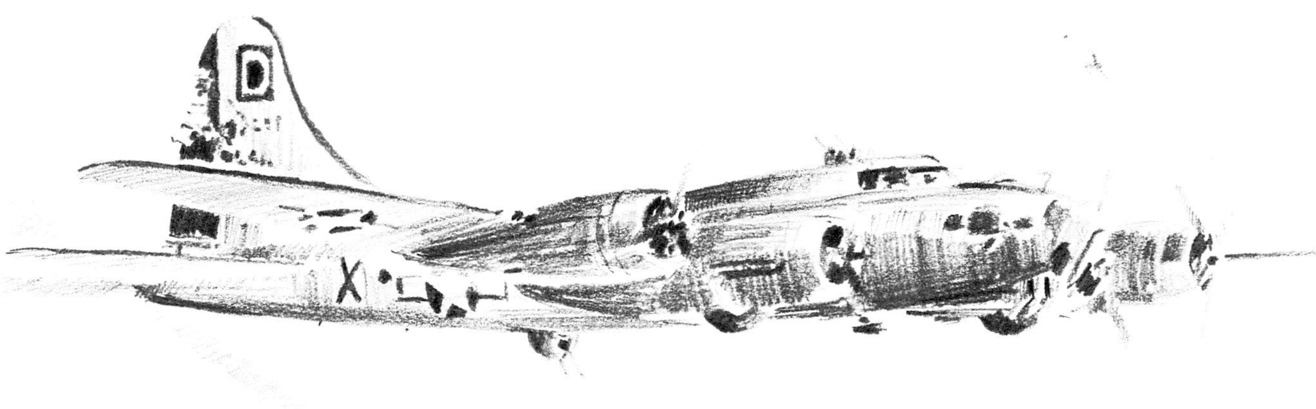

During the great daylight raids the bombers flew at high altitude, in fairly tight formations. The principle of defence was to stick together concentrating the considerable firepower of each aircraft, making it difficult for enemy fighters to penetrate the formation. The practice was to some extent successful and certainly the air gunners had considerable success against the enemy fighters. However when a bomber was hit, and started to lose height, it became totally vulnerable to the marauding fighters. It was around these 'winged' aircraft that many of the ferocious dogfights developed.

The FW190 pilots were aggressive and determined, but so were the crews of the protecting fighters and bombers. My painting shows such a scene. Several B-17s have been hit, are losing height and have dropped from the relative protection of the formation, seen contrailing high above. A bunch of FW190 fighters have attacked the stragglers, and P51s and Spitfires have joined the battle. In the foreground a P-51 has thwarted the FW190 attack on the lowest of the B-17s whilst below a Spitfire pulls hard around to get on the tail of a second FW190.

To endeavour to obtain the 'gathering in the air' feeling, I portrayed a concentration of aircraft in the centre of the picture. The P-51 and the FW190 are very close together – as often happened in air combat. With both in very tight turns, I was able to build up the 'speed' with the use of vortex from the wing tips. From a composition point of view it is not usually entirely satisfactory to have both main subjects in an aviation painting 'going away' from the viewer, but in this case I was happy with the effect achieved. To keep up the action, I painted a FW190 coming almost straight at me, having made a pass at the B-17 at the right of the picture, with the Spitfire turning to get on his tail. In the background several individual dog fights are engaged around the other stragglers.

The P-51 is a beautiful aircraft and looks good from almost any angle, so there was no problem here. The FW190 was more difficult to paint because the angle had to be precisely right so as to indicate that his pass at the B-17 had been thwarted, yet he had managed to avoid the guns of the P-51 on his tail. There was some difficulty in positioning the larger of the B-17s to get the right balance in the picture. In fact I painted it and removed it several times before becoming satisfied.

The scene is late in the day, which enabled me to bring in some warm evening colours. The light at 20,000 feet is still good; however, below, dusk is approaching and beneath the clouds it all looks very foreboding. It is possible to create great drama with the cloud formations painted into an aerial picture. One can use clouds to suggest all manner of moods in a painting. Here it was my aim, by painting the dark colours below, to imply a hostile environment down there – an area to avoid at all costs. Looking down into the gloom one can imagine the unfriendly reception awaiting the crews should their luck run out.

The painting below features a FW190 and was one of a set of six completed for reproduction on fine porcelain china plates. The series comprised six of the most outstanding fighter aircraft of World War II. My brief was in each case a picture bearing in mind that the centre section, including obviously the aircraft would be 'removed' from the painting in order to be reproduced on the circular plate. As I worked on each painting I used a scaled-up tracing of the plate to ensure that, although I was painting a rectangular picture, the circular composition in the centre remained 'complete'.

The FW190 became a front line fighter in 1941. Powered by a bulky aircooled BMW radial engine, it gave Luftwaffe pilots a temporary superiority over the MkV Spitfires, until the Mark IX came into service. The FW190D–9 long-nose variant which came into service in 1944 had a top speed of 426 mph and was generally considered to be the best of Germany's piston engined fighters during the war.

Fw 190

In the collection of Mr and Mrs J Kettlety

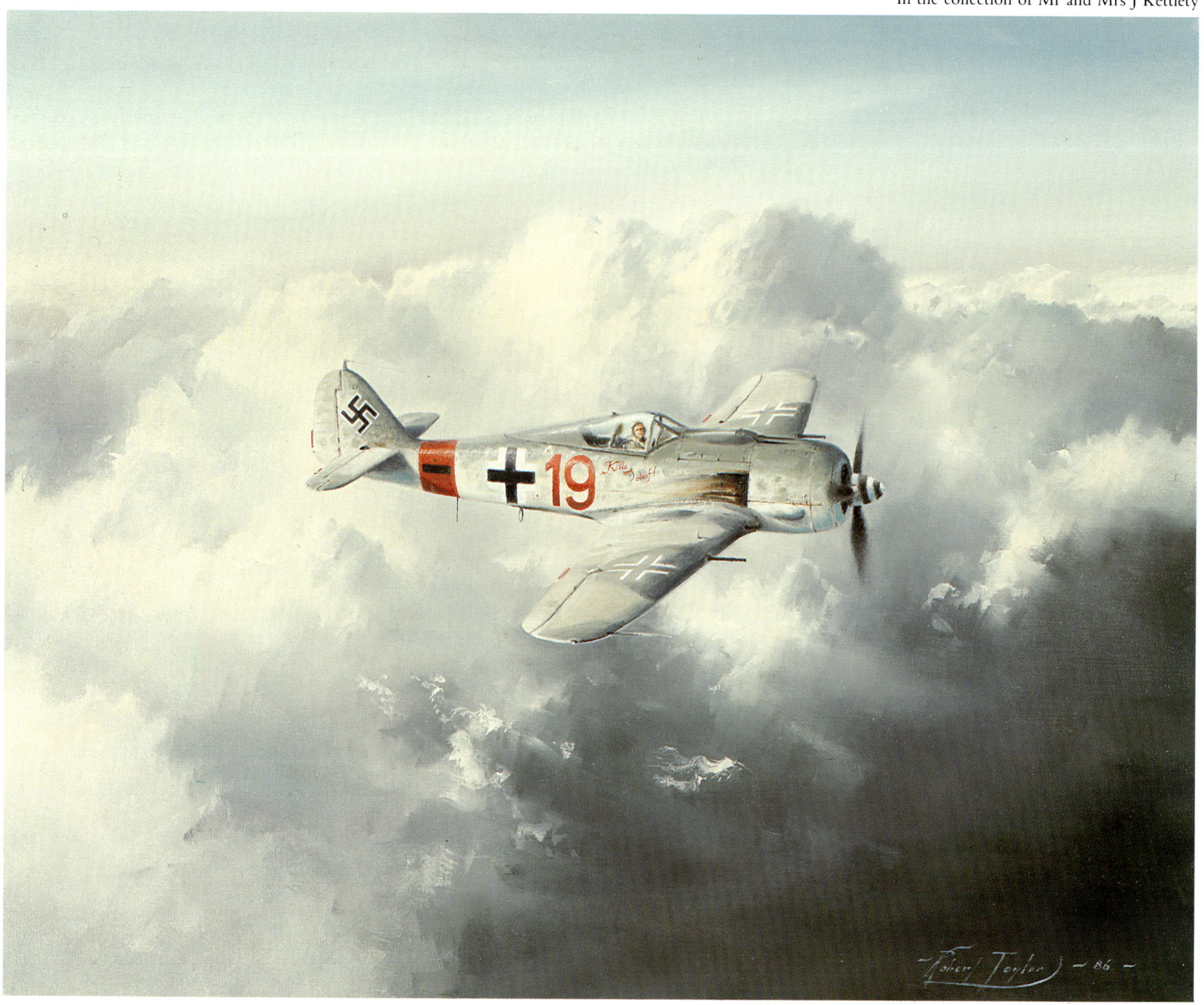

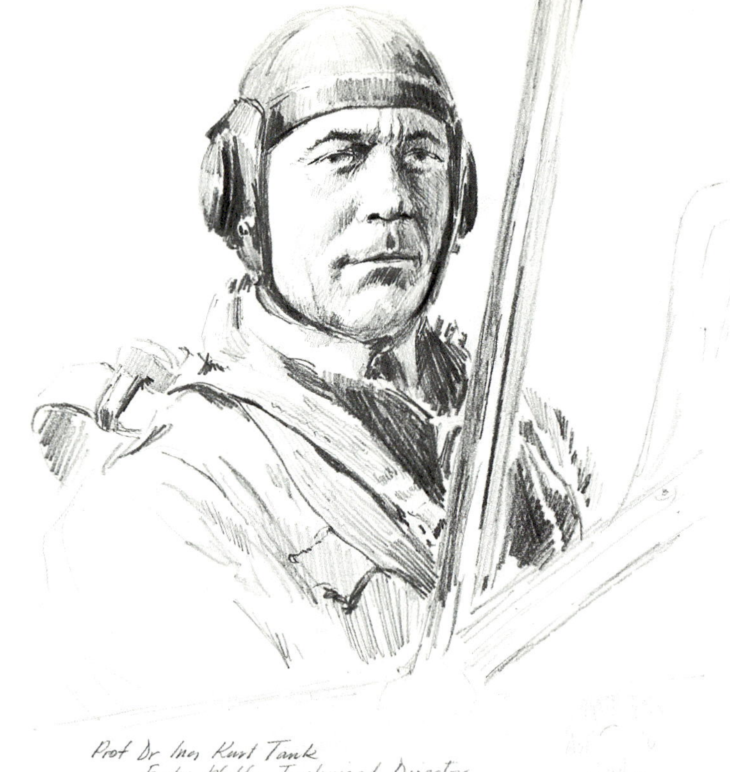

Prof Dr Ing Kurt Tank
Focke Wulfs Technical Director
who often took part in the flight test programmes

All the paintings in this book were painted in oil. I am sometimes asked if I ever paint in acrylics or water colour. The answer is No, not any more. I have painted only in oil for the past twelve years. As with many amateur artists, most of my early paintings were watercolours but during my time as a picture restorer I became so enamoured with oil that I have painted in this medium ever since.

There are many variations among the ways in which different artists work with oil paint. I rarely mix anything else with my paints and like to keep the pallet fairly clean whilst working.

If I want to alter something I have painted I nearly always remove what is on that part of the canvas, before starting again. This is another legacy of my restoring days, when I remember often working on old canvases where the underpaint had, after many years, started to show through. I know that sometimes people find it interesting to be able to look at an artists's mistakes a few hundred years later, but I would prefer to remove any of mine as I go!

I like to prepare and stretch my own canvases. I have done this ever since I started painting in oil. I use a fine tooth linen canvas to which I like to apply at least two coats of oil primer before I start. Paintings are not varnished for at least six months after completion. This avoids the varnish having a softening effect on the paint and retarding the drying.

Even though I work much of my time in a studio atmosphere I never tire of that distinctive aroma that is peculiar to freshly-mixed oil paint.

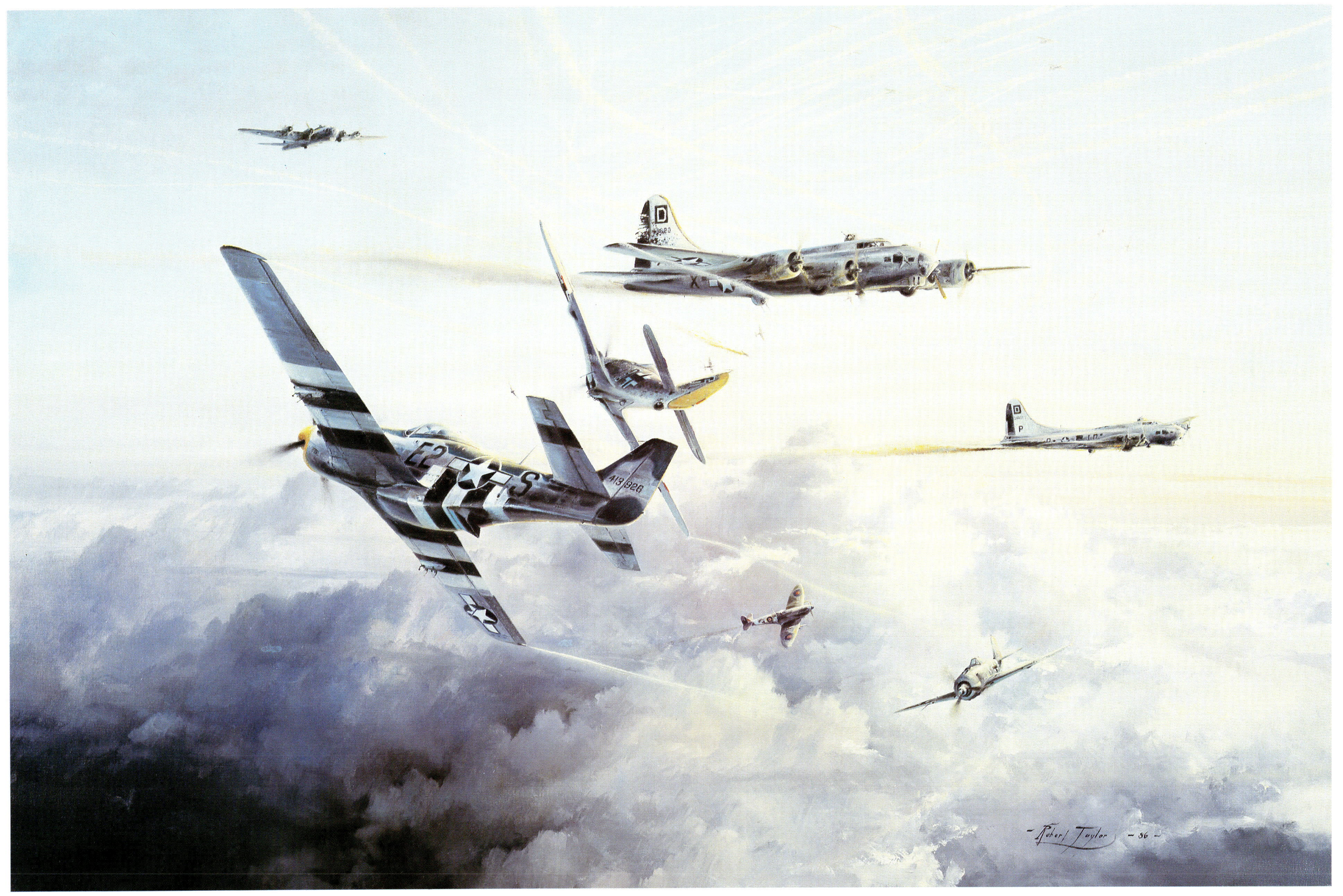

GATHERING OF EAGLES
In the collection of The Military Gallery

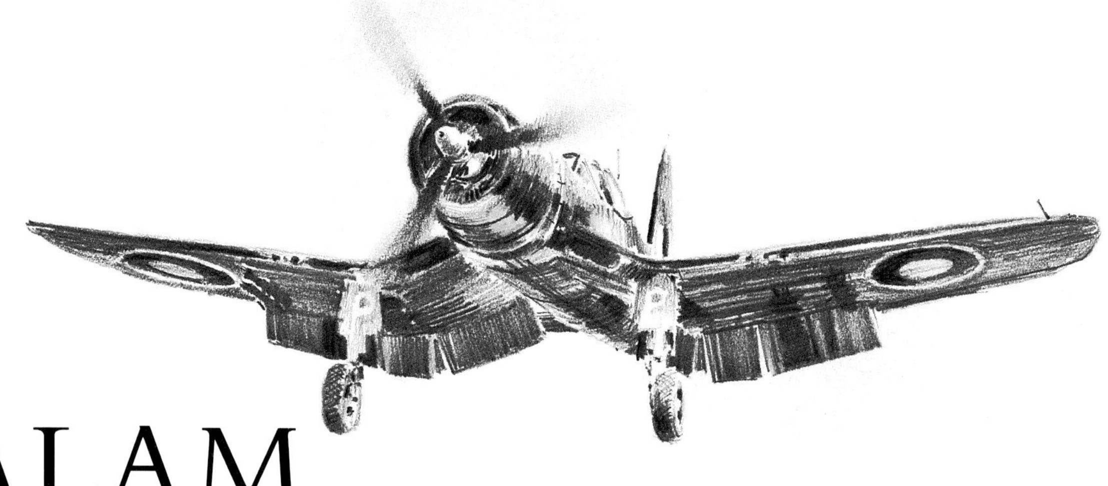

THE PUTTALAM ELEPHANTS

The Corsair was designed and built by Chance Vought as a shipboard fighter. It first flew on 25 June 1942 but it was a further two-and-a-half years before it was to be considered suitable for shipboard operations by the American Navy. The F4U Corsair was a fast, powerful aircraft with a very distinctive profile – easily recognised by its gull-shaped wings. It had a huge 2,000 hp engine and the longest propeller ever seen on a fighter. Its landing characteristics were its major problem: it tended to bounce violently and lose directional stability on landing, and this wasn't helped by the very poor cockpit visibility. It was no wonder the US Navy was wary about having it land on their aircraft carriers, and more than a little surprising that it was in service with the Royal Navy some nine months before the Americans declared it safe for its navy pilots.

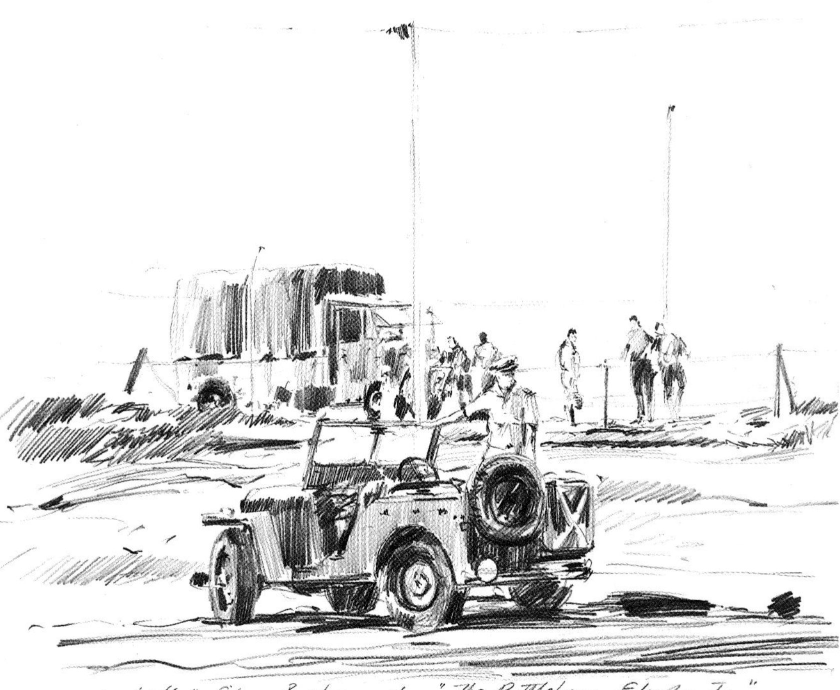

The F4U Corsair first saw active service in the hands of US Marine Corps pilots, flying from shorebases on the island of Guadalcanal in February 1943, and within six months all Marine Corps fighter squadrons in the South Pacific had been equipped with the aircraft. It was indeed the Marine pilots who finally formed the first carrier-based squadron equipped with F4Us in April of 1943. Meanwhile, the Royal Navy continued to equip steadily with the aircraft and before the war in the Pacific ended had a total of nineteen squadrons flying the Corsair.

I have talked to a number of pilots who flew the F4U Corsair in combat and it seems that it was one of those aircraft that a pilot either loved or hated. Either way pilots always appeared to have a fund of graphic stories about the fighter so it seems that it was an airplane with great character. One pilot told me that the only good view he ever got out of the cockpit was looking straight up! The drawing above shows an F4U Corsair making its final approach. Bearing in mind my friend's comments, and knowing of the limited forward vision on approach, one can imagine how hard the pilot is working during these moments just before touch down. Another remarked that the cockpit was so large a pilot could take evasive action by undoing his harness and dodging about inside!

Criticised for its handling though the F4U may have been, it was one of the fastest naval fighters of the war. It was a tough aircraft which could absorb a great deal of punishment and its engine had a reputation for reliability. In any case, from an artist's point of view, the F4U Corsair with its huge engine, gull wings, bubble canopy, short fuselage and high tail, provides plenty of interesting shapes to work with.

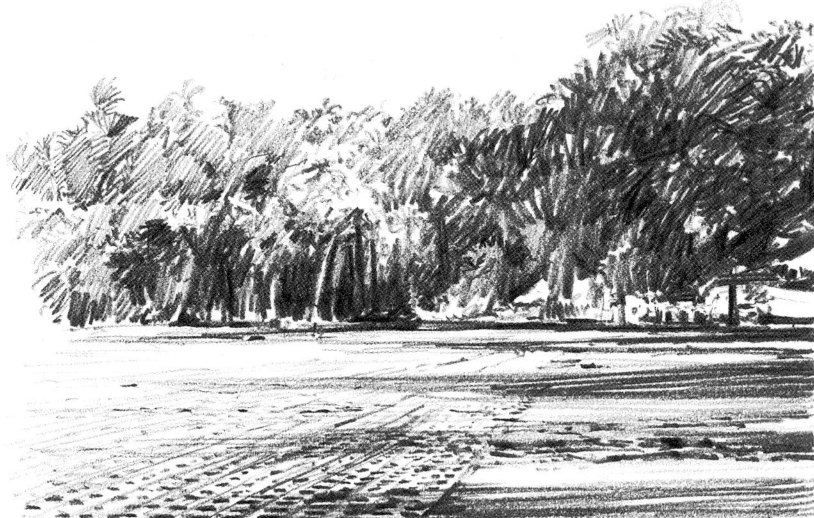

Thus it was with more than a little excitement that I listened to the story about the Puttalam elephants and discovered that the aircraft concerned were F4Us. I had painted elephants before but not Corsairs!

After the painting was completed, it was presented by its owner to the Fleet Air Arm Museum, where it now hangs. I received a telephone call some months later from an ex-Corsair pilot who had been stationed at Puttalam. He asked me how I had known he was there for I had, he told me, portrayed him accurately in my painting!

The drawing on this page was prepared with the aid of the information given in the letter and diagram reproduced below. Both were provided by one of the pilots who had served at Puttalam. I had already obtained a first-hand account of the scene from Commander Sam McDonald-Hall, who had also flown Corsairs at Puttalam, and who had given me the idea for, and commissioned, the painting.

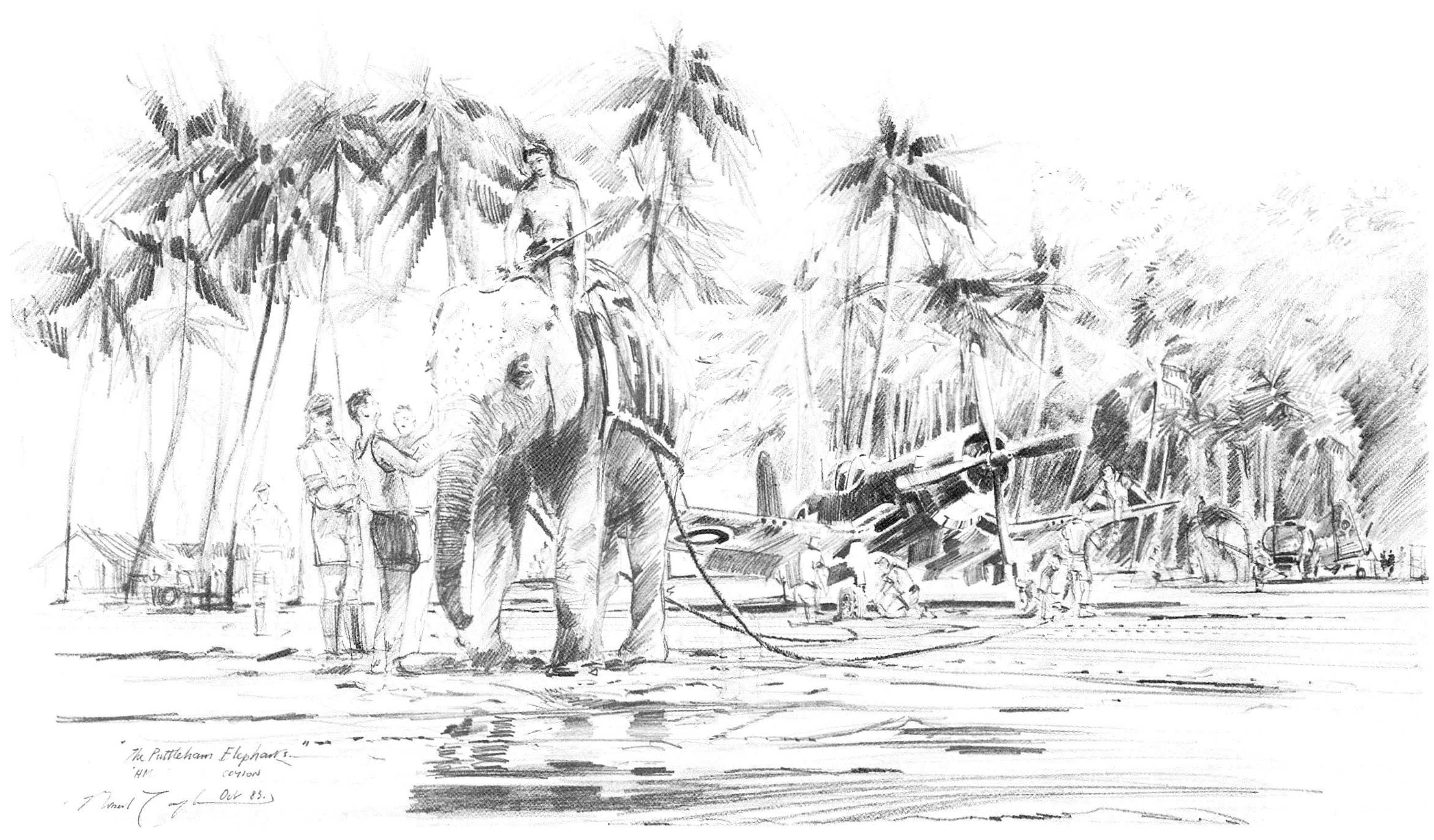

With regard to Puttleham (H M S Rigolia) I regret that I have no photographs, but I remember it as follows.

The airfield was a circle cut out of the jungle, with a single "Somerfeld" tracking runway down the centre.

It was lined, on the seaward side by a row of tall palm trees (very dicey in no wind).

The other three sections of the circle were dense jungle.

Off the runway was sand which turned to mud after rain.

After a shower the runway (steel strips) turned to ice. You stamped on the brakes, locked the wheels, and the Corsair slid gracefully into the sand.

Call for the duty elephant. One was named "Fifi" and had this painted on her side, amidships, in white letters.

Ropes were fixed to the Jumbo's collar, and led to the U.C. legs (Corsair) just above the wheels.

To get the outfit back on the runway, Fifi had to pull from the opposite side, as Jumbo did not like padding around on the metal tracking.

The jockey (Mahout) sat on the elephants neck, clad only in a loin cloth.

The aircraft should be a Corsair Mark IV, suggest a dark green jungle background, and the pilot sitting on the wing.

The elephants also towed the petrol bousers.

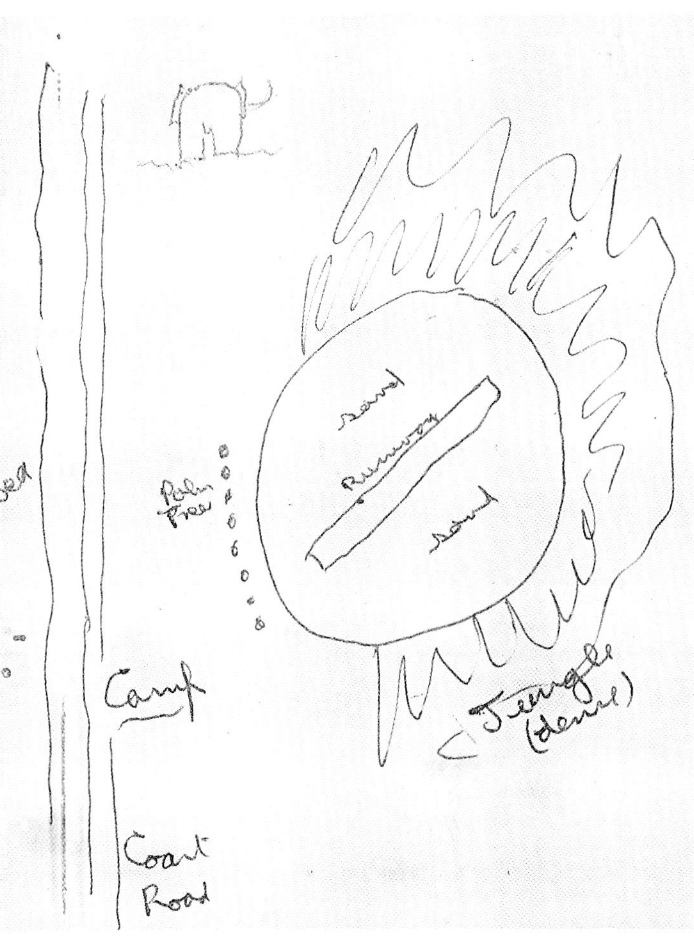

The information contained in these two items represents vital research material and exactly the type I try to obtain. Whilst there was no graphic reference to work with, all the information was provided by people who had been stationed at Puttalam.

After *Puttalam Elephants* had been presented to the Fleet Air Arm Museum I remember being asked by the admiral at Yeovilton if I had found it difficult to paint the elephant – my being an aviation and marine artist. It was a perfectly natural question, but it took me by surprise at the time because in fact I had found it to be one of the easiest parts of the painting. I had more trouble with the Somerfield tracking! What the admiral did not know at the time was that I had painted animals, including elephants, off and on for years before I started painting professionally, and I painted almost nothing but animals during my first six months as a professional painter.

There is a great freedom about painting animals which is not available to the same extent when painting the more technical subjects such as aircraft. Whilst this freedom is enjoyable, on balance I have to admit I much prefer the challenge of trying to portray the great man-made machines and their surroundings.

The unique thing about Puttalam, a shore-based Royal Naval operational fighter station in Ceylon, was its elephants. The makeshift runways, which were constructed of steel mesh plates, became very slippery after rain. The ground beyond the runway became a quagmire during the monsoon season. It was common for aircraft to slide off the runway after landing – that old instability problem – and become stuck in the mud. Fifi and her elephant companions performed valuable duties recovering bogged-down Corsairs on these occasions and the painting records Fifi in action. The detail below highlights the area of the painting devoted to the Mk IV Corsair aircraft. Naturally, however, Fifi is the star of the show!

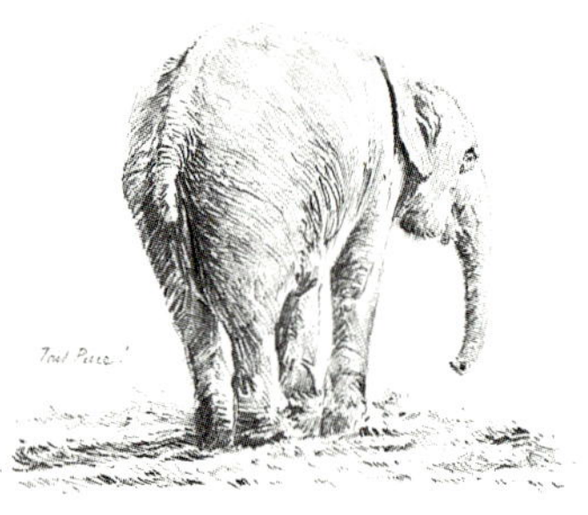

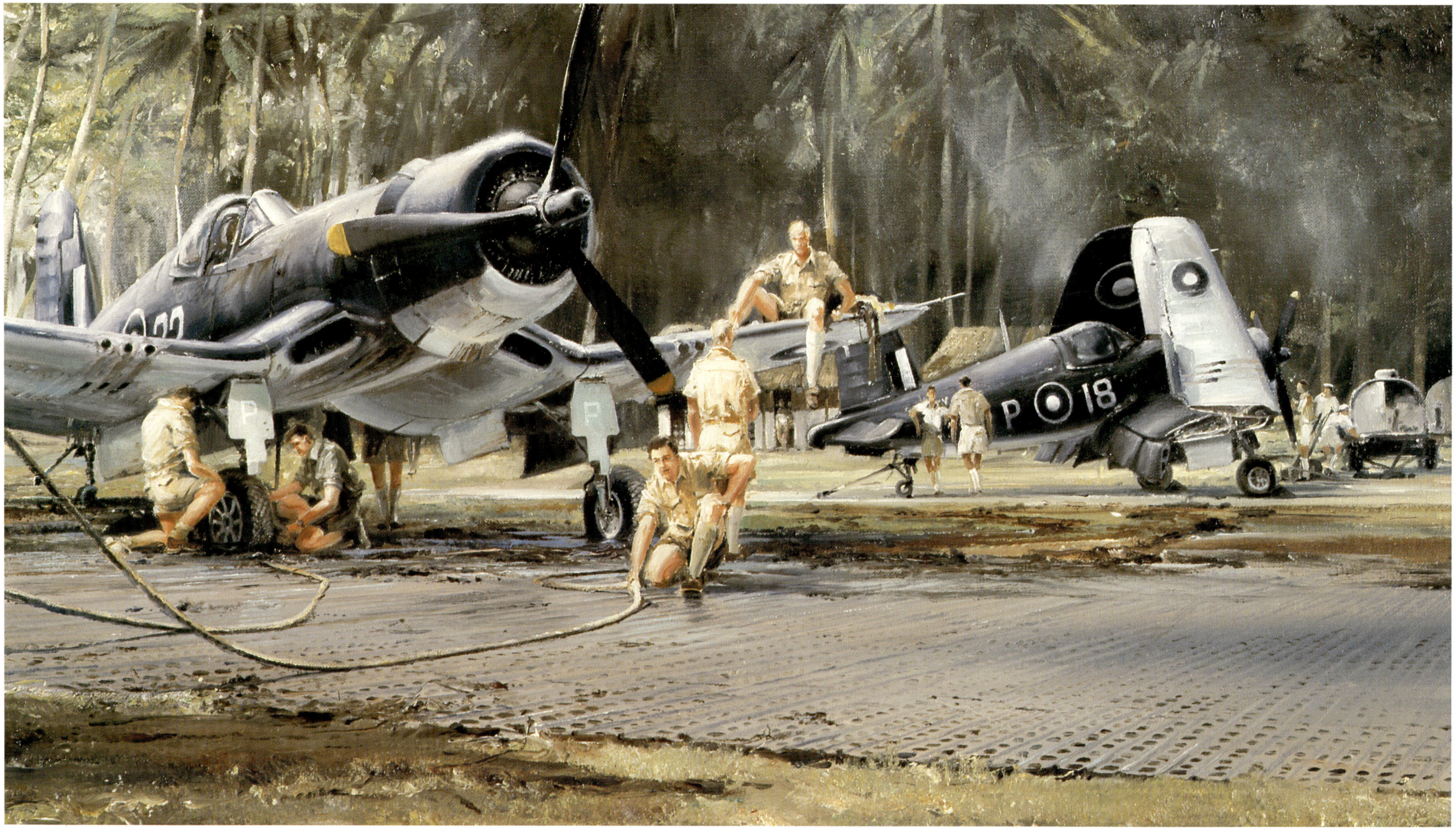

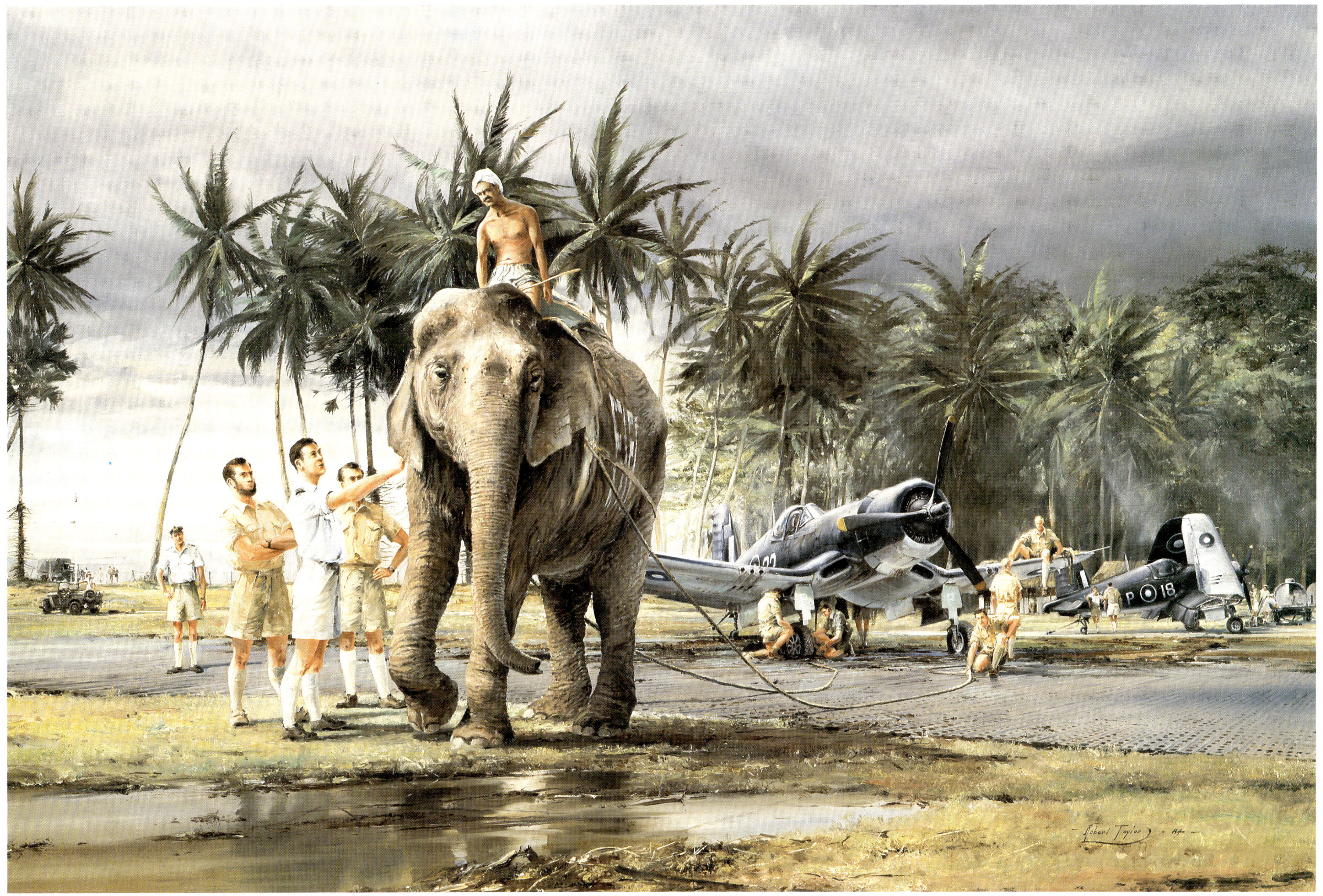

PUTTALAM ELEPHANTS

In the collection of The Fleet Air Arm Museum, Yeovilton

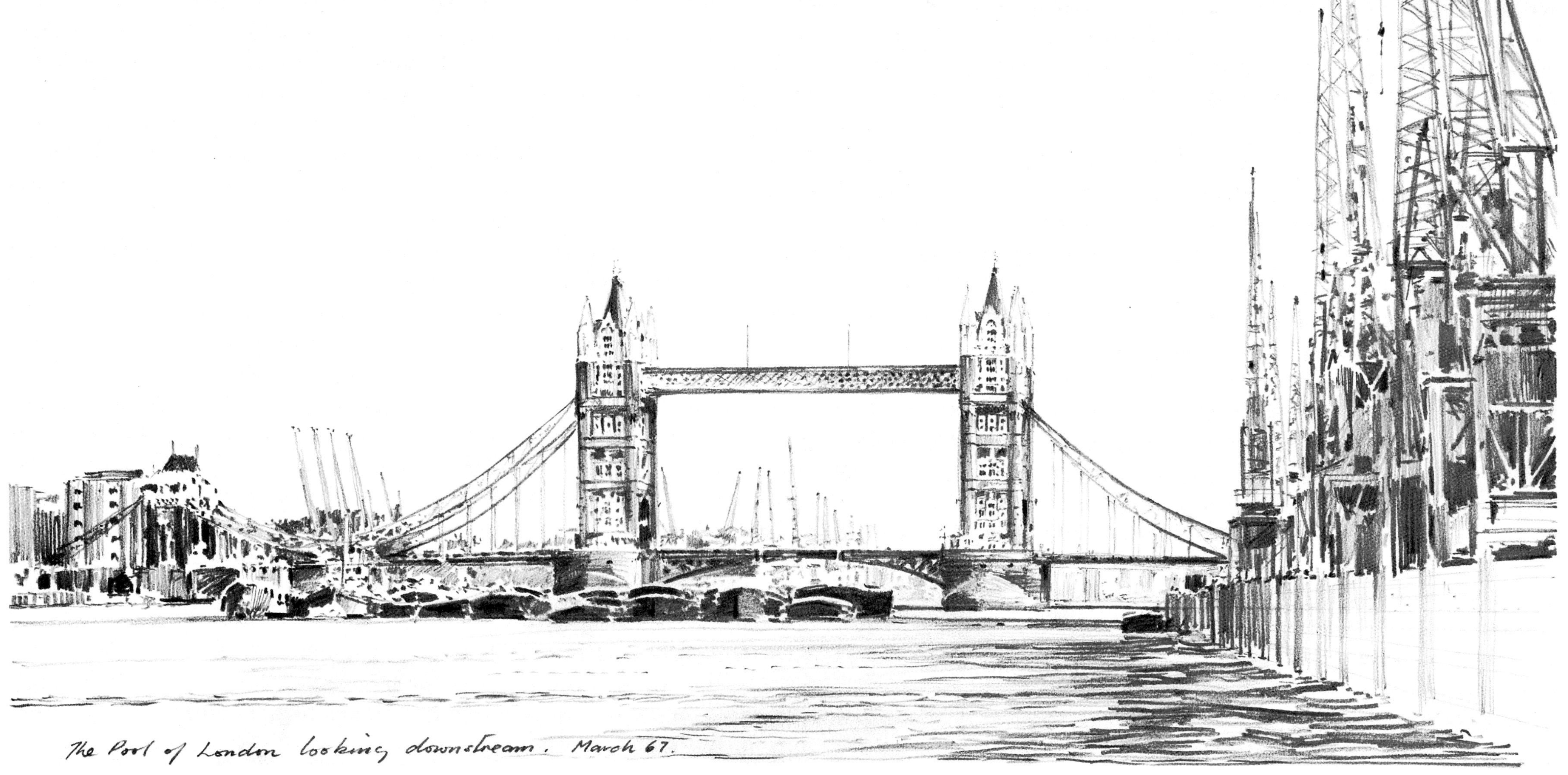

VICTORY SALUTE OVER LONDON

In 1985 most of Europe celebrated the fortieth anniversary of the end of World War II and forty years of peace in Europe. I was asked by The Military Gallery to paint a picture that would in some way commemorate this landmark. Choosing the subject for the painting was not an easy task. So many people were involved in the war – in fact, in their own way, everybody old enough contributed something. To select a subject that might in some way symbolise this combined effort, and sacrifice, taxed me to the full.

All the major campaigns of the war came under consideration, in particular those which most affected the population of Britain. That the British Isles were not invaded in 1940 was almost a miracle. Had the Battle of Britain not been won there is no doubt that an invasion would have taken place. When the Luftwaffe resorted to bombing Britain's large cities, the war at home touched almost everybody. Even my own home city of Bath.

Though the population of many cities suffered greatly during this period of the war it seemed to me that London should be featured in order to symbolise best the steadfastness of the British people.

The Military Gallery had indicated that they would like the principle subject matter to be aviation. It was obvious to me that it was going to be impossible to paint a picture that featured everybody, so my mind started revolving around some kind of painting depicting London from the air. If this were to be so then the aircraft would of necessity be the Spitfire and the Hurricane, for it was their pilots who had won the Battle of Britain, and prevented the certainty of invasion.

Whilst thinking about the painting I had cause to visit HMS *Belfast*, moored in the Thames opposite the Tower of London, by Tower Bridge. *Belfast* is the only surviving World War II Cruiser and is beautifully maintained by the Imperial War Museum as a museum ship. Whilst aboard her the idea that I was looking for appeared. I would paint a Spitfire and a Hurricane, in close formation, over Tower Bridge with London stretched out across the canvas, flying a Victory Salute to the city below. London would be depicted as she is today, after forty years of peace, and HMS *Belfast* would be included in the painting!

Obtaining my reference for the aircraft would be easy, as it seemed appropriate to use aircraft from the Battle of Britain Memorial Flight. But Tower Bridge and a vista of London looking west 1,000 feet above the city was going to be a problem. I knew that somehow I was going to have to get up there!

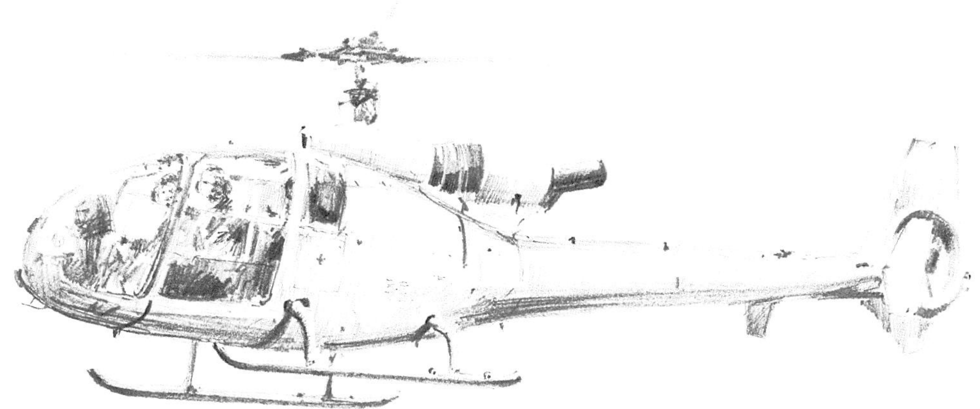

The Military Gallery were enthusiastic about my idea for the painting and we discussed the problem of looking at London from 1,000 feet above the Thames. Pat Barnard made some telephone calls. Within a short time I was climbing aboard a Gazelle helicopter at Westland's airfield in Yeovil – bound for London. I had flown before many times, but not in a helicopter, and was immediately impressed by the fantastic all-round vision.

Piloted by Simon Smith, we headed for the west London heliport, making a stop at Fairoaks to collect some urgently required parts (for another aircraft I am pleased to say!). Once over the Thames we followed the river, winding its way east through the capital city, past Parliament, Blackfriars, Tower Bridge and on down to the new Thames barrier. Here we turned to retrace our path upstream, much more slowly. This was the direction from which the painting would be viewed, and the shutter of my camera was working overtime. After displaying much patience and considerable piloting skill in the twenty-knot wind Simon made a gentle landing at the heliport. The half-hour stop gave me time to scribble a few pages of notes and sketches and we were airborne again, heading west for Yeovil. Thanks to Westland Helicopters I had gathered the vital reference needed for the painting.

After completing the pre-painting drawings to my satisfaction I decided, at the very last moment, to tilt the horizon. Tilting the angle of the horizon is sometimes a useful technique in an aviation painting I think it adds interest and helps remind the viewer that from an aircraft one sees the horizon at a multitude of changing angles. I did not bargain for the problems this would cause – all the buildings had to be painted off the perpendicular! However, having made the commitment I was reluctant to change the plan. Having finished the painting I was very glad I had not taken the easy way out, as I felt the angled horizon helped the flow of the aircraft in the foreground.

I have used backlighting in the picture as I wanted to limit the visibility to some extent. There is usually a haze over Britain, especially London, up to about 5,000 feet, on all but the very clearest of days. By backlighting this haze I was able to make the two aircraft stand out against the mass of buildings below. At the same time I was able to achieve the feeling of warmth which I wanted in the picture.

Backlighting an aviation painting has to be carefully judged. Too strong a light will put the aircraft in virtual silhouette, which in most cases is best avoided. It is, however, a very effective way to create atmosphere and warmth in a picture and enables one to emphasise some lovely reflections of light on canopies, wings, the tops of fuselages, and from rivers or the sea below. In addition it provides the artist with great scope for painting clouds, showing the effect of the sunlight filtering through.

On the subject of lighting, I like best to portray the morning and evening colours in my skies. This is not always possible of course, particularly when painting a specific event where the authenticity of the prevailing weather is of paramount importance. However, given the freedom to choose my time of day, morning or evening always wins! The morning light is more subtle than that of the evening, but both treat us to a paradise of outstanding changing colours, with no two scenes ever the same. This spectacle of nature provides artists with the most beautiful and readily-available form of reference imaginable for their paintings. It is my constant endeavour to make use of this beautiful treasure-house of material to the best of my ability.

Victory Salute over London was acquired by an American collector who generously loaned it to the Smithsonian National Air and Space Museum in Washington DC, where it now hangs.

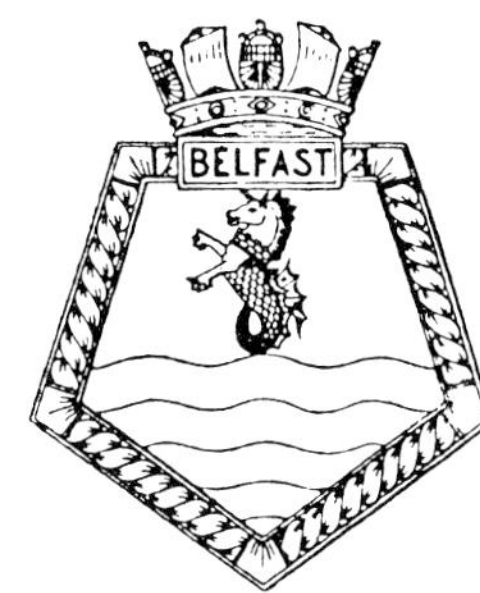

HMS BELFAST

HMS *Belfast* was one of the few ships of the Royal Navy to see the war right through. Introduced in 1938 as one of the Southampton class, the *Belfast*, was built to a stronger pattern than the previous new cruisers. The guns were more numerous – twelve instead of six 4-inch anti-aircraft guns – and the armour was heavier.

Earlier in the war *Belfast* fell victim to one of the first magnetic mines encountered and broke her back. After a thoroughgoing rebuild she was back in action in 1942.

Her most famous engagement was that against the German battleship the *Scharnhorst*, in whose destruction she played a key rôle. It was December 1943 and, leading two other cruisers, the *Norfolk* and the *Sheffield*, the *Belfast* was ordered to protect an eastbound convoy from the threat of the *Scharnhorst*, which had just left its base in Northern Norway. With the aid of her highly advanced radar, and the despatch of 393 shells, the *Belfast* was the major contributor to the demise of this significant enemy ship. Her reward has been the unique status she now enjoys as the only World War II cruiser still afloat. She went into reserve in 1963 and then in 1971 was permanently berthed in the Pool of London as a museum ship.

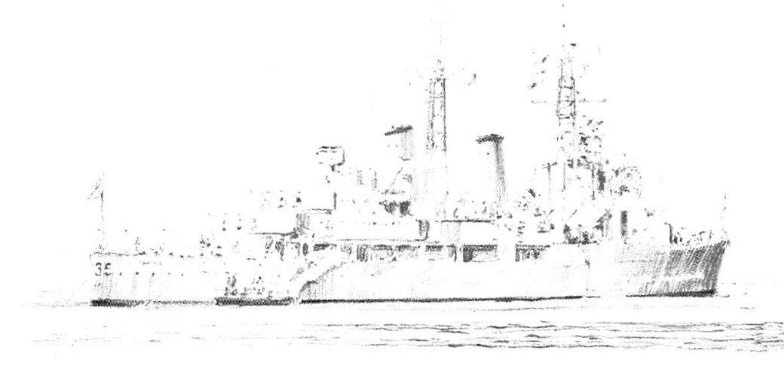

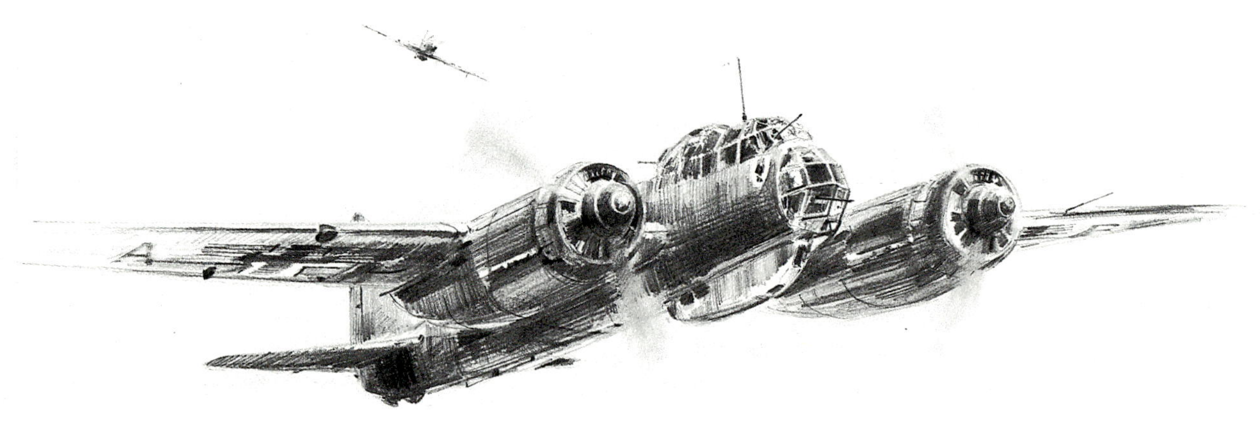

He111's OVER LONDON

In the collection of Mr James Kline

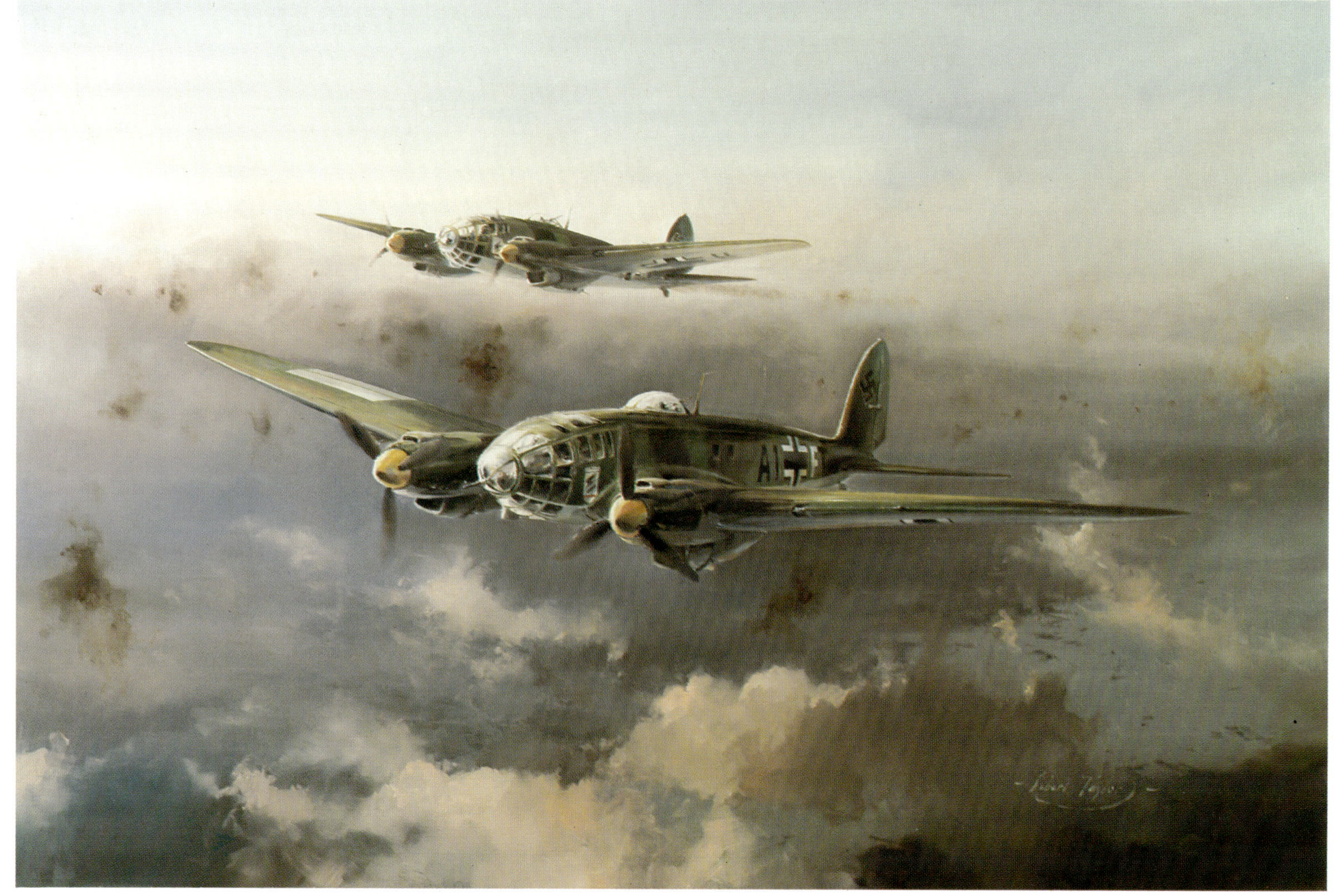

During the research for *Victory Salute* I read a number of books and articles on the Luftwaffe raids over Britain in 1940. These started with the daylight raids on coastal installations and ports, followed by a programme of attacks on the fighter stations in the south east and daylight bombing of London – the dock areas east of the City being the prime target. The bombing raids culminated with the massive night-bombing raids of London itself, and other major cities. I painted the picture on the left of Heinkel bombers over London some years ago, in 1980 I think, and in it tried to convey the feeling of hostility of the bomber aircraft – the He111 depicted was a particularly sinister-looking airplane I always thought, though with all the glass in the nose and its general shape, quite lovely to paint. It is seen flying west at about 12,000 feet with the river Thames and the Isle of Dogs visible below.

The Heinkel He111 first flew in 1935 and, although obviously designed as a medium bomber, attempts were made by the German authorities to present it as a civilian passenger aircraft at the time.

I have over the years painted many of the best known Luftwaffe aircraft. Reviewing these from an aesthetic standpoint – an artist's prerogative! – they comprise an excellent collection of shapes and designs.

For me the Junkers 88, which seemed to have a greenhouse stuck on the front of its fuselage, was only exceeded in its ugliness by the Junkers Ju87 dive bomber. Both give the artist plenty to work with!

The three-engined Dornier Do24T was a lovely-looking seaplane and reminiscent of the wonderful old Catalina. The Focke-Wulf FW190 had nice lines, especially the long-nosed version, and the Me262 jet looked as fast as it was. Of all those aircraft which flew with the Luftwaffe during World War II, for me the most enjoyable to paint is that archetypal fighter – the Me109.

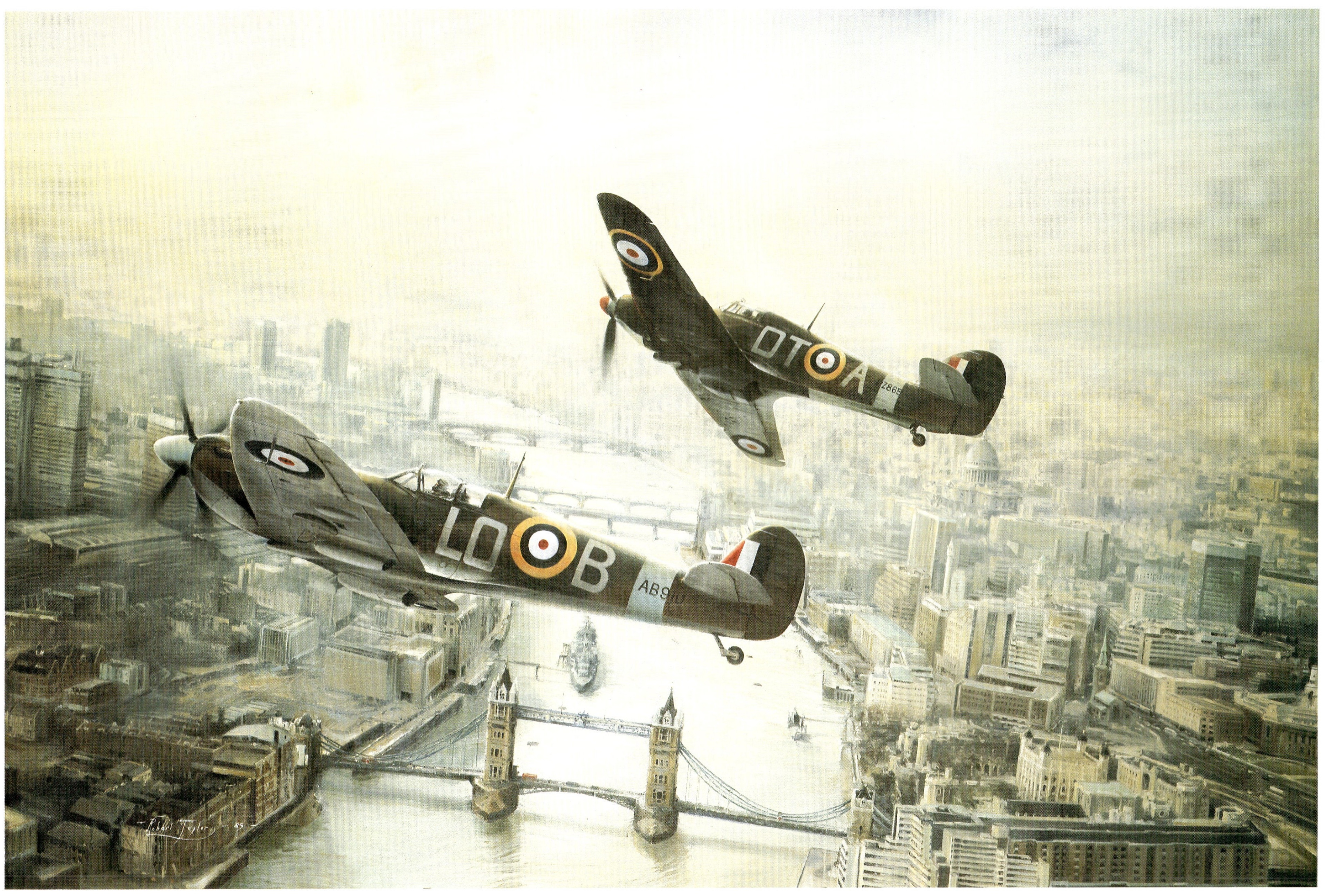

VICTORY SALUTE
In the collection of Mr N Maggos

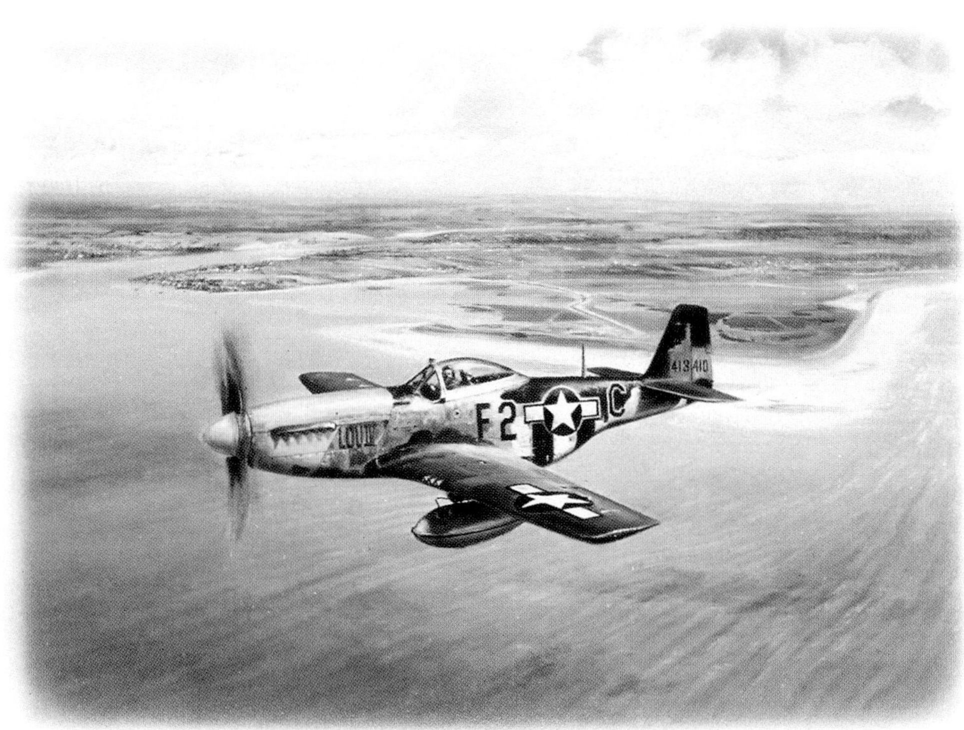

ACKNOWLEDGEMENTS

When publishers, David and Charles, approached me with the idea of producing this book I had no idea just how much time would be involved, or how many people would be concerned with its production. It has been an eye-opener for me. So many people have contributed to this volume apart from myself that I feel a little embarrassed that only my name appears on the cover.

I am honoured that Air Vice-Marshal Johnnie Johnson should have written the foreword to this book. I am one of his greatest admirers and thus feel greatly flattered by the kind words he has said.

I must express a debt of gratitude to Robert Weston for the time and care he devoted to write about me. I think he flatters me too much, but nevertheless thank him for his kindness, patience, and attention to detail.

I would like to thank all those distinguished people, many of whom are the subjects of my paintings, for the invaluable help and encouragement given me during the research for the paintings featured in the book. Sadly some of them are no longer alive, but I cherish the memories of the time spent with all of them. I am particularly grateful to those who have kindly contributed to this book by writing specially for it: Air Vice-Marshal Johnnie Johnson, Group Captains Peter Townsend and Hamish Mahaddie, Wing Commander Bee Beamont, Commanders Dennis White and 'Sharkey' Ward, and from Germany, General Adolf Galland.

The staff of David and Charles, who have published this book, have been kind and considerate and have given me my way on so many aspects of the book. David Porteous who controlled its production has been especially sympathetic and helpful, and it is due to his skill in co-ordination that the whole book has come together. I am also grateful to David Thomas, the publisher's Chairman, for taking a personal interest in the book.

I must pay a special tribute to my art publishers, The Military Gallery, Pat Barnard and all the Gallery staff with whom I have worked so closely over the years. Most of the paintings featured in this book have been reproduced as fine art prints by The Military Gallery during the past decade, and it is largely due to them that this book has been made possible. My special thanks to Pat Barnard who was personally responsible for the overall design of my book.

I also appreciate the help provided by John Price of R. A. Muddimers, the printing company which has been responsible for the production of so many of the prints. Their help in the provision of colour transparencies for this book has been of great assistance. John King of Bristol has also been of great assistance with his excellent photography.

Many other friends have helped during the monumental task of gathering together all the material featured in the book, and I offer my sincere thanks to all of them. My particular appreciation goes to Commander Dennis White, OBE, Director of the splendid Fleet Air Arm Museum at Yeovilton, to Jenny Loasby, Peter Cooke, Paul Beaver, Ray Callow, and Virginia Bader.

I am also grateful to the collectors of my paintings reproduced in the book, whose names appear below the colour plates, and hope they will enjoy reading the stories behind the paintings.

Finally I acknowledge the enormous support which my wife Mary has given me throughout my career, and in particular her encouragement when, with three children to provide for, I took the plunge and became a full time professional painter back in early 1977.

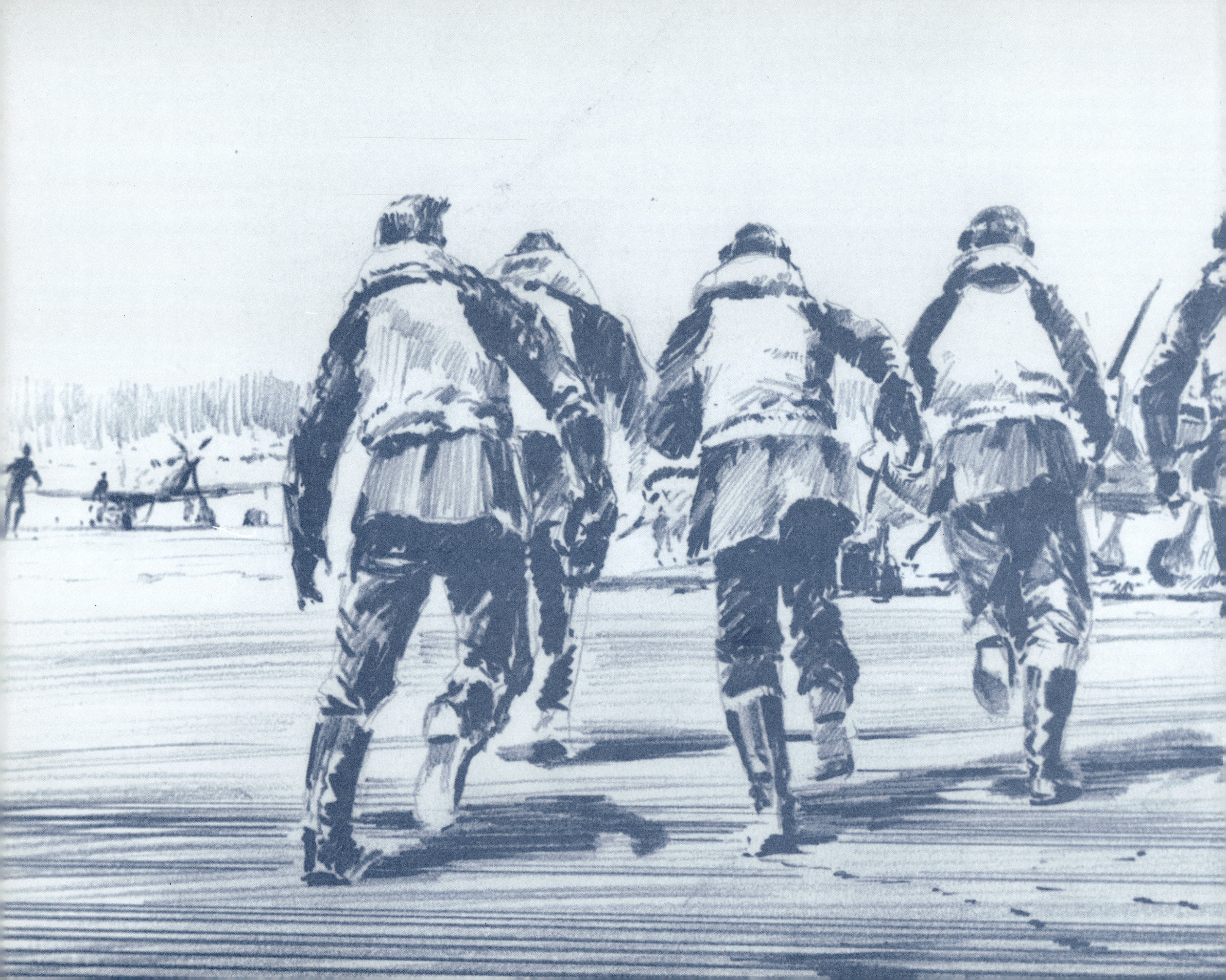